Fundamentalism and Gender

POSTMODERN ETHICS SERIES

Postmodernism and deconstruction are usually associated with a destruction of ethical values. The volumes in the Postmodern Ethics series demonstrate that such views are mistaken because they ignore the religious element that is at the heart of existential-postmodern philosophy. This series aims to provide a space for thinking about questions of ethics in our times. When many voices are speaking together from unlimited perspectives within the postmodern labyrinth, what sort of ethics can there be for those who believe there is a way through the dark night of technology and nihilism beyond exclusively humanistic offerings? The series invites any careful exploration of the postmodern and the ethical.

Series Editors:
Marko Zlomislić (Conestoga College)
David Goicoechea (Brock University)

Other Volumes in the Series:
1. *Cross and Khôra: Deconstruction and Christianity in the Work of John D. Caputo* edited by Neal DeRoo and Marko Zlomislić
2. Agape *and Personhood with Kierkegaard, Mother, and Paul (A Logic of Reconciliation from the Shamans to Today)* by David Goicoechea
3. *The Poverty of Radical Orthodoxy* edited by Lisa Isherwood and Marko Zlomislić
4. Agape *and the Four Loves with Nietzsche, Father, and Q (A Physiology of Reconciliation from the Greeks to Today)* by David Goicoechea

Fundamentalism and Gender

Scripture—Body—Community

EDITED BY
ULRIKE AUGA, CHRISTINA VON BRAUN,
CLAUDIA BRUNS, AND JANA HUSMANN

⌐PICKWICK *Publications* · Eugene, Oregon

FUNDAMENTALISM AND GENDER
Scripture—Body—Community

Copyright © 2013 Wipf and Stock Publishers. All rights reserved. Except for brief quotations in critical publications or reviews, no part of this book may be reproduced in any manner without prior written permission from the publisher. Write: Permissions, Wipf and Stock Publishers, 199 W. 8th Ave., Suite 3, Eugene, OR 97401.

Pickwick Publications
An Imprint of Wipf and Stock Publishers
199 W. 8th Ave., Suite 3
Eugene, OR 97401

www.wipfandstock.com

ISBN 13: 978-71-62032-392-2

Cataloguing-in-Publication data:

    Fundamentalism and gender : scripture—body—community. / edited by Ulrika Auga, Christina von Braun, Claudia Bruns, and Jana Husmann

    x + 288 pp. ; 23 cm. Includes bibliographical references.

    ISBN 13: 978-71-62032-392-2

    1. Religious fundamentalism. 2. Women and religion. 3. Gender Identity. I. Title.

BL458 F87 2013

Manufactured in the U.S.A.

The article by Jasbir Puar, "Citation and Censorship: The Politics of Talking About the Sexual Politics of Israel," was first published in *Feminist Legal Studies* 19/2 (2011) 133–42. With kind permission from Springer Science and Business Media. © Springer Science+Business Media B.V. 2011.

Contents

Contributors | vii
Preface | ix

Fundamentalism and Gender—An Introduction | 1
  Ulrike Auga, Christina von Braun, Claudia Bruns, and Jana Husmann

Literalism, Religion, and Science

Religion and Science—An Opposition? | 33
  Christina von Braun

Fundamentalism and Gender: Comments of Two Useful Concepts | 57
  Martin Riesebrodt

Jesus Enters the Battle of the Sexes | 74
  Vincent Crapanzano

Literalism and Anti-Semitism: Positions within the (German) Bibelbund during the 1930s | 92
  Jana Husmann

The Qur'ān in the Field of Conflict between the Interpretative Communities: An Attempt to Cope with the Crisis of Qur'ānic Studies | 109
  Angelika Neuwirth

Nation, State, and Community

Belonging to Halakhic Judaism: On the Sense of Matrilineal Descent | 131
  Micha Brumlik

Race, Gender, and Religious Fundamentalism: Debates between Christians and Jews at the End of the Weimar Republic. The Case of Hans Blüher and Hans-Joachim Schoeps | 145
Claudia Bruns

Antifundamentalism as Fundamentalism: Reading Thilo Sarrazin through Joseph McCarthy. Some Thoughts on Supremacy, Secularism, Gender, and Culturalization | 171
Gabriele Dietze

Citation and Censorship: The Politics of Talking About the Sexual Politics of Israel | 190
Jasbir Puar

Body, Life, and Biopolitics

Queer Theologies and Sacred Bodies | 205
Lisa Isherwood

Seminal Reasoning: Ultra-Orthodoxy and the Biopolitics of Medically Assisted Reproduction in Israel | 220
Carmel Shalev

Daughters are Diamonds: When Honor Precludes Reflexivity | 244
Shafinaaz Hassim

"No Other Means"? Fundamentalisms, Religion, Survival, and Biopolitical Counterdiscourses | 264
Ulrike Auga

Contributors

Ulrike Auga, Professor of Religious Studies, Intercultural Theology, Ecumenics and Gender at the Faculty of Theology, Humboldt University, Berlin.

Christina von Braun, Professor Emerita of Gender and History at the Institute for Cultural History and Theory, Humboldt University, Berlin; Head of the Center for Jewish Studies Berlin-Brandenburg.

Micha Brumlik, Professor of Education at the Institute of Pedagogy, Goethe University, Frankfurt am Main.

Claudia Bruns, Professor for History of Knowledge and Gender at the Institute for Cultural History and Theory, Humboldt University, Berlin.

Vincent Crapanzano, Distinguished Professor of Comparative Literature and Anthropology at the Graduate Center, the City University of New York.

Gabriele Dietze, Adj. Professor of American Studies; Research Fellow at the Research Unit "Cultures of Urban Insanity," Berlin, funded by the German Research Foundation (DFG).

Shafinaaz Hassim (MA), Biographer and Lecturer in Sociology at the School of Social Sciences, University of the Witwatersrand, Johannesburg.

Jana Husmann, Postdoctoral Researcher and Lecturer in Gender Studies and Cultural History and Theory, Berlin.

Contributors

Lisa Isherwood, Professor of Feminist Liberation Theology and Director of the Institute of Theological Partnerships at the University of Winchester.

Angelika Neuwirth, Senior Professor at the Seminar for Semitic and Arabic Studies, Free University, Berlin.

Jasbir Puar, Professor in the Department of Women's & Gender Studies at the School of Arts and Sciences, Rutgers University, New Brunswick.

Martin Riesebrodt, Professor Emeritus of the Sociology of Religion in the Divinity School and in the Department of Sociology, University of Chicago.

Carmel Shalev (JSD Dr), Adjunct Professor at the Faculty of Law, Haifa University.

Preface

This book is the result of a conference held in December 2010 at the Humboldt University in Berlin and dedicated to the theme "Fundamentalism and Gender: Scripture—Body—Community." Scholars from Germany, Israel, South Africa, and the United States presented their work on one of three different panels focused on the following topic clusters: (1) Literalism, Religion, and Science; (2) Nation, State, and Community; and (3) Body, Life, and Biopolitics. The interdisciplinary approaches taken to the subject included perspectives from cultural history and theory, religious studies, Christian theologies, Islamic studies, history, social sciences, anthropology, comparative literature, and women and gender studies. We are pleased that most of these contributions are available here in written form.

We give special thanks to all those who took part in the conference and contributed to a productive series of discussions. For financial support of this publication we would like to thank the PhD Research Training Group "Gender as a Category of Knowledge," funded by the German Research Foundation (Deutsche Forschungsgemeinschaft, DFG). Our special thanks also go to Leah Chizek for translation and editing assistance, and to Viola Beckmann and Julia Eckhoff for assistance with both editing and formatting.

The editors,
Berlin, September 2012

Fundamentalism and Gender— An Introduction[1]

ULRIKE AUGA, CHRISTINA VON BRAUN,
CLAUDIA BRUNS, JANA HUSMANN

Why pursue the relationship between gender and fundamentalism? Initially, at least, this question might appear to be self-explanatory when one considers the ways such topics have been present in the Western media during recent years and their significance with respect to a number of geopolitical events. Springing most readily to mind, perhaps, are the populist associations between Islamism and the oppression of women. And yet issues pertaining to Christian fundamentalism—premarital abstinence, homophobia, and conservative family values—have become a source of increasing interest in the Western public sphere over the last few years as well. Parallel to this is a renewed sense of scholarly engagement with the interrelations between religion and secularism, a critical endeavor that is focused largely on examining the Western discourse about fundamentalism itself.[2] On a meta-level, this means questioning Western myths about the secular, which subsume it into a progressive teleology that imagines secularism as a force both separate from and ultimately prevailing over religion. According to these critiques, teleological narratives of this kind fail to recognize the extent to which religious heritage and concerns continue to exercise their influence on modern Western

1. Translated from German by Leah Chizek.
2. Asad et al., *Is Critique Secular?*

societies.³ Not least the diverse manifestations of Christian fundamentalism underscore a return of the religious in secular Western contexts.

However, the notion that secularism represents a progressive form of overcoming religion has a particularly strong effect on Western discourses about Islamic fundamentalism. Critiques that examine the stereotypical conflation of fundamentalism with "Islam" unveil a host of neo-occidental stereotypes according to which the Muslim Other embodies religious backwardness, while the West is said to represent secular progress and emancipation (from religion). Such stereotypes go together with neo-racist processes of othering and new modes of occidental self-affirmation, as has been illustrated repeatedly.⁴ Authors such as Judith Butler, Saba Mahmood, Jasbir Puar, and Joan Scott examine the ambivalent position assigned to Western feminism in this Islamophobic context, in which feminism and gay rights are instrumentalized by anti-Muslim discourse and thereby permitted to feed into polarizing notions of identity and geopolitical strife.⁵ With an eye toward the contemporary wars waged in the name of liberating women, Linda M. Alcoff and John D. Caputo invoke Gayatri C. Spivak's famously pithy definition of colonial legitimation strategies as "[w]hite men saving brown women from brown men"⁶ in order to underscore its ongoing pertinence in today's context, where such strategies are ideologically recoded under the sign of the (anti)religious.⁷ These various examinations of Western discourse about fundamentalism—about its generalizing and legitimizing functions—on the one hand illustrate how Western feminism is assimilated into hegemonic structures of power; yet on the other, they also illustrate the critical and (self-)reflexive potential resid-

---

3. Butler, "Sensibility of Critique," 119–20; Mahmood, "Religious Reason," 71–72; Mahmood, "Secularism"; Taylor, "Redefinition of Secularism"; Taylor, *Secular Age*. On the secularization of religious thought, see Braun, *Schwindel*, 438. On the relation between religion and secularism, see also Butler et al., *Power of Religion*; Casanova, *Public Religions*; Casanova, "Secularization"; Warner et al., *Secularism*.

4. On the previous concept of occidentalism in the context of postcolonial theory, see Coronil, "Beyond Occidentalism." On the concept of critical occidentalism in relation to islamophobia and neo-racism, see Dietze, "Okzidentalismuskritik"; Dietze et al., *Okzidentalismus*.

5. Butler, "Sensibility of Critique," 126–34; Mahmood, "Religion"; Puar, *Terrorist Assemblages*; Scott, *Politics of the Veil*.

6. Spivak, "Subaltern," 296.

7. Alcoff and Caputo, "Introduction," 2.

ing in the feminist production of knowledge, which calls into question the tendency of such rhetoric to view (Western) feminism as a monolithic entity. In this context, the various feminist and (self-)critical interventions alluded to here do not make religious fundamentalism their object of analysis but instead criticize the problematic creation of stereotypes and legitimizing strategies used by Western discourse about fundamentalism. Yet, as Gabriele Dietze argues in this volume, the political and secular positions behind antifundamentalism can betray a fundamentalist character of their own. In a similar way, Alcoff and Caputo speak of "secular Fundamentalism" with regard to "ethnocentric nativism" and "anti-Muslim policies of exclusion."[8]

Of course, these various feminist interventions into polarized conceptions of "Islam" versus "the West" do not obviate the need to question the unjust structures that pervade religious fundamentalisms of every shade and reconsider the complex pictures of the enemy they construct and that cut across various geopolitical factions. Thus, in present-day conflicts between Islam and the Western world—whether the latter defines itself as Christian or secular—we find again a number of potent images at work that were already in use in anti-Semitism of the nineteenth century. Some of these images are directed against Moslems, whereas others have Muslim origins and are directed against Christians or the Western world in general; still others are directed against Jews and Israel, making use of images from the anti-Semitic journal *Der Stürmer* we thought we would never see again. All of these present conflicts have in common that they are highly emotional, replace reflection by polemics and, in doing so, they also make ample usage of gender categories.

Gender Research and the Term Fundamentalism

Historically, at least, religious fundamentalism is not unilaterally associated with Islamism the way it often is today; rather, it has much more commonly been understood as a Western and Christian phenomenon: The term fundamentalism has its origins in the context of American fundamentalism, where it initially served as a means of positive self-description.[9] In the research on fundamentalism, the concept has

---

8. Ibid.

9. The term "fundamentalism" was coined in the 1920s by the Baptist pastor Curtis Lee Laws (1868–1946). The multivolume work *The Fundamentals: A Testimony to*

meanwhile been applied in a number of additional, largely monotheistic religious contexts, though it has also been used with reference to non-monotheistic religions such as Hinduism.[10] At the same time, the term fundamentalism has also been applied to secular phenomena.[11] This more expansive usage is not without controversy. Contentious, though, is the question as to whether—and if so, to what extent—the Protestant concept of fundamentalism should even be applied to other religions in the first place when it is historically associated with the specific criterion of (Protestant) literalism (i.e., a literal understanding of the Bible). There are, after all, alternative concepts available to describe the dogmatic, archconservative, and/or extremist tendencies of other religions—"Catholic integralism," for example, or the "extreme traditionalism" of ultra-Orthodox Judaism.[12] These objections notwithstanding, fundamentalism has since also become established as a transreligious concept, which is attested to by the diverse spectrum of applications it has received within the context of gender research.

Gender-theoretical studies focus on both specific cultural and religious dimensions, as well as on transreligious elements in their discus-

---

the Truth (1910–1915) represents the founding text of American Protestant fundamentalism. The first institutionalized forms of Protestant fundamentalism are linked to the founding of the World's Christian Fundamentals Association in 1919. On the history of Protestant fundamentalism in the United States see, e.g., Barr, *Fundamentalism*; Bendroth, *Fundamentalism and Gender*; DeBerg, *Ungodly Women*; Marsden, *Fundamentalism*; Pieh, "Fight like David"; Riesebrodt, *Pious Passion*.

10. Numerous interdisciplinary anthologies and various interreligious reflections on fundamentalism testify to this. See, e.g., Bielefeld and Heitmeyer, *Politisierte Religion*; Brink and Mencher, *Mixed Blessings*; Caplan, *Fundamentalism*; Hawley, *Fundamentalism & Gender*; Jäggi and Krieger, *Fundamentalismus*; Kepel, *Revenge*; Kienzler, *Fundamentalismus*; Kindelberger, *Fundamentalismus*; Lehmann and Iqtidar, *Fundamentalism*; Marty and Appleby, *Glory*; Meyer, *Fundamentalismus*.

11. Thus, for example, Bamforth and Richards take into account the "historical originalism in American constitutional interpretation" in their definition of a "source-based fundamentalism" (Bamforth and Richards, *Patriarchal Religion*, 280). See also Crapanzano, *Serving*. Jäggi and Krieger discuss the term fundamentalisms with regard to Marxism and certain fractions of the Green Party in Germany. See Jäggi and Krieger, *Fundamentalismus*, 138–46. Prokop relates the term to right-wing policies. See Prokop, "Rechtsradikalismus." Albrecht links it to National Socialism. See Albert, *Religiöser Fundamentalismus*.

12. For a critical treatment on the use of the term fundamentalism in the Jewish context see, e.g., Harris, "Fundamentalism"; Wagner-Rau, "Suche," 20–21; on Catholicism, see Wagner-Rau, "Suche," 16–18; on Islam, see Riesebrodt, *Pious Passion*, 12–14.

sions of gender and fundamentalism. The Christian fundamentalism of the early twentieth century has thus been linked to a rearticulation of patriarchal structures. In particular are those sociological, ethnological, and historico-scientific perspectives that attribute the rise of Christian fundamentalism to the momentous changes brought about by Western modernity. These include the historical restructuring of gender relationships in the context of industrialization and urbanization, as well as the foundation of the first Western women's movement. In much the same token, historian Margaret Lamberts Bendroth has interpreted Protestant fundamentalism as a defensive reaction to the growing significance of women within evangelical organizations toward the end of the nineteenth century.[13] And in a similar vein, sociologist Martin Riesebrodt has described both Christian *and* Islamic fundamentalism as two versions of a "patriarchal protest movement" in reaction to modernity.[14] Various works of feminist theology shed additional light on the strategies of theological reasoning that has been deployed in support of fundamentalist-patriarchal structures.[15] The revival of Protestant fundamentalism since the 1970s has also been described on numerous occasions as a conservative "rollback" that goes hand in hand with sexism in its struggles against societal liberalization.[16] In the introduction to their anthology *Fundamentalism & Gender* (1994), John Stratton Hawley and Wayne Proudfoot conceptualize the meaning of gender in the context of fundamentalism as generally linked to a "conservative ideology of gender."[17] In contrast to more usual, one-sided theses positing oppression of "the woman" Judy Brink and Joan Mencher emphasize in their reader *Mixed Blessings: Gender and Religious Fundamentalism Cross Culturally* (1997) how women have been politically and socioeconomically integrated into different fundamentalist communities.[18] Ran-

13. Bendroth, *Fundamentalism and Gender*.

14. Riesebrodt, *Pious Passion*, 206. The term "patriarchal protest movement" (*patriarchalische Protestbewegung* in German) is also part of the book title to the German edition of Riesebrodt's *Pious Passion* and describes one of the book's main arguments. See Riesebrodt, *Fundamentalismus*.

15. Schüssler Fiorenza, *Searching*.

16. Ostendorf, "Conspiracy Nation," 163–65; Riesebrodt, "Protestantischer Fundamentalismus," 12–13.

17. Hawley and Proudfoot, "Introduction," 4.

18. Mencher, "Introduction." See also Riesebrodt, "Fundamentalismus, Säkularisierung," 83–86.

dall Balmer calls attention to the cultural-historical specificity behind the religious and social ideals of femininity informing fundamentalist constructions of gender.[19] And in her study of conservative evangelicals in the US, Dagmar Herzog demonstrates that religious conservatism does not invariably lead to the general suppression and silencing of sexuality; rather it succeeds in generating new discursive positions through its discussions of putatively right and wrong sexualities as the emergence of the evangelical "multimillion-dollar Christian sex industry" indicates.[20] With regard to conservative Catholicism and theories of New Natural Law, which serve to legitimize heteronormative constructions of gender and sexual politics, Bamforth and Richards thus see a form of fundamentalism constituted by "moral absolutes."[21]

These various examples show how questions concerning the social construction of gender and sexual politics have acquired substantial significance for research on fundamentalism in many different ways. In their various attempts to describe the exact nature of the relationship between basic religious tenets of faith, its holy writings and/or dogmas, and the establishment of sociocultural norms, such studies also arrive at different answers. For example, Hawley and Proudfoot juxtapose the literalist belief in biblical inerrancy with social themes of gender, reading them together through the lens of the abortion debate. In doing so, they establish a position that illustrates just how impossible it is to apply a *literal* reading of the Bible to this issue.[22] They ultimately reach the conclusion, "As American fundamentalism has prospered over the last two decades, its most powerful message has been one of social, not scriptural, inerrancy."[23] Rather differently, a substantial connection between gender and literalism can also be ascertained that clearly extends further than social constructions of gender. This, in any case, is one of the points driven home by Vincent Crapanzano, who describes Christian literalism as a modern "style . . . of interpretation"[24] that is coded as

---

19. Balmer, "American Fundamentalism."

20. Herzog, *Sex in Crisis*, blurb. The "Christian sex industry" includes in particular the wide field of Christian literature of advice on sexual behavior.

21. Bamforth and Richards, *Patriarchal Religion*, 279.

22. Hawley and Proudfoot, "Introduction," 3–4.

23. Ibid., 4.

24. Crapanzano, *Serving*, xvii.

masculine by its "pragmatic, tough minded realism."²⁵ By asking what role gendered forms of knowledge play in the fundamentalist context and what relationship they have to modernity and its social constructions of gender, Crapanzano's reflections on literalism as a "masculine" system of knowledge help to broaden the interpretive framework of gender-theoretical analysis.

Against this background, defined by the multifarious and mutual relationships between fundamentalism and gender, the conference "Fundamentalism and Gender: Scripture—Body—Community,"²⁶ on which this anthology is based on, raised a number of overarching questions: For what reasons are all (religious) fundamentalisms constituted to a substantial degree by (normalizing) definitions of sexuality, gender roles, and intergender relations? Why do sexual politics constitute a common denominator of religious fundamentalisms that otherwise radically differ? To what extent and why does the category gender play a role (or not) in definitions of fundamentalism? What understanding of religion, politics, society/community, and the individual subject are implied by different fundamentalisms and in critical discussions about them? In what way do gender and sexual politics play a role in secular criticisms of religious fundamentalism? And finally, how are forms of secular fundamentalism characterized by gender constructs and sexual politics?

As these questions show, one of the overarching research interests behind this anthology is in the analytical diversification of the term *fundamentalism* and its various intersections with the category gender. On the one hand, the focus is on the historical and current specificity of religious fundamentalisms within the three Religions of the Book (Judaism, Christianity, and Islam). On the other hand, consideration is also given throughout to those Western secular means and methods of self-affirmation that are structured with recourse to discursive knowledge production about (religious) fundamentalism. Analytical perspectives that make use of the term fundamentalism with regard to secular phenomena are also included. Accordingly, consideration is given to what is or has been understood by fundamentalism in various disciplines and political or religious contexts.

25. Ibid., 24.
26. The conference was held in December 2010 at the Humboldt University in Berlin. For the conference website, see www2.hu-berlin.de/gkgeschlecht/fundamentalismus.

For the anthology, then, the diverse possibilities for applying the concept of fundamentalism and its various alternatives were purposefully left open. On the whole, however, this publication makes no claims to be complete or give equal weight to different forms of fundamentalism (religious and secular). If anything, an overview of the various contributions here suggests that they might better be understood as an invitation to sound out the limits and possibilities offered by the term fundamentalism and discuss related themes from the various perspectives afforded by religious and cultural studies and history, as well as by sociopolitical points of view.

In terms of content, a certain conceptual premise entailed here involves reflecting in more detail on the relationships between (religious) fundamentalism and modernity. To be sure, conflicts between religions have always existed—and especially between the three Religions of the Book. But paradoxically, these conflicts seem to have grown both in amplitude and forcefulness since large parts of the world have turned *away* from religion and toward a secular understanding of itself. Why is that? Why is religious fundamentalism on the rise in the so-called modern world? One of the answers is, of course, that fundamentalism appears where the fundaments themselves have given way; and it is true that the loss of religious fundaments can be felt as an abyss, which creates the need for a lot of new concrete and high walls intended to separate one's own group from all others. Against this background, many works have understandably sought to describe fundamentalism primarily as an antimodern phenomenon. Yet, an overarching conceptual focus for this book lies in critically questioning approaches that seek to define and understand (religious) fundamentalism as a *strict* form of antimodernism and in doing so imagine a realm of religious irrationality—approaches that are structured by simplified dichotomies between enlightenment versus religion, rationality versus irrationality, reason versus unreasonableness.[27] So even if religious fundamentalisms are frequently associated with conservatism and the rhetoric of antimodernism, they must also be understood at the same time—as will be

---

27. Instructive in this context is, e.g., the title of an anthology published by Thomas Meyer: *Fundamentalismus in der modernen Welt: Die Internationale der Unvernunft*. See also Hubbert, *Fundamentalismus*. In their strict antireligious attitude, the works of Richard Dawkins can also be problematized in this respect. See Dawkins, *God Delusion*. On Dawkins, see von Braun in this volume.

underscored here—as a *result* of modernity and thus deeply imbricated with modern developments. Along these same lines, Gottfried Küenzlen speaks of fundamentalism as a form of "modern antimodernism."[28] That religious fundamentalisms are by no means categorically opposed to modernity, science, and new technologies is evident not least of all in their use of modern media, a fact that has been repeatedly highlighted.[29]

The interconnections between religious fundamentalism and modernity also become particularly apparent in the case of fundamentalist gender ideals: while the impression is often aroused in the context of (religious) fundamentalism that prevailing, normative notions of gender should be timeless constants independent of culture, the universal results of divine creation, they can—in contrast to such a-historical assumptions—only be understood in historical hindsight against the rise of modernity. For in the Western context, the cultural construction of a naturalized sexual dichotomy and the heteronormative nuclear family are the results of discursive processes engendered in bourgeois society—the outcome of a historical interplay between scholarly, cultural, and economic discourses and societal practices of modernity.[30]

By challenging both historical and ongoing relationships between science and religion, as well as between secular and religious thought, this anthology focuses on interdependent structures of modern religious and secular knowledge productions about gender and asks how this intrinsically intersects with other modern/secular categories of power and difference, most notably race and nation. The book therefore uses gender and religion as analytical and intersectional categories that embrace both sociopolitical and symbolic levels of analysis. It furthermore gives rise to an analysis of gender as a category of knowledge in context of both religious and secular knowledge production and their intersections. On the epistemic level, this implies asking to what extent modern religious and secular claims to objectivity not only diverge but also correlate.

In the next section, we would like to summarize the basic conceptual concerns behind the three thematic foci and chapter divisions in the present volume—"Literalism, Religion, and Science," "Nation,

28. Küenzlen, "Fundamentalismus," 53, 56.

29. Tibi, *Islamischer Fundamentalismus*; Marty and Appleby, *Glory*; Riesebrodt, "Protestantischer Fundamentalismus."

30. Frevert, *Mann und Weib*; Hausen, "Polarisierung."

Literalism, Religion, and Science

Thematizing the connections between literalism, religion, and science is indebted, firstly, to the observation that religious literalism, meaning the belief in the literal truth of the holy scriptures, constitutes one of the usual definitional criteria for religious fundamentalism. Accordingly, from a gender-theoretical perspective the relationships between literalism and social constructions of gender are subject to negotiation. Previous research has thus devoted itself to breaking down and contextualizing literalist interpretations of individual passages from the Bible and the Koran through the varied lenses of theology, social politics, the history of religion, and cultural history.[31] This includes critical studies of fundamentalist positions on a variety of sociocultural norms, adjacent attempts to find an appropriate religious rationale for these positions, and the various discrepancies that can accompany literalist claims to truth (see Crapanzano in this volume).

Simultaneously, this focus on belief in the written word draws on analyses from both cultural and religious studies dedicated to understanding the ways gender is encoded in both the oral and written traditions of knowledge associated with the three Religions of the Book.[32] Beyond the religious context, however, literalism also poses questions about the extent to which religious and secular forms of loyalty to the written word and literal hermeneutics may even be compared. Making the analogy between science and religion, Erich Geldbach has described (Christian) literalism as a factual way of reading the Bible, a practice he associates with a so-called "theology of facts."[33] In contrast to this purely allegorical connection between science and religious literalism, Christina von Braun's article pursues a more concrete comparison of the religious and scientific-secular belief in the written word, which she

---

31. Balmer, "American Fundamentalism"; Balmer, *Kingdom*; Mernissi, *Veil*; Schüssler Fiorenza, *Searching*.

32. Ahmed, *Border Passage*; Braun and Mathes, *Verschleierte Wirklichkeit*.

33. Geldbach, *Fundamentalismus*, 45.

illuminates in more detail for a Western context in terms of its religious and cultural history.

Basically, the conflicting relationships between literalism, religion, and science imply a need to examine literalist claims to objectivity more closely and ask questions about the ambivalent relationship between (religious) literalism and (secular) science. While religious literalism is usually perceived as being separate from modern secular science, religion has still made a number of attempts to appropriate science for specific agendas, as the much discussed concept of Creationism continues to demonstrate. And while literalist recourse to holy scriptures is often depicted as both a salutary return to fundamentals and a turning away from modern societies perceived to be in crisis, the relationship between religious fundamentalism and modernity is on the whole far more ambivalent than this (see Riesebrodt in this volume).Examining literalist claims to objectivity also entails problematizing religious reasons and explanations of secular (scientific) configurations of knowledge. At issue is the need to clarify the cultural and temporal specificities that inform literalist knowledge production, as can be seen in the case of historical literalist attempts to justify modern anti-Semitic and racist knowledge bases (see Husmann in this volume).

A final topic relevant to the relationship between literalism, religion, and science consists in the ways scholarly work in religious studies access the holy scriptures. With this, the various lines of conflict between different hermeneutic traditions and textual understandings become the subject of negotiation, as Angelika Neuwirth demonstrates in her discussion of Western-European and Muslim Qurʾānic scholars.

Nation, State, and Community

Most obviously, the concerns comprising the focus on "Nation, State, and Community" result from nationally specific versions of different religious fundamentalisms. For example, the peculiarities of fundamentalist religious movements in the US, Iran, and Israel have all been examined in terms of the local (socio)political developments in these countries during the 1970s and 80s.[34] Likewise, the gender-political as-

---

34. Marty and Appleby, *Glory*; Much and Pfeifer, *Bruderzwist*; Kepel, *Revenge*; Riesebrodt, *Pious Passion*. For further historical and national contexts see, e.g., Gaier, *Muslimischer Nationalismus*; Goldberg, *Kingdom Coming*; Rausch, *Zionism*; Schied,

pects of fundamentalism have been linked to these individual national contexts.[35] At the same time, however, we find transnational commonalities between different fundamentalisms, for example their manifestation as "patriarchal protest movements," as already mentioned above.[36]

All in all, the creation of fundamentalist movements poses essential questions about the cultural and political processes behind religious community-building. At issue is the extent to which gender plays a role in this context, on a symbolic as well as a social level. Contrary to the static and ideal notions advanced by fundamentalist communities, it therefore seems necessary to highlight the historical evolution and elasticity that ultimately inform religious constructions of community and their various depictions of gender. Micha Brumlik's article on the historical development of the matrilineal principle in Judaism offers an illustrative example of this fundamentally fluid character and the historico-cultural contextuality of religious community-building.

Yet another cluster of themes connected to questions concerning fundamentalism, nation, and community deals with issues of nationalism, anti-Semitism, and/or racism, as well as religious anti-Judaism and anti-Islamism within religious fundamentalisms. Here, the interrelationship between religious and secular constructions of community comes to the fore, which in turn also necessitates considering the gendered dynamics behind such group formations. In addition to this, the nexus between nationalism and racism also touches on the matter of secular fundamentalisms. This includes those approaches that regard nationalism itself *as* fundamentalism.[37] In this context, for example, even National Socialism has been described as a form of "[r]eligious fundamentalism" on account of its various sacral elements.[38] In order to

Nationalismus. On the relationship between nationalism and fundamentalism, see also Lintl, *Fundamentalism*; Marx, "Fundamentalismus"; Mehmet, *Fundamentalismus*; Moaddel, *Islamic Modernism*.

35. In this regard, many scholars point to the connections between Protestant fundamentalism and the American New Right movement in reaction to gender-political liberalizations. See Herzog, *Sex in Crisis*; Ostendorf, "Conspiracy Nation"; Riesebrodt, "Protestantischer Fundamentalismus." On the differences between evangelical and militant right-wing fundamentalist groups like "Christian Identity," see Zickmund, "Verschwörungstheorien."

36. Riesebrodt, *Pious Passion*.

37. Breuer, *Ästhetischer Fundamentalismus*; idem, *Moderner Fundamentalismus*.

38. Albert, *Religiöser Fundamentalismus*.

break down the connections between nationalism, racism, and secular fundamentalism, Claudia Bruns' article examines the Christian-Jewish dialogue during the Weimar Republic era and looks at the underlying correlations between national/nationalist, rascist, and religious constructions of community.

Lastly, questions about nationalism and racism also become relevant to critical reflections on Western discourse about fundamentalism and are examined through the theoretical framework of a Critical Occidentalism (*Kritischer Okzidentalismus*).[39] Here, the Western modes of self-affirmation and homogeneous images of community generated through secular forms of knowledge about religious Islamic fundamentalism are themselves subject to scrutiny. Considered through the lens of theories of racism this leads to a number of questions: To what extent are new manifestations of "neo-racism"[40] relevant in this context? How are the categories of culture and religion bound in newly essentializing ways? And lastly, in what ways are traditional Western self-understandings of "race" and "ethnos" projected onto religion? Examining occidentalist notions of community and related sexual-political discourses in the contemporary German context, Gabriele Dietze offers fresh insights into the extent to which occidentalist antifundamentalism can itself be analyzed as a form of (political) fundamentalism. Belonging to this same cluster of themes are analyses that focus on the imagination of communities and regulatory state practices brought about by Western political discourses of a "war on terror." Through recourse to the idea of homonationalism, Jasbir Puar has investigated the sexual-political dimensions of this political discourse in two respects: on the one hand, with a view to the political absorption of queer politics in the context of American nationalism, and on the other with a view to sexualized stereotypes of the fundamentalist Other.[41] Puar's article here pursues the idea of homonationalism and instrumentalizations of sexual-political discourses with reference to the Israeli-Palestinian conflict.

---

39. Dietze, "Critical Whiteness Theory"; Dietze et al., *Okzidentalismus*.
40. Balibar, "Neo-Racism."
41. Puar, *Terrorist Assemblages*.

Body, Life, and Biopolitics

In the context of fundamentalism, the thematic focus on "Body, Life, and Biopolitics" encompasses a broad field of questions related to social practices normalizing the individual body, the ways the collective bodies of the self and other are imagined, and the various biopolitical regulations centering on both the body and the concept of life.

Belonging to this particular constellation of themes is a classic field of feminist intervention, namely the struggle with culturally-sanctioned powers of control over the (female) body. Accordingly, connected to this are the study of religious-fundamentalist strategies for legitimizing gender hierarchies and the critical illumination of cultural bans and precepts regulating life conduct. This also leads to questions concerning the discrepancies evident between religious imperatives and culturally passed-down practices of hierarchization (see Hassim in this volume). Additional questions concern lastly the various discrepancies between (female) religious figures, metaphors, symbols, and social constructions of gender, questions that were given early emphasis within the field of religious studies.[42]

A closer examination of the category of the body furthermore ensues against the background of numerous gender-theoretical works that attempt to sound out the relationship between the individual and the collective body in more detail: this includes research in the fields of cultural studies, religious studies, and history, all of which investigate the metaphorical and allegorical gendering of collective bodies[43] and/or analyze how the body is imagined in sexualized, racist, and anti-Semitic discourse.[44] An additional point of theoretical approach to the body lies in the ways Queer Theory and related methodologies critically reflect the cultural production of bodily norms that characterize the heterosexual matrix.[45]

---

42. See, e.g., the classic reader by Bynum et al., *Gender and Religion*; Bynum, "Introduction."

43. Lanwerd, "Religion"; Wenk, *Versteinerte Weiblichkeit*.

44. Braun, "Feind"; McClintock, *Imperial Leather*; Mosse, *Image of Man*. For its part, the "white body as feminist fetish" has also been subject to critical reflections on race. See Lorey, "Körper."

45. Butler, "Bodies." On the scientific history behind bipolar body images, see Laqueur, *Making Sex*.

Against this backdrop, the most diverse inroads appear for further possible research on fundamentalism. This means asking, among other questions, what religious, secular, and organic metaphors of the body are invoked by fundamentalist constructs of the self and the other, as well as what interrelations play a role between the individual body, the collective body, and the (holy) body of text. By examining the normative processes that serve to engender, (de)sexualize, and heteronormalize the body, questions arise over religious-fundamentalist efforts to justify a normative model of the (two) sexes, together with attendant symbolic and sociopolitical functions. Applying the methods of "queering" in this context, Lisa Isherwood examines theological-patriarchal and fundamentalist Christian approaches to interpreting the bodies of the sexually marginalized as well as the symbolic body of the earth itself and contemplates both the underlying and alternative conceptions of "life."

An additional thematic constellation centers on the relationship between fundamentalism, the concept of life, and biopolitical strategies of regulation, which includes questions about the appropriate use of new technologies. At stake are fundamental questions about the way religions distinguish between lives that can be lived, are worth preserving, and are capable of procreation. Where the question is a matter of defining life, religious-fundamentalist positions are mostly perceived as "anti-emancipatory" ones that adopt contrarian attitudes toward the technological advances offered by science; this figures into debates over cloning, stem cell research, artificial insemination, and abortion, but also into more secular controversies over issues like kinship, (gay) marriage, and adoption rights. Frequently, too, (religious) conflicts over the status and definition of life remain ethical rather than becoming biopolitical in nature. In contrast to this, however, one can also consider exactly the opposite scenario—in other words, the extent to which religious fundamentalisms indeed regulate the sexual politics of gender and the body. This requires close examination of fundamentalist influences on scientific theory and practice of the sort undertaken by Carmel Shalev in her study of ultra-Orthodox interpretations of Jewish *halakah* and their implications for the practice of reproductive medicine in Israel.

On another level, the concept of human life can also assist with the project of theorizing the relationship between theological-fundamentalist regulations on human life on the one hand, and resistive subject formations on the other. Thus, in her proposal of a "critical bio-theology," Ulrike Auga negotiates various political and philosophical concepts of power, knowledge, and agency in order to conceptualize the religious sphere itself as a possible site of resistance—one that is equally capable of permitting new, temporary, and performative concepts of life.

If the individual contributions to this volume have already been touched upon in part above, we would now like to introduce them as such by summarizing their basic arguments.

Article Overview

Section 1: Literalism, Religion, and Science

Christina von Braun opens the first section with her article "Religion and Science—An Opposition?" Here, von Braun reveals a number of structural similarities pertinent to all forms of fundamentalism—be they of religious or secular origin. She puts special emphasis on one characteristic in particular: the manner in which the written word, especially the sacred texts, are confounded with historical truth and reality. This "literalism"—the act of taking the printed word for reliable truth—has already been pointed to by other scholars. Christina von Braun additionally demonstrates that this phenomenon is closely related to specific historical changes prompted by the alphabets—the writing system that became the basis for all three "Religions of the Book." And yet the Enlightenment also proclaimed a deep belief in the written word—a factor to reflect upon when we think of modern fundamentalism.

By contrast, *Martin Riesebrodt* focuses on the concept of fundamentalism solely in the context of religion. Taking his departure point from its historical status as a Protestant phenomenon, Riesebrodt theorizes the extent to which fundamentalism can apply to a diverse spectrum of religious groups and cultural contexts. Gender and fundamentalism are understood as complementary categories of social and historical analysis. His article underscores the structural similarity between different fundamentalisms, which then becomes visible through processes of centralization and the patriarchal regulation of gender relations and sexual moralities. At the same time, Riesebrodt also pleads for a differentiated view that considers the diversity of cultural gender-regimes and critically assesses ideal-typical characterizations against concrete manifestations of fundamentalism.

Vincent Crapanzano brings an ethnological perspective to his study of various strains of Protestant fundamentalism in the United States. His article "Jesus Enters the Battle of the Sexes" takes a critical look at contemporary forms of biblical counseling, evangelical self-help literature (best-selling books of advice on marital relations and sexual behavior), and the practice of sanctification. Crapanzano stresses the significance accorded to Jesus as a mediating figure in fundamentalist gender relations and problematizes the inherent hierarchization and mechanization of sexual relationships. At the same time, his analysis takes into account literalism's underlying modes of interpretation and spells out the discrepancies that arise between the interpretive claims of literalism and fundamentalist paraphrasings of Holy Scripture.

Jana Husmann also focuses on forms of Protestant fundamentalism but examines it in the historical context of Germany during the 1930s. She analyzes the various interrelationships between fundamentalism, literalism, and anti-Semitism, which are then exemplified by the German *Bibelbund* (Bible Confederation). Beginning with the contemporary conflicts centered on the Old Testament's status as Christianity's Jewish legacy, Husmann discusses how the Bibelbund positioned itself toward National-Socialist racial ideology. In doing so she inquires into the ways religion is racialized while secular categories are sacralized, processes that become potently effective in the context of religious anti-Semitism. This is accompanied by reflections on the intersections of religion, race, nation, and gender, which pertain to concrete forms of literalist knowledge production on the one hand and affect both literalism as a system of knowledge and its ambivalent relationship to science on the other.

Starting with the observation that "the West" and "Islam" are often presented as two distinct monolithic blocks, both in the Western public sphere and in the scholarly field of Qur'ānic studies, *Angelika Neuwirth* investigates the conflicts and hermeneutical barriers that persist between Western European and Muslim Qur'ānic scholars. Throughout, she thematizes the present-day conflicts that give rise to different scriptural understandings of the Qur'ān and its genesis: these include juxtaposing notions of a transcendent *ur-schrift* or protoscript on the one hand, and those conceiving of the Qur'ān as a failed "imitation of the Bible" on the other. Neuwirth reveals the historical development of such antagonisms. Unlike narrower, Eurocentric interpretations, she makes a case for reintegrating the Qur'ān and Early Islam into the epoch of Late Antiquity, thereby stressing the common theological and cultural history of the three monotheistic religions and their "scriptural communities."

Section 2: Nation, State, and Community

Section 2, "Nation, State, and Community," opens with *Micha Brumlik's* article "Belonging to Halakhic Judaism: On the Sense of Matrilineal Descent." Concentrating on how, when, and why the matrilineal principle of Jewish descent developed as it did, Brumlik traces the historical lines and breaks in the development of Jewish identity formation and in the historically variable criteria that define Judaism and being Jewish following the First Temple's destruction in 587 BCE. With recourse to biblical and Talmudic sources, Brumlik discusses the "ethnogenesis"—the relationship between Jewish religion and ethnicity—and demonstrates why this should be understood as the result of both exile and anti-Semitism. The implementation of the matrilineal principle during the rabbinic era can be understood as an effect of internal political strife during the period of Early Judaism. Brumlik's commentary on the complex historical processes of Jewish belonging thus point to the paradox constituted by matrilineal geneaology and legal restrictions on women, a paradox that becomes operative through a series of historical episodes.

Claudia Bruns considers the extent to which racist elements in the Christian-Jewish dialogue at the start of the twentieth century can be read as a sign of fundamentalist tendencies and asks how tightly the connections between fundamentalism, racism, and gender can be ascertained here. On the basis of a Christian-Jewish dispute between Hans Blüher and Hans-Joachim Schoeps, published in 1933 under the title "Streit um Israel," the author drives home just how deeply the categories of race, gender, and national identity penetrated religious discourse at the end of the Weimar Republic and contributed to its fundamentalization. In addition to this, the close imbrication of religious and racial discourses in the present day is also revealed, laying bare how the German nation is created and conceived anew as an ethno-racial unity primarily through a strategic focus on religious differences.

In her article on "Antifundamentalism as Fundamentalism," *Gabriele Dietze* directs her attention to forms of secular political fundamentalism, exemplified on the one hand, she says, by the anticommunism of the McCarthy era in the United States during the 1950s and on the other by contemporary anti-Islamic discourse in Germany. Dietze's basic thesis is that antifundamentalist political agitation—whether against Maoism and/or communism as a kind of secular fundamentalism, or Islamist fundamentalism and "Islam as culture"—exhibits characteristic features of fundamentalism in its own right. In the process, Dietze underscores the relevance of sexual politics to antifundamentalist discourse and shows how German anti-Islam discourse makes connections between gender constructs, neo-racism, and occidentalist visions of nation and community.

Jasbir Puar devotes her attention to forms of homonationalism and the so-called "pinkwashing" she claims are practiced by the state of Israel. Her concern is to work out the complex imbrication of sexual politics, specifically with regard to gay and lesbian rights, in the Israeli-Palestinian conflict. Taking up the example of the "Brand Israel" campaign, Puar pursues the thesis that Israeli self-images of "gay-friendliness" become politically intrumentalized: according to this, dualistic constructs are used to stage Israel as gay-friendly, progressive, and Westernized while making Islamic nations appear backward, repressive, and homophobic—images that correspond to stereotypes about Islamist fundamentalists. The title of her article, "Citation and Censorship: The Politics of Talking About the Sexual Politics of Israel," furthermore alludes to the debates that preceded the conference and were spurred largely by Puar's original lecture title—"Beware Israeli Pinkwashing"—as well as another article she wrote for *The Guardian* on "Israel's gay propaganda war," which appeared in July of 2010. This was the context in which Puar was compelled to contend with accusations of anti-Semitism. Contrary to her depiction of events, however, it was not the organizers of the conference who accused Puar of anti-Semitism but some of the doctoral students from the PhD Research Training Group "Gender as a Category of Knowledge," among whom these claims were also quite controversial. The purportedly anti-Semitic elements of Puar's critical view of Israel were also claimed by certain activist groups in Berlin and were discussed critically in some sectors of the Berlin public sphere. The conference organizers' attempt to communicate the ensuing controversy to Puar prior to the conference left her understandably confused due to the short notice she received and the unclear formulation of the complaint. Responding to the accusations of anti-Semitism, Puar argues in her article for a distinction between criticisms of Israeli state practice and anti-Semitism as a form of racism directed against Jewish people. While the organizing committee had already rejected the accusations of anti-Semitism against Puar prior to the actual conference, her critique of Israel nonetheless remained contentious. In an interview, for example, Christina von Braun positioned herself against Puar's argument in the *Guardian* article. Puar interpreted this interview as well as the additional events leading up to the conference as the dynamic between "Citation and Censorship." Her theses that the Israeli state practices "pinkwashing" as well as the initial discussions about it consequently led to controversies at the conference. These debates implied mainly two problematic aspects of handling the subject: Firstly, and generally, they revealed the difficulty of discussing the Middle East conflict in a German context without resorting to polemics; and secondly, the conference discussions disclosed the limitation of those identity politics that confine questions of power and hegemony solely to (post-)coloniality and leave little or no space for more nuanced political views of the Middle East conflict, nor for an analytical differentiation of "whiteness" and "white hegemony" that would include critical reflections on anti-Semitism. More complex attempts to consider and differentiate between historical and contemporary power relations, different experiences of violence, and intermediate positions within the framework of (identity) politics remain challenging, to be sure—especially, though not exclusively, in discussions about the conflict in the Middle East.

Section 3: Body, Life, and Biopolitics

The third section, "Body, Life, and Biopolitics," begins with *Lisa Isherwood's* article "Queer Theologies and Sacred Bodies." Isherwood looks at bodies that resist patriarchal and fundamentalist Christian theologizing. She gives an outline of fundamentalist monotheistic eschatology and its absurd endeavor to "strip the planet of all its resources"—intended to clear space for the messiah's act of total re-creation—and also considers the ways these ideas have influenced both policy making and various processes of "othering." Isherwood draws on Marcella Althaus-Reid's notion of the Bi/Christ, as well as on the ways transpeople—transgendered individuals, transsexuals, and transvestites—challenge the reigning gender orthodoxy. She proposes a eucharistic love that has no investment in the heteronormative "arrangement" of body parts. Rendering what could be termed a "queer cosmology," Isherwood traces the shift in metaphors of the earth as a body or organism in order to reread the creation narrative through a decolonizing lens—one that leads away from an all-powerful father who instantaneously "zaps" out the world and toward a subtler, more enticing ethic of "chaos seeking enfleshment" characterized by emanations, *energeia*, and *dynamis*—in other words, the buried treasures of a post-Augustinian Christian tradition. Isherwood thus aims to send a shock wave through fundamentalist, dualist theologies, shattering their manifold alliances with neoliberalism.

Carmel Shalev brings together great expertise in medical, cultural, political, and religious scholarship in her complex study in order to discuss the fundamentalist, patriarchal, and ultra-Orthodox views informing various halakhic concepts of fertilization and reproduction. Israel, of course, is the example of choice where progressive policies toward reproduction and liberal application of new biomedical technologies are concerned. Shalev traces the correlations between medical progress and a national sense of mission by examining religious responses to and reconceptualizations of "health," "healing," and the biblical command to "be fruitful and multiply." She focuses on the biblical prohibition against "wasting seed," arguing that this obsession with sperm results in a preference for medical technologies that are ultimately more intrusive and more drastically violate women's bodies. Shalev demonstrates several cases in which restrictions enforced by halakhic kinship laws interfere with contemporary law and policy making and dictate how concrete clinical practice affects ultra-Orthodox couples—namely by engendering a form of "postmodern" fundamentalism that instrumentalizes women's bodies.

Shafinaaz Hassim skillfully reframes the traditional but objectifying saying that "women are diamonds," referring to her study *Daughters are Diamonds: When Honour Precludes Reflexivity* (2007). Setting her findings against the background of "honor killings" in Pakistan, Hassim draws on case studies featuring biographical narratives from six women in Johannesburg's Indian Muslim community. She focuses on the correlations between patriarchal structures, "honor," "shame," and "self-reflexivity." Throughout her exploration of these themes, a drastic imbalance becomes apparent in attempts to reconcile rereadings of religious texts (rereadings that understand the Qurʾān as "egalitarian" and "antipatriarchal") with juridical forms of reorganization on the one hand, and with the deeply inscribed social customs in countries with ties to Islamic faith and culture on the other. Hassim maps out the "loss of reflexivity" in honor- and shame-based social constructs by addressing their reliance on "terror," "stigma," and the "internalization of values." The biographical data she presents forms a continuum revealing both pressure to conform as well as more liberating experiences of self-realization—in any case, each of these women's lives are predominantly determined by a tight, visceral, and efficacious network of social control.

Ulrike Auga addresses the "troubled relationship" that queer, leftist, feminist, and other critical theories have with "religious" and theological discourses, which they deem conservative and restrictive. Combining religiopolitical theory and political theology, Auga aims to undermine the artificial dichotomy between the "secular" and "religious," which has only served to aggravate reinvigorated strains of fundamentalism worldwide. She demonstrates how the secular—no less than the religious—must be understood as a construct and category of knowledge that pits the "rational, scientific, enlightened, non-believing" against the "oppressive," "terrorist," and "obsolete" elements that are said to characterize (religious) faith. Auga looks at theoretical contributions by Spivak, Mbembe, and Puar, as well as their various reappropriations of fractured and marginalized bodies, the bodily language of suicide, and acts of self-destruction versus the (creation of a) Western Foucauldian subject. At the same time, however, she claims that the various theorists she discusses themselves fail to escape the visible configurations of agency and subject formation offered by Western discourse and unfortunately refuse to sufficiently attend to the religious aspects of their argument. Auga's project, a critical biotheology engaged in a critique of power and epistemic violence on the level of human life itself, also seeks to opens spaces for subject formation and agency, particularly within the religious sphere. Together with Saba Mahmood, Auga opts for new forms of life, unusual temporal alliances, and nonunivocal contextual performances—an array of future-oriented projects dedicated to human flourishing.

Conclusion of Conference Discussions

Looking back on the conference "Fundamentalism and Gender: Scripture—Body—Community," it can be concluded that the various contributions and the ensuing discussions about them resulted in a number of complex insights into the relationships between gender and fundamentalism as well as the interconnections between religious and secular traditions of thought, and encouraged critical reflections on the very concept of fundamentalism. Moreover, the broadening of the latter term to include secular fundamentalisms underscores how a strict dichotomy between religion and secularism falls short when thematizing the phenomenon. At the same time, the conference discussions also betrayed some potentially problematic issues, which could be seen partly in the attempts to extend the concept of fundamentalism beyond a religious framework: in any case, the claims that fundamentalism potentially loses much of its analytical function when applied to secular forms of knowledge will surely remain a controversial point for future discussions.

The impulse behind the conference—to reflect on the ways gender and fundamentalism mutually constitute and reinforce one other—was productively examined and discussed with an eye to the complex connections that ensue between religion, gender, sexuality, nation(alism), anti-Semitism, and racism. The most controversial discussions—those dealing with the Middle East conflict—also revealed the need within gender research to more strongly consider the various theoretical connections between postcolonialism, anti-Semitism research, Queer Theory, and Queer Politics in order to work against the possible pitfalls of one-sided intersectional research and simplistically political polarizations. In this regard, the conference not only delivered numerous insights into the relationship between gender and fundamentalism but also stimulated the kind of critical and controversial impulses necessary to further the ongoing development of gender-theoretical theories of intersectionality and interdependencies.

Bibliography

Ahmed, Leila. *A Border Passage: From Cairo to America—A Woman's Journey*. New York: Penguin, 1999.

———. *Women and Gender in Islam: Historical Roots of a Modern Debate*. New Haven: Yale University Press, 1992.

Albert, Hans. "Religiöser Fundamentalismus und Drittes Reich. Zur Analyse der Nationalsozialistischen Weltanschauung." In *Fundamentalismus "interdisziplinär,"* edited by Kurt Salamun, 85–116. Wien: LIT, 2005.

Alcoff, Linda Martin, and John D. Caputo. "Introduction: Feminism, Sexuality, and the Return of Religion." In *Feminism, Sexuality, and the Return of Religion*, edited by Linda Martin Alcoff and John D. Caputo, 1–16. Bloomington, IN: Indiana University Press, 2011.

Alcoff, Linda Martin, and John D. Caputo, editors. *Feminism, Sexuality, and the Return of Religion*. Bloomington, IN: Indiana University Press, 2011.

Alkier, Stefan, et al., editors. *Religiöser Fundamentalismus: Analysen und Kritiken*. Tübingen: Narr Francke Attempto, 2005.

Asad, Talal. "Free Speech, Blasphemy, and Secular Criticism." In Talal Asad et al., *Is Critique Secular? Blasphemy, Injury, and Free Speech*, 20–63. Berkeley: University of California Press, 2009.

Asad, Talal, et al. *Is Critique Secular? Blasphemy, Injury, and Free Speech*. Berkeley: University of California Press, 2009.

Auga, Ulrike, and Christina von Braun, editors. *Gender in Conflicts: Palestine—Israel—Germany*. Berlin: LIT, 2006.

Balibar, Etienne. "Is There a 'Neo-Racism'?" In *Race, Nation, Class: Ambiguous Identities*, edited by Etienne Balibar and Immanuel Wallerstein, 17–28. London: Verso, 1991.

Balmer, Randall. "American Fundamentalism: The Ideal of Femininity." In *Fundamentalism & Gender*, edited by John Stratton Hawley, 47–62. Oxford: Oxford University Press, 1994.

———. *Thy Kingdom Come: How the Religious Right Distorts the Faith and Threatens America. An Evangelical's Lament*. New York: Basic, 2006.

Bamforth, Nicholas, and David A. J. Richards. *Patriarchal Religion, Sexuality, and Gender: A Critique of New Natural Law*. New York: Cambridge University Press, 2008.

Barr, James. *Fundamentalism*. London: SCM, 1981.

Bendroth, Margaret Lamberts. *Fundamentalism and Gender: 1875 to the Present*. New Haven: Yale University Press, 1993.

Bendroth, Margaret Lamberts, and Virginia Lieson Brereton, editors. *Women and Twentieth-Century Protestantism*. Urbana, Chicago: University of Illinois, 2002.

Bielefeldt, Heiner, and Wilhelm Heitmeyer. "Einleitung: Politisierte Religion in der Moderne." In *Politisierte Religion. Ursachen und Erscheinungsformen des modernen Fundamentalismus*, edited by Heiner Bielefeldt and Wilhelm Heitmeyer, 11–36. Frankfurt: Suhrkamp, 1998.

Bielefeldt, Heiner, and Wilhelm Heitmeyer, editors. *Politisierte Religion. Ursachen und Erscheinungsformen des modernen Fundamentalismus*. Frankfurt: Suhrkamp, 1998.

Braun, Christina von. "Und der Feind ist Fleisch geworden. Der rassistische Antisemitismus." In *Der ewige Judenhaß: Christlicher Antijudaismus, Deutschnationale Judenfeindlichkeit, Rassistischer Antisemitismus*, 2nd ed., edited by Christina von Braun and Ludger Heid, 149–213. Berlin: Philo, 2000.

———. *Versuch über den Schwindel: Religion, Schrift, Bild, Geschlecht*. Zürich: Pendo, 2001.

Braun, Christina von, et al., editors. *"Holy War" and Gender: Violence in Religious Discourses—"Gotteskrieg" und Geschlecht: Gewaltdiskurse in der Religion*. Berlin: LIT, 2006.

Braun, Christina von, and Bettina Mathes. *Verschleierte Wirklichkeit: Die Frau, der Islam und der Westen*. Berlin: Aufbau, 2007.
Breuer, Stefan. *Ästhetischer Fundamentalismus: Stefan George und der deutsche Antimodernismus*. Darmstadt: Primus, 1995.
———. *Moderner Fundamentalismus*. Berlin: Philo, 2002.
Brink, Judy, and Joan Mencher, editors. *Mixed Blessings: Gender and Religious Fundamentalism Cross Culturally*. New York: Routledge, 1997.
Butler, Judith. *Bodies That Matter: On the Discursive Limits of Sex*. New York: Routledge, 1993.
———. "Is Judaism Zionism?" In Judith Butler et al., *The Power of Religion in the Public Sphere*, edited by Eduardo Mendieta and Jonathan VanAntwerpen, 70–91. New York: Columbia University Press, 2011.
———. "The Sensibility of Critique: Response to Asad and Mahmood." In Talal Asad et al., *Is Critique Secular? Blasphemy, Injury, and Free Speech*, 101–36. Berkeley: University of California Press, 2009.
Butler, Judith, et al. *The Power of Religion in the Public Sphere*, edited by Eduardo Mendieta, and Jonathan VanAntwerpen. New York: Columbia University Press, 2011.
Bynum, Caroline Walker. "Introduction: The Complexity of Symbols." In *Gender and Religion: On the Complexity of Symbols*, edited by Caroline Walker Bynum et al., 1–20. Boston: Beacon, 1986.
Bynum, Caroline Walker, et al., editors. *Gender and Religion: On the Complexity of Symbols*. Boston: Beacon, 1986.
Caplan, Lionel, editor. *Studies in Religious Fundamentalism*. Albany: SUNY Press, 1987.
Casanova, José. *Public Religions in the Modern World*. Chicago: University of Chicago Press, 1994.
———. "Rethinking Secularization: A Global Comparative Perspective." *Hedgehog Review* 8/1–2 (2006) 7–22.
Castelli, Elizabeth, and Rosamond C. Rodman, editors. *Women, Gender, Religion: A Reader*. New York: Palgrave, 2001.
Ceming, Katharina. *Gewalt und Weltreligionen: Eine interkulturelle Perspektive*. Nordhausen: Traugott Bautz, 2005.
Coronil, Fernando. "Beyond Occidentalism: Toward Nonimperial Geohistorical Categories." *Cultural Anthropology* 11/1 (1996) 51–87.
Crapanzano, Vincent. *Serving the Word. Literalism in America from the Pulpit to the Bench*. New York: New, 2000.
Dawkins, Richard. *The God Delusion*. London: Bantam, 2006.
DeBerg, Betty A. *Ungodly Women: Gender and the First Wave of American Fundamentalism*. Minneapolis: Fortress, 1990.
Di Blasi, Luca. "Das Nicht-Hermeneutische und der Fundamentalismus: Schnittflächen zwischen kulturellen und religiösen Valorisierungen des Alphabets." *TRANS: Internet-Zeitschrift für Kulturwissenschaften* 16 (2006). N.p. Online: http://www.inst.at/trans/16Nr/06_7/diblasi16.htm.
Dietze, Gabriele. "Critical Whiteness Theory und Kritischer Okzidentalismus: Zwei Figuren hegemonialer Selbstreflexion." In *Weiß—Weißsein—Whiteness: Kritische*

Studien zu Gender und Rassismus/Critical Studies on Gender and Racism, edited by Martina Tißberger et al., 219–48. Frankfurt: Lang, 2006.

Dietze, Gabriele, et al., editors. *Kritik des Okzidentalismus. Transdisziplinäre Beiträge zu (Neo-)Orientalismus und Geschlecht.* Bielefeld, Germany: transcript, 2009.

Dingel, Irene, editor. *Feministische Theologie und Gender-Forschung: Bilanz—Perspektiven—Akzente.* Leipzig: Evangelische Verlagsanstalt, 2003.

Frevert, Ute. *"Mann und Weib, und Weib und Mann." Geschlechter-Differenzen in der Moderne.* München: Beck, 1995.

The Fundamentals: A Testimony to the Truth (1910–1915). 4 vols. Edited by The Bible Institute of Los Angeles, 1917. Reprint: Grand Rapids: Baker, 1993. Online: http://www.xmission.com/~fidelis/index.php.

Gaier, Malte. *Muslimischer Nationalismus, Fundamentalismus und Widerstand in Pakistan: Die Bewegung Jama'at-i-Islami.* Berlin: LIT, 2012.

Geldbach, Erich. *Protestantischer Fundamentalismus in den USA und Deutschland.* Münster: LIT, 2001.

Goldberg, Michelle. *Kingdom Coming: The Rise of Christian Nationalism.* New York: Norton, 2007.

Habermas, Jürgen. *Glauben und Wissen: Friedenspreis des Deutschen Buchhandels 2001. Laudatio: Jan Philipp Reemtsma.* Frankfurt: Suhrkamp, 2001.

Harris, Jay M. "'Fundamentalism': Objections from a Modern Jewish Historian." In *Fundamentalism & Gender,* edited by John Stratton Hawley, 137–73. New York: Oxford University Press, 1994.

Hassim, Shafinaaz. *Daughters are Diamonds: Honour, Shame and Seclusion—A South African Perspective.* Wandsbeck, South Africa: Reach, 2007.

Hausen, Karin. "Polarisierung der Geschlechtscharaktere: Eine Spiegelung der Dissoziation in Erwerbs- und Familienleben." In *Sozialgeschichte der Familie in der Neuzeit Europas: Neue Forschungen,* edited by Werner Conze, 363–93. Stuttgart: Klett, 1976.

Hawley, John Stratton, editor. *Fundamentalism & Gender.* Oxford: Oxford University Press, 1994.

Hawley, John Stratton, and Wayne Proudfoot. "Introduction." In *Fundamentalism & Gender,* edited by John Stratton Hawley, 3–46. Oxford: Oxford University Press, 1994.

Heimann, Horst. "Marxismus als Fundamentalismus?" In *Fundamentalismus in der modernen Welt: Die Internationale der Unvernunft,* edited by Thomas Meyer, 213–30. Frankfurt: Suhrkamp, 1989.

Herzog, Dagmar. *Sex in Crisis: The New Sexual Revolution and the Future of American Politics.* New York: Basic, 2008.

Holthaus, Stephan. *Fundamentalismus in Deutschland: Der Kampf um die Bibel im Protestantismus des 19. und 20. Jahrhunderts.* Bonn: Kultur & Wissenschaft, 2003.

Höpflinger, Anna-Katharina, et al., editors. *Handbuch Gender und Religion.* Göttingen: Vandenhoeck & Ruprecht, 2008.

Isherwood, Lisa. *Introducing Feminist Christologies.* London: Continuum, 2001.

Isherwood, Lisa, editor. *Patriarchs, Prophets and Other Villains.* London: Equinox, 2007.

Jäger, Margarete, and Jürgen Link, editors. *Macht—Religion—Politik: Zur Renaissance religiöser Praktiken und Mentalitäten*. Münster: Unrast/Edition Diss, 2006.

Jäggi, Christian J., and David J. Krieger. *Fundamentalismus: Ein Phänomen der Gegenwart*. Zürich: Füssli, 1991.

Julé, Allyson, editor. *Gender and the Language of Religion*. New York: Palgrave Macmillan, 2005.

Kepel, Gilles. *The Revenge of God: The Resurgence of Islam, Christianity and Judaism in the Modern World*. Cambridge: Polity, 1994.

Kienzler, Klaus. *Der religiöse Fundamentalismus. Christentum—Judentum—Islam*. 2nd ed. München: Beck, 1999.

Kindelberger, Kilian, editor. *Fundamentalismus: Politisierte Religionen*. Brandenburgische Landeszentrale für politische Bildung Potsdam, 2004. Online: http://www.politische-bildung-brandenburg.de/publikationen/pdf/fundamentalismus.pdf.

King, Ursula, editor. *Religion and Gender*. Oxford, Cambridge, MA: Blackwell, 1995.

King, Ursula, and Tina Beattie, editors. *Gender, Religion, and Diversity: Cross-Cultural Perspectives*. London: Continuum, 2004.

Krämer, Gudrun. *Hasan al-Banna*. Oxford: Oneworld, 2010.

Krämer, Gudrun, and Sabine Schmidtke, editors. *Speaking for Islam: Religious Authorities in Muslim Societies*. Leiden: Brill, 2006.

Küenzlen, Gottfried. "Fundamentalismus: Moderner Antimodernismus. Kulturhistorische Überlegungen." *Praktische Theologie* 29/1 (1994) 43–56.

———. *Die Wiederkehr der Religion: Lage und Schicksal der säkularen Moderne*. München: Olzog, 2003.

Lanwerd, Susanne. "Religion, Repräsentation und Geschlecht: Religionswissenschaftliche Bemerkungen zur Funktion weiblicher Körperbilder." In *Handbuch Gender und Religion*, edited by Anna-Katharina Höpflinger et al., 209–24. Göttingen: Vandenhoeck & Ruprecht, 2008.

Lanwerd, Susanne, and Márcia Elisa Moser, editors. *Frau—Gender—Queer: Gendertheoretische Ansätze in der Religionswissenschaft*. Würzburg: Königshausen & Neumann, 2010.

Laqueur, Thomas. *Making Sex: Body and Gender from the Greeks to Freud*. Cambridge, MA: Harvard University Press, 1990.

Lehmann, David, and Humeira Iqtidar, editors. *Fundamentalism and Charismatic Movements*. 4 vols. New York: Routledge, 2011.

Lintl, Peter. *Fundamentalismus—Messianismus—Nationalismus: Ein Theorievergleich am Beispiel der jüdischen Siedler des Westjordanlandes*. Hamburg: Diplomica, 2012.

Lorey, Isabell. "Der weiße Körper als feministischer Fetisch. Konsequenzen aus der Ausblendung des deutschen Kolonialismus." In *Weiß—Weißsein—Whiteness: Kritische Studien zu Gender und Rassismus*, edited by Martina Tißberger et al., 61–83. Frankfurt: Lang, 2009.

Mahmood, Saba. "Can Secularism Be Other-wise?" In *Varieties of Secularism in a Secular Age*, edited by Michael Warner et al., 282–99. Cambridge, MA: Harvard University Press, 2010.

———. "Religion, Feminism, and the Empire: The New Ambassadors of Islamophobia." In *Feminism, Sexuality, and the Return of Religion*, edited by Linda Martin Alcoff and John D. Caputo, 77–102. Bloomington, IN: Indiana University Press, 2011.

———. "Religious Reason and Secular Affect: An Incommensurable Divide?" In Talal Asad et al., *Is Critique Secular? Blasphemy, Injury, and Free Speech*, 64–100. Berkeley: University of California Press, 2009.

Malone, Mary T. *Women & Christianity*. Vol. 3, *From the Reformation to the 21st Century*. Maryknoll, New York: Orbis, 2003.

Marsden, George M. *Fundamentalism and American Culture*. 2nd ed. Oxford, New York: Oxford University Press, 2006.

Marty, Martin E., and R. Scott Appleby. *The Glory and the Power: The Fundamentalist Challenge to the Modern World*. Boston: Beacon, 1992.

Marty, Martin E., and R. Scott Appleby, editors. *The Fundamentalism Project*. 5 vols. Chicago: University of Chicago Press, 1991–95.

Marx, Christoph. "Fundamentalismus und Nationalstaat." *Geschichte und Gesellschaft* 27/1 (2001) 87–117.

McClintock, Anne. *Imperial Leather: Race, Gender, and Sexuality in the Colonial Contest*. New York: Routledge, 1995.

Mehmet, Özay. *Fundamentalismus und Nationalstaat: Der Islam und die Moderne*. Hamburg: Europäische Verlagsanstalt, 2002.

Mencher, Joan. "Introduction." In *Mixed Blessings: Gender and Religious Fundamentalism Cross Culturally*, edited by Judy Brink and Joan Mencher, 1–8. New York: Routledge, 1997.

Mernissi, Fatima. *The Veil and the Male Elite: A Feminist Interpretation of Women's Rights in Islam*. Translated by Mary Jo Lakeland. Reading, MA: Addison-Wesley, 1991.

Meyer, Thomas. "Fundamentalismus. Die andere Dialektik der Aufklärung." In *Fundamentalismus in der modernen Welt: Die Internationale der Unvernunft*, edited by Thomas Meyer, 13–22. Frankfurt: Suhrkamp, 1989.

Meyer, Thomas, editor. *Fundamentalismus in der modernen Welt: Die Internationale der Unvernunft*. Frankfurt: Suhrkamp, 1989.

Moaddel, Mansoor. *Islamic Modernism, Nationalism, and Fundamentalism: Episode and Discourse*. Chicago: University of Chicago Press, 2005.

Mosse, George L. *The Image of Man: The Creation of Modern Masculinity*. New York: Oxford University Press, 1996.

Much, Theodor, and Karl Pfeifer. *Bruderzwist im Hause Israel: Judentum zwischen Fundamentalismus und Aufklärung*. Wien: Kremayr & Scheriau, 1999.

Neuwirth, Angelika, et al., editors. *The Qur'ān in Context: Historical and Literary Investigations into the Qur'ānic Milieu*. Leiden: Brill, 2010.

Ostendorf, Berndt. "Conspiracy Nation. Verschwörungstheorien und evangelikaler Fundamentalismus: Marion G. (Pat) Robertsons 'Neue Weltordnung.'" In *Politisierte Religion: Ursachen und Erscheinungsformen des modernen Fundamentalismus*, edited by Heiner Bielefeldt and Wilhelm Heitmeyer, 157–87. Frankfurt: Suhrkamp, 1998.

Pally, Marcia. *The New Evangelicals: Expanding the Vision of the Common Good*. Grand Rapids: Eerdman, 2011.

Pieh, Eleonore. *"Fight Like David—Run Like Lincoln." Die politischen Einwirkungen des protestantischen Fundamentalismus in den USA.* Mit einem Geleitwort von Klaus Beyme. Münster: LIT, 1998.
Prokop, Ulrike. "Rechtsradikalismus als politischer Fundamentalismus." In *Die halbierte Emanzipation? Fundamentalismus und Geschlecht*, edited by Elisabeth Rohr et al., 173–202. Königstein: Helmer, 2007.
Puar, Jasbir K. "Israel's gay propaganda war." *Guardian*, July 1, 2010, n.p. Online: http://www.guardian.co.uk/commentisfree/2010/jul/01/israels-gay-propaganda-war.
———. *Terrorist Assemblages: Homonationalism in Queer Times*. Durham, NC: Duke University Press, 2007.
Rausch, David A. *Zionism within Early American Fundamentalism, 1878–1918: A Convergence of Two Traditions*. New York: Mellen, 1979.
Riesebrodt, Martin. *Fundamentalismus als patriarchalische Protestbewegung. Amerikanische Protestanten (1910–28) und iranische Schiiten (1961–79) im Vergleich*. Tübingen: Mohr/Siebeck, 1990.
———. "Fundamentalismus, Säkularisierung und die Risiken der Moderne." In *Politisierte Religion: Ursachen und Erscheinungsformen des modernen Fundamentalismus*, edited by Heiner Bielefeldt and Wilhelm Heitmeyer, 67–90. Frankfurt: Suhrkamp, 1998.
———. *Pious Passion: The Emergence of Modern Fundamentalism in the United States and Iran*. Translated by Don Reneau. Berkeley: University of California Press, 1993.
———. "Protestantischer Fundamentalismus in den USA: Die religiöse Rechte im Zeitalter der elektronischen Medien." EZW-Texte: Informationen Nr. 102, 1–24. Stuttgart, 1987. Online: http://www.ekd.de/download/EZWINF102.pdf.
———. *Die Rückkehr der Religionen: Fundamentalismus und der Kampf der Kulturen*. München: Beck, 2000.
Rohr, Elisabeth, et al., editors. *Die halbierte Emanzipation? Fundamentalismus und Geschlecht*. Königstein: Helmer, 2007.
Salamun, Kurt, editor. *Fundamentalismus "interdisziplinär."* Vienna: LIT, 2005.
Sánchez, María Carla, and Lisa Schlossberg, editors. *Passing: Identity and Interpretation in Sexuality, Race, and Religion*. New York: New York University Press, 2001.
Schied, Michael. *Nationalismus und Fundamentalismus in Indien: Der Ayodhya-Konflikt*. Saarbrücken: VDM, 2008.
Schüssler Fiorenza, Elisabeth, editor. *Searching the Scripture*. Vol. 2, *A Feminist Commentary*. London: SCM, 1995.
Scott, Joan Wallach. *The Politics of the Veil*. Princeton: Princeton University Press, 2007.
Spivak, Gayatri Chakravorty. "Can the Subaltern Speak?" In *Marxism and the Interpretation of Culture*, edited by Cary Nelson and Lawrence Grossberg, 271–313. London: Macmillan, 1988.
Spohn, Willfried, editors. *Politik und Religion in einer sich globalisierenden Welt*. Wiesbaden: VS Verlag für Sozialwissenschaften, 2008.
Stadler, Nurit. *Yeshiva Fundamentalism: Piety, Gender, and Resistance in the Ultra-Orthodox World*. New York: New York University Press, 2009.

Taylor, Charles. *A Secular Age*. Cambridge, MA: Harvard University Press, 2007.
Tibi, Bassam. *Islamischer Fundamentalismus, moderne Wissenschaft und Technologie*. Frankfurt: Suhrkamp, 1992.
Tißberger, Martina et al., editors. *Weiß—Weißsein—Whiteness: Kritische Studien zu Gender und Rassismus/Critical Studies on Gender and Racism*. Frankfurt: Lang, 2006.
Trimondi, Victor, and Victoria Trimondi. *Krieg der Religionen: Politik, Glaube und Terror im Zeichen der Apokalypse*. München: Fink, 2006.
Turk, Horst, et al., editors. *Kulturelle Grenzziehungen im Spiegel der Literaturen: Nationalismus, Regionalismus, Fundamentalismus*. Göttingen: Wallstein, 1998.
Unger, Tim, editor. *Fundamentalismus und Toleranz*. Hannover: Lutherisches Verlagshaus, 2009.
Wagner-Rau, Ulrike. "Die Suche nach einem Fundament: Eine Einführung in die fundamentalistische Frömmigkeit." In *Die halbierte Emanzipation? Fundamentalismus und Geschlecht*, edited by Elisabeth Rohr et al., 11–28. Königstein: Helmer, 2007.
Walgenbach, Katharina, et al. *Gender als interdependente Kategorie: Neue Perspektiven auf Intersektionalität, Diversität und Heterogenität*. Opladen: Budrich, 2007.
Warner, Michael, et al., editors. *Varieties of Secularism in a Secular Age*. Cambridge, MA: Harvard University Press, 2010.
Wenk, Silke. *Versteinerte Weiblichkeit: Allegorien in der Skulptur der Moderne*. Köln: Böhlau, 1996.
Zickmund, Susan. "Religiöse Verschwörungstheorien und die Milizen in den USA." In *Politisierte Religion: Ursachen und Erscheinungsformen des modernen Fundamentalismus*, edited by Heiner Bielefeldt and Wilhelm Heitmeyer, 301–19. Frankfurt: Suhrkamp, 1998.

Literalism, Religion, and Science

Religion and Science— An Opposition?[1]

Christina von Braun

Some General Remarks on Terminology

We generally associate the term fundamentalism with religion, and I will attempt here to show how this notion is expressed in the three "religions of the book": Christianity, Judaism, and Islam. I shall limit my discussion to these religions for two reasons: first of all because this is where "literalism" is most marked, and second of all because literalism in turn is the point of reference for the phenomenon of fundamentalism in modern, nonreligious political movements as well as the sciences, which I will address in the final section of my remarks. Despite much common ground, great differences naturally exist between the various fundamentalist movements: thus fundamentalism may be allied with the state (for example, in Iran), or in opposition to it (for instance, in Algeria); it may also simply be a phenomenon with more or less influence on politics at different times, as is the case with the fundamentalism of the American Bible Belt. Such differences are usually a result of

---

1. Translated from German by Pamela Selwyn.

historical circumstances and, while significant in individual cases, not necessarily helpful in trying to understand fundamentalism as a mindset. Having said this in order to prevent misunderstandings, I shall now attempt some generalizations:

The various religious fundamentalisms share certain characteristics:

1. A low tolerance for ambivalence that goes hand in hand with notions of the purity of the social body or the compulsive need to purify it—not merely by distancing oneself from "Others" (and other social bodies) but also by expelling anything alien and erasing all that is "impure" and that "poisons" the social body. The reference to purity and notions of disease is instructive here.

2. A "backward-looking utopia," or what Martin Riesebrodt refers to as "utopian regress"[2]: Riesebrodt specifies that fundamentalist thinking is shaped by an "experience of crisis" and locates the causes in an abandonment of the eternal, divine, and written or orally transmitted principles once practiced in a "golden age."[3] The term "utopia" is illuminating here, because it was a Western invention, first of all, and closely associated with the written word. Utopias are models of an ideal world designed on paper and demanding realization. All Western utopias—whether Plato's *Republic*, Thomas More's *Utopia*, or Francis Bacon's scientific utopia *Nova Atlantis* became reality in the twentieth century in one form or another. The fundamentalist proceeds from a complete conformity between text and life.

3. This backward-looking utopia is associated with a belief in written texts that is sometimes referred to as "literalism" and sometimes also as "scripturalism."[4] This belief lacks the usual elements of belief in texts, since it is generally accompanied by an animosity toward intellectuals and artists:

4. Despite a clearly anti-modernist impetus, the modern media—and especially radio and television—play an important role for fundamentalisms. One might be tempted to see this as a countermovement to a belief in texts, since these media appear as a return to

---

2. Riesebrodt, *Fundamentalismus als Protestbewegung*, 21.
3. Ibid., 19–20.
4. Harwazinski, "Fundamentalismus/Rigorismus," 431–32.

orality in modern society. This assessment would be a wrong, however. Media theorist Vilém Flusser has written that technical images (photography and film) were invented in the nineteenth century so as "to re-charge the texts with magic."[5] However, this was preceded by a process of abstraction, which led away from material reality through reading and writing. Photography and other visual technologies succeeded in lending these abstract texts a "body" again. We should understand the use of modern means of mass communication in a similar way: radio and television are not means of overcoming the written word; instead, they restore to letters a "body that matters," to borrow Judith Butler's book title. They are a means of giving writing that corporeality from which the alphabets—as phonetic writing system—once led us away. All three religions of the book are based on holy scriptures using alphabetic writing systems.[6] An alphabetic writing system, in which spoken sounds are translated into visual signs and speech is thus abstracted from the body, implies an intense relationship between orality and the written word. I shall return to this point later.

5. An important component of all fundamentalisms is the call for a return to traditional gender roles. While this call is rooted in "utopian regress," gender roles—much like the oral modern mass media—also represent a mode of rematerializing abstract language. Thus, on the one hand we have the belief in texts, and on the other a belief in the "mother tongue" perceived as "orality." This may explain a paradox common to all fundamentalist movements: although the call for a return to traditional gender roles also entails restricting women's rights, fundamentalist movements often receive massive support from women—within all three religions; that said, the leaders or spiritual heads are usually men.

6. Contrary to a widespread notion that says otherwise, fundamentalists usually have quite a high level of education. But this

---

5. Flusser, *Philosophie der Fotografie*, 16.

6. The strict monotheism of the Jewish religion originated once the Semitic alphabet had been thoroughly developed; Christian teachings developed out of Greek philosophy, which was indebted in turn to the "complete" Greek alphabet, which also wrote vowels. In line with this, the written codification of Christian teachings was realized using both Greek and Latin alphabets. The Arabic alphabet only first developed into a sovereign written system following the revelation and written recording of the Koran.

education is very specific: often consisting of religious education, of course, fundamentalists will also enter fields like engineering, the natural sciences, or medicine. What fundamentalists avoid if not loathe, however, are the humanities: those fields that teach a person to reflect on oneself or one's knowledge, as well as to understand that there may be more than one truth. This resistance is extreme in the case of Christian and Islamic fundamentalists but even applies to Jewish fundamentalists, who may well have no great difficulty accepting Darwin and evolution theory—already Philo of Alexandria and Maimonides had declared that the history of the Bible should not necessarily be read literally—and yet still avoid the humanities for the aforementioned reasons.

7. Finally, the role of the martyr could also be considered common to all three religious fundamentalisms. Here, too, writing is associated with corporeality: the word martyr actually means "witness." In the figure of the martyr, ink becomes blood and the tale is tied to the deed.[7] It is debatable, however, whether the figure of the martyr is essential to fundamentalism or not[8]—for which reason I will leave it aside here.

Historically, the term fundamentalism comes from the Christian context. It was coined in the early twentieth century by the American Baptist Curtis Lee Laws. Proponents of the Princeton Theology created the so-called Princeton Doctrine, according to which the text of the Bible was verbally inspired by God and thus inerrant. In 1910, the highest body of the Presbyterian Church of North America formulated what it called the Five Fundamentals:

1. The inerrancy of the Bible as the revelation of the word of God
2. The bodily resurrection of Jesus Christ
3. The virgin birth
4. The doctrine of Jesus Christ's substitutionary atonement
5. The bodily second coming of Jesus Christ

---

7. Huhnholz, "Kulturalisierung des Terrors," 75.
8. Preißler, "Märtyrer," 385.

These principles were disseminated in the early years in a series of publications financed by wealthy businessmen and called *The Fundamentals: A Testimony of the Truth*. They were distributed free of charge in a print run of three million, mainly at schools and universities, which fundamentalists regarded as the main source of modernism. In their definition, modernism referred chiefly to critical biblical exegesis and Darwin's theories. When the group known as the World's Christian Fundamental Association was founded in Philadelphia in 1919 and thereby poised for the launch of its massive anti-evolution crusade, fundamentalism became its self-described sensibility. This same crusade offered ample points of connection for the Ku Klux Klan and the ideology of the Aryan Nations, which conceived God as white. By the mid-1940s, fundamentalists had a strong presence on the (American) airwaves, and the association known as the National Religious Broadcasters was founded. In the 1950s, this expanded to include television and television preachers such as Jerry Falwell and Billy Graham: "Televangelism and the 'electronic church' had been born."[9]

In the 1970s, the movement joined forces with extreme conservatives to form the organization Moral Majority. Its declared enemies were Communism, secular humanism, equal rights for women, sex education in the schools, and gay liberation. By 1981, the Moral Majority was present in all fifty states; it encompassed around one hundred thousand pastors and four hundred radio stations with daily programming and conducted gigantic media campaigns.[10] Soon, it had also enlisted three hundred universities and twenty-five thousand schools. Adherents included not just Protestants but also Catholics and Jews, including former homosexuals of both genders who had "'converted' to heterosexuality."[11] Patriotism, anti-Semitism, anti-modernism, and gender issues play an important role in the "experiential worship services" of the TV church. The TV church cannot offer congregational life but instead replaces this with emotionally-charged, professionally-staged shows featuring faith healing or spontaneous conversions and usually inflected with a populist chord of anti-intellectualism. In short, the history of Bible Belt fundamentalism exhibits all of the traits I have

---

9. Harwazinski, "Fundamentalismus/Rigorismus," 429.
10. Ibid., 431.
11. Ibid.

mentioned as common to fundamentalism: the belief in a "golden age" and the call for a return to traditional gender roles, a belief in texts combined with use of the mass media, and a low tolerance for ambivalence, expressed most clearly in animosity toward intellectuals.

Literalism

The chief commonality among the various fundamentalisms is the relationship between text and deed, or idea and blood. Nearly all political actions pursue the aim of creating consistency between the book and life; however, this is also where the differences between the fundamentalisms of the three religions of the book emerge—and they are closely tied to the differences between the three alphabets. Simply put: while in the Jewish and Muslim traditions—because of the consonantal alphabets—we find a high value placed upon spoken language alongside the holy scriptures, the traditions of thought that emerged from Hellenism and later shaped Christianity placed a higher value upon the written word; at the same time, orality was devalued. This had gender implications: medieval scholars referred to the Latin texts as the "father tongue" while the regional dialects were considered "mother tongues." The vocalized alphabet implies a higher degree of abstraction, and it was this very "dematerialization" (from *mater*, or mother) of language for which mass communication technologies sought to compensate. It is no accident that these techniques were all invented in the West. The fact that the mass media are also used nowadays by the other two religious fundamentalisms means either that they are quite compatible with their own oral traditions or that, perhaps unwittingly, a Western tradition has been adopted. Should the latter be true, this would mean that a dominant belief in texts has emerged here, too, despite the consonantal alphabets.

Literalism and Judaism

Historically, one cannot speak of Jewish fundamentalism before the second half of the twentieth century. To be sure, in the late eighteenth century an orthodox movement emerged with its rejection of the hermeneutical practice that had accompanied the Jewish religion since the beginning of the Diaspora. This orthodoxy had little to do with modern fundamentalism, however. Nevertheless, it was a form of literalism. Up to that point, apart from the foundational thirty-six Holy Scriptures (the Pentateuch, the nineteen books of the prophets, and the twelve writings), Judaism had always included the tradition of the "oral Torah." On the one hand, it was understood as revelation independent of written teaching, passed down orally in an uninterrupted chain from Moses on Mount Sinai until its codification in the second century in the Mishna (which means "teachings," or more precisely "repetition" and "review"). On the other, the oral Torah also referred to the interpretations in the Talmud, which sought to update the text of the Holy Scripture for every epoch and cultural situation. The Talmud juxtaposed various interpretations. Despite great controversies among scholars, the interpretations were never mutually exclusive. For instance, during the late nineteenth century in Vilnius, a large edition was printed containing various versions of the Talmud with marginal commentaries, supercommentaries, and corrections incorporating different readings. This diversity was the opposite of fundamentalist unambiguousness.

A break with this tradition began to appear in the late eighteenth century, that is, at the beginning of European modernity. At stake was no longer a learned dispute within the tradition but the tradition itself. Three movements emerged at this time: Hasidism, a form of popular piety that questioned the values of rabbinical scholasticism; the opponents of Hasidism, represented among others by Elia ben Salomo (1720–1797) in Vilnius; and the Jewish Enlightenment (*Haskala*), associated with Moses Mendelssohn (1729–1786). The latter promoted the preservation of the Jewish way of life but sought connection with modern Europe through secular education and enlightenment.

This split within Judaism lent fundamental significance to the question of the written word, a circumstance that only became clear after the Shoah. The neo-Orthodox movements in particular moved away from the tradition of interpretive diversity and toward unambiguousness. This was rooted in the shock of the Shoah, which led to a return to Jewish sources and traditions. But the new belief in texts was also nourished by a *rapprochement* with Western traditions. Haym Soloveitchik, who teaches Jewish history and theology at Yeshiva University in New York, describes the emergence of a new Jewish orthodoxy around 1950 as follows: "If I were asked to characterize in a phrase the change that religious Jewry has undergone in the past generation, I would say that it is the new and controlling role that texts now play in contemporary religious life."[12] He attributes this dominance of texts to a process of acculturation resulting from emigration to the United States, adaptation to modern ways of life, and a "dramatic rise in intermarriage."[13] Before the modern age, Eastern European Jewish life consisted of lived tradition and unconscious rituals passed from one generation to the other. The next generation of young Jews, above all men, replaced these lost customs with a set of rules: "A way of life has become a *regula,* and behavior, once governed by habit, is now governed by rule."[14] It is interesting that Soloveitchik uses the term regula in this description. The term was originally coined by Holy Benedict, the so-called father of monastic life in Europe. In 540, he created the regula according to which monks should live, which essentially implied work, prayer, and a general disciplining of the body. It was the first written law of this kind and became the standard for all of later monastic life in Europe—Christian monastic life, of course. From the very beginning, the regula was always linked to a text, a written rule considered to be opposed to custom. Says Soloveitchik, "Custom *is* potent, but its true power is informal. It derives from the ability of habit to neutralize the implications of book knowledge."[15]

According to Soloveitchik, the increasingly textual orientation of Judaism was a result of the fact that the new generation raised in the United States drew the knowledge they needed for their professional and everyday lives from books and now also looked to books—manuals and primers written in English or modern Hebrew—for access to religion. This development represented a break with oral tradition, which he locates largely in Yiddish: "Yiddish was used for common speech and all oral instruction; Hebrew for prayer and all learned writing."[16] Now, however, English—and not Yiddish—became the mother tongue; and like the modern society in which religious Jews live, English is dominated by "written rules," implying a "shift of authority to texts . . . as the sole source of authenticity."[17] This development had consequences

12. Soloveitchik, "Rupture and Reconstruction," 65.
13. Ibid., 78–79.
14. Ibid., 71.
15. Ibid.
16. Ibid., 83.
17. Ibid., 87.

for the definition of Jewish identity and religious learning: "Zealous to continue traditional Judaism unimpaired, religious Jews seek to ground their new emerging spirituality less on a now unattainable intimacy with Him, than on an intimacy with His Will . . . Having lost the touch of His presence, they seek now solace in the pressure of His yoke."[18] This "yoke" is the belief in texts. Soloveitchik's description thus clearly underscores that modern Jewish fundamentalism, as it has developed in some Jewish communities in the United States or Israel, stems from an overemphasis on the written word over orality. This is not actually in keeping with Jewish tradition; rather, the overvaluation of the text is a characteristic of Western or Christian thought and to that extent implies the adoption of outside traditions. The same is true of nationalism with which—above all in Israel—the new belief in texts goes hand in hand. While all fundamentalist movements in Israel agree on the struggle against "Western culture," this does little to change the fact that the national idea itself originated in the post-Christian world and was disseminated with the Enlightenment: this, too, was a legacy borrowed from non-Jewish traditions that brought forth—for the first time in history, we might add—such a thing as Jewish fundamentalism.

Literalism and Islam

Like the Jewish tradition, Islam—across the wide range of Islamic movements—places a high value on orality. This expresses itself not in a diversity of interpretations, however, but through joy in the act of recitation or prayer. Muslims are "very receptive to the spoken word, which, in combination with rhetoric, religious associations, and references to the early Islamic period can lead to the audience becoming highly emotionalized."[19] Many Muslims cannot understand the texts written in classical Arabic, but "musical and poetic recitations of Quranic verses serve as an introduction to every community event." Muslims "experience deep aesthetic pleasure from listening to the rich, resonant, rhyming prose with its repetitions and subtle inflections."[20] The masters among Quran reciters compete in public contests and "are held in an

---

18. Ibid., 103.
19. Fuess, "Islamische Schlachtrede," 56.
20. Esposito, *Everyone Needs*, 9.

esteem comparable to that of opera stars in the West."[21] The significance of orality also influences the culture of memory. This is evident in the *hadith*, the collection of traditions relating the life of the Prophet, which provide the norm for the proper way of life. The authenticity of these narratives is documented not by the fact that they exist in writing but rather by the "verification of the chain of transmitters."[22] In order to be considered "authentic," a narrative must be traced along an oral chain that goes back to Mohammed himself or to one of his actual companions. Great attention is paid to the issue of whether the individuals in question could really have known their informants personally. "If the chain of transmitters could be proven possible, then the hadith was accepted as authentic."[23] This kind of chain of memory and "authentification" concerned with knowledge passed on not in writing but verbally is a typical example of oral memorial traditions.

Here, too, the encounter with Western modernity brought about a break with traditions, and this had a direct influence on the appearance of Islamic fundamentalism. I would like to illustrate this with three examples:

Leila Ahmed, who grew up in Egypt, now teaches at Harvard, and has written a nuanced work on the history of the Islamic gender order,[24] describes in her memoirs the close relationship in her own childhood between the gender order, orality, and religion. At her grandmother's house in Alexandria, women had their own understanding of Islam that differed from the men's "official Islam," which was transmitted in written form. Women passed down an Islamic experience expressed not by rules or prohibitions but "by a touch, a glance, a word":

> And all of these ways of passing on attitudes, morals, beliefs, knowledge—through touch and the body and in words spoken in the living moment— . . . profoundly shape the next generation, but they do not leave a record in the way that someone writing a text about how to live or what to believe leaves a record. Nevertheless, they leave a far more important and, literally, more vital, living record. Beliefs, morals, attitudes passed on to and impressed on us through those

---

21. Ibid., 10.
22. Ibid., 13.
23. Ibid., 14.
24. Ahmed, *Women and Gender*.

fleeting words and gestures are written into our very lives, our bodies, our selves, even into our physical cells and into how we live the script of our lives.[25]

The "subculture" that accompanied the oral transmission of Islam—a subculture without "spiritual guidance"—permitted the adoption of cultural peculiarities in different regions. "Textual Islam," or "men's Islam," by contrast, was created by a minority: "The Islam they developed in this textual heritage is very like the medieval Latinate textual heritage of Christianity. It is as abstruse and obscure and as dominated by medieval and exclusively male views of the world as are those Latin texts."[26] Ahmed holds the Arabic alphabet responsible for the lively tradition of Islam: "A set of consonants can have several meanings and only acquires final, specific, fixed meaning when given vocalized or silent utterance (unlike words in European script, which have the appearance, anyway, of being fixed in meaning). Until life is literally breathed into them, Arabic and Hebrew words on the page have no particular meaning."[27] This Islam, passed down orally and which speaks of a truth "only here and now, for this body,"[28] is in Ahmed's opinion on the retreat, gradually being displaced by textual Islam which, in turn, has spawned fundamentalist Islam, "textual Islam's more narrow and more poorly informed modern descendant."[29] This signals, however, an adaptation to Western thought with its dominance of the written word, and Ahmed draws our attention to the not insignificant role that western Islamic studies has played in this development. It has contributed to the legitimation and authorization of textual Islam and the suppression of oral traditions, since Western scholarship focuses largely on written texts and official institutions such as the mosque.[30]

The second example refers to the research of Amira Sonbol, who teaches Islamic history, law, and society at Georgetown University. Sonbol has studied the records of Egyptian courts from the period of quadi justice and compared them to legislation introduced in the nineteenth

25. Ahmed, *Border Passage*, 121–22.
26. Ibid., 126.
27. Ibid., 127.
28. Ibid., 128.
29. Ibid.
30. Ibid., 128–29.

century under the influence of European legal norms.[31] Contrary to widespread notions about women's powerlessness under old Shari'ah law, these records paint quite a different picture of women's rights. Thus women could negotiate their own marriage contracts, for example: "Although the Shari'ah law allowed the husband to take four wives, that right was frequently waived as a wife's condition for marriage."[32] Women could also divorce their husbands or practice a profession without their consent. They acted as their children's legal guardians, owned and managed property, and were active in all branches of the economy. They "served as heads of guilds of physicians, weavers and other employments. They lent and borrowed money, owned and ran coffee shops and even ran pawn businesses."[33] In other words, "Shari'ah court records illustrate that women participated widely in almost all aspects of the market place and that the quadis did not question a woman's right to work on a particular job."[34] Things changed radically after legal reform: "Modern laws not only require a husband's permission before his wife takes a job, the wife must waive her husband's financial support of her if she works."[35] These reforms were introduced under the influence of a concept of the nation-state adopted from the West. This "was not surprising since the reformers themselves were either British advisors to the Egyptian government or Egyptian graduates of French and British law schools . . . The reforms helped modernize the legal system by standardizing legal procedures and applying principles of legal process and the rule of law. By streamlining the legal system, laws became more homogenous."[36]

What set the Western understanding of the law apart from jurisprudence under the quadis? Among other things, a strict belief in texts (which in the West also frequently leads to conflicts between law and justice). This understanding of the law has developed historically in the West in conjunction with the nation-states and doubtless has its advantages and validity. In Egypt, however, it became associated with a form of legal practice that had not existed previously. While justice as

---

31. Sonbol, "Women in Shari'ah Courts."
32. Ibid., 242.
33. Ibid., 249–50.
34. Ibid., 251.
35. Ibid.
36. Ibid., 230.

dispensed by the quadi was highly flexible, since the notion of law was adapted to social realities—for example, when it came to women's capacity to engage in business—the new jurisprudence subordinated social realities to the law. This had grave consequences for women, since the new laws were formulated and codified according to the strictest interpretations of Shari'ah. Sonbol concludes that

> [d]econstructing the historical image of women shows that the controls under which they live today are really State-made and differ from practices before the modernization of law. This does not mean the pre-modern system was not patriarchal. It was a different type of patriarchy than exists today where State-power is used to enforce legal patriarchal rules that confine the activities and rights of women. Put differently, it is not a question of God's laws that cannot be changed; rather it is a patriarchal State that refuses to change laws controlling gender and family. The pretext that this is in fulfillment of God's wishes is an excuse that is put into question once the specificities of women's history and the history of legal practices are brought to light.[37]

We are thus dealing with a phenomenon similar to that noted by Leila Ahmed in order to describe the gradual overpowering of oral by "textual" Islam, which in turn produced fundamentalism, "textual Islam's narrower and more poorly informed modern descendant."[38]

The third example refers to a study conducted in 2007 at Oxford University, which clearly demonstrates that the emergence of violent Islamist fundamentalism is by no means associated with a lack of education. Sociologists Diego Gambetta and Steffen Hertog explored the question of why engineers constitute such a large number of members belonging to violent Islamist groups. According to the authors, a preponderance of technical professions in radical Islamist groups is a worldwide phenomenon: based on an analysis of all terrorist groups, the authors found that approximately 40 percent of their members had an engineering background. At the same time, the proportion of engineers in the terrorists' countries of origin was very low: only three percent of the overall population and less than 18 percent of students. The authors have examined the reasons for this curious concentration

---

37. Ibid., 251–52.
38. Ibid.

of engineers in radical movements. With convincing arguments, they reject a number of other possible reasons for this concentration of engineers and technicians (such as the technical skills needed to construct bombs) and conclude that engineering attracts people who are guided by strict principles of order and authority. Other studies have shown that a higher proportion of conservative and narrow religious views are to be found among Western engineering students than students of other disciplines.[39] This means that on the one hand violent fundamentalism requires a high degree of technical education and on the other a belief in order and authority that points to the low tolerance for ambivalence mentioned at the beginning of my article. This example is quite telling in regard to the links between fundamentalism and the avoidance of fields close to the humanities.

These examples show that present-day Islam, like Judaism, includes a tendency toward textual dominance with little precedent in its own religious traditions. This development began for the Jewish community around 1800 (with the emergence of Orthodox Judaism) and for Islam in the twentieth century. What brought about this change? In both cases, the development of Christian society exerted decisive influence: The Jewish Enlightenment—like Orthodox Judaism—represented a response to the Christian Enlightenment. On the one hand, the Enlightenment led to a new tolerance toward other religions, which meant that Jews were permitted to become full citizens of the state; on the other, it also transferred belief in the text from the theological to the secular realm. The Jewish Enlightenment responded to this challenge by turning to secular education and scholarship. At the same time, a new Jewish figure emerged, which the historian Yosef Hayim Yerushalmi, using the case of Freud, has described as the "psychological Jew"[40]: a secular definition of "Jewish identity." While this development affected Jews living within Christian communities early on, its influence on Islam began only in the mid-nineteenth century: first through colonialism, and then with the emergence of nation-states, which paradoxically brought both independence from Western powers but also the adoption of Western standards—including the dominance of text over orality. This was to become one of the bases of fundamentalism. I am not arguing that Islamic

---

39. Gambetta and Hertog, "Engineers of Jihad."
40. Yerushalmi, *Freud's Moses*, 10.

or Jewish fundamentalism is a product of Western thought but merely pointing out the role that the written word, so highly prized in Western thought, has played in this process.

Literalism and Enlightenment

What exactly was the Christian Enlightenment? Apart from the call for a secular state, for legislation independent of the church, it was also the beginning of compulsory school attendance accompanied by the spread of universal literacy. What emerged in this process was not a *belief* in texts; instead, the written word itself became part of social and economic reality. The written word took possession of the social and the individual body. Both were recorded in an unprecedented manner in numbers, statistics, measurements, and norms. At the same time, paper money arose, representing a "text" that created material reality: the economist Hans Christoph Binswanger has demonstrated very convincingly that Goethe's sole topic in *Faust Part II* is the way in which physical reality—including soil—was produced by written documents and paper money.[41] The French Revolution would have failed without the *assignats*, just as American independence would never have been established without paper money. Paper money also created the preconditions for the emergence of the market economy in which, as Karl Polanyi has noted, the economy was for the first time no longer embedded in society, but society in the economy.[42]

In other words: The Enlightenment was a symptom of Christian society's transition into a society immersed in writing. It was no accident that the Enlightenment occurred in the Christian cultural sphere, which was wholly shaped by the "complete alphabet" and in which the printing press was invented. Indeed, the invention of the printing press was connected with requirements that had arisen within the church: toward the end of the Middle Ages, many monasteries had become more or less copy centers, the monks performing as writing machines. There was, at first, an *ecclesiastical* interest in the printing press. As it turned out, of course, it became the motor of scientific scholarship, nonreligious cultivation, and enlightenment. But let me remind you that the word "clerk"—the bureaucrat of modern secular states and enterpris-

41. Binswanger, *Money and Magic*.
42. Polanyi, *Great Transformation*.

es—is derived directly from clerics and the clergy. In short: what I am trying to get at is that, contrary to frequent assertions, the Enlightenment did not arise in opposition to Christianity but is causally linked with the history of the church.

The history of writing and the printing of books are but one example. Two others are mechanical clocks and optical devices. Like the invention of the printing press, we owe the invention of clockwork to the requirements of Christian monasticism. The French word for clock, *horloge*, comes from *hora lego*, or prayer hour. By the seventh century, the Cluniac Reforms had led to a stronger division of time through the seven hours. Beginning in the fourth century, monasteries were established in which the entire daily routine was conceived as communal life: monks and nuns ate, prayed, and worked together, as well as lived together in communal spaces. The Cistercians took up this objective in the tenth and eleventh centuries. They introduced the ideal of homogeneity into their monasteries. David Landes, who has written a history of the mechanical clock, describes the process as one of "depersonalization" and "de-individuation": the aim of monastic life was "uniformity of practice."[43] The most important thing was to appear punctually to communal prayer, this being not only associated with the transcendent but also contributing to bodily discipline. Since prayers also had to be said at night, the monks needed a mechanical clock, which was invented around 1300.

Like the printing press, the mechanical clock soon extricated itself from its monastic context. People outside the monasteries also learned to live according to the stroke of the clock. This was particularly true in the cities, where people began to synchronize their lives.[44] Court society profited from this, but still more so the bourgeoisie and entrepreneurs. The clock created a decisive precondition for the gradual process of mechanization and industrialization that would accompany the history of the West from the late Middle Ages on. According to Lewis Mumford, the mechanical clock "dissociated time from human events and helped create the belief in an independent world of mathematically measurable sequences: the special world of science."[45] That means that

---

43. Landes, *Revolution in Time*, 58.
44. Ibid., 74.
45. Mumford, *Technics and Civilization*, 15.

the cities and industry with their synchronic timing accepted the monastic legacy and created communities in the secular realm that were subject to the discipline of the clock: "Bells sounded for start of work, meal breaks, end of work, closing of gates, start of market, close of market, assembly, emergencies, council meetings, end of drink service, time for street cleaning, curfew, and so on through an extraordinary variety of special peals in individual towns and cities."[46]

The clock wandered from the tower to the living room, and then—with smaller and smaller mechanisms and springs—came to be worn on the body itself. Punctuality replaced temporal compulsion. Paraphrasing Weber, Landes writes, "What the clock was to the cloistered ascetics of the Middle Ages, the watch was to the in-the-world ascetics of post-Reformation Europe."[47] Most clockmakers were Protestants, even in majority Catholic France: when Louis XIV revoked the Edict of Nantes, he drove two hundred clockmakers out of France—and the domestic clock industry collapsed.[48] Many clockmakers fled to Switzerland, where they contributed to the flowering of Swiss clock manufacturing. Nineteenth-century industrial capitalism would be unthinkable without mechanical clocks, and Lewis Mumford thus correctly noted that the clock, not the steam engine, was the key machine of the industrial age.[49] Its origins, however, lay in the monastery.

The third example makes clear that the church's influence on the sciences was based not just on lifestyle habits but also on theological doctrine. Beginning in the late Middle Ages, the Christian world witnessed an intense reception and incorporation of Arab knowledge—in mathematics and medicine, among other fields—which helped to launch the scientific Renaissance. However, in one area—quite apart from printing—Christian society created something all its own: the techniques of visuality; and here, too, religion played a central role.

In both Judaism and Islam, God is hidden and may not be represented—he thus remains shrouded. The believer cannot enter into direct contact with him. Both Moses and Mohammed cover their heads before receiving the word of God. As a religion of revelation, Christian-

---

46. Landes, *Revolution in Time*, 76.

47. Ibid., 96. Thus in Nuremberg, for example (where there were both, Protestants and Catholics), 87.3 percent of all clockmakers were Protestants (ibid., 97).

48. Ibid., 97.

49. Mumford, *Technics and Civilization*.

ity follows a different logic. The Greek word for revelation is *apokalypsis*—literally, unveiling—and is composed of *kalypta*, a veil-like covering, and the prefix *apo* (= away, distant). The Latin term *revelatio* also understands revelation as a symbolic act of unveiling (*velum* = veil, curtain). The idea of unveiling implies the ability to see and understand the truth of Christ, that is, the secret of God, undisguised. In contrast to the two other religions of the book, Christianity is a religion of *disclosure*. At its center is a God who assumed concrete form in his son.

This Christian topos of *revelatio*—as access to truth and secrets—deeply influenced Western science: In search of scientific "truth," the Occident developed a plethora of optical devices and technique—central perspective, the telescope, the microscope, the camera obscura, and later photography—that set new scientific paradigms and facilitated discoveries. Western science's thirst for exposure also had sexual aspects, which reveal how tightly interconnected the gender and knowledge orders are. Thanks to the new optical devices, scientists could penetrate unknown worlds and bring "dark continents" to light: whether the object of knowledge was the human body, Nature, or foreign continents, it was imagined as a female body to be "deflowered" and uncovered by science. We can observe this impetus very well in the gradual undressing of the female body in public space. The process begins in the Renaissance with fantasies of penetrating the female body with the eyes—an idea for which Titian, with his images of Venus, gives us a pertinent example. It continues in the anatomical representations of the seventeenth and eighteenth centuries and leads around 1800 to the imagination of a voluntary "unveiling" of Nature before the eyes of science. When photography emerged in the mid-nineteenth century as the "pencil of life," a medium capable of revealing the "naked truth," uncovering is no longer conceived of in allegorical terms but leads to an actual undressing of the female body—a process that reached a preliminary highpoint in 1946 with the advent of the bikini. It would come to symbolize Western "decadence" in the eyes of other cultures, and yet ultimately this skimpy item of clothing—revealing more than it conceals—merely serves to emphasize the power of the gaze and its technically-armed eye.

Religion and Science

These examples demonstrate that Christian religion and Enlightenment or science are far more closely associated with each other than we are accustomed to thinking of them, and that modern science—at least the paradigms according to which research and progress function—are by no means as religiously neutral as some of their adherents would like to believe. Modern science did not develop in opposition to the Christian church; rather, many of its leading paradigms emerged from Christian teachings. The Catholic philosopher Charles Taylor has shown that some modern secular states adhere more closely to Christian principles than was the case for societies before the Enlightenment.[50] In science, the lines of tradition leading from the church to the laboratory are sometimes of a technical nature (as with the printing press and mechanical clock) but sometimes also rooted in theology, as I have tried to show with the example of optical techniques. Similarly, one could point out that in vitro fertilization and other techniques of modern (and now frequently applied) reproductive medicine have turned a theological phantasm of the Christian religion into scientific reality: conception without the sexual act. There is, so to speak, a direct line from Saint Peter to the Petri dish, if I may be allowed the pun.

If Christianity and the Enlightenment are not that far removed from one another, what does this mean for the conflict between Christian fundamentalism and evolution, Enlightenment or atheism? As we know, the Evangelical Christian fundamentalists claim that life as it is described in the Bible arose a few thousand years ago, and not 2.5 to 3.5 billion years ago as geologists, paleontologists, and bioscientists are now able to demonstrate. The Creationist movement has succeeded in introducing the compulsory teaching of intelligent design—instead or alongside evolutionary theory—in the public schools of some US states. The individuals seeking to reconcile Holy Scripture and life are by no means uneducated. Rather, many natural scientists and technicians adhere to the doctrine of intelligent design. Five hundred scientists recently signed a petition rejecting evolution. They included seventy-six chemists, sixty-three physicists, twenty-four medical doctors, and some one hundred biologists.[51]

---

50. Taylor, *Säkulares Zeitalter*.

51. Kenneth Chang, "Few Biologists but Many Evangelicals Sign Anti-Evolution Petition," *The New York Times*, Feb 21, 2006, D2, http://www.nytimes.com/2006/02/21/

This means that we are dealing with a phenomenon similar to that of the large proportion of engineers among fundamentalist Islamist terror groups: among Creationists, education and fundamentalism are not mutually exclusive but appear to be compatible.

The fiercest (and most widely read) crusader *against* the anti-evolution crusade is Richard Dawkins; but strangely enough, his images, too, are highly instructive. Not only does he cite the very categories of disease so popular among fundamentalists when he calls his book against religion *The God Delusion,* or when he writes, "Atheism nearly always indicates a healthy independence of mind and, indeed, a healthy mind"[52]; he also redeploys the Christian topic of "unveiling the truth," when he announces that "Darwin seized the window of the burka and wrenched it open, letting in a flood of understanding."[53] With this image of the ignorance concealed behind the burka—which he comes back to several times in his book—he also resorts to a cliché frequently deployed in the West to stigmatize Islamic fundamentalism.

Dawkins accuses religion of rigorism: "When a science book is wrong, somebody eventually discovers the mistake and it is corrected in subsequent books. That conspicuously doesn't happen with holy books."[54] He does not for a moment consider that the entire Talmud is one gigantic attempt to imbue Holy Scripture with ever new meanings and allow more contradictions to coexist than science ever did. The natural sciences in particular set great store by replacing contradiction and ambiguity with definite answers. Dawkins would like to see the same applied to religion: "Did Jesus have a human father, or was his mother a virgin at the time of his birth? Whether or not there is enough surviving evidence to decide it, this is strictly a scientific question with an answer in principle: yes or no."[55] One answer is, of course, that it was precisely modern science that proved that, indeed, virgin motherhood is possible. What's's more, Christian theology and religious studies do indeed have an answer to this question: the doctrine of the incarnation was only formulated three hundred years after the lifetime of Jesus. It

science/sciencespecial2/21peti.html?pagewanted=all.

52. Dawkins, *God Delusion*, 3.
53. Ibid., 367.
54. Ibid., 282.
55. Ibid., 59.

is thus dogma, not reality. Religious *history*, however, has no place in Dawkins's scientific worldview.

Dawkins's remarks on the deism of a Voltaire or Thomas Paine are also quite illuminating:

> Compared with the Old Testament's psychotic delinquent, the deist God of the eighteenth-century Enlightenment is an altogether grander being: worthy of his cosmic creation, loftily unconcerned with human affairs, sublimely aloof from our private thoughts and hopes, caring nothing for our messy sins or mumbled contritions. The deist God is a physicist to end all physics, the alpha and omega of mathematicians, the apotheosis of designers; a hyper-engineer who set up the laws and constants of the universe, fine tuned them with exquisite precision and foreknowledge, detonated what we would now call the hot big bang, retired and was never heard from again.[56]

This deist God, who is a physicist and a mathematician, a technician and a hyper-engineer, who operates with precision and hangs his "private thoughts and hopes" in the cloakroom before entering the laboratory—this God has a surprising amount in common with the ideal of the modern scientist in whom Dawkins clearly sees the God of the modern age: "Indeed, wouldn't the designer of the universe *have* to be a scientist?"[57] Naturally it is not my intention here to criticize Dawkins's struggle against the Creationists or his defense of the theory of evolution. The point I am trying to make is that this, too, is a form of literalism—a literalism expressed in the image of the "healthy atheist" who would like to see the categories of natural science applied to religion. This literalism is the result of the very same Western belief in texts that brought forth religious and political fundamentalism. Here is Dawkins again: "Fundamentalists know they are right because they have read the truth in a holy book and they know, in advance, that nothing will budge them from their belief . . . Books about evolution are believed not because they are holy. They are believed because they present overwhelming quantities of mutually buttressed evidence."[58]

It is interesting to note that this mode of argumentation is also often criticized by gender studies (which I understand as a discipline

56. Ibid., 38.
57. Ibid., 104.
58. Ibid., 391.

dedicated to questioning canonical knowledge): Pieces of evidence that supplement one another so neatly are often nothing but self-fulfilling prophecies. Hypotheses verify each other, metaphors provoke experimental designs, and "paradigm shifts" frequently prove to be mere reformulations of old presuppositions. Erwin Panofsky referred to Gothic cathedral architecture, with its mutually supporting columns and pillars meant to ensure the statics of the entire structure, as "scholasticism in stone": scholastic thought, which was based on a "system of logical subordination" and sought to explain faith by reason, also became the principle of Gothic architecture, he writes.[59] Scholasticism, in which one "rational" text supports the other, is a form of belief in texts— a belief that assumed material form in the cathedral.

Something similar applies to the relationship between genetic sciences and computer technology, the modern form of writing—except that here, the belief in texts becomes materialized in corporeality itself. In genetic technology, says science scholar Hans-Jörg Rheinberger, "the laboratory, that privileged forge of epistemic things, is transferred into the organism itself and thus becomes potentially immortal, since it begins to write with its own typewriter of life."[60] Nowadays, computer technology has taken the place of the scholastic system of theories:

> The script of life is transported to the scriptorium of the laboratory, and turned into an epistemic thing, brought into the world of the middle dimensions, in which our sensory organs operate. As a research scientist, the biologist no longer works with the cell's genes—he knows as little as anyone else what that "really" is—he works with graphemes produced experimentally in a representational space. If he wants to know what they mean, his only option is to interpret this articulation of graphemes through another one. The interpretation of a sequencing gel can never be anything other than a further sequencing gel.[61]

It seems as if modern science has learned from scholasticism—and that way from the medieval cathedral to the modern natural sciences is quite direct.

---

59. Panofsky, *Gothic Architecture*, S. 32–33, 38.
60. Rheinberger, "Alles, Inskription," 272.
61. Ibid., 273.

To summarize my thesis concerning the relation of fundamentalist religion and the belief in science in a single sentence: I would say that intelligent design and authors like Dawkins represent two opposite forms of the belief in texts. In the case of the Creationists, the belief in texts refers to the historical truth of the Bible; in the case of Dawkins, the belief in texts fails to recognize that certain scientific paradigms can arise from historical circumstances and consequently also from religion. He uses scientific arguments to combat the belief in God, yet in a historical perspective it seems evident that religions arise when there is a historical necessity for this manner of understanding the world. Contrary to their own claim to eternity, we know fairly precisely when each of the three religions of the book arose and how their holy scriptures were formulated. Consequently, we also know that there was a historical reason for the emergence of these religions. But what is true of religion must also be true of science. There was apparently a historical necessity for the Enlightenment and Darwin's theory of evolution. And—without wishing to propose a monocausal argument—the advent of both the three religions of the book and the Enlightenment was closely tied to the history of alphabets. Just as the alphabets were the force behind the emergence of these three world religions, the growing importance of the written word was also the force behind the Enlightenment and the dismissal of the religions. A science, however, that regards itself as a-historical "truth" readily mutates into a "Holy Scripture" and takes on the features of literalism. In short, the absence of historicity is a potential common denominator between religion and science—and history happens to be one of those fields of the humanities that fundamentalists avoid wherever they can.

Bibliography

Ahmed, Leila. *A Border Passage: From Cairo to America—A Woman's Journey*. New York: Farrar, Straus & Giroux, 1999.

———. *Women and Gender in Islam: Historical Roots of a Modern Debate*. New Haven: Yale University Press, 1992.

Binswanger, Hans Christoph. *Money and Magic: A Critique of the Modern Economy in the Light of Goethe's Faust*. Chicago: University Press of Chicago Press, 1994.

Dawkins, Richard. *The God Delusion*. London: Bantam, 2006.

Esposito, John L. *What Everyone Needs to Know about Islam*. New York: Oxford University Press, 2002.

Flusser, Vilém. *Für eine Philosophie der Fotografie*. 5th ed. Göttingen: European Photography, 1991.

Fuess, Albrecht. "Die islamische Schlachtrede und die 'Geistliche Anleitung.'" In *Terror im Dienste Gottes: Die 'geistliche Anleitung' der Attentäter des 11. September 2001*, edited by Hans Gerhard Kippenberg et al., 55–66. Frankfurt: Campus, 2004.

Gambetta, Diego, and Steffen Hertog. "Engineers of Jihad." Oxford Sociology Working Paper 10, 2007. Online: http://www.nuff.ox.ac.uk/users/gambetta/engineers%20of%20jihad.pdf.

Harwazinski, Assia Maria. "Fundamentalismus/Rigorismus." In *Metzler-Lexikon Religion: Gegenwart—Alltag—Medien*, edited by Christoph Auffarth et al., 1:427–34. Stuttgart: Metzler, 1999.

Huhnholz, Sebastian. "Kulturalisierung des Terrors. Das dschihadistische Selbstmordattentat als Stereotyp islamischer Kampfkultur." *Zeitschrift für Kulturwissenschaft* 1 (2010) 69–80.

Landes, David S. *Revolution in Time: Clocks and the Making of the Modern World*. Cambridge, MA: Belknap, 1983.

Mumford, Lewis. *Technics and Civilization*. New York: Harcourt, Brace & World, 1963.

Panofsky, Erwin. *Gothic Architecture and Scholasticism*. 3rd ed. Latrobe, PA: Archabbey, 1956.

Polanyi, Karl. *The Great Transformation: Politische und ökonomische Ursprünge von Gesellschaften und Wirtschaftssystemen*. Translated by Heinrich Jelinek. Frankfurt: Suhrkamp, 1990.

Preißler, Holger. "Märtyrer." In *Metzler-Lexikon Religion: Gegenwart—Alltag—Medien*, edited by Christoph Auffarth et al., 2:382–85. Stuttgart, Weimar: Metzler, 1999.

Rheinberger, Hans Jörg. "Alles, was überhaupt zu einer Inskription führen kann." In *Wissensbilder: Strategien der Überlieferung*, edited by Ulrich Raulff et al., 265–78. Berlin: Akademie, 1999.

Riesebrodt, Martin. *Fundamentalismus als patriarchalische Protestbewegung: Amerikanische Protestanten (1910–28) und iranische Schiiten (1961–79) im Vergleich*. Tübingen: Mohr, 1990.

Soloveitchik, Haym. "Rupture and Reconstruction: The Transformation of Contemporary Orthodoxy." *Tradition* 28/4 (1994) 64–130.

Sonbol, Amira. "Women in Shari'ah Courts: A Historical and Methodological Discussion." *Fordham International Law Journal* 27/1 (2003) 225–53.

Taylor, Charles. *Ein säkulares Zeitalter*. Translated by Joachim Schulte. Frankfurt: Suhrkamp, 2009.

Yerushalmi, Yosef Hayim. *Freud's Moses: Judaism Terminable and Interminable*. New Haven: Yale University Press, 1991.

Fundamentalism and Gender

Comments of Two Useful Concepts

MARTIN RIESEBRODT

In a rather influential article Joan Scott called "gender" a useful category for historical analysis. Few would disagree with her. Gender studies have established themselves as an important field over the last decades and have made major contributions to many disciplines. Evolving from women's studies, gender studies have succeeded in developing earlier approaches further by focusing not just on women—though such a focus was indeed overdue and meant to make up for the prior disregard of women's historical agency—but on the complex interrelationships between "male" and "female" as well.

A second concern of gender studies was the distinction between sex and gender. Whereas sex was referring to "natural" or "biological" differences, gender was supposed to refer to the culturally and socially constructed dimension. Although I would find it somewhat naïve to treat "nature" or "biology" as objectively given and not also as socially constructed, what people probably had in mind was the distinction between visible physical differences on the one hand and their cultural interpretation and significance on the other. For example, the fact of female menstruation—however it may be called and understood in other cultures—must be clearly distinguished from its frequent cultural valuation as "polluting" as well as the implications and possible consequences of such a construction. However, such a distinction between an "objective" scientific dimension and a cultural value dimension is hardly universal. Usually, both dimensions of observable fact and valuation are embedded in one overarching model. To my mind, then, the concept of sex should not be opposed to gender but subsumed under the broader category of gender.

In short, Joan Scott argues convincingly that gender is a very useful concept indeed for the study of any social phenomenon so long as one understands it as a relational category analyzing the ways distinctions between male and female are made and transformed into a cognitive order and system of social relations.

This is especially true when we turn to the notion of fundamentalism. Here, gender is not just a useful category but an indispensable one. One cannot appropriately understand and explain fundamentalism without making use of the concept of gender. I will therefore try to show that "gender" and "fundamentalism" complement each other as useful categories of analysis. Indeed, gender and sexual morality, as well as ideals and norms of "manhood" and "womanhood," are very much at the core of the ideologies I would characterize as "fundamentalist."[1]

But here we run into trouble: whereas most scholars may agree that "gender" is a useful concept, many object to the idea that "fundamentalism" is also a useful and legitimate general concept for historical and sociological analysis across various religious traditions. Where does this opposition come from, and what are its arguments? What are my reasons for defending the concept of fundamentalism, and what are its benefits?

Fundamentalism as an Analytical Concept

As we all know, the term fundamentalism emerged in the early twentieth century in the context of American Protestantism to designate an alliance of orthodox groups opposing—among other things—biblical criticism, the social gospel, the teaching of evolutionism, Nietzsche's philosophy, and German beer. Until the 1970s, the term fundamentalism referred almost exclusively to such movements within Protestantism.

---

1. Riesebrodt, *Pious Passion*.

By the late 1980s, however, the Fundamentalism Project, organized by Martin E. Marty and Scott Appleby at the University of Chicago,[2] identified fundamentalisms not just in Protestant Christianity but also in Judaism, Islam, and Hinduism, and even in Buddhism and Confucianism. What had happened during this decade?

In the United States, Protestant fundamentalism had reorganized itself in part in reaction to the Civil Rights movement, often using mass media quite successfully. This same Protestant fundamentalist camp organized a coalition with other religious forces, the Religious Right and the Moral Majority, which also consisted of Catholics, Jews, and Mormons. This coalition supported the election of Ronald Reagan and has since gained major influence in the Republican Party.

At the same time, Islamism was emerging in Iran, Afghanistan, and Palestine, to mention just a few examples. Islamism staged the revolution in Iran and organized the Afghan resistance against Soviet occupation. In Lebanon and Gaza, Hezbollah and Hamas emerged. In Egypt, Islamists assassinated Anwar al-Sadat.

In Israel, too, a Religious Right was on the rise, which was responsible for the assassination of Yitzhak Rabin and has gained great influence especially among settlers. In India, we witnessed the assassination of Indira Gandhi by radical Sikhs as well as growing tensions between Hindu nationalists and Muslims. What all these movements and events supposedly had in common was not always quite clear from the start, but the term fundamentalism seemed to capture notions of antimodernism and religious radicalism they apparently all exhibited.

Unfortunately, the Fundamentalism Project did not begin with either a clear general definition of fundamentalism or a focus on what fundamentalism might mean in each of these various religious traditions in order to develop a more general concept. Instead, it worked with a fuzzy notion of "family resemblances." This lack of clarity led to the impression that fundamentalism is a catchall term for all kinds of religious movements that have little in common except being disliked by more enlightened people. Still others, who defined fundamentalism as a political attitude of rigidity and intolerance, only confused matters even more by psychologizing the concept.

---

2. Marty and Appleby, eds., *Fundamentalism Observed*; idem, *Fundamentalisms and Society*; idem, *Fundamentalisms and the State*.

It therefore came as no surprise that scholars criticized the concept of fundamentalism from various points of view. Some objected morally, while others insisted on the religious and cultural differences between traditions and civilizations. What irked people in particular was the inflationary journalistic and political use of the term; and since terms used in public discourse do not always make good analytical concepts, it is quite understandable that many scholars reject the term fundamentalism for various reasons.

Mark Juergensmeyer, for example, has criticized the use of the concept to label all kinds of religious movements in order to justify their suppression and persecution.[3] I do not doubt that this is a correct observation but would hesitate to draw the conclusion that this disqualifies the usefulness of fundamentalism as a scholarly concept. Who, after all, would suggest giving up the concepts of communism or fascism, although they have been used in similar ways?

Other objections against fundamentalism as a general concept are based on cultural relativism. Different religious traditions are considered to be so unique that comparisons are only deemed legitimate so as to determine the profound differences between them. Admittedly, there are religious traditions that might not know fundamentalist versions. But general terms never imply that social phenomena have to be universal. Aside from this, the charge of cultural relativism has its flaws in that it assumes a homogeneity within religious traditions that is empirically false. Within all religious traditions, there exists a broad spectrum of beliefs and practices and various "syncretisms" are the rule rather than the exception. Moreover, the claim to uniqueness is an argument for comparisons and general concepts rather than against them, since uniqueness can actually only be established through comparisons, which can be conducted under the perspectives of similarity, difference, or both.

There are also in-between positions. Some find any extension of the term fundamentalism beyond Protestantism objectionable; others, like Bruce Lawrence, include the Abrahamic traditions of Judaism, Christianity, and Islam, since they identify fundamentalism with literalist interpretations of sacred scriptures, although they find its application

---

3. Juergensmeyer, "Antifundamentalism."

to Asian religions objectionable.[4] Still others accept the application of general concepts only where indigenous equivalents exist.

However, this is a dangerous objection since it applies to almost all analytical concepts. All concepts have emerged under specific historical circumstances; but they do not necessarily remain bound to their historical genesis. The category of gender also emerged under very specific circumstances, namely in discourses within the women's movement in the West, and yet there is hardly even an equivalent for gender in other languages. Nevertheless, the concept of gender has been immensely useful across historical and cultural boundaries for analyzing male-female relations in societies that do not have such a term in their own languages. Few people have rejected this term with the same argument and vigor they have rejected fundamentalism. The legitimacy and usefulness of concepts should therefore not be judged *a priori*.

Not only scholars but also people adhering to various non-Protestant groups resent the term fundamentalism. They understand themselves as representatives of true Judaism, true Islam, or true Hinduism but see no relation whatsoever to Protestant fundamentalism. They obviously have a point: all of these movements certainly express features that are very particular to the religious traditions in which they have emerged.

But there is also a widespread lack of understanding what general concepts are supposed to achieve. Remember the crab in William James's *Varieties of Religious Experience*, which is outraged because it has been categorized as a crustacean. The crab cries out, "I am no such thing . . . I am MYSELF, MYSELF alone!"[5] However, from a scholarly point of view, similarity and difference are not objectively given, thereby impressing themselves on the minds of scholars, but effects of the perspective one employs. Different disciplines make different assumptions about similarities and differences and have different interests in analyzing them. For a biologist, the category "mammals," which lumps humans and animals together, is absolutely reasonable and useful. For an anthropologist, however, each human culture should be studied in its own right and not lumped together with others.

Obviously, it is also a scholarly decision to analyze various religious ideologies from the perspective of either similarity or difference.

4. Lawrence, *Defenders of God*.
5. James, *Varieties of Religious Experience*, 9.

Of course, nothing prevents us from analyzing religious fundamentalist movements primarily from the perspective of their singularity based on the religious tradition they identify with. The frame of reference for Protestant fundamentalism would then be Protestantism or Christianity in general; for Islamism, it would be Islam; for Hindu religious nationalism, Hinduism, and so forth.

However, we can also analyze these movements from a comparative, cross-cultural perspective, emphasizing commonalities, for example, in their social composition, leadership, organizational forms, or ideologies. Both generalizing and particularizing perspectives ask different questions and therefore provide different kinds of answers. But both are equally legitimate and—in my mind—indispensable for our attempts at understanding and explaining fundamentalisms. We should not refrain from cross-cultural comparisons just because the present orthodoxy says that traditions are so unique that comparisons are futile or even illegitimate. For example, the well-documented obsession that fundamentalisms of every kind have with issues of gender and sexual morality should stimulate our curiosity and compel us to inquire into the reasons for such similarities. The *a priori* assumption that this must mean different things in different cultures is actually rather banal and empty. Only a careful comparison could establish what is actually unique.

Do we need the term fundamentalism for our analysis? Of course not. We could even replace it with a different term, if we find one that scholars can agree upon. However, we are in need of a concept that helps us frame such a comparative analysis. Since the term fundamentalism is widely used, I prefer to give it more analytical precision instead of replacing it with yet another term no one understands.

Let me introduce a concept of fundamentalism I find useful for comparative analysis: fundamentalism refers to the ideologies and practices of religious groups and movements that attempt to overcome a perceived moral crisis through a strict, often "literal," return to principles and modes of behavior regarded as sacred and eternally valid. In contrast, "progressive" movements tend to emphasize the "spirit" of those principles. The sacredness of those principles stems either from tradition, the religion's founder, their divine origin, or a combination thereof. Usually, the moral crisis of the present is seen as the result of an apostasy from such principles, and only a return to them is believed to rectify the situation.[6] Such principles explicitly or implicitly express typical views of history, ethics, social order, and anthropology.

The fundamentalist view of history rejects the enlightenment historical narrative of progress and reform through human reason and effort and counters it with a narrative of apostasy and decline. Fundamentalists view history as salvation history. Human beings can contribute to their salvation by rejecting the arrogance of the Enlightenment project and returning to an eternal truth. In terms of ethics, fundamentalists tend to adhere to a strict ethic of law and ritual observance. The law as they define it is timeless and unchanging; since it is sacred, it must be obeyed and strictly enforced.

In terms of their anthropological assumptions, fundamentalists reject modern, gender-neutral individualism and counter it with the doctrine of gender dualism according to which men and women are created or naturally designed in relation to each other.

Fundamentalists are often regarded as being antimodern, and with respect to their views of history and anthropology, they certainly are; in other respects, however, they are actually innovative. They have made creative use of modern mass media and have at times borrowed arguments from competing ideologies, like nationalism, liberalism, or Marxism. Socially, fundamentalists have formed novel kinds of associations and movements, often integrating people from diverse social backgrounds and different class segments.

In their self-understanding, fundamentalist movements are not class movements but cultural ones, held together by a social and moral critique of contemporary society and by a vision of an ideal social order based on religious principles. This might explain why their ideologies have remained relatively stable in spite of changes in their social composition.

My definition and further description implies that fundamentalisms can be identified neither with particular religious traditions nor with definite organizational forms. They organize themselves as communes and subcultures, religious movements and social protest-movements, secret societies, and political parties. In other words, more or less all religious traditions have the potential to become fundamentalist, and no organizational form is more typical than others. To put it as clearly as possible: fundamentalism is neither an exclusively Christian

---

6. Riesebrodt, *Pious Passion*, 15–17.

nor even an Islamic phenomenon, and it is not principally linked to militancy and violence.

Initially, the political mobilization of fundamentalism often makes use of charismatic structures of authority. In such cases, a new kind of leadership by preachers or lay demagogues articulates the grievances and demands of social groups who feel widely excluded from political participation. In these instances, fundamentalists do not represent traditional authority but rather undermine it.

In order to better understand and explain fundamentalist movements and groups, however, it would be misleading to focus too much on political mobilization; for very often, the point is instead to mobilize for the sake of religious goals. Fundamentalists often stress pious life conduct and the cultivation of a specifically religious ethos, as, for example, Saba Mahmood has shown in her study of Egyptian women: people from lower classes and women are often enlisted into such efforts.[7] Since such practices also profoundly influence principles of socialization, their actual cultural and social significance might become more visible in future generations.

Fundamentalism as Radical Patriarchalism

Although the ways of life and ideologies of different fundamentalist groups can vary considerably in various respects, they all tend to idealize patriarchal structures of authority and morality. They all seem to share an advocacy of a god-given or "natural" gender dualism. Men and women are created different, because they were created for each other. The family is a sacred institution, which expresses this purpose of creation. The god-given or "natural" task of women is to bear and raise children; their natural sphere is the domestic one. The god-given or "natural" task of men is to father children, protect the family, and provide the resources necessary. Their natural sphere is the extradomestic one. The female body must be decently covered so that it does not arouse the male passions. In an Islamic context, this may involve veiling, while in a Protestant context, it may refer to the length of the skirt. Whatever its cultural forms, the patriarchal family, patriarchal authority, and gender dualism are central to fundamentalist identity. And

---

7. Mahmood, *Politics of Piety*.

fundamentalists share the belief that only a return to such principles can overcome the present crisis.

Although fundamentalism exposes a rather strict patriarchal ideology and advocates the submission of women to patriarchal authority, it also has activated women to rethink the religious tradition on their own and come up with a redefinition of their social roles. In conjunction with higher levels of education and greater access to the labor market, this has led to a renegotiation of gender relations within fundamentalist milieus. In some instances, it has not only produced less rigid practical arrangements of patriarchal relations but even to the (unintended) development of an indigenous religious feminism.

The basic patriarchal principles also apply to the economic and political sphere. The economic ideals of the first generation basically consist of a traditionalist, personalistic type of capitalism based on the family model, which is much more comfortable with local and regional economic relations than with national, international, or even global ones. Although fundamentalists are often religious nationalists, they also wish to limit the state's economic and political interference in local and regional affairs and tend instead to emphasize its role as a guardian of the social moral order and shield against competition and organized labor. Within the second generation of fundamentalists, some share these ideals while others advocate the more comprehensive involvement of a theocratic state in social life.

Although the program of fundamentalist movements and groups cannot be reduced to questions of gender, gender still plays a very central role in probably all fundamentalist movements. Understood as a moral system of social relations based on distinctions between male and female, gender defines proper manhood and proper womanhood, male and female rights and duties, and proper sexual relations. Deviations from such norms are condemned and—where possible—sanctioned, often quite brutally indeed; this is especially true in cases of adultery, prostitution, and homosexuality, as well as "nakedness," which is usually a synonym for "indecent" styles of dress.

The obsession with the female body and sexual morality is a common denominator of fundamentalist movements across religious traditions. The case of Islam is obvious, and debates about "veiling" have been prominent over the last few decades.[8] Already the Fedayani Islam, a militant Iranian group of the 1940s and 1950s, write with reference to unveiled women: "Flames of passion rise from the naked bodies of immoral women and burn humanity into ashes."[9]

It is important to notice that this kind of thinking is not at all peculiar to Islam. John R. Straton, a New York pastor active mostly in the 1920s, for example, wrote many tracts like "The Connection Between Women's Dress and Social Vice" and "The Scarlet Stain of Sexual Impurity." He also proposed a "national costume" for women designed to preserve propriety.[10] And a leading Protestant fundamentalist journal, *The King's Business*, writes in 1919: "There is a full-fledged rebellion under way, not only against the headship of man in government and church but in the home . . . The cultivation of the modern woman's idea of 'my individuality' in bound to be a destroyer of the home life and a breeder of divorces."[11]

Today's Hindu nationalists argue similarly. For example, Mridula Sinha, ex-president of the BJP Mahila Morcha, stated in an interview by the magazine *Savvy* (April 1994): "I oppose women's liberation as it is another name for 'loose morals.' We oppose equal 'rights' for both sexes. There is nothing wrong with domestic violence against women: very often it is the women's fault. We advise women to try and adjust, as her 'non-adjustability' creates the problem. Women's future lies in perpetuating the present, because no where else are women 'worshipped' as they are in India."[12] And as the female BJP leader Vijaya Raje Scindia argues: "[I]t is the fundamental right of Hindu women to commit sati, as it is in preservation of our past glory and culture."[13]

The recent protests by ultra-Orthodox Jews in Israel wearing fake KZ clothes and yellow stars were also directed against the equality of women and demand gender separation in public: women should take back seats in buses, use different ballot boxes in elections, dress "decently," and should not walk in front of synagogues. Altogether, the New

---

8. Ahmed, *Quiet Revolution*.
9. Ferdows, *Religion*, Appendix, 9.
10. Straton, *Menace of Immorality*, 49–50.
11. K. L. B., "Woman Suffrage," 701.
12. Quoted in Puniyani, *Communal Politics*, 222.
13. Quoted in Louis, *Emerging Hindutva Force*, 88.

York Times remarks on January 14, 2012, "Israelis [are] facing a seismic rift over [the] role of women."[14]

Fundamentalists of all traditions also strongly oppose homosexuality. Radical Hindus have protested against the Delhi High Court ruling that decriminalized homosexuality. And according to *Asian News International*, VHP activist Vijay Pal Singh says, "[w]e strongly oppose homosexuality and we consider this as human deformity. Only a mad person can order legalising it."[15]

Protestant, Jewish, and Muslim preachers have explained earthquakes, tsunamis, and other disasters as the result of immorality. Jerry Falwell, one of the most prominent Protestant fundamentalist leaders, explained the 9/11 attacks this way in an interview: "I really believe that the pagans, and the abortionists, and the feminists, and the gays and the lesbians who are actively trying to make that an alternative lifestyle, the ACLU, People For the American Way, all of them who have tried to secularize America. I point the finger in their face and say 'you helped this happen.'"[16]

Falwell's Jewish counterpart Yehuda Levin, an Orthodox rabbi from Brooklyn, New York, has gained notoriety for his strong opposition to abortion and gay rights—he even blamed the earthquake in Haiti on homosexuality. In the last elections, Levin had originally supported the Republican candidate for governor of New York, Carl Paladino. But after he had learned that Paladino had apologized for his earlier antigay remarks, Levin withdrew his support. According to the *New York Times* he said, "I was in the middle of eating a kosher pastrami sandwich . . . While I was eating it, they come running and they say 'Paladino became gay!' I said 'What?' And then they showed me the statement. I almost choked on the kosher salami . . . He discovered now he has a gay nephew? . . . Mazel tov! We'll make a coming-out party!"[17] Evidently Levin was so shocked that he even forgot whether he was eating a pastrami or salami sandwich.

14. Bronner and Kershner, "Israelis Facing a Seismic Rift Over Role of Women."
15. "VHP Demonstration Against Decriminalising Homosexuality."
16. Falwell, "You Helped This Happen."
17. Harris, "Rabbi Breaks With Paladino Over Apology."

But enough of these examples: I hope they have sufficiently illustrated that gender issues are at the heart of fundamentalist ideologies, as I have defined them above, across religious traditions.

Why the Centrality of Gender?

How can one explain this prominence of gender in fundamentalist ideologies? Given the multiplicity of structural changes in all social spheres over the last century—from technological revolutions to globalization—why is it that fundamentalism is so preoccupied with gender relations and sexual morality? Of course, it is impossible to give a satisfying answer here to such a complex question. Therefore, I only want to offer some preliminary suggestions of an admittedly all too general nature.

As opposed to an explanation that reduces everything to economic dynamics, changing gender relations should be taken seriously as mobilizing forces. The focus on gender is not an expression of a "false consciousness"; it is not just a sideshow symbolizing "real" socioeconomic issues. Instead, it represents a very real concern over quite dramatic changes that have taken place.

Women have been enfranchised: their legal position has been strengthened, they have gained access to higher education, and they have entered the labor market in huge numbers. Sexual mores have changed dramatically. Women have increasingly gained control over their bodies through contraception and the legalization of abortion. Homosexuality has been decriminalized. Gay marriage is on today's agenda. There are love parades and gay parades, events that would have been unthinkable fifty years ago. Given all this, fundamentalists are not deluded but addressing observable facts.

Furthermore, these changes in gender relations and sexual morality have been implemented by a "progressive milieu" consisting of a liberal political class, a secular state bureaucracy, and people who are generally better off in terms of income and education. Accordingly, these changes have become symbols of that milieu and—for non-Western societies—symbols of the West.

Moreover, our Western discourse has increasingly made women's rights the measure of modernity and human rights. Our political class finds public approval by criticizing and expressing concern about the rights of women in other countries. And Islamophobia is by no means limited to the political Right but also widespread among liberals and leftists because of it.

Fundamentalists have organized their own milieu in opposition to the "progressive milieu," and particularly in opposition to the secular state as its most powerful agent. In their view, the state has been instrumental in transforming patriarchal structures of authority and morality in which men are in control of home and family into bureaucratic ones based on gender indifference and formal equality, where the state is in control. This transformation has also created great ambiguity regarding gender relations and sexual morality. Not only has male authority been weakened, but some of the traditional ways of exerting this authority vis-à-vis women and children have also been outlawed, whereas formerly outlawed modes of behavior have become acceptable, like homosexuality or "nakedness" in public places, advertising, TV, and film.

Obviously, this shift in power from patriarchs to bureaucrats and from men to women has provoked strong reactions. Most importantly and not surprisingly, fundamentalist milieus have formulated and institutionalized visions of gender relations and sexual morality that stand in strict opposition to the bureaucratic levelling of gender differences. These visions emphasize strict patriarchal structures of authority and morality legitimized as representing God's eternal law or a sacred tradition.

This makes advocates and representatives of the new gender regime and sexual morality enemies of God, betrayers of tradition, traitors of the nation, apostates—you name it. This scenario, which envisions an apocalyptic battle between the Party of God and the forces of evil, not only re-establishes patriarchs but creates opportunities for dramatizing manhood in the forms of heroism and martyrdom. These forms of manhood are diametrically opposed to the dominant culture of bureaucratic rule, welfare, and "wellness."

However, fundamentalism is by no means a return to tradition but rather represents an invention of tradition or a radicalized traditionalism. It forges a new milieu that includes mobilized traditional groups as well as other people who see themselves as victims of the secular state. In the early beginnings, fundamentalists come from the traditional middle, lower middle, and working classes, but over time the modern middle classes come to predominate—engineers, students, disenchanted bureaucrats, or unemployed university graduates whom the bureaucracy can no longer absorb. Obviously, this is not only a struggle about cultural ideals and values but also about political control.

Of course, women are part of the fundamentalist milieu and often actually an active one. What has surprised many observers the most is the fact that often quite educated, modern, middle-class women have voluntarily joined fundamentalist or extremely traditionalistic religious associations, as, for example, Kelly Chong has shown in her excellent study of South Korean converts to Evangelicalism, or Lynn Davidman and Debra Kaufman in their analyses of Judaism.[18]

Last but not least, gender issues have also gained symbolic significance in the culture war between the secular state and the progressive milieu on the one hand and those who feel that they have become politically, socially, economically, and culturally marginalized on the other. Since they often do not share other common interests, gender politics and sexual morals allow them to articulate their various frustrations in a unified language. Moreover, nothing seems to upset the modernist milieu more than offenses against its own view of gender relations and sexual morals, like the rights of women and of homosexuals. Therefore these topics are ideal for the purpose of creating and maintaining group boundaries.

Varieties of Fundamentalisms and Gender Regimes

I hope I have successfully argued that fundamentalism is a useful analytical concept, especially when it is combined with and related to the concept of gender. But so far my characterization of fundamentalism obviously represents an ideal-typical overgeneralization in need of critical confrontation with the historical realities of various fundamentalisms. Otherwise, ideal types could become stereotypes. Although this is not the place to actually confront ideal types and history, let me briefly indicate in which direction further elaboration should proceed.

The concepts of fundamentalism as well as patriarchalism are useful in order to establish a conceptual frame, but they obviously cover a lot of ground and initially tend to homogenize. Therefore, in order to engage in any meaningful analysis of gender regimes, one must acknowledge the internal variety of fundamentalisms and their historical dynamics.[19]

18. Chong, *Deliverance*; Davidman, *Tradition*; Kaufman, *Rachel's Daughters*.
19. Riesebrodt and Chong, "Fundamentalisms."

Max Weber once analyzed the affinities the various classes have for different structures of religious plausibility.[20] Peasants, artisans and traders, warriors, bureaucrats, and intellectuals all develop different attitudes toward religion and different kinds of religiosity. In similar fashion, one should expect different kinds of fundamentalism to develop according to rationalities and irrationalities typical of various life-worlds. Furthermore, one should also differentiate between fundamentalist gender regimes in the context of various countries and regions as well as religious traditions.

The gender regime of the Taliban is different from that of Iran or Arab Muslim immigrants in Berlin; likewise, the gender regime of Mormon fundamentalists in rural and small-town Utah is different from that in Salt Lake City or Frankfurt, Germany, and the gender regimes of Pentecostals in Venezuela,[21] Ghana, and Italy are not exactly alike. Moreover, all fundamentalisms have features that are quite specific to their religious traditions. There might, for example, be features that are only typical of Jewish, Christian, Muslim, or Hindu fundamentalists and that vary across time and geographical location.

In order to further explore and assess fundamentalist gender regimes, one should relate them to the practiced alternatives against which they emerge instead of utopian modern Western ideals. Otherwise, one fails to understand their meaning to their members, especially in the case of voluntary participation by women. For example, if the alternative to patriarchal structures of authority and morality is *machismo*, then a woman might be better off with a sober and hard-working fundamentalist husband than with a secular drunkard who beats her up and gambles his wages away.[22]

Historical Dynamics of Gender Regimes

I began my article with a reference to Joan Scott, who called gender a useful concept for historical analysis. Here, I would like to emphasize "historical": not only do fundamentalisms show a great variety of gender regimes, but these gender regimes are also not static. They change

---

20. Weber, *Sociology*, 80–117.
21. Smilde, *Reason to Believe*.
22. Brusco, *Reformation of Machismo*.

over time, often when women renegotiate their position by transforming and reinterpreting patriarchal structures from within.

Depending on the historical and political context and social dynamics, each regime might open or close opportunities for such changes in unique fashion. In particular, it is of great interest to observe the reproduction of fundamentalist milieus with regard to the changes each new generation might contribute. For example, wearing a headscarf might mean quite different things for different generations.[23]

Such detailed studies should also prevent us from using the specter of fundamentalism as a cheap excuse for our own complacency. Focusing on the patriarchalism of "the other" does not excuse us from critically analyzing the gender regime(s) of our liberal society. To what extent are our gender relations simply adaptations to economic market pressures and the logic of market relations? What are the effects on children of various gender regimes?

The sheer absence of fundamentalism and patriarchalism does not automatically guarantee a morally founded and legitimate system of social and gender relations. Therefore, we should resist naturalizing modern Western ideals of gender equality and sexual tolerance by treating all other ideals as aberrations. Instead, gender relations and sexual morality should be the objects of an ongoing discourse among responsible citizens and critical scholars.

Bibliography

Ahmed, Leila. *A Quiet Revolution: The Veil's Resurgence, from the Middle East to America*. New Haven, London: Yale University Press, 2011.

Bronner, Ethan, and Elizabeth Kershner. "Israelis Facing a Seismic Rift Over Role of Women." *New York Times*, Jan 14, 2012. Online: http://www.nytimes.com/2012/01/15/world/middleeast/israel-faces-crisis-over-role-of-ultra-orthodox-in-society.html?pagewanted=all.

Brusco, Elisabeth E. *The Reformation of Machismo: Evangelical Conversion and Gender in Colombia*. Austin: University of Texas Press, 1995.

Chong, Kelly H. *Deliverance and Submission: Evangelical Women and the Negotiation of Patriarchy in South Korea*. Cambridge, MA: Harvard University Press, 2008.

Davidman, Lynn. *Tradition in a Rootless World: Women Turn to Orthodox Judaism*. Berkeley: University of California Press, 1991.

Falwell, Jerry. "'You Helped This Happen.' Jerry Falwell and Pat Robertson React to the September 11 Terrorist Attacks on American Soil." Beliefnet, partial transcript of comments from the Sept 13, 2011 edition of the "700 Club," n.p. Online: http://

---

23. Ahmed, *Quiet Revolution*.

www.beliefnet.com/Faiths/Christianity/2001/09/You-Helped-This-Happen.aspx.

Ferdows, Adele. "Religion and Iranian Nationalism." PhD diss., Indiana University, 1967.

Harris, Elizabeth A. "Rabbi Breaks With Paladino over Apology." *New York Times*, Oct 13, 2010. Online: http://www.nytimes.com/2010/10/14/nyregion/14paladino.html.

James, William. *The Varieties of Religious Experience: A Study in Human nature*. 28th ed. London: Longmans, Green, 1917.

Juergensmeyer, Mark. "Antifundamentalism." In *Fundamentalisms Comprehended*, edited by Martin E. Marty and R. Scott Appleby, 353–66. Chicago: University of Chicago Press, 1995.

Kaufman, Debra Renee. *Rachel's Daughters: Newly Orthodox Jewish Women*. New Brunswick, NJ: Rutgers University Press, 1991.

K. L. B. "Woman Suffrage and the Bible." *The King's Business* 10/8 (1919), 700–702.

Lawrence, Bruce B. *Defenders of God: The Fundamentalist Revolt Against the Modern Age*. San Francisco: Harper & Row, 1989.

Louis, Prakash. *The Emerging Hindutva Force: The Ascent of Hindu Nationalism*. New Delhi: Indian Social Institute, 2000.

Mahmood, Saba. *Politics of Piety: The Islamic Revival and the Feminist Subject*. Princeton: Princeton University Press, 2005.

Marty, Martin E. and R. Scott Appleby, editors. *Fundamentalisms and Society: Reclaiming the Sciences, the Family, and Education*. Chicago, London: University of Chicago Press, 1993.

———. *Fundamentalisms and the State: Remaking Polities, Economies, and Militance*. Chicago, London: University of Chicago Press, 1993.

———. *Fundamentalisms Observed*. Chicago, London: University of Chicago Press, 1991.

Puniyani, Ram. *Communal Politics: Facts Versus Myths*. New Delhi: Sage, 2003.

Riesebrodt, Martin. *Pious Passion: The Emergence of Modern Fundamentalism in the United States and Iran*. Translated by Don Reneau. Berkeley: University of California Press, 1993.

Riesebrodt, Martin, and Kelly Chong. "Fundamentalisms and Patriarchal Gender Politics." *Journal of Women's History* 10/4 (1999) 55–77.

Scott, Joan W. "Gender: A Useful Category of Historical Analysis." *The American Historical Review* 91/5 (1986) 1053–75.

Smilde, David. *Reason to Believe: Cultural Agency in Latin American Evangelicalism*. Berkeley: University of California Press, 2007.

Straton, John Roach. *The Menace of Immorality in Church and State: Messages of Wrath and Judgment*. New York: Doran, 1920.

"VHP Demonstration Against Decriminalising Homosexuality." *Asian News International*, July 21, 2009. Online: http://www.thefreelibrary.com/VHP+demonstration+against+decriminalising+homosexuality.-a0204108469.

Weber, Max. *The Sociology of Religion*. Translated by Ephraim Fischoff. Boston: Beacon, 1964.

Jesus Enters the Battle of the Sexes

Vincent Crapanzano

Gender studies have, for the most part, been argued in binary terms: "male" versus "female." In so doing, they have failed to consider the mediation of a third. By "third" I am not referring to inter- or trans-sexuals (though they may, of course, play a mediating role) but to an interlocutory (technically, a metapragmatic) function.[1] Put simply, the parties to any interlocution, say, a dialogue, negotiate, if not explicitly then implicitly, the communicative and interpersonal conventions (language, grammar, genre, style, modes of figuration, law, etiquette, discretion, and decorum) that will apply to their exchange. Think, for example, of negotiations over which language to speak, between people with different mother tongues but who speak each other's language. Will they speak English or German? Or will they arrive at some idiosyncratic accommodation, speaking English when they are chatting, for example, and German when they are arguing? This function may be incarnated— again implicitly if not explicitly—in a deity, saint, spirit, totem, fetish, king, priestess, or any other figure of authority, including on occasion the more authoritative interlocutors. The King's English might be an example. The degree to which such embodiments are personified, the authority attributed to them, the level and mode of engagement they "demand" will vary from occasion to occasion, from culture to culture. The role that Jesus Christ plays in the lives of believing Christians var-

---

1. As I have discussed "the third" in a number of publications, I will resist the temptation to repeat my argument in detail. The reader is referred to Crapanzano, *Hermes' Dilemma*.

ies, for example, significantly. For some it is intermittent, distant, and rarely intrusive. For others, say, Christian fundamentalists, it is—in the ideal—immediate, intense, intimate, constant, and suppliant. Insofar as such tertiary figures affect the relations between people engaged with each other, they influence the images each one has of the other in his or her particularity and generality. I want to suggest that the intimate role Jesus plays in the lives of Christian fundamentalists configures their images of each other, as man and woman, and their marital and sexual relations in ways that challenge the binary images of gender and gender relations, indeed of self and other, that are presumed in most prevailing studies of gender and sexuality.

Let me begin with an incident from my research on American Christian fundamentalism, whose relevance to my argument will, hopefully, become clear in the course of this essay. I had made an appointment to interview a professor at a conservative evangelical seminary in Los Angeles. I arrived early and, as I was waiting, I talked to his secretary, whom I'll call Emily. Emily was very young, perhaps nineteen or twenty, soft-spoken, innocent, timid but not exactly shy, and excessively polite even for a woman who had grown up in a fundamentalist household. Her eyes, I remember, were anemic—without sparkle. When, after calling for his next appointment, the professor saw me, he turned angrily to Emily, asked who I was, and then accused her of making a double appointment. "But he's come all the way from New York," she started to say, but before she could finish, he turned as angrily to me and without apologizing said he had no time to see me. Fortunately, his other appointment arrived—his colleague in the next office who was meeting him as usual for lunch—and said that they could meet for lunch anytime. The interview that followed was hardly productive. When I was quite literally dismissed, Emily started to apologize for the mix-up. I told her that it was not her fault, that I had in fact seen my name clearly written on the professor's agenda, but, as though she had not heard me, she continued to apologize.

This is, of course, a familiar story, but it is unique in several respects. I never encountered such a display of anger—displaced anger—among any of the fundamentalists I met. Although Emily's insistent apology was not unusual, she herself was. She had told me, as I was waiting for the interview, that she had gone to the East Coast for the first time a few weeks earlier—with her father who had decided, after struggling with the idea and much prayer, to attend his twenty-fifth class reunion at Princeton, where he, along with several classmates, had been baptized by the Holy Spirit. "He was embarrassed seeing his former classmates," Emily said without comment. I asked her if she had gone or was planning to go to college. She answered, "Oh, no. I'd like to, but my dad doesn't want me to." I was surprised since fundamentalists, certainly of her background, do send their daughters to college, if only to become good homemakers. I must have shown my disapproval, for Emily quickly changed the subject, telling me that she had grown up in Brazil where her father had been a financial advisor to a missionary society. When I said a few words to her in my broken Brazilian Portuguese, her eyes lit up, her voice deepened and became more confident, her manner almost flirtatious. The transformation was quite dramatic, but it did not last.

A few weeks later, back in New York, I received a call from Emily in which she again apologized for the mix-up. I asked her if she had been told to call me by the professor and reluctantly she said yes. Again, I assured her it was not her fault and then—quite inappropriately, perhaps—I told her that the professor's blaming her seemed unchristian to me. After a long silence, and then without much enthusiasm, Emily said she would have to think about that, and with a "God bless" said goodbye and hung up. My last words were "Please be courageous."

The professor, who taught at a very conservative evangelical, that is a fundamentalist, seminary was not representative of his colleagues there or at other similar institutions. They were all men—friendly, warm at times, helpful, and concerned, I believe, with my salvation. Unlike some of the students, they made no effort to proselytize—to witness to me, as they say—but preferred, as I did, to maintain a collegial attitude. We were both professors. I think that some of them actually enjoyed talking to me, for I represented a secular, humanistic world with which they had little contact, though they were highly critical of it, more accurately of the image they had of it. They were not as extreme as the faculty at the very conservative Bob Jones University, who advocate two degrees rather than one degree of separation from non-Christians—that is, not being friendly with non-Christians as opposed to not being friends with Christians who were friendly with non-Christians. They form a community apart.[2] (I am using "Christian" here and throughout this essay as the evangelical Christians do—exclusively, to refer only to those Christians who are reborn.)

The seminary where I met the professor and where I did a lot of my research was on a large campus with a church that seated several thousand, a primary and secondary school, a college, and a bible-counseling service that had at the time more than thirty biblical counselors, working full-time. The church complex was founded by a highly respected preacher of enormous energy whom I will call William. William ran the church, delivered three sermons on Sundays, wrote countless books and articles, traveled extensively to preach at other churches or participate in evangelical meetings. He had taught at another bible seminary, but left it when its counseling program took a psychodynamic approach. William thought the turn to psychoanalysis was unchristian, among other reasons, because of psychoanalysis's focus on the past, thereby perpetuating sin by not recognizing the redemptive powers of Christ. He shared this view with many conservative evangelicals.

Each of William's Sunday services was devoted to an explication of a passage from the Bible. He was progressing slowly, verse by verse, though all the books of the New Testament and some, I believe, of the Old Testament. He focused far more on textual exegesis, citing at times the Greek, than most of the preachers I have heard, who immediately applied the text they were reading to the present day. (Indeed, despite their commitment to literalist interpretation, many of them would read a passage from Scripture, paraphrase it, and then comment on their paraphrase as if it were the text itself.) William's services reminded me of a Victorian classroom. One was provided with paper and pencil and expected to take notes during the service. Many church members attended all three services and between them special workshops, some devoted to biblical exegesis, some to problems of working with non-Christians in the workplace, some to the meaning of Christian marriage, to raising children in a non-Christian environment, to proselytizing, and to the role of women in the church. The church also organized study groups during the week and encouraged bible-study groups at people's homes. I met fundamentalists who, aside from going to church,

---

2. See Crapanzano, *Serving the Word*, for a detailed account of my research on American fundamentalism.

attended three or even four of these home-study groups each week. Often they used workbooks based on a book or manual offering advice on how to be a good Christian.

Aside from organized study groups, many fundamentalists have or at least have had family meetings each evening in which they discussed the spiritual and moral problems they had that day, their failures, the sins they (may) have committed, and passages in Scripture that might help them resolve their problems. The daily meeting begins and ends with prayer. Jay Adams, a biblical counselor admired by William, is a staunch believer in these meetings, particularly if the family or a family member is in crisis. He suggests that the family sit around a table—the "conference table," he calls it—that is ideally used only for this purpose.[3] It marks a special occasion in which Christian communication occurs or can be restored. "Tables tend to draw people together,"[4] Adams writes in one of his most important books on biblical counseling. They "soon become a symbol of hope."[5] He spells out the rules of these meetings—rules that reflect the fundamentalists', indeed, the evangelicals', ideal family. The father as "head of the home" calls the conference; the mother acts as secretary. The children are instructed and frequently admonished. Adams notes that since one of the most prevalent marriage problems is a reversal of the roles of husband and wife, these table meetings should aim at structuring or restructuring the proper relationship between husbands and wives and their children. I have met former fundamentalists who remember dreading these meetings as children, particularly those in which their fathers assumed a harsh, punitive role. It is clear that the restoration of Christian communication, a primary goal of these meetings, is hierarchically structured in such a way that wives, as secretaries, are forced into a submissive role.

In comparison to many other fundamentalist churches, particularly the nondenominational ones, which are found throughout small-town America and in working-class urban neighborhoods, William's is rigorously Calvinist. He emphasizes original sin and man's depraved imagination—a consequence of Adam's, always Adam's, sin. Insofar as depraved imagination can be contained, it is by a strict adherence to the

3. Adams, *Competent to Counsel*, 231–36.
4. Ibid., 231.
5. Ibid.

literal—"the plain, ordinary, commonsense"—meaning of Scripture. William is suspicious of figurative language and condemns "the promiscuous allegorization of Roman Catholicism." Personal salvation rests on God's grace only. Like other fundamentalists, he focuses on Christ's Second Coming and preaches a pretribulational premillennialism; that is, the belief that Christ will raise up and rapture the born-again Christians before the seven years of tribulation, or the outpouring of God's wrath, which precedes Christ's Second Coming and the ensuing millennium. Premillennialists argue that the demonic element in history is on the increase and that the present age will end in catastrophe. William's view is not as bleak as that of some fundamentalists. He gives priority to saving souls over any attempt to improve the world through political, social, economic, or physical means. Yet I never heard him discourage such attempts, provided it was understood that they would not lead to one's salvation. Unlike more moderate evangelicals, who are playing a dominant role in American politics, William insists on the separation of church and state. I never saw political tracts in his church, though I often saw them in other conservative evangelical churches.

It is important not to lump all evangelicals together. They range from the strict fundamentalists to the popular Pentecostalists. The majority of American evangelicals—around seventy million by some estimates—find themselves somewhere in the middle. They all insist on a literal reading of Scripture, Christ's Second Coming, personal salvation, a commitment to biblical life, an intimate, prayerful relationship with Jesus, and a responsibility to proselytize. They all have had or long to have, at some point in their lives, a revelatory experience—a conversion or the intensification of belief: rebirth. Yet, there are important differences in their understanding and evaluation of theology in their services, in their styles of preaching, in the manner in which they minister to others, in their biblical counseling, and in their attitudes toward psychology. Fundamentalists, like William, who are particularly suspicious of heightened emotional—"spiritual"—experiences, disapprove of charismatic Christians, like the Pentecostalists, particularly those who claim that speaking in tongues and other gifts of the Spirit are signs of having been saved.[6] William is critical of their insistence on the simultaneous occurrence of rebirth, justification, and complete sanctification.

6. MacArthur, *Charismatic Chaos*.

For William, as for most strict fundamentalists, sanctification is a lifelong discipline. It is an aspect of the order of salvation, the *ordo salutis*, of Reformed theology.[7] This is not the place to rehearse that order, which is differently interpreted by different evangelical theologians. Suffice it to say that sanctification is usually paired with justification: that is, an act of grace by which the sinner, formerly condemned by God, now has His blessing. It elevates the believer to a "realm of full acceptance and divine privilege in Jesus Christ."[8] It declares, in other words, a change of status, but it effects no actual change in the believer. "At justification we surrender the principle of sin and self-rule,"[9] William says. "In sanctification we relinquish the practice of specific sins as we mature in Christ."[10] Theological niceties aside, sanctification is understood by most fundamentalists as making your life as biblical as possible.

I have stressed sanctification here because the discipline it requires figures or, perhaps more accurately, refigures gender, sexual, and family relationships in purportedly biblical terms. I will not focus, however, on scriptural references but on the practice of sanctification, on the ground, in family situations, for example, in guides to behavior, and in biblical counseling. Given the dramatic nature of regeneration (conversion), it has not always received the attention it deserves in scholarly studies of evangelical Protestantism.

Before proceeding, I should point out a contradiction in the fundamentalists' hermeneutics that constitutes the space—the arena—in which sanctification is carried out. Put simply, fundamentalists are caught, despite themselves, in a figurative trap. Like William, they accept the traditional hermeneutical distinction between explication, interpretation, and application. Unlike contemporary philosophical theories of interpretation—those of Heidegger and Gadamer, for example—that stress the recursive relationship between these phases or aspects of hermeneutic practice, they insist, in accordance with their literalism, on their separation. It is, of course, possible to make a case for a literalist approach to explication and interpretation, but not to application. Insofar as there is a temporal gap between the text under consideration and

---

7. Crapanzano, *Serving the Word*, 101–2.
8. MacArthur, *The Gospel According to the Apostles*, 71.
9. Ibid., 90.
10. Ibid.

the practice to which that text is applied, as between Scripture and actual circumstances, it is impossible to avoid metaphor or analogy. Scripture can speak to the present only in figurative terms, though figuration is often masked by reading passages in Scripture as imperatives even if they are neither in the imperative mood nor substantive commands. In making one's life as biblical as possible, one has either to accept the figurative and the risks it entails stemming from depraved imagination and sinful desire—ultimately, from Satan—or one has to find a way to abolish or at least diminish the temporal gap through sanctification—by making one's life, indeed one's perception and cognition, as biblical as possible. In extreme cases one sacrifices experience to text.[11]

Sanctification is, however, not limited to making one's life as biblical as possible but also to "maturing in Christ." It requires the acceptance of Christ, who in the ideal is ever-present in the believer's world. A. W. Tozer, one of the earlier theologians William likes to quote, understands the acceptance of Christ in terms of both an all-inclusive and an all-exclusive attachment to Him. All-inclusively, "the true believer owns Christ as his All in All without reservation," Tozer writes. "He also includes all of himself, leaving no part of his being unaffected by the revolutionary transaction [that is acceptance]."[12] All-exclusively, Tozer goes on to observe, the believer "orbits around Christ as the earth around the sun, held in thrall by the magnetism of His love, drawing all his life and light from Him. In this happy state he is given other interests, it is true, but these are all determined by his relation to the Lord."[13] As a goal, the attachment to Christ, it would seem, penetrates deeply into believers' lives, affecting their self-image, their sense of self, their attitude toward others, their image of men and women, and their relations—their sexual relations—with one another. This leads to subtle and at times not so subtle changes in language—in the meaning, evaluation, and affective weight of referents—and in consequence possible misunderstandings between "Christians" and non-Christians.

Lest this seem too abstract, let me quote from Larry Crabb's *The Marriage Builder: A Blueprint for Couples and Counselors*, a book that has sold over 400,000 copies. Crabb is a biblical counselor, who had studied

---

11. Crapanzano, *Serving the Word*, 118–21.
12. Tozer, *That Incredible Christian*, 18–19.
13. Ibid.

psychology at university and practiced psychotherapy before becoming a biblical counselor. Though committed to a literalist interpretation of Scripture, he is theologically less rigid than William and appears to be slightly more tolerant of some of the assumptions of secular psychotherapies. He has, in fact, been criticized for being too psychological. According to Crabb, obedience to God's command is a prerequisite for a successful marriage. Marital problems result primarily from a loss of personal significance and security. Whether or not a married person is made to feel significant and secure by his or her spouse, true significance and security can only come from Christ—through His love. Unlike Adams, Crabb does not stress role reversal as the primary cause of marital problems, though several of the cases he discusses do revolve around a wife's assuming a husband's role in the family, the husband being forced into a submissive role or withdrawing his affection and love for his wife.[14] Many of Crabb's case snippets—and those of other biblical counselors—on marital problems revolve around the failure of communication between spouses. This may in part be the result of the presumptive role husbands play—and have to defend—in the family and the submissive role wives are given. Crabb understands the problem in terms of manipulation—of trying to change one's spouse—rather than ministering to him or her.

> When people do not depend fully on the Lord to satisfy their essential needs, they necessarily turn to others. Their purpose becomes to arrange their worlds of people and things in a way that brings some sense of satisfaction. The goal of manipulation—attempting to change whatever does not satisfy so that it will satisfy—is set in motion. Husbands try to make their wives lose weight, stop nagging, be more cooperative sexually, and acquiesce to their opinions. Wives work hard to get their husbands to play less golf, help more with housework, be more romantic, spend more time with the children, and share feelings more openly.[15]

14. We should remember the Promise Keepers' insistence that men once again assume the leadership of the family, which they have surrendered to women, especially feminists. The Promise Keepers was founded in 1990 by Bill McCartney, the head football coach at the University of Colorado, Boulder. It describes itself as "a Christ-centered organization dedicated to introducing men to Jesus Christ as their Savior and Lord, helping them grow as Christians." It has been on the wane since suffering financial difficulties following its famous rally in Washington, D.C. in 1997. Feminists have criticized it for fostering male superiority and encouraging inequality in marriage.

15. Crabb, *Marriage Builder*, 98.

The list is indicative of prevailing values among conservative evangelicals—and no doubt among many other Americans, though they would probably not emphasize God's role in their intimate life. Indeed, Crabb even stresses the role of one's attachment to Christ for a successful sexual life. Christ's love is a prerequisite for a loving sexual relationship, which Crabb, like other counselors, distinguishes from "fun sex." The relationship between the two loves is palimpsestic.

Though Crabb is far more careful to consider sympathetically women and the difficulties they encounter in their families, with their friends, and in the workplace (if they are so economically hard pressed as to have to work) than many other biblical counselors. His attitude, its underside at least, is revealed in this case anecdote. "A little girl is molested by her father," Crabb begins. "This confusing, painful experience may teach her that men are a source of hurt and must never be trusted." She grows up believing that she has "to protect herself from rejection" by distancing herself from men. She marries. "Her husband is looking forward to their first night together. When he approaches her . . . she freezes inside, she feels nervous, tight. Her husband struggles to be patient but cannot conceal his disappointment and frustration. She feels terrible. She wonders what is wrong with her." She "withdraws from sexual involvement," eager to avoid the emotional pain. After trying a "few lackluster seductions," her husband gives up and "settles into a pattern of mechanical release whenever her guilt prompts her to 'service' him." Whenever the couple sits in church, "a jointly held hymnbook is the extent of their oneness."[16] Crabb's perfunctory attitude toward the abuse and its effects, the simplistic treatment he suggests, and the role he gives to Jesus, however compassionate and loving it may be, all serve to thrust responsibility on the woman. The damage lies simply in what she believes—the threat sexual closeness poses to her security as a woman. She must bear the "legitimate pain" she feels from her husband's rejection—not the abuse she suffered; for her need for security will be fully met by "Christ's unchanging faithfulness."[17] It is she who may have to "reestablish some sort of relationship with her dad" (rather than his coming to her). It is she who must approach her husband for

16. Ibid., 96.
17. Ibid., 97.

sex, perhaps by snuggling up to him "on the couch during a TV show rather than busying herself in the kitchen."[18]

However insensitive, indeed grotesque, we may find Crabb's attitude, our interest is in the image of woman it reveals: one of total submission to the Lord, mirrored, if not explicitly then implicitly, in a woman's relationship to her husband and, despite her submissiveness, the responsibility—the pain even—she is made to bear. Although Crabb does not cite Ephesians 5:22–23 here, his position reflects Paul's words (or the author of that epistle)—words that are cited repeatedly by family-value evangelicals: "Wives, be subject to your husbands as you are to the Lord. For the husband is the head of the wife just as Christ is the head of the church." True, Crabb, like other biblical counselors, insists on a man's—a husband's—total obedience to the Lord, but if you read carefully, if you listen carefully, you will find, facilitated by the asserted belief in Christ's love, a woman's being caught in a paradoxical situation in which she has to be submissive as she must assume responsibility for the failure of her relationship with her husband. Christ, believed in or not, plays, as a *tertium quid,* a rhetorical role in the articulation of this relationship. Indeed he penetrates the most intimate of their relations.

There are two other connected dimensions of the fundamentalist's image of women, marriage, and sex I want to consider. The first is the mechanization of relationships, particularly sexual ones; the second is the shallowness of the image of both men and women and their relationship. Both relate to the fundamentalists' insistence on absolute sexual purity. Not only do they consider premarital sex a sin but also lustful thoughts which, in the case of men, will lead inevitably if not to fornication then to masturbation, and masturbation will have dire effects on marital relations and—more importantly—on one's relationship with God. "Victory is more than stopping masturbation," Arterburn and Stoeker write in *Every Young Man's Battle*: "It's starting to experience God in those moments that would have been dedicated to sex. It's finding God and His help in the midst of every struggle and even every failure. It's not about extinguishing masturbation as much as it's about igniting a new passion for God, with sexuality integrated into your life in a balanced way."[19] The authors, who stress the importance of visual

---

18. Ibid.

19. Arterburn and Stoeker, *Young Man's Battle*, 169.

stimulation in men advise them to look away whenever they see an attractive woman or, needless to say, pornography, or even lingerie ads in the newspaper. Women need touching, sharing, hugging, and deep communication: "Sex isn't so much a physical act as it's an emotional act for women."[20] "Guys give emotion so they can get sex,"[21] they write summarily. "Girls give sex to get emotions."[22] Throughout their book, they assume that women desire sex less often than men.

In both my interviews and informal conversations with fundamentalists, especially men, there was an assumption that if a man were left alone with a woman, or danced with her, a sexual relationship or an attempted one would ensue. Of course, men and women have often been left alone with each other or danced with each other without any sexual consequences. But in preaching, in gossip, in sex education, and in conservative biblical counseling, any suggestion of intimacy was immediately eroticized—more accurately, sexualized. Belief and reality were but poorly bridged in this respect, sometimes with dire consequences, as when a respected member of a church, found alone with a woman in the parish, was immediately expelled from the church. The woman—who was not expelled from the church—was tainted. I have met more than one woman who left the church, indeed the community, to flee the stigma attached to her.

Jay Adams, whom I mentioned earlier, is the founder of nouthetic counseling, which is practiced by the counselors in William's church and in many other fundamentalist communities. It is a confrontational, admonishing approach to the troubled and afflicted. ("Nouthetic" comes from the Greek *nouthesis*, reproof, admonishment, teaching.) Adams is ardently opposed to psychoanalysis, which, by attempting to release the individual from personal guilt, without recognizing original sin, encourages the promiscuity and irresponsibility that prevail today in this premillennarian age.[23] He asks: "Is the fundamental problem of persons who come for personal counseling sickness or sin?"[24] Nouthetic counseling achieves its goal by means of prayer, by confronting the counselee with

20. Ibid., 207.
21. Ibid., 208.
22. Ibid.
23. See also MacArthur and Mack, *Introduction to Biblical Counseling*.
24. Adams, *Competent to Counsel*, 19.

the sins he or she has camouflaged, which are taken to be the source of his or her malaise, through reproof, admonishment, and teaching—nouthesis—and by assigning "homework" of a practical nature, which is based on relevant biblical passages. Many of these are from Proverbs. Other than searching for the etiological sinful acts, the nouthetic counselor gives little attention to the counselee's past. Adams puts it this way: We are not interested in the why (as psychoanalysis is). We already know the answer to that: man's sinful nature. We are interested in the what.[25] Rarely lasting more than a few weeks or months, the counseling is focused on the present and future. At the heart of Adams's counseling, one of his critics says, quoting Adams himself, is "You can't say 'can't.'"[26]

Like the cases in most other counseling books I have seen, Adams's are little more than anecdotes. His *Casebook* consists of case reports of less than a page, followed by questions that the counselor should ask him- or herself. He gives no answers. Adams gives each of them provocative titles: "The Affair," "He Molested Our Daughter," "What Can You Do for a Single Girl Who Wants To Be Married?", "Can't Control His Wife," "Depression," and "The Locked Door"—to name a few. Most of the cases concern marital problems, sexual addiction, drinking, work problems, lack of commitment, and faulty communication. Some edge on the prurient, as, for example, a couple who cannot have sex for a while because the husband has ringworm on his penis. As they both want to have sex, they ask their pastor if mutual masturbation is permissible. Adam's vignettes illustrate not only his approach to counseling but his view of marriage, women, men, and sex. They are shared by other nouthetic counselors and by many of the conservative evangelicals with whom I spoke. How characteristic they are of evangelicals generally, indeed of the American working and (lower) middle classes, from which the majority of evangelicals come, I cannot say.

In "What Do I Do Now?" a Mrs. Williams—she and her husband are professed Christians—has come to seek advice from a pastor in a neighboring church. She asks, "What is my responsibility to my husband now that he has filed for a divorce?"[27] Reggie left her six months earlier and obtained a legal separation. She explains: "'Before the sep-

---

25. Ibid., 48–49.
26. Ibid., 133.
27. Adams, *Christian Counselor's Casebook*, 76.

aration we counseled with our pastor for about five months. He only listened to us; never told us what to do or how to get out of the mess. Reggie finally quit and left. Reggie says that he does not love me any more. Can you help me?'"[28] Adams adds that Mrs. Williams explained that she has legal rights to the children, that her husband has stopped going to church, and that when he comes to visit the children, he wants to have sex with her. She wonders if she should agree. "What Do I Do Now?" is one of many of the cases that involve the sexual demands of the husband. Many other case vignettes focus on the inevitability of the husband's sexual needs without discussing his behavior and attitudes or the wife's needs.

In "Please Listen," Lena, a fourteen-year-old girl, is tricked by her girl friends into seducing a married man. They each promise to do so, but she is only one who follows through. When she reports back to her friends, they drop her. To show them, she decides to sleep with each of their fathers. To her surprise, they did, each paying her ten dollars to keep quiet, as the first man she seduced had. "In time," Adams writes, "her 'exploits' became a way of life which led to prostitution, two illegitimate children, three abortions, and now her doctor has told her she has cancer. 'There is just no hope for me at all,'" Lena says. "'My life is too messed up, and I am too far gone to do anything about it all!'"[29] The four questions that follow the case are: "1.) Beyond her need for the gospel, what is Lena's greatest need? 2.) How would you seek to evangelize her? 3.) Assuming that she became a Christian, how would you want to help her afterwards? 4.) What place could your local congregation play in helping Lena?"[30] One wonders whether the pastor would have helped her if she were not to become a Christian. Adams has been criticized, even by some of his followers, for lacking compassion. He insists that counselors not go soft and sentimental.

Aside from seeking the appropriate biblical passages that will help the counselees, and which they must study and discuss over the conference table as they open themselves up to their spouses and children, the advice that Adams gives is simplistically practical. A man who is troubled by masturbation is told not to walk by "art films"—pornographic

28. Ibid.
29. Ibid., 96.
30. Ibid., 97.

ones—on his way back from work. An inconsiderate husband is told to open the car door for his wife. A married airline attendant, who has a man at each port of call, is told to call her husband as soon as she arrives at the hotel in the town where the plane has landed. Most counselees are asked to write lists of the sins they committed each week.

Even teenage guides for leading a Christian life, written by evangelicals who are far more open-minded than Adams, Crabb, and preachers like William, share with them an equally mechanical view of sex and gender. Shannon Ethridge and Stephen Arterburn's *Every Young Woman's Battle: Guarding Your Mind, Heart, and Body in a Sex-Saturated World*, a volume in a series devoted to "Win[ning] the War on Sexual Temptation at Every Age" that has sold over three million copies, stresses the importance of remaining a virgin until marriage.[31] Ethridge and Arterburn write openly about sex, discussing, among other things, the way young women convince themselves that they are preserving their sexual purity by remaining technically a virgin while engaging in masturbation, oral and anal sex, and lesbian relations. (These practices are, according to the authors, frequent among teenage girls.) The authors are concerned that such practices can lead to sexual addiction—a term that has recently become fashionable among secular psychologists and sexologists in the United States. They argue that while most girls have masturbated at some point in their lives, its repeated practice can lead eventually to disappointment in their sexual relations with their husbands and to marital difficulties, for they (like men) may find greater satisfaction in masturbation. They praise self-control. They advise young women not to flirt or wear provocative clothing because it can excite men to the point of taking them by force. In *Every Young Women's Battle* at least, Ethridge and Arterburn assume that men have less control over their sexuality than young women. They write:

> The next time you are tempted to flirt "just for fun" remember that there is Someone you can whisper your heart's desires to and have fun with who isn't going to jeopardize your integrity but instead strengthen it. If you are looking for a safe relationship to pour your attentions and affections into, you don't have to look any further than Jesus Christ. He can delight your

---

31. Arterburn and Stoeker, *Young Man's Battle*, which I quoted earlier, is also in the series.

heart and soul and satisfy every fiber of your being much more than any boy on the planet.

If you are thinking, *No way will talking to God ever excite me like talking to a guy* then you haven't allowed yourself to be courted by our Creator. The same God whose words possessed the power to form the entire universe longs to whisper words into your heart that have the power to thrill you, heal you, and draw you into a deeper love relationship than you ever imagined possible.[32]

I think it likely that strict fundamentalists such as William, Adams, and even Crabb, would look askance at the eroticization of one's relationship to God—the sensual language in which they write. What is striking about these counseling practices and the theology that lies behind them is the focus on the present and future. They lack historical or even biographical depth, and, coupled with their mechanistic understanding of sexual and marital relations, their stereotypy of men and woman, their interest—in Adams's words, "in the what and not the why"—and their insistence on the sinful nature of men and women that lies at the root of all their clients' guilt and affliction leads to a superficial understanding of motivation and consequent behavior. I should note, in addition, the influence of behaviorism on their stress on the habitual and, when sinful, its correction. (Adams had studied with the behaviorist psychologist O. Hobart Mowrer.) Through Christ's redemption and the inevitability of sinfulness, the counselees are freed or can be freed of the burdens of the past, often enough, if we can trust the observations of the biblical counselors who spend little time with them and have only brief, if any, follow-ups. They attribute their success to the Holy Spirit—the force, as they see it, behind biblical counseling—and their faith in Christ's love. It is not for us to question the power of faith, but I believe we have to recognize the way in which, through sanctification (of which counseling is but a moment), Christ comes to so occupy—to so penetrate—their lives, at least in the ideal, that the very image of the person—man or woman—cannot be separated from His presence. Crabb puts it this way: The spirit oneness—the con-union—of the believer's relationship to Christ is a prerequisite for soul oneness—the con-union—of the married couple. Of course, spirit oneness and soul oneness are an ideal that is in constant struggle with the demands—the challenges—of the secular world—the sex-saturated

---

32. Ethridge and Arterburn, *Young Women's Battle*, 102–3.

world, as the conservative evangelicals see it—of the average American, or better the image of themselves that Americans perpetuate. It is in this context, I believe, that the fundamentalists' image of women has to be understood. Whether they achieve their goal or not, it is their struggle that is formative.

In conclusion, let me return to Emily and her last words, "God bless," before hanging up. We can take them simply as a conventional good-bye or as a mark of her Christianity or as a gift of God's blessing. But to whom was it addressed? She did not say "God bless you." It free-floated, like "have a good one" that has become a common way of saying good-bye among Americans. It had no direct object. We were, I suppose, all incorporated in God's blessing—in a world in which her faith had been challenged by the unchristian anger, the injustice, of the professor whose Christianity she was supposed to admire. She was caught then in the paradoxical situation in which she had at once to be submissive to the professor and yet bear the responsibility for his error—his sinning. God—Christ—was invoked in what I presume was a restorative gesture—to give her the strength to manage the paradox in which she found herself. "I'll have to think about that." In Emily's eyes, no doubt, her faith in the Lord rendered my last words, "Please be courageous," both puzzling and needless.

Bibliography

Adams, Jay E. *The Christian Counselor's Casebook: Applying the Principles of Nouthetic Counseling.* Grand Rapids: Zondervan, 1974.

———. *Competent to Counsel: Introduction to Nouthetic Counseling.* Grand Rapids: Zondervan, 1970.

Arterburn, Stephen, and Fred Stoeker. *Every Young Man's Battle: Strategies for Victory in the Real World of Sexual Temptation.* Colorado Springs: Waterbrook, 2002.

Crabb, Lawrence J. *The Marriage Builder: A Blueprint for Couples and Counselors.* Grand Rapids: Zondervan, 1982.

Crapanzano, Vincent. *Hermes' Dilemma and Hamlet's Desire: On the Epistemology of Interpretation.* Cambridge, MA: Harvard University Press, 1992.

———. *Serving the Word: Literalism in America from the Pulpit to the Bench.* New York: New, 2000.

Ethridge, Shannon, and Stephen Arterburn. *Every Young Woman's Battle: Guarding Your Mind, Heart, and Body in a Sex-Saturated World.* Colorado Springs: Waterbrook, 2004.

MacArthur, John F. *Charismatic Chaos.* Grand Rapids: Zondervan, 1992.

———. *The Gospel According to the Apostles: The Role of Works in the Life of Faith.* Nashville: Nelson, 2000.

MacArthur, John F., and Wayne A. Mack, editors. *Introduction to Biblical Counseling: A Basic Guide to the Principles and Practice of Counseling.* Dallas: Word, 1994.

Tozer, A. W. *That Incredible Christian.* Harrisburg, PA: Christian, 1964.

Literalism and Anti-Semitism

Positions within the (German) Bibelbund during the 1930s[1]

JANA HUSMANN

Introduction

The German Bibelbund[2] was founded in 1894 and brought together various factions of German Protestant fundamentalism, including proponents of Christian literalism.[3] A major objective in founding the Bibelbund was to counteract the growing influence of liberal theology

---

1. A similar version of this paper is published in German. See Husmann, "Problem Judentum." This version translated from German by Leah Chizek and Jill Denton.

2. In English: *Bible Confederation*.

3. In the Christian context, literalism is defined as the (fundamentalist) belief in the absolute inerrancy of the Bible, according to which the Holy Scripture is understood in the *literal* sense as the incontrovertible truth of God. Though the teaching of biblical inerrancy is also said to be an "old legacy" (Joest, "Fundamentalismus," 732), the specific nature of modern religious literalism lies in its opposition to modern liberal theology, historico-critical biblical science and its diagnosis of a larger societal decay of the Christian faith: "The dogma of the Bible's verbal inspiration and complete freedom of error was called upon now in protest of these developments, acquiring a sharply apologetic accent and . . . indeed the full significance of a fundamental tenet on which all remaining aspects of belief now depended" (ibid., 733). On literalism, see also Crapanzano, *Serving*; Riesebrodt, *Rückkehr*, 54. On the idea of a "theology of facts," see Geldbach, *Fundamentalismus*, 45–46.

and Higher Criticism, or more precisely, of historico-critical approaches to the Bible. The Bibelbund's statutes thus declared that

> 1. Members profess their belief that the Holy Scripture of the Old and New Testament is and is therewith the sole guide to our faith and in our lives. 2. They are allied in a concerted effort to thoroughly research the biblical books, individually and in their entirety, so as to defend the respect rightfully due to the Holy Scripture as the Word of God from its opponents. 3. Publications by the *Bibelbund* thereby include: a) scholarly works on language, exegesis, biblical history, geography, archaeology etc., b) on the critique of criticism in particular c) popular works in the aforementioned areas.[4]

The Bibelbund's official publication was the journal *Nach dem Gesetz und Zeugnis* (According to Law and Testament), which is still available today under the title *Bibel und Gemeinde* (Bible and Parish).[5] In 1938–1939, the journal's editor-in-chief Wilhelm Möller[6] (1872–1956) published a treatise in serial form entitled "On Building Bridges between State and Church: Suggestions and Wishes, Particularly Regarding the

---

4. The Bibelbund's statutes are part of every issue of the journal *Nach dem Gesetz und Zeugnis*. Here quoted and translated from *Nach dem Gesetz und Zeugnis* 1 (Apr 1912): "1. Die Mitglieder bekennen sich zu dem Glauben, daß die Heilige Schrift Alten und Neuen Testamentes nach ihrem Zeugnis über sich selbst das durchaus und in allem einzelnen wahre und von jedem Irrtum freie Wort Gottes und darum die einzige Richtschnur unseres Glaubens und Lebens ist. 2. Sie verbinden sich zu einer gemeinsamen Arbeit, die biblischen Bücher im einzelnen und im ganzen zu durchforschen, das der Heiligen Schrift, als dem Wort Gottes, gebührende Ansehen ihren Gegnern gegenüber zu verteidigen . . . 3. Die Veröffentlichungen des Bibelbundes sind daher: a) wissenschaftliche Arbeiten der Sprachforschung, der Exegese, der biblischen Geschichte, Geographie, Altertumskunde usw., b) besonders auch Kritik der Kritik, c) populäre Arbeiten auf den vorgenannten Gebieten."

5. The journal *Nach dem Gesetz und Zeugnis* appeared from 1901 to 1939. In 1939 it was prohibited. The journal began publication anew in 1950 and was published under the new title *Bibel und Gemeinde* as of 1954.

6. Wilhelm Möller was an Old Testament biblical scholar who gained a certain international prominence in Christian fundamentalist circles. In the famous series of treatises *The Fundamentals: A Testimony to the Truth* (1910–1915), he is mentioned as a converted academic who left his further historico-critical approaches to the Bible behind and turned to a fundamentalist believe in the Holy Scripture: "Wilhelm Möller, who confesses that he was once 'immovably convinced of the irrefutable correctness of the Graf-Wellhausen hypothesis,' has revised his former radical conclusions on the ground of reason and deeper research as a Higher Critic" (Hague, "Higher Criticism," 40).

Question of Judaism and the Old Testament."[7] The following analysis of this treatise seeks to clarify certain of the Bibelbund's positions on National Socialist ideologies of state and race. The primary interest thereby is the Bibelbund's contradictory and often conflict-ridden endeavors to adapt its agenda to accommodate National Socialist policy, endeavors that centered largely on a vindication of the Old Testament[8]—in other words, of the Hebrew Bible. This vindication of the Old Testament must be seen in context, and very especially in relation to the Religious Movement of the German Christians (*Glaubensbewegung Deutsche Christen*), which was closely connected to the Nazi Party.[9] As early as 1933, the German Christians had called for the abolition of the Old Testament (which they defamed as Jewish heritage).[10] The Bibelbund—for reasons evident in the aforementioned statutes—remained opposed to this key point, since its defense of a literalist stance rested on a faith in divine inspiration[11] and in the absolute inerrancy of the Holy Scriptures in their entirety. Yet it would be a mistake nonetheless to read the Bibelbund's stance on the "German-völkisch movement" simply as "cautious" as theologian Stephan Holthaus, a present-day member of the Bibelbund does—not generally, but in specific reference to the Bibelbund's defense of the Old Testament.[12] Möller's efforts to defend the Holy Scriptures in their entirety rather clearly attest to "völkisch" goals when he concludes that "one cannot possibly imagine or wish for better allies in the war against Judaism than the Old Testament and the Bible."[13]

    7. Möller, *Brückenbau*.

    8. The term "Old Testament" has been criticized for its anti-Judaistic connotation according to which the Hebrew Bible is antiquated and only gains its value and worship in relation to the "New Testament." See e.g., Deutsche Bibelgesellschaft, "Einleitung." I will use the term Old Testament in this paper in view of its historical usage by Möller and his theological and political context.

    9. On the German Christians see, e.g., Bergen, *Twisted Cross*; Heschel, *Aryan Jesus*.

    10. So, for example, at a "spectacular mass rally held by the German Christian faith movement at the Berliner *Sportpalast* (Nov 13, 1933)," at which pastor D. Krause "vilified the Old Testament and the Pauline version of the Bible as Jewish machinations" (Broszat, "Kirchengemeinden," 372).

    11. On the idea of divine "verbal inspiration" see, e.g., Wagner-Rau, "Suche," 15, 25, Ann. 2.

    12. Holthaus, "100 Jahre," §4.

    13. Möller, *Brückenbau*, 18: "[M]an [kann] sich keinen besseren Bundesgenossen im Kampf gegen das Judentum wünschen und denken . . . als das Alte Testament und die Bibel überhaupt."

In the following analysis, I will address three interwoven anti-Semitic elements in Möller's defense of the Old Testament: Firstly, an anti-Semitic construction of the Jew; secondly, a "de-Jewification" of the Hebrew Bible and its interpretation as an anti-Semitic document; and thirdly, an anti-Semitic approach evident in Möller's critique of Higher Criticism, or rather historico-critical approaches to the Bible. The following basic questions outline my focus when interpreting Möllers text: To what extent are religious and secular forms of knowledge entangled? How does literalism come into play as a specific "style . . . of interpretation"[14] and as a specific form of modern religious knowledge production? In what way(s) are the racialization of religion and the re-sacralization of the secular categories race and nation interwoven? To what extent do anti-Judaism, anti-Semitism and anti-intellectualism play a role in the literalist assertion of supposedly true and false interpretations of the Scriptures? And in which way(s) do they ally themselves with *gendered* constructs of knowledge?

In response to these questions, my paper is structured in two parts: In the first part, titled "Anti-Semitism and the Defense of the Old Testament," I will discuss Möller's main strategies for presenting the Hebrew Bible as an anti-Semitic document. In the second part, titled "Anti-Semitism, Anti-Rationalism and the Critique of Higher Criticism," I will outline the anti-Semitic impact of Möller's critique of modern historico-critical approaches to the Bible and his related notions of rationalism. At the end of the paper, I will briefly draw some conclusions.

Anti-Semitism and the Defense of the Old Testament

As a matter of principle, leading members of the Bibelbund greeted the rise of National Socialism and hailed Adolf Hitler as the "God-sent leader (*Führer*)."[15] Editor-in-chief Wilhelm Möller thus ascertains in 1939 that "Hitler knows he is pursuing a divine mission, and so the people [*das Volk*] welcome him as a special gift from God."[16] In this same context,

---

14. Crapanzano, *Serving*, xvii.
15. Holthaus, "100 Jahre," §4.
16. Möller, *Brückenbau*, 29: "Hitler weiß sich als von der Vorsehung beauftragt, und das Volk nimmt ihn als ein besonderes Gottesgeschenk an." For appraisals of Adolf Hitler and National Socialist politics in *Nach dem Gesetz und Zeugnis* during the years 1938/39, see also Ramge, "Führer"; Ramge, "Deutschland"; Ramge, "Krieg";

Möller expresses wholehearted approval of the anti-Semitic policies of the National Socialist state.[17] Indeed, as early as 1926 he had spoken, as Holthaus has critically pointed out, "at a Bibelbund conference of 'Judaism's destructive impact on the world of nations [*Völkerwelt*].'"[18]

It is therefore evident that any conflict between the Bibelbund's agenda and the National Socialist worldview was not of a general nature. Furthermore, the agreement with National Socialism was directly addressed in the defense of the Old Testament. A strategic line of argument was to draw a parallel between the allegedly true and valid *writings* or, to be more precise, the scriptural fundaments of Christian Protestantism and of National Socialism. "If Christianity is to be of any use to the people [*Volk*], then naturally, it cannot rest on just any kind of common or garden-variety writings [*Allerweltschriftentum*] but must be solely the type of Christianity that has its origins and its standards in the Bible, just as the Third Reich is rooted in Hitler's book *Mein Kampf* and in the mandates of National Socialist policy."[19] Moreover, according to Möller the so-called Jewish Question (*die Judenfrage*) constitutes a common thread in Christian and National Socialist creeds: "It is in any case certain that the Bible takes the Jewish question seriously, even more so than National Socialism does; insofar there is little reason to fear a conflict between the State and Church on this point, so long as the Church stands by biblical pronouncements."[20]

It is this idea of turning to the "pure" Word of God, the idea of an objective reading of the Scripture and an understanding of the Bible as a book of objective, timeless norms and facts that already gives a hint of the relevance the concept of religious literalism has within Möller's

Bilderbote; and further articles by Heinrich Cornelius (editor in chief) and August Fliedner (member of the Bibelbund).

17. Möller, *Brückenbau*, 14.

18. Holthaus, "100 Jahre," §4.

19. Möller, *Brückenbau*, 34: "Soll das Christentum dem Volk etwas nützen, so kann es natürlich andererseits nicht ein Allerweltschriftentum sein . . . sondern nur das Christentum, das an der Bibel seinen Ursprung und seine Norm hat, wie das 3. Reich an Hitlers Buch 'Mein Kampf' und an den Artikeln des nationalsozialistischen Programms."

20. Ibid., 19–20: "Jedenfalls ist soviel sicher, daß die Bibel die Judenfrage noch viel ernster nimmt als selbst der Nationalsozialismus; von hier aus ist also ein Konflikt zwischen Staat und Kirche wirklich nicht zu befürchten, wenn die Kirche bei der biblischen Verkündigung bleibt."

argumentation. This goes together with the claim to and the belief in a "pure" literality that corresponds to an a-temporal "theology of facts"— a critical term Erich Geldbach introduces in his current work on Christian fundamentalism.[21]

How does Möller's argumentation function in detail? How does he bring together the contemporary Jewish Question with his professedly objective reading of the Old Testament? The following three strategies and propositions can be identified in Möller's "vindication" of the Old Testament:

The first strategy implies an anti-Jewish and anti-Semitic rereading of God's election of Israel: According to Möller, the biblical doctrine of the election of Israel as well as Israel's significance in the context of salvation history are linked to Israel's own "misunderstanding" of the election.[22] Essentially, it is argued, the election of Israel was a result not of the virtues but rather of the "inferiority" of the Bible's chosen people—insofar, it is telling evidence of the Lord's extraordinary mercy.[23]

The second strategy can be described as a conflation of biblical "truth" and contemporary historical "reality": The Bible is said to generally offer insight into Jews' character and present-day situation. Möller thus assesses the "punishment (persecution, exile)," "hardness of heart," "curse," and "conversion" of the Jews both in terms of their meaning for salvation history and as an actual historical expression.[24] It follows that contemporary anti-Semitic notions (such as Judaism's association with the "most unscrupulous and villainous of spirits" and with "Bolshevism") appear to be a historically consistent and 'real' expression of "Israel's [biblical] sin."[25] These supposedly "valid expressions" of the Jewish character simultaneously serve, in Möller's eyes, to confirm the historical and prophetic truth of the (entire) Bible.[26]

21. Geldbach, *Fundamentalismus*, 45. The expression "Theologie der Tatsachen" (theology of facts) is also a book title published by the German theologian August F. C. Vilmar in 1856; see Vilmar, *Theologie*.

22. Möller, *Brückenbau*, 17, 23.

23. Ibid., 17, Ann. 1.: "Daß Gott sich ein minderwertiges Volk für seine Zwecke aussuchte, stellt seine Gnade nur in ein um so helleres Licht; denn dann dürfen auch die gesunkensten Völker noch auf Gnade hoffen."

24. Ibid., 19–20: "Strafe (Verfolgung, Zerstreuung)," "Verstockung," "Fluch" and "Bekehrung."

25. Ibid., 17: "skrupellosestem Verbrechergeist"; "Bolshewismus"; "Sünde Israels."

26. Ibid.

The third strategy underlying Möller's argumentation is a (re)sacralization of "völkisch" concepts and the "völkisch" nationalization of religious concepts/categories: concepts briefly treated by Möller hereby include "race"[27]; "blood"[28]; "bloodlines/line of succession"[29]; "heredity"[30]; "soil [*Boden*]"[31]; "honor"[32]; "conception of God"[33]; "regard for earthly life"[34]; "nation [*Volk*]"[35]; and the "concept of 'chosen peoples.'"[36]

All three strategies and propositions are linked with an objectification of knowledge that is based on a way of reading the Bible quite unique to (modern) literalism, namely the practice of *dehistoricizing* the Bible. The logic inherent to this practice enables a historically specific and hegemonic form of racist and anti-Semitic discourse to be conceived of as a supposedly timeless and neutral form of biblical knowledge. In this sense, Möller's approach to the Bible is also an example of what Randall Balmer—in his work on Christian fundamentalism in the US—has called "selective literalism,"[37] this being a thematically selective approach to certain passages in the Bible and the inscription of contemporary discourse into the Holy Scripture from an interpretive standpoint that remains "invisible."

Furthermore, given that many of the terms and concepts mentioned above—"race,"[38] for instance—do not even occur in the Bible,

27. Ibid., 24: "Rasse."

28. Ibid., 24–25: "Blut."

29. Ibid., 25: "Blutzusammenhang nach rückwärts und vorwärts, Geschlechterfolge."

30. Ibid., 25–26: "Vererbung."

31. Ibid., 26: "Boden."

32. Ibid., 27: "Ehre."

33. Ibid.: "Der Gottesbegriff."

34. Ibid.: "Die Schätzung des irdischen Lebens."

35. Ibid., 27–28: "Volk."

36. Ibid., 29: "Erwählungsgedanke."

37. Balmer, *Kingdom*, 9, 10.

38. Möller uses the idea of race in relation to the three sons of Noah, who he understands as the founding fathers of three different races of people. See Möller, *Brückenbau*, 24. This exemplifies the extent to which Möller's argumentation is characterized by a resacralization of secular structural categories. As Peter Martin has shown, the Noah legend concerning the curse of his son Ham plays a decisive role in explanations typical of early race theory. See Martin, *Schwarze Teufel*, 283–88. Möller therefore invokes the encoding of religious traditions into secular race-theoretical

literalism's interpretive claim to literal truth, based as it is on absolute loyalty to the written word, is bound to fail. And even those concepts that *are* found in the Bible ("blood," for example) obviously cannot be linked literally—which is to say, *from within* the biblical text—to National Socialism's blood and soil mythology. Möller thus follows a rhetorical strategy, initially pinpointing only the concepts' contemporary significance in the National Socialist context before later indicating their general significance in the Bible. Should these concepts or terms not occur in the Bible at all, Möller looks for conceptual and/or visual analogies. For example, he dwells at length on the notion of "soil" (*Boden*), as in the racist mythology of blood and soil, merely in order to bring up the garden of Eden, which appears to correspond to, historically anticipate, and legitimize the conceptual significance of soil for National Socialism.[39]

Thus, in Möller's argumentation, anti-Semitic constructs of the Jew, the creation of "völkisch" and racialized categories per se, and a rereading of the Hebrew Bible as an anti-Jewish document become mutually interdependent factors. Insofar the racist nationalization of the Holy Scripture, a racialization of Christianity, and a resacralization of racialized German Christian identity go hand in hand. Given this background, it is not exactly astonishing that Möller's treatise also refers to the term German Christian in the more positive sense of self-identification. While the German Christians' rejection of the Old Testament was precisely the position Möller opposed in his treatise, he nevertheless uses the term German Christian to combine both—his own understanding of racialized Christian identity and his plea for acceptance of the Holy Scripture in its entirety.[40] Last but not least, Möller presents

taxonomies yet in doing so he presupposes the category of race, which is only later established. On the naturalization of religious traditions of thought in the context of race theory and racism, see the detailed discussion in Husmann, *Schwarz-Weiß-Symbolik*.

39. Möller, *Brückenbau*, 26.

40. "We should make an effort to understand the rightful . . . motive of the German Christians, who stand fully grounded on the soil of the Third Reich and who will not tolerate any unbearable and adverse effects sought after or attained in the name of Christianity. At the same time, though, we must make an effort to appreciate the rightful place of German Christians within the Confessing Church [Bekenntniskirche], for they flock to the Gospel and will not let meddlesome forces from outside interfere with its message" (Man sollte sich bemühen, das berechtigte . . . Moment der Deutschen Christen zu verstehen, die ganz auf dem Boden des Dritten Reiches stehen und nicht dulden wollen, daß durch das Christentum irgendwelche untragbare und

the Christian renunciation of the Old Testament as a Jewish aspiration to destroy the unity of Christianity and the German people (*Volk*). The intrafactional Christian conflict centering on whether to reject or retain the Old Testament accordingly appears to be the result and expression *not* of contemporary anti-Semitism but of the "intellectual influence" of the Jews themselves.[41]

Anti-Semitism, Anti-Rationalism, and the Critique of Higher Criticism

A further context in which anti-Semitic constructs are functionalized within Möller's treatise is the Bibelbund's opposition to the influence of Higher Criticism. Here, anti-Semitic constructs appear in order to support the *critique* of biblical criticism, and thereby constitute the Bibelbund's Christian self-understanding in its unique fundamentalist specificity. Likewise, the "Jewish spirit" has an instrumental role in immunizing the latter against historico-critical approaches to the Bible. The following quotation illustrates this with reference to Old Testament criticism:

> From this angle Judaism's link to criticism of the Old Testament and vice versa is clear ... This [criticism of the Old Testament] nevertheless has ... such a destructive quality so thoroughly in line with the destructive Jewish character I suspect that, on the personal level, many of the researchers and reviewers who influenced it perhaps have a hint of the Jew in their blood while on the professional level this criticism, owing to its connections with the rationalists, the encyclopaedists, and the spirit of the French Revolution, can be traced back even more closely—and perhaps unbeknownst to it—to Jewish influences. Investigations to that end would be very desirable on both counts. National Socialism, however, would have two reasons not to get caught in the fray of this so-called 'science.'[42]

verkehrte Beeinträchtigung erstrebt oder versucht werde. Ebenso aber sollte man sich bemühen, das berechtigte Moment der Deutschen Christen in der Bekenntniskirche zu würdigen, die sich um das Evangelium scharen und sich in diese Botschaft nichts Verkehrtes von außen einmischen lassen wollen); ibid., 34.

41. Ibid., 23.

42. Ibid.: "Nach diesen Seiten hin ist der Zusammenhang des Judentums mit der alttestamentlichen Kritik und umgekehrt klar ... Diese [alttestamentliche Kritik] hat aber ... einen derartig zersetzenden Charakter, der so ganz mit der jüdisch zersetzenden Art zusammenstimmt, daß ich vermute, einmal nach der persönlichen Seite

Here, biblical criticism appears as a "Jewish science," while the anti-Semitic identification of the "destructive Jewish character" calls into question the scientific legitimacy of biblical criticism per se.[43] At the same time, rationalism is portrayed as a false form of knowledge and functions as a code word for "Jewish thought." Möller thus taps into a contemporary current of anti-Semitism as anti-intellectualism, according to which "the Jew" is identified with the "falsifying" logic of abstract thought and "cold" intellect.[44] In this way, a further parallel with the National Socialist worldview is established. The defamation of "rationalists" and "encyclopaedists" also implies their incorrect relationship with the written word/letter, which is to say, their incorrect handling and usage of script(ure). Here, the (encyclopaedic) historicization of terms and ideas as well as, in the wider sense, a deconstructive style of reading is the counterpoint to Christian-literalist belief in the written word of God. The subsequent defamatory reference to the "spirit of the French Revolution" historicizes the rationalism considered here to be false and thus turns against the enlightened impetus of reason and rationality. This implicit reference to the traditions of the Enlightenment therefore comprises an indirect rebuke of modern biblical criticism's scientific-historical origins and a denial, broadly speaking, of universalist demands for equality.

Möller's identification of the "evil Jewish spirit,"[45] as he describes it, with "destructive rationalism" and in particular with a supposedly wrong way of handling and interpreting the Holy Scripture implies both a redefinition of anti-Judaistic traditions and a religious version of anti-Semitism. As Lisa Lampert-Weissig has pointed out, in the context of

---

hin, viele Forscher oder Gewährsmänner, die Alttestamentler beeinflußten, möchten einen jüdischen Einschlag in ihrem Blut haben, und nach der fachlichen Seite hin, die Kritik gehe durch ihren Zusammenhang mit den Rationalisten, Enzyklopädisten und dem Geist der französischen Revolution noch viel enger auf jüdische, vielleicht ihr selbst unbewußte Einflüsse zurück. Dahingehende Untersuchungen wären nach beiden Seiten hin dringend erwünscht. Der Nationalsozialismus hätte aber doppelten Grund, nicht in den Geleisen dieser 'Wissenschaft' einherzufahren."

43. This anti-Semitic interpretation of historico-critical Bible research, made by another member of the Bibelbund in 1939, is a clear reference to Baruch de Spinoza (1632–1677), the founder of modern biblical criticism. See Gahr, "Baruch Spinoza."

44. On the connection between anti-Semitism and anti-intellectualism, see Braun, *Schwindel*, 466–79; Nordmann, "Intellektuelle."

45. Möller, *Brückenbau*, 14.

Christian anti-*Judaism* the Jews were associated with a "'useless' style of interpreting texts" and "depicted as blind readers who read without understanding. They are regarded merely as custodians of the Old Testament and associated with the literal text."[46] This traditional anti-Judaistic stereotype is connected with the image of the misguided "Jewish spirit" that connotes a false faith and a false understanding of scripture. Here, to associate the Jews with the *literal text* is simultaneously to defame them for "misapprehending" the true spirit of Christ. While these Christian anti-Judaistic images also influenced the secular anti-Semitic construct of the Jew as an intellectual, Möller's specific religious approach to this anti-Semitic construct not only draws on the appeal of earlier Christian traditions; taking into account that Möller posits the "evil spirit" of Judaism in terms of its secularized dimensions (namely as "destructive Jewish rationalism") and simultaneously in the context of Christian salvation history, one could instead speak of a resacralization of secular anti-Semitism. I will briefly elaborate on this thought, firstly by touching on the relations between sin and sickness and racialization and resacralization, and secondly by considering the *gendered* repercussions of Möller's anti-Semitic notion of anti-rationalism in more detail.

It first has to be stated that the anti-Semitic image of the Jew as an intellectual is connected as such with the anti-Semitic vision of a "sick mind" residing in a "sick body," which serves as the symbiotic antithesis to the racialized notion of a "healthy mind" in a "healthy body."[47] Möller revives these racialized visions and their connection with notions of the contamination, infection, and cleansing of images of the body in a dual sense—namely, in terms of the racialized *individual* body as well as in terms of the *collective* body. This becomes clear when he links rationalism to the influence of "Jewish blood," suggesting, as in the quote above, that rationalists, or rather, the "researchers . . . who influenced it [Higher Criticism of the Old Testament] perhaps have a hint of the Jew in their blood."[48] Regarding the collective body, Möller speaks of the "Jew-infested state."[49] In this sense and as an overarching metaphor for destructive rationalism, the "evil Jewish spirit" threatens to contaminate

---

46. Lampert-Weissig, "'Frau' und 'Jude,'" 172.

47. Hödl, *Pathologisierung*, 178–80. On fascist constructs of ideal masculinity, see Mosse, *Image of Man*.

48. Möller, *Brückenbau*, 23.

49. Ibid., 14: "jüdisch verseuchten Staat."

the racialized Christian nation as well as the (fundamentalist) Christian faith itself.[50] The process of resacralization underlying Möller's narrative patterns becomes palpable when one considers that Christian notions of sin and sinfulness have been transposed to secular typologies of illness throughout the historical course of European secularization.[51] Thus, in Möller's religiously-construed version of racist anti-Semitism, the "evil Jewish spirit"—stigmatized as destructive and infectious—is evaluated *in turn* as an expression of sinfulness, that is, of Israel's "biblical guilt."

As historical research on anti-Semitism, gender, and sexuality has broadly indicated, the racialized construct of the Jew is linked intrinsically with corresponding notions of sickness, sexual aberration, and an "abnormal" gender identity—sexualized constructs of the racialized Other that serve to establish a normative racialized self. Such research emphatically demonstrates that the historical stereotype of the Jewish intellectual invoked by Möller is characterized by a gendered logic of pathological inversion. The notion of a "false" masculine intellectualism is connected here to a corporeal feminization or emasculation of the Jewish male as well as to a masculinization or defeminization of the Jewish female (intellectual).[52] What has to be stressed here is a complex and variable interplay of gendered images of racialized "Jewish physicality," gendered codifications of knowledge, and their racialized embodiment. This also means that in anti-Semitism, the traditionally male-codified rationalism is linked with racialized images of a bodily wrong masculinity that gives rise in turn, to a racialized notion of rationalism as a false and destructive male-identified spirit.

While it should by now have become clear that Möller's anti-Semitic elaboration of rationalism is evidently meant to immunize his position against Higher Criticism and the related rationalist-scientific approach to the Holy Scripture, the underlying separation of religion and science as well as the significance of rationalism itself provoke further questions. This ultimately leads to paradoxical elements where Möller's anti-Semitic defamation of rationalism is concerned—and therewith to the vital connection between reason, rationalism, and religious liter-

50. On the shift in cultural-historical paradigm toward a devaluation of intellect and reason at the end of the nineteenth century, see Braun, *Schwindel*, 476.

51. On the relationship of religious anti-Judaism to racist anti-Semitism in this context, see Braun, "Feind"; Gilman, *Difference*; Hödl, *Pathologisierung*.

52. Braun, *Schwindel*, 429–33, 466–79.

alism's own faith in the word. Indeed, the religious literalist recourse to the (factual, neutrally conceived) "pure" and timeless Word of God, which seems to evade any kind of symbolism or multivalent meaning, suggests the paradox of a (modern) rationalist form of religious knowledge. It appears much more to be an outcome of modern Western traditions of scientific thinking and claims to objectivity and rationality than is ever admitted. This is also to keep an eye on the intrinsic rationalist strategies of objectifying religious knowledge as well as its mutual transfers with secular and secularized knowledge bases. Considered in this light, the literalist impact within Christian Fundamentalism also fits into Gottfried Küenzlen's definition of religious fundamentalism as "*modern* anti-modernism."[53]

Finally, and with respect to gendered constructs of knowledge, this means that two differently inflected forms of male-coded rationalism ultimately inform Möller's remarks: on the one hand is the notion of a "false" masculinity underlying anti-Semitic anti-rationalism and anti-intellectualism; on the other, a positive reference is made precisely to a male-coded rationalism corresponding with a (fundamentalist) "theology of facts."[54] In this regard, modern Christian literalism can also be understood as a modern form by which Protestant Christianity undergoes symbolic (re)masculinization.

Conclusion

When Stephan Holthaus, writing on the history of the Bibelbund, summarily claims that the Bibelbund under National Socialism found "no answer . . . to the essential challenges of the day and to the Jewish question,"[55] his phrasing is misleading to say the least; for the Bibelbund had indeed found a *specific* answer, one intended to harmonize the relationship between church and state. As the case of Möller shows, fundamentalist belief in the absolute inerrancy of the Holy Scriptures went hand in hand with belief in the absolute infallibility of National Socialist policy (on state and race).

---

53. Küenzlen, "Fundamentlismus," 53, 56.

54. Geldbach, *Fundamentalismus*, 45. On the relationship between literalism, rationalism, and the encoding of gender, see Crapanzano, *Serving*, 24.

55. Holthaus, "100 Jahre," §4.

Möller's attempt to defend the Old Testament thereby reveals a complex interplay of narrative strategies: nationalization of the Holy Scriptures, racialization of the individual and the collective body, and resacralization of the National Socialist Christian community. The religious anti-Semitism that underpins Möller's argumentation is thus evidently connected to the production of *secular* knowledge on race and nation. But it simultaneously reveals National Socialism itself to be a "secular religion"[56] in the truest sense of the term: for Christian elements appear in National Socialist knowledge production in secularized and racialized forms. Blood is just one such highly significant example: in the Christian tradition, it appears as a *symbolic* marker for Christian Community (one linked to the sacred and pure blood of Christ); and in the secular context of racial theories, it is transformed into a *secular* marker for the *racialized* (German) Christian Community.

The secularization of Christian elements within National Socialism might also explain the latter's ambivalent, skeptical and partly even hostile stance on the relation between church and state. Thus, as Christina von Braun suggests, it was no longer possible from the National Socialist perspective for "two religions of such similarity to coexist alongside one other."[57] Conversely, as I have endeavored to show, it was nevertheless perfectly conceivable from the standpoint not only of the German Christians but also from the standpoint of Protestant fundamentalism to rewrite Christianity—including the Hebrew Bible—as a National Socialist history of salvation in which the racialized category of the "German Christian" indeed found its place.

Accordingly, the interpretative method used by Möller exposes the respective cultural-historical and political contexts on which modern literalist knowledge production and fundamentalist readings of modernity, a "theology of facts," and its relation to scientific thinking depend. Möller's contradictory approach to rationalism and modernity is thus also shaped in three different ways by the ambivalent relation of religion to science: his approach first appears as a religious/fundamentalist *rejection* of modern science, that is, of Higher Criticism; secondly, and implicitly, as an *inclusion* of supposedly scientific (anti-Semitic) constructs

---

56. Braun, "Feind," 150. On the concept of National Socialism as a secular religion, see also Bärsch, *Politische Religion*; Mommsen, "Nationalsozialismus"; Schoeps, "Erlösungswahn"; Voegelin, *Religionen*.

57. Braun, "Feind," 150.

of race, gender, and nation; and thirdly, as a *methodological combination* of religion and science that constructs religious literalism as a modern style of interpretation and a "theology of facts."

When, in his work on literalism, Crapanzano suggests that in the American context "the emphasis on the literal is a male preoccupation—a sign, if you will, of the pragmatic, tough-minded realism that Americans attach to the male persona,"[58] then this crucial hint as to the intrinsic impacts of gender within literalism also relates to the European context in several ways: it relates to the occidental traditions of gendered structures of knowledge, the symbolic gender codification of rationality and irrationality, and not lastly the European processes of secularization by which these symbolic codifications become naturalized and hence shape modern Western gender identities. The male-identified "pragmatic, tough-minded realism" within literalism also relates to Geldbach's definition of a "theology of facts," with its underlying link to modern scientific thinking. Furthermore, it fits into Martin Riesebrodt's definition of "legalistic-literalistic Fundamentalism," which he distinguishes from "charismatic Fundamentalism" and rather "'emotional-irrational' forms of religious experience."[59] Taking this differentiation into account, literalism and its link to a "symbolic (re)masculinization" (as I have been calling it) is only one side of the gender dualism within fundamentalism as a gender-codified system of knowledge. And finally, as Möller's anti-Semitic impact shows, this specific relationship between literalism and gender may be crisscrossed by various interdependent factors, factors that shape gender as an *intersectional* category of knowledge—each in its respective ways, depending on the particular time, place, and political positioning.

Bibliography

Balmer, Randall. *Thy Kingdom Come: How the Religious Right Distorts the Faith and Threatens America. An Evangelical's Lament*. New York: Basic, 2006.

Bärsch, Claus-Ekkehard. *Die politische Religion des Nationalsozialismus: Die religiösen Dimensionen der NS-Ideologie in den Schriften von Dietrich Eckart, Joseph Goebbels, Alfred Rosenberg und Adolf Hitler*. München: Fink, 2002.

Bergen, Doris L. *Twisted Cross: The German Christian Movement in the Third Reich*. Chapel Hill: University of North Carolina Press, 1996.

58. Crapanzano, *Serving*, 24.
59. Riesebrodt, *Rückkehr*, 54.

Der Bilderbote. Sonderausgabe [Special issue, commemorative issue in honor of Adolf Hitler's fiftieth birthday, 1939], Berlin: Evangelischer Preßverband für Deutschland [supplement in: *Nach dem Gesetz und Zeugnis* 39/1–2 (Apr–May 1939)].

Braun, Christina von. "Und der Feind ist Fleisch geworden. Der rassistische Antisemitismus." In *Der ewige Judenhaß: Christlicher Antijudaismus—Deutschnationale Judenfeindlichkeit—Rassistischer Antisemitismus*, edited by Christina von Braun et al., 149–213. Berlin: Philo, 2000.

———. *Versuch über den Schwindel: Religion, Schrift, Bild, Geschlecht*. Zürich: Pendo, 2001.

Broszat, Martin. "Teil IV Zur Lage evangelischer Gemeinden. A. Berichte der Kapitelsbeauftragten für Volksmission 1933/34: Einführung." In *Bayern in der NS-Zeit: Soziale Lage und politisches Verhalten der Bevölkerung im Spiegel vertraulicher Berichte*, edited by Martin Broszat et al., 369–76. München: Oldenbourg, 1977.

Crapanzano, Vincent. *Serving the Word: Literalism from the Pulpit to the Bench*. New York: New, 2000.

"Einleitung zur Bibelkunde des Alten Testaments. Begriffsbestimmung AT." Deutsche Bibelgesellschaft, 2010, n.p. Online: http://www.bibelwissenschaft.de/bibelkunde/altes-testament/.

Hague, Canon Dyson. "The History of Higher Criticism." In *The Fundamentals: A Testimony to the Truth*, edited by Reuben Archer Torrey et al., 9–42. Grand Rapids: Baker, 2000.

Gahr, Christian. "Baruch Spinoza, der Vater der geschichtlich-kritischen Bibelforschung." *Nach dem Gesetz und Zeugnis* 39/1–2 (1939) 8–13.

Geldbach, Erich. *Protestantischer Fundamentalismus in den USA und Deutschland*. Münster: LIT, 2001.

Gilman, Sander L. *Difference and Pathology: Stereotypes of Sexuality, Race and Madness*. Ithaca, NY: Cornell University Press, 1985.

Hödl, Klaus. *Die Pathologisierung des jüdischen Körpers. Antisemitismus, Geschlecht und Medizin im Fin de Siècle*. Vienna: Picus, 1997.

Holthaus, Stephan. "100 Jahre Bibel und Gemeinde." *Bibel und Gemeinde* (2000) n.p. Online: http://www.bibelbund.de/htm/2000-1-054.htm.

Joest, Wilfried. "Fundamentalismus." In *Theologische Realenzyklopädie*, edited by Gerhard Krause and Gerhard Müller, 11:732–38. Berlin: de Gruyter, 1983.

Husmann, Jana. "Das 'Problem Judentum und Altes Testament': Literalismus und Antisemitismus im Bibelbund. Ein Textbeispiel aus den Jahren 1938/39." In *Dämonen, Vamps und Hysterikerinnen: Geschlechter- und Rassenfigurationen in Wissen, Medien und Alltag um 1900*, edited by Ulrike Auga et al., 185–96. Bielefeld, Germany: transcript, 2011.

———. *Schwarz-Weiß-Symbolik: Dualistische Denktraditionen und die Imagination von "Rasse": Religion—Wissenschaft—Anthroposophie*. Bielefeld, Germany: transcript, 2010.

Künzlen, Gottfried. "Fundamentalismus: Moderner Antimodernismus. Kulturhistorische Überlegungen." *Praktische Theologie* 29/1 (1994) 43–56.

Lampert-Weissig, Lisa. "'Frau' und 'Jude' als hermeneutische Strategie: Zu den gemeinsamen Wurzeln von Frauenfeindlichkeit und Antisemitismus." In

Kritik des Okzidentalismus: Transdisziplinäre Beiträge zu (Neo-)Orientalismus und Geschlecht, edited by Gabriele Dietze et al., 171–85. Bielefeld, Germany: transcript, 2009.

Martin, Peter. *Schwarze Teufel, edle Mohren: Afrikaner in Geschichte und Bewußtsein der Deutschen*. Hamburg: HIS, 2001.

Möller, Wilhelm. *Zum Brückenbau zwischen Staat und Kirche: Winke und Wünsche mit besonderer Berücksichtigung des Problems: Judentum und Altes Testament*. Brieg/Bez. Breslau, 1939. [Sonderdruck (Special Edition). From: *Nach dem Gesetz und Zeugnis* 38/4–5—39/5–7 (1938-1939).]

Mommsen, Hans. "Der Nationalsozialismus als säkulare Religion." In *Zwischen "Nationaler Revolution" und Militärischer Aggression: Transformationen in Kirche und Gesellschaft 1934–1939*, edited by Gerhard Besier, 43–53. München: Oldenbourg, 2001.

Mosse, George L. *The Image of Man: The Creation of Modern Masculinity*. New York: Oxford University Press, 1996.

Nordmann, Ingeborg. "Der Intellektuelle. Ein Fantasma." In *Antisemitismus: Vorurteile und Mythen*, edited by Julius H. Schoeps and Joachim Schlör, 252–59. München: Piper, 1995.

Ramge, Karl. "An den Führer unseres deutschen Volkes!" *Nach dem Gesetz und Zeugnis* 39/1–2 (1939) 1.

———. "Deutschland und Österreich wieder ein Reich!" *Nach dem Gesetz und Zeugnis* 37/1–2 (1938) 1.

———. "Krieg." *Nach dem Gesetz und Zeugnis* 39/5–7 (1939) 88.

Riesebrodt, Martin. *Die Rückkehr der Religionen: Fundamentalismus und der Kampf der Kulturen*. München: Beck, 2000.

Schoeps, Julius H. "Erlösungswahn und Vernichtungswille: Der Nationalsozialismus als politische Religion." In *Zwischen "Nationaler Revolution" und Militärischer Aggression: Transformationen in Kirche und Gesellschaft 1934–1939*, edited by Gerhard Besier, 55–63. München: Oldenbourg, 2001.

Vilmar, August Friedrich Christian. *Die Theologie der Tatsachen wider die Theologie der Rhetorik: Bekenntnis und Abwehr*. 3rd ed. Marburg: Elwert, 1857. Reprint, Erlangen: Luther, 1938, with an introduction by D. Hermann Sasse.

Voegelin, Eric. *Die politischen Religionen*. 3rd ed. München: Fink, 2007.

Wagner-Rau, Ulrike. "Die Suche nach einem Fundament: Eine Einführung in die fundamentalistische Frömmigkeit." In *Die halbierte Emanzipation? Fundamentalismus und Geschlecht*, edited by Elisabeth Rohr et al., 11–28. Königstein: Helmer, 2007.

The Qur'ān in the Field of Conflict between the Interpretative Communities

An Attempt to Cope with the Crisis of Qur'ānic Studies

ANGELIKA NEUWIRTH

Introduction: The Current Situation

In recent years, talking about the Qur'ān in Germany has become a *politicum*, the divulgation of a political statement. The controversy surrounding the status of Muslims in Europe, kindled by the high-profile publication of Thilo Sarrazin's polemical book in 2009,[1] is still making massive waves. It has brought to light the profoundly essentialist perception of Islam that prevails in broader social circles—a perception that makes it easy to forget that, until only recently, inclusive umbrella terms like "the three Abrahamic religions"[2] or "the three scriptural religions" were in fact popular. In many circles, it seems as if these terms have given way to a dichotomy between monolithic blocks like Europe, or "the West," and "Islam." This controversy has spilled over to academic Qur'ānic studies as well. In the following, I

---

1. Sarrazin, *Deutschland schafft sich ab*.
2. Kratz and Nagel, *Abraham unser Vater*, 133–49.

will briefly survey the current situation and then propose a new and more inclusive approach to the Qurʾān.

The exclusivist stance is by no means limited to parts of the Western public. In academic circles, a form of exclusivism has spread in the East *and* the West alike. Because of hermeneutical barriers, Western European and Muslim Qurʾānic scholars, who in fact should be particularly reliant upon one another at a time when Islam has long become a part of everyday life in Europe, are today more divided than ever before. Western researchers reproach Muslims with succumbing to the bias of their tradition, whereas Muslims often perceive their Western colleagues as triumphalist, revealing an utter lack of empathy for Islam. While in the interwar years Arab universities offered posts to European scholars of Islam and guest lectureships of German Qurʾānic scholars were welcome in Jordan and Egypt into the 1970s and 1980s, such mutual curiosity and openness has been consigned to history in today's climate. Between now and then there lies a series of drastic political events and developments, such as the Iranian Revolution, but above all the seemingly perpetual lurking of inner crises that have led to the currently ubiquitous phenomenon of a *sahwa islamiyya*, or "Islamic awakening." In the academic realm, however, it was scholarly debates—veritable "text wars"—which led to a significant cooling of East-West relations and a breach of mutual trust: foremost of all, the simultaneous publication in 1977 of two works in English declaring the transmitted Qurʾān text *in toto* to be nothing but an anonymous compilation. While it is undeniable that critical remarks articulated by earlier Western scholars of Islam met with distrust amongst Muslims,[3] it is just as clear that these two works,[4] penned by highly-regarded academic (both of whom attempted to prove that the entire Islamic tradition was historically baseless and thus reveal the genesis of Islam to be nothing more than a subsequent mythologizing), triggered an upheaval in relations between scholars on both sides. They were followed by other revisionist theses put forward by French and German academics.[5] The consequence, still resonant today, is a progressive self-ghettoization of research on early Islam in the Near East. But the new model had a grave

---

3. See for example Mingana, *Syriac Influences*.
4. Wansbrough, *Qurʾanic Studies*; Crone and Cook, *Hagarism*.
5. Lüling, *Über den Ur-Qurʾan*; Luxenberg, *Die syro-aramäische Lesart*.

impact in the West as well. Degraded to an anonymous compilation of texts whose origin(s) cannot be determined in terms of time and place, the Qur'ān seemed inaccessible to genuine historical concerns; it vanished, as it were, for about thirty years from the horizon of research.[6]

In practical terms, this means that European and more generally Western scholars are hermeneutically unable to achieve the competence, accumulated over centuries of learned practice, of their Muslim colleagues, and conversely, that the benefit the latter can gain from academic work by Western researchers is very limited. Qur'ānic studies is a divided terrain. We therefore face a pressing task: namely, to reconsider our approach to the Qur'ān.

Let us begin by asking: What is so different about the Western and Islamic approach to and study of the Qur'ān? Often the difference is seen in the religious beliefs of the researcher, who is either a "believer" or an "unbeliever." There seems, however, to be another, more fundamental difference—one related to the researcher's openness or anxiety regarding the historicity of religion as such. Unlike in Islam, religions are regarded in Western research as historical phenomena calling, like many other such phenomena, for scholarly investigation—a critical position spawned by historical conditions. Such a point of view, though shared by a number of modern Muslim intellectuals, remains alien to more conservative Islamic circles, who see the founding document of their religion in a completely different light.

The Obsession with Transcendence in Traditional Islamic Circles

A normal everyday event can illuminate this: A few years ago, an international conference on Qur'ānic Studies was held in Medina. The one Western expert who was invited—Stefan Wild, a professor at the University of Bonn—later wrote about the conference in the *Frankfurter Allgemeine Zeitung*.[7] The fact that only a single guest from the West was present fit the basic mood of the scholars gathered there, who viewed any studies on the Qur'ān from the West with great skepticism. Among the various reproaches directed against Western studies, one of

---

6. See the research report on Qur'ānic Studies in Neuwirth, *Der Koran als Text der Spätantike*, 68–119.

7. Wild, "Drei Tage in Medina."

the objections to outsiders initially sounds harmless enough: Western experts, it was claimed, speak of the Holy Book of the Muslims simply as "the Qur'ān," whereas Islamic usage generally speaks of *al-qur'ān al-karīm*, the "noble Qur'ān," adding the honorific qualification "noble" to its name. This observation is by no means a trifle, as it may appear to be; on the contrary, it in fact encapsulates a difference which indeed separates the Islamic view of the Qur'ān from the Western one. The designation *al-qur'ān al-karīm* is loaded with implications. It goes back to a verse in Q 56:77, where we read: "This is truly a noble *Qur'ān* preserved in a protected Record [*innahu la-qur'ānun karīm fī kitābin maknūn*]." Elsewhere, this record is described as a "preserved Tablet," in *sūrat al-burūj*, Q 85:22: "This is truly a glorious Qur'ān [written] on a preserved Tablet [*bal, innahu qur'ānun majīd—fī lawḥin maḥfūẓ*]." The Qur'ān thus has its origin and rightful location in a transcendent protoscript; indeed, it appears as a kind of excerpt from that heavenly source.

But what does this transcendent dimension mean practically? For over thirteen hundred years of Islamic history it has proven its effectiveness, above all in prayer and specific rituals of everyday life; it has by no means, however, dominated scholarly dealings with the Qur'ān. The claim that there is a transcendent dimension to the Qur'ān, even in its function as a subject of research, is an instance of modern self-censorship. It can nonetheless invoke the doctrine of the Qur'ān's "non-createdness," which emerged in the ninth century and claims that the Qur'ān is not only preexistent but also eternal, like God. Accordingly, the Arabic language in which it is clad is not seen as originating in social convention but posited and instilled by God[8] and in the Qur'ān; the meanings of the text therefore cannot be severed from what the prophet himself has laid down in his sayings, in "oral tradition." In consequence of this ruling, Qur'ānic exegesis would have been consigned to the narrow boundaries of veritative, "literal" interpretation had the ruling consequently been heeded in practice. However, it never succeeded in extinguishing creative exegetical thought, as disclosed by many centuries of interpretative tradition—theological, poetological, often allegorical, and at times even historical. The present and striking phenomenon that sees some circles insisting on the Qur'ān's transcendent character and forbidding its reinterpretation in light of contemporary needs is thus

---

8. Schöck, "Der moderne Islam," 88–90.

something new and amounts to a politically-conditioned retreat into essentialist self-ghettoization. Throughout history, the Qur'ān was factually both at once: a document of transcendent origin and a this-worldly center for a way of life.

The Qur'ānic Position vis-à-vis a Plurality of Scriptures

Furthermore, this attempt to monopolize transcendent origins for the Qur'ān alone is by no means in accordance with the Qur'ānic text itself, which in fact insists on the shared origin of all three monotheistic scriptures and invites Jews and Christians, as the older "people of the book" (*ahl al-kitāb*), to recognize the common genealogy of the monotheistic religions, which, as the Qur'ān says, all derive from one and the same transcendent protoscript. Here, the Qur'ān even assumes a pioneering position: for as the American scholar William Graham emphasizes,[9] the idea of Sacred Scriptures external to one's own religion, first made familiar in the West during the nineteenth century, is self-evident for the Qur'ān. Countless verses speak of the heavenly scripture (*kitāb*) but also manifestations of it already established in this world—the scriptures (*kutub*) of other religions, namely those of the Jews and Christians. The Qur'ān describes a "community of Scripture," encompassing Jews, Christians, and proto-Muslims.

This openness, evident from the very beginning in the Qur'ānic text, continues to prevail in classical Islam. What is characteristic of the Islamic reading of the Qur'ān is an immense diversity that admits contradicting and even mutually exclusive views. As the vast literature that has emerged from this scholarly exchange attests, scholars ensured that the text was met with an astounding degree of openness. Even the Qur'ān itself was received not in one but in fourteen slightly different versions, transmitted side by side and subject to the same philological practices. That the tendency toward conformist exegesis, toward interpretations serving consensus formation, is so dominant today is to a great extent due to social factors but perhaps also to the ideal of a unified text, which gained currency under colonial rule.[10] The obsession with the transcendent nature of the Qur'ān in some conservative circles is just one indicator that the ideal of diversity has

9. Graham, "Scripture and the Qur'ān."
10. See the recent study of Bauer, *Die Kultur der Ambiguität*.

been lost along with the ambiguity of tradition so cherished in premodern Islamic scholarship.

Two Distorting Mirrors: Teleology and Epigonality

Let us now turn to the Western counterpart of Islamic learning. Already in the nineties, Aziz al-Azmeh,[11] lamenting the fact that the Qur'ān was not submitted systematically to the set of methodological steps pursued in Biblical studies, could not imagine any reason for that failure other than the Qur'ān's exceptional position as a nonbiblical scripture, its alleged "alterity." Western Qur'ānic studies, according to al-Azmeh, partake in the "orientalist discourse" that tends to decontextualize Near Eastern cultural phenomena, thus allowing scholars to dispense with the rigid laws applied in related Western fields of academic research. What is orientalist is the exotic perception of the Qur'ān,[12] which fails to acknowledge it as a scripture of monotheism like the other scriptures (i.e., texts that have acquired an extraordinary position in their communities through the particular process of being canonized). William Graham's definition of scripture puts this in more precise terms: "Scripture is not a literary genre but a religio-historical one. No text is authoritative or sacred apart from its functional role in a religious community and that community's historical tradition of faith. The sacred character of a book is not an a priori attribute but one that develops and achieves widespread recognition in the lives of faithful persons who perceive and treat the text as holy or sacred. In other words, the scriptural characteristics of a text belong not to the text itself but to its role and standing in a religious community."[13] What is striking in the Qur'ānic case is that such

11. Azmeh, "The Muslim Canon."

12. A quite different critique of Qur'ānic Studies has been presented by Arkoun, *Islam: To Reform or to Subvert?* Arkoun pleads for a crossing of the "epistemic and epistemological threshold" (ibid., 77) to update Qur'ānic Studies and achieve a deconstructionist analysis of the Qur'ān. Though he unilaterally favours linguistic and psychological approaches without sufficiently regarding the still existing desiderata in historical-philological scholarship, his plea for a diversification of "the methodologies and the enlargement of the scope of a compared history of religions, coupled with the elaboration of an anthropological frame of understanding" (ibid.) is certainly in line with the claim raised in this article.

13. Graham, "Scripture and the Qur'ān," 559. It is true that "scripture as a particularistic concept seems to have first developed fully in Jewish and Christian contexts and it was in later phases of these and, most recently, in secular contexts primarily

a generic and relational understanding of scripture as that which is now common in the study of religion is—according to Graham—"largely compatible with the Qur'ān's own frequent use of kitāb, kutub, to refer to scriptural revelations given by God to previous prophets or messengers, before the bestowing of the Qur'ān upon Muhammad as his kitāb."[14] This observation implies that the Qur'ān constitutes an exception among scriptures, insofar as the scriptural character of the Qur'ānic text is not due to a later development but is an intrinsic feature of the Qur'ān itself. In Graham's words:

> It is . . . the generic use of kitāb/kutub to refer to earlier scriptures and to the Qur'ān itself that is special, or even unique, about the Qur'ānic notion of scripture. Typically, the other sacred texts of the world's religions that we call scriptures were not written with any similar consciousness of belonging themselves to a category of texts called scripture. Most if not all great scriptural texts other than the Qur'ān are unconscious of being even potentially scriptures, for scripture or any analogous concept is usually a category developed ex post facto.[15]

If this is true, then the "widespread recognition in the lives of faithful persons" that bestow the text with its scriptural character is not that of the later Muslim community but the group involved in the first Qur'ānic communication process. This conclusion is of momentous consequence for Qur'ānic studies. It implies that no serious study of the Qur'ānic text—which goes beyond external, linguistic, and grammatical aspects—can dismiss the Qur'ān's "scripturality," which is inscribed in its precanonical text. Yet the distinction between the precanonical text that was informed by scripturality and communicated to the first listen-

within the Western world (especially those of the modern academy) that generic use of the term was subsequently developed to refer commonly not only to particular Jewish or Christian biblical texts but also to the sacred texts of other religious communities . . . This is not to say that in other religions traditions there are no analogous concepts that might be adduced, rather it is to note that the inclusion of the Qur'ān (or Veda or Lotus Sutra) under the rubric of the Latinate word 'scripture' is not terribly old historically and was relatively infrequent until the past century or so—at least since the 1879–1894 publication of Max Müller's edited series *Sacred Books of the East*. Such generic usage is now much more common, but scripture as a phenomenon occurring in diverse religious contexts and traditions is still something that has only begun to be studied comparatively and globally in any adequate way" (ibid., 558).

14. Ibid., 559.
15. Ibid., 560.

ers and the later canonized official text of the Muslim community has continuously been glossed over in Qur'ānic scholarship.[16] The unique claim raised by the Qur'ān itself to constitute a scripture and thereby closely belong to the *trias* of monotheist scriptures originating from the late antique Near East, still awaits discussion and to be employed moreover as a point of departure for rethinking the Qur'ān's position in modernity. In what follows, I will first try to outline what in my view is problematic in current Qur'ānic studies, then turn to the development that preceded and perhaps induced the present crisis, and, as a conclusion, propose some ideas how to cope with the problem.

Western Stumbling Blocks: The Qur'ān's Stigma of Epigonality

Turning to the second impediment that stands in the way of properly valorizing the Qur'ān in Western scholarship, we must take a brief look back some two hundred years. A strong awareness of scripture as a metahistorical charter of truth *mutatis mutandis* had prevailed in premodern Christian and Jewish Biblical studies. However, Western scholarly preoccupation with the Bible had crystallized into a highly sophisticated theology and anthropology whose theoretical potential had been enhanced through the challenges of Reformation and Enlightenments. The Bible was thus familiar in virtually all its facets of meaning, when, in the eighteenth and nineteenth centuries the epistemic revolution occurred that modern scholars refer to as a "major break in Biblical studies": this was the introduction of historical critical scholarship, when—to quote Robert Wilken—"biblical scholarship

---

16. It is not acknowledged by William Graham either, who discusses the relation between "Scripture and Qur'ān" as applied to both the precanonical and the postcanonical text without differentiating between them. Such a distinction is to some degree discouraged by a current more general skepticism toward historical approaches to scriptures. Thus, Biblical Studies have recently seen a move, spearheaded by Brevard Childs, away from tradition and redaction history toward a growing interest in the final version of the Biblical text as it has become canonical within the Christian church. A similarly "synchronic" approach to the Qur'ān has been advocated by Daniel Madigan, among others. Even though both positions are by no means a-historical—after all, the final version of the text is viewed as having come into being at a particular moment in time—they privilege the final stage in what they recognize to be an extended process of textual genesis over preliminary stages and do so by virtue of the fact that it is the canon in its final shape which has been accepted as binding.

acquired a life of its own as a historical enterprise independent of the church and of the synagogue."[17]

This methodological innovation, which may be viewed as a critical turn and innovation in Biblical studies, was neither a turn nor a renewal in Western Qur'ānic scholarship but the very beginning of academic preoccupation with the text. The text at this time in Europe was virtually unknown as a religious foundational document; it had never been seriously considered in terms of its final form but had been read as a rule as a conglomerate of doctrines inviting refutation in missionary circles. It was only in the nineteenth century that the Qur'ān was freed from the shackles of bias and submitted to a purely scholarly investigation.

This development took place within the context of Jewish studies (*Wissenschaft des Judentums*),[18] a German Jewish intellectual movement starting in the nineteenth century and was primarily concerned with the historicization of Jewish religious traditions. Judaism in this movement is regarded as a religion bearing universal values, applicable in any given place or time. It is here that scholars with a solid philological training turned to the Qur'ān—no longer to refute it as had been the case with their Christian contemporaries but to apply the newly acquired tools of historical research to the text. It would, however, be an exaggeration to claim that the initiative targeted Islam in the same way as it targeted Judaism (i.e., as another religion to be acknowledged as bearing universal values). The purpose of their enterprise was "to recover earlier Jewish sources and kernels of ideas that had imbedded themselves in new (Muslim) literary environments: Jewish themes in Muslim texts."[19]

One of the founders of the *Wissenschaft des Judentums*, Abraham Geiger, had already taken particular interest in the history of the Qur'ān. In 1832, he won a contest sponsored by the philosophy department at the University of Bonn, which had called for an inquiry into those themes in the Qur'ān that were derived from Judaism; within one year, he presented his famous work—originally in Latin—under the German title *Was hat Mohammed aus dem Judenthume aufgenommen?*[20]

---

17. Wilken, "In Defense of Allegory," 199.
18. Lassner, "Abraham Geiger."
19. Ibid., 112.
20. Geiger, *Mohammed*. For the English translation see idem, *Judaism and Islam*.

Geiger's title not only presupposes the Qurʾān's material dependence on Judaism but also an auctorial intention on Muhammad's part. In Geiger's view, Muhammad consciously looked to the Jews and the Jewish past when establishing his own faith and formulating a Muslim world view.[21] Geiger refers to the Qurʾān as "the product of a seventh-century Arab's literary imagination and oracular skill."[22] Yet, Geiger "in opposition to a long established Christian tradition did not regard the Islamic prophet as a self-serving adventurer. 'Muhammad seems to have been a genuine enthusiast [*Schwärmer*] who was himself convinced of his divine mission.'"[23]

Yet Geiger's approach to Qurʾānic studies—though pioneering in terms of contemporary methodologies—was to set the epistemological course for a narrow and simplified perception of the Qurʾān. The assumption that Muhammad authored the Qurʾān apodictically negates the interaction of the multiple agencies involved in its genesis: the Prophet, the emerging community of his listeners, and those adjacent groups who acted as transmitters of the multiple traditions current in the late antique Near East. To reduce this polyphonic scenario to one individual agent would mean laying the hermeneutical burden of reformulating the multiple traditions reflected in the Qurʾān on the shoulders of the one person Muhammad, who—in view of the frequent Qurʾānic divergences from those traditions—is consequently to be blamed for innumerable "misunderstandings." It was the negation of the Qurʾān's scripturality that kept scholars of the *Wissenschaft des Judentums* blind to the intrinsic, discursive dimension of Qurʾānic references to earlier traditions and thus to the Qurʾān's rank as an autonomous new paradigm. Yet it needs to be acknowledged that the scholars of the movement—Abraham Geiger, Hartwig Hirschfeld,[24] Josef Horovitz,[25] and Heinrich Speyer,[26] to mention only the most prominent[27]—introduced a vast number of Qurʾānic intertexts, indispensable for understand-

21. Hartwig, "Wissenschaft des Judentums: Geiger."
22. Lassner, "Abraham Geiger," 114.
23. Ibid., 106.
24. Hirschfeld, *Beiträge*; Hirschfeld, *Jüdische Elemente im Koran*; Hirschfeld, *New Researches*.
25. Horovitz, *Koranische Untersuchungen*.
26. Speyer, *Die Biblischen Erzählungen*.
27. Hartwig, "Wissenschaft des Judentums: Perspektiven."

ing the Qur'ān's situatedness. Qur'ānic scholarship has never recovered from the violent disruption of their work brought about by the Nazis' expulsion of Jewish scholars from German universities in the 1930s.

It is, however, hard not to realize that the historical approach, with its focus on the older traditions reflected in the Qur'ān and favored over the Qur'ān's own message, ultimately put the Qur'ān down as an epigonal text. No differently than biblical texts, the Qur'ān was immediately subjected to procedures of textual archaeology—with results that were to prove more than ambivalent. One must remember that historical-critical scholarship is not least a quest for the prototexts of Scripture[28]—a quest that for the Bible had resulted in the unearthing of a large number of ancient Oriental traditions relevant to individual biblical texts. These traditions—like the legal code of Hammurabi in the case of Deuteronomy—were apt to throw light on the historical setting of the Bible. They could, however, rarely seriously compete with their theologically far more sophisticated counterparts, shaped by the biblical authors. The Bible remained the most authoritative text. In the Qur'ānic case, the opposite is true: what was discovered was not a set of pagan, religiously "preliminary" texts but the most prestigious ancient text imaginable—the Hebrew Bible itself, together with its exegetical ramifications. What scholars like Geiger perceived in the Qur'ān was, at best, an anthology of innumerable biblical and postbiblical traditions, which the Qur'ān's supposed "author," the Prophet Muhammad, had "borrowed" from Judaism in order to compose a work of guidance for his community. Since deviation from such an authoritative *prototext* could only be a distortion, the Qur'ān emerged—to put it into somewhat exaggerating terms—as a failed imitation of the Bible. This stigma of imitation, the taint of epigonality, has clung to the Qur'ān in Western research down to the present day. The Qur'ān is not approached or read as being on par with the two other scriptures; instead, it is still regarded as an exotic text, as the symbol of a "completely different culture." This impression, which arises from the imbalance of the Western perspective, demands reconsideration.

---

28. Barton, "Historical-Critical Approaches."

In Search of a Solution: Reflections on an Inclusive Approach to the Qur'ān

We are used to viewing the Qur'ān as the "Islamic text" *par excellence*. But is this really justified? Before the Qur'ān became the founding document of Islam, it was proclaimed orally for over twenty years. This Qur'ānic proclamation did not yet address Muslims—who became such only after receiving and embracing the Qur'ānic teachings—but was directed at pre-Islamic listeners, who are best described as persons "versed" in the traditions of late antiquity. If we wish to understand the Qur'ān from its origin and earliest development, as communicating a message to an audience that was not yet Islamic, we have to read the Qur'ān as a set of answers responding not to the core questions of Islam but of late antiquity. This is a time in which Jewish and Christian theologians, rabbis, church fathers, and pagan philosophers were discussing pivotal problems, for instance whether the image of God resembled man or not, whether there was divine intervention in history, and how to understand transcendent retribution and the guilt-obliterating power of sacrifice—in other words, precisely those issues that are pivotal in the Qur'ān. Viewed from this perspective, the Qur'ān emerges as another, new voice in the "concert" of those debates conducted between learned men in late antiquity and which went beyond religious barriers, or in fact took place before the establishment of such barriers. Read in this way, the Qur'ān is a kind of record or transcript of a propagation process. Such a process is indeed clearly reflected in the text, which provides information on whether the listeners accept its new teachings or not. For instance, we can read their reactions to certain commandments they are expected to obey, which are initially formulated in rigorous terms, only to then be tempered by an amendment of some sort. Think of the instruction to hold extended nightly prayers in Q 73:1–9. The amendment (v. 20) represents the new version of the commandment, adjusted to meet listener expectations that have transpired during the proclamation process: vigils need not be extended half the night, as was initially demanded, but may be shortened due to new social circumstances. The voice of the congregation who should have expressed its plight is thus unmistakably present in the Qur'ān.[29] We need to imagine that the Prophet was attracting a steadily growing

---

29. For details, see Neuwirth, *Der Koran: Handkommentar*, 347–58.

audience, and together they gradually formed their own new thinking on the basis of the biblical and pagan traditions they were familiar with—and which were general knowledge during late antiquity. While much of this, for example, the forms for praising God, is closely related to the well-known psalms, other elements of biblical tradition are rigorously reinterpreted—for instance, the very human-like biblical imagination of God in the Qur'ān is much more abstract—or they are categorically rejected, as is the case in the idea of the guilt-obliterating sacrifice, which was extremely influential in Judaism and Christianity at the time but excluded from Qur'ānic thinking through a verse in Q 22:36–37 that discusses the Hajj sacrifice and explicitly states, "The flesh and blood of the sacrificial animals will not reach God, but your piety will reach him." The significance of this verse as a clear statement against the forms of mythopoiesis prevailing in neighboring religious cultures can hardly be overestimated. The Qur'ān thus reflects the successive "negotiations," the community's adoptions as well as its modifications and rejections of biblical and postbiblical traditions. Viewed in this way, the Qur'ān is cast in a very different light: no longer an anthology of isolated suras, which, according to the Western view, Muhammad is purported to have written, or, as traditional Islam itself sees it, a divine book sent from heaven, the Qur'ān emerges as the mirror of a drama of human endeavor not least of all, the attempt to articulate a new form of monotheism, purged above all of mythical elements and national religious entanglements, and arrives at a universal faith appealing to human reason. This perspective does not reduce the Qur'ān to a purely secular, temporally-determined text precluding its divine origin. What is does do, however, is return the Qur'ān to history and thus accord with the view of scholars such as Nasr Hamid Abu Zaid,[30] Mohamed Arkoun,[31] and Ömer Özsoy.[32] This perspective furnishes a European interpretative proposition, which springs from the Western hermeneutical tradition and does not demand its adoption by Muslims but may be taken by them as a view complementary to their own. It is only with the arsenal provided by the methods developed here that the long-running

---

30. Kermani, *Offenbarung als Kommunikation*.
31. Arkoun, "The notion of revelation."
32. Özsoy, "Geschichtlichkeit."

international debate on the genesis of the Qur'ān, on its originality or epigonality, can ever be understood and then played out.

A Case Study: Negotiating the Jewish and the Christian Creeds

For the audience of the Qur'ān to become a scriptural community, the rereading of the core texts of the older traditions and their adaption to the newly developing worldview as well as to the Arabic linguistic standards was of essential importance. But whereas biblical traditions had been current and easily accessible as part of common knowledge at Mecca, at Medina these traditions became a matter of dispute, of religious and even political rivalry, since at this stage the historical heirs of biblical tradition, learned Jews and Christians, appeared on stage to reclaim their monopoly on the exegesis of biblical tradition. Debates over particular issues have left their traces in the Qur'ān. A particularly telling example, Q 112—"The Pure Belief" (sūrat al-ikhlās)—will be briefly discussed:

Qul huwa llāhu aḥad	Say, he is God, one
Allāhu ṣ-ṣamad	God, the absolute
lam yalid wa-lam yūlad	He did not beget, nor is he begotten
wa-lam yakun lahu kufuwan aḥad	And there is none like him.

The Qurʾān in the Field of Conflict between the Interpretative Communities 123

Nicene Constantinopolitan Creed		Deuteronomy 6,4		Qurʾān, Sura 112 (al-Iḫlāṣ)	
We believe in one God,	Πιστεύομεν εἰς ἕνα Θεόν	Hear, Israel, the Lord is our God, the Lord is One.	שְׁמַע יִשְׂרָאֵל: יְהוָה אֱלֹהֵינוּ, יְהוָה אֶחָד	Say: He is God, one,	قُلْ هُوَ اللَّهُ أَحَدٌ
the Father **Almighty**, Maker of heaven and earth, and of all things visible and invisible	Πατέρα παντοκράτορα, ποιητὴν οὐρανοῦ καὶ γῆς, ὁρατῶν τε πάντων καὶ ἀοράτων.			God the absolute,	اللَّهُ الصَّمَدُ
And in one Lord Jesus Christ, **the only-begotten Son of God**, begotten of the **Father** before all worlds (æons), Light of Light, very God of very God, **begotten, not made**,	Καὶ εἰς ἕνα κύριον Ἰησοῦν Χριστόν, τὸν υἱὸν τοῦ θεοῦ τὸν μονογενῆ, τὸν ἐκ τοῦ Πατρὸς γεννηθέντα πρὸ πάντων τῶν αἰώνων, φῶς ἐκ φωτός, θεὸν ἀληθινὸν ἐκ θεοῦ ἀληθινοῦ, γεννηθέντα οὐ ποιηθέντα,			He did not beget, nor is He begotten,	لَمْ يَلِدْ وَلَمْ يُولَدْ
being of one substance with the Father;	ὁμοούσιον τῷ πατρί			And there is none like Him.	وَلَمْ يَكُنْ لَهُ كُفُوًا أَحَدٌ

This graphic has been produced by the team of Corpus Coranicum Project, Berlin.

It is hard to miss the fact that verse one, "Say, God is One [*qul, huwa llāhu aḥad*]" echoes the Jewish credo "Hear Israel, the Lord, our God, is One [*Shemaʿ Yisraʾel, adonay elohenu adonay eḥad*]." It is striking that the Jewish text remains audible in the Qurʾānic version, which—against grammatical norms—adopts the Hebrew-sounding noun *aḥad* instead of the more pertinent adjective *wāḥid* for the rhyme. This "ungrammaticality" cannot go unnoticed. I am referring to the notion analyzed by Michael Riffaterre, meaning the awkwardness of a textual moment that semiotically points to "another text" where the same element is "normal"—a text that therefore provides a key to deeper understanding of the text in question; in our case, this other text is the Jewish credo.[33]

This striking translingual quotation is part of the Qurʾānic negotiation strategy, which strives to appropriate the Jewish credo. Not by taking it over, however, but through a process of negotiation. The biblical version in the Qurʾān is substantially modified in that it is uni-

33. Riffaterre, *Semiotics of Poetry*, 92.

versalized—no longer addressing Israel, exclusively, but any believer in general. Yet it continues—through the sustained sound presence of the Jewish credo—to partake in the older text's authority. The biblical credo is altered to fit not only Jewish believers but men universally.

But there is yet another credo involved: verse three, "He did not beget nor is he begotten [*lam yalid wa-lam yūlad*]," is a reverse echo of the Christian creed formulated at the council of Nicea, where the Jewish creed had been translated into trinitarian language. With verse three, the Qurʾānic formula, which had already rejected the exclusivist Jewish claim, now proceeds to reject the equally exclusivist Christian claim. The emphatic affirmation of Christ's sonship—"begotten, not made," or *genethenta, ou poiethenta* in the Christian formula—is countered by a no less emphatic double negation in the Qurʾān: *lam yalid wa-lam yūlad*. This negative theology is summed up in verse four: "And there is none like Him [*wa-lam yakun lahu kufuwan aḥad*]." That verse not only inverts the Nicene formula of Christ's being of one substance with God, *kufuwun* with him, so to say—*homoousios to patri*—but moreover forbids one to think of any being equal in substance to God, let alone a son. Though these verses negate the essential statement of the Nicene Creed, they nonetheless "re-sound" the older text by adopting its rhetorical strategy of parallelism and intensification. The older texts thus remain present to bestow their authority on the new text. Theology is negotiated or even rejected—and rhetoric is maintained.

Conclusion

Our attempt to relocate the genesis of the Qurʾān in late antiquity, our "European reading," is not seeking to deliver a master key for the Qurʾān. In the first instance, we are looking to become relevant in terms of cultural criticism, and this for both sides of the divide—the European and the Middle Eastern. The new approach agrees in substantial points with concerns expressed by avant-garde Arab intellectuals who—like the Lebanese historian Samir Kassir—denounce the construction of an epochal boundary between late antiquity and Islam as being calamitous. According to the dominant Islamic view, relevant Arab history first begins with the Qurʾānic revelation; as Kassir puts it, "this view is left with merely a chaotic picture of the preceding ages, a picture concentrated in the concept of *jāhilīya*, understood as the 'age of ignorance' or 'barbarism.'"³⁴ Leading everything back to the role played by the prophet Mohammad, this myth of origins turns the antecedent history of Islam into a dark foil of comparison for the new civilization brought into being by Islam. Kassir considers the revision an urgent step—he goes so far as to claim that a Copernican revolution is needed to break the monopoly of the notion of a Golden Age ushered in with the emergence of Islam.

Kassir's demand for a new contextualization of Arab Islamic history, setting it in relationship to Jewish-Christian and pagan late antiquity, is, however, only one side of the equation posed by the necessary reconsideration: the question of how to evaluate pre-Islam, the *jāhilīya*, so virulent in current Islamic discussion, has its counterpart in debates on the Western construction of late antiquity. *Jāhilīya* and late antiquity are two sides of the same coin, though it is difficult to bring them together. For its part, the Western construct of late antiquity used to exclude Islam, which was considered a factor in a cultural breach responsible for the "decline" of the pluralistic older cultures of the Middle East that had survived into late antiquity—a construct that has only recently begun to be supplanted by a more inclusive perspective. At present, it is solely the Qur'ān itself which could not yet be located in late antiquity.

To contribute to this overdue revision of two obsolete historical constructs, where from the Muslim perspective the genesis of Islam marks the dawn of something "absolutely new" while from the European perspective something substantially "different" begins, demands a historical rereading of the Qur'ān itself. This work, of course, cannot take place in isolation from the Muslim heirs of their own rich tradition; on the contrary, it is imperative that a language be found which is capable of discursively connecting both approaches—the Western and the Middle Eastern. At first, however, a kind of division of labor is required: with good reason, Middle Eastern scholars insist that the canon of knowledge taught in Islamic scholarship must be acknowledged and studied by Western academics. The Islamic tradition has preserved an archive of linguistic and cultural knowledge indispensable for any serious critical study of the Qur'ān. Without it, any attempt to understand the Qur'ān would be baseless, a pure construct. An important step in the direction of integrating this canon into our own research horizon

---

34. Kassir, *Das arabische Unglück*, 38–40.

is the recommendation put forward by the German Council of Science and Humanities to establish institutes for Islamic theology. Five of these have already been founded and started to work. In the future—at least, so we hope—a model of "working toward one another" will assert itself and allow Islamic scholars to focus their vast corpus of learned literature on the Qur'ān, bringing new methods and lines of inquiry, in particular textual hermeneutics, to bear on their own tradition. In tandem with this, Western scholarship will calibrate its proper historical domain by rereading the Qur'ān in the light of the traditions of Late Antiquity, of Jewish, Christian, and pre-Islamic provenance. Both sides stand to gain enormously: by reintegrating the Qur'ān and early Islam into the epoch of late antiquity—traditionally monopolized by Europe—new horizons of their history, long blocked, would open up for Muslims, while for Europeans the Qur'ān's still ignored contributions to a shared theological and cultural history would finally become discernible. Above all, however, this reintegration would put into concrete practice what is currently being recognized as a pressing task, most recently articulated by former federal president Christian Wulff: that our exclusive notion of a solely Jewish-Christian Europe, ultimately anchored in a truncated understanding of Late Antiquity, needs to be reconsidered. It needs to be altered into the concept of a Jewish-Christian-*Islamic* Europe.

Bibliography

Arkoun, Mohamed. *Islam: To Reform or to Subvert?* London: Saqi Essentials, 2006.

———. "The Notion of Revelation from Aahl al-Kitab to Societies of the Book." *Die Welt des Islams* 28 (1988) 62–89.

Azmeh, Aziz al-. "The Muslim Canon from Late Antiquity to the Era of Modernism." In *Canonization and Decanonization*, edited by Arie van der Kooij et al., 191–228. Leiden: Brill, 1998.

Barton, John. "Historical-Critical Approaches." In *The Cambridge Companion to Biblical Interpretation*, edited by John Barton, 1–6. Cambridge: Cambridge University Press, 1998.

Bauer, Thomas. *Die Kultur der Ambiguität: Eine andere Geschichte des Islam*. Berlin: Verlag der Weltreligionen, 2011.

Crone, Patricia, and Michael Cook. *Hagarism: The Making of the Islamic World*. Cambridge: Cambrigde University Press, 1977.

Geiger, Abraham. *Judaism and Islam*. Translated by F. M. Young. Madras: MDCSPK, 1898. Reprint. New York: KTAV, 1970. Prolegomenon by Moshe Pearlman.

———. *Was hat Mohammed aus dem Judenthume aufgenommen? Eine von der Königlich-Preussischen Rheinuniversität gekrönte Preisschrift*. Bonn: Baaden, 1833.

Graham, William. "Scripture and the Qur'ān." In *Encyclopaedia of the Qur'ān*, edited by Jane Dammen MacAuliffe, 4:558–69. Leiden: Brill, 2004.

Hartwig, Dirk. "Die Wissenschaft des Judentums und die Anfänge der historisch-kritischen Koranforschung: Abraham Geiger und die erste Generation jüdischer Koranforscher." In *Jüdische Existenz in der Moderne: Abraham Geiger und die Wissenschaft des Judentums*, edited by Christian Wiese et al, 297–320. Berlin: de Gruyter, 2013.

———. "Die Wissenschaft des Judentums und die Anfänge der kritischen Koranforschung: Perspektiven einer modernen Koranhermeneutik." *Zeitschrift für Religions und Geistesgeschichte* 61 (2009) 234–56.

Hirschfeld, Hartwig. *Beiträge zur Erklärung des Korans*. Leipzig: Schulze, 1886.

———. *Jüdische Elemente im Koran*. Berlin: Im Selbstverlag, 1878.

———. *New Researches into the Composition and Exegesis of the Qoran*. London: Royal Asiatic Society, 1902.

Horovitz, Josef. *Koranische Untersuchungen*. Berlin: de Gruyter, 1926.

Kassir, Samir. *Das arabische Unglück*. Translated by Ulrich Kunzmann. Berlin: Schiler, 2006.

Kermani, Navid. *Offenbarung als Kommunikation: Das Konzept waḥy in Nasr Hamid Abu Zayds Mafhum an-nass*. Frankfurt: Lang, 1996.

Kratz, Reinhard G., and Tilman Nagel, editors. *"Abraham unser Vater": Die gemeinsamen Wurzeln von Judentum, Christentum und Islam*. Göttingen: Wallstein, 2003.

Lassner, Jacob. "Abraham Geiger: A Nineteenth-century Jewish Reformer on the Origins of Islam." In *The Jewish Discovery of Islam: Studies in Honor of Bernard Lewis*, edited by Martin Kramer, 103–36. Tel Aviv: Moshe Dayan Center for Middle Eastern and African Studies, Tel Aviv University, 1999.

Lüling, Günter. *Über den Ur-Qur'an: Ansätze zur Rekonstruktion vorislamischer christlicher Strophenlieder im Qur'an*. Erlangen: Lüling, 1974.

Luxenberg, Christoph. *Die syro-aramäische Lesart des Koran: Ein Beitrag zur Entschlüsselung der Koransprache*. Berlin: Das arabische Buch, 2000.

Mingana, Alphonse. *Syriac Influences on the Style of the Kur'ān*. Manchester: University Press, 1927.

Neuwirth, Angelika. *Der Koran als Text der Spätantike: Ein europäischer Zugang*. Berlin: Verlag der Weltreligionen, 2010.

———. *Der Koran: Handkommentar mit Übersetzung*. Vol. 1, *Frühmekkanische Suren: poetische Prophetie*. Berlin: Weltreligionen, 2011.

Özsoy, Ömer. "Die Geschichtlichkeit der koranischen Rede und das Problem der ursprünglichen Bedeutung von geschichtlicher Rede." In *Alter Text—neuer Kontext: Koranhermeneutik in der Türkei heute*, edited by Felix Körner, 78–98. Freiburg: Herder, 2006.

Riffaterre, Michael. *Semiotics of Poetry*. Bloomington, IN: Indiana University Press, 1978.

Sarrazin, Thilo. *Deutschland schafft sich ab: Wie wir unser Land aufs Spiel setzen*. München: Deutsche Verlags-Anstalt, 2010.

Schöck, Cornelia. "Der moderne Islam zwischen Traditionalismus und Rationalismus: Geistesgeschichtliche Hintergründe der aktuellen Krise." In

Soziale und kulturelle Herausforderungen des 21. Jahrhunderts, edited by Karl Acham, 83–98. Vienna: Passagen, 2005.

Speyer, Heinrich. *Die Biblischen Erzählungen im Qoran.* Gräfenhainichen: Schulze, 1937.

Wansbrough, John. *Quranic Studies: Sources and Methods of Scriptural Interpretation.* Oxford: Oxford University Press, 1977.

Wild, Stefan. "Drei Tage in Medina: Als Ungläubiger unter Korangelehrten." *Frankfurter Allgemeine Zeitung*, Nov. 30, 2006.

Wilken, Robert L. "In Defense of Allegory." *Modern Theology* 14 (1998) 197–212.

Nation, State, and Community

Belonging to Halakhic Judaism

On the Sense of Matrilineal Descent[1]

Micha Brumlik

Preliminary Remarks

How to define Judaism and the Jews and how one becomes a Jew are all questions that clearly transcend religious concerns. To cite just a few relevant examples: For years now, Israel has adjusted its Law of Return (*Chok ha Schwuth*) in order to accommodate the complex familial relationships of Jewish immigrants from the (former) Soviet Union; more recently, the Central Council of Jews in Germany has begun offering special courses to the children of Jewish fathers willing to convert; and in the United States, Reform Judaism—unlike in Europe—has long since permitted the biological children of Jewish fathers to become *Bat* or *Bar Mitzvah* provided they have had a Jewish upbringing.

A Jew is most commonly someone whose birth mother is Jewish or who has formally converted before a recognized rabbinical court after an exhaustive education in the Torah, the Talmud, the Halakah, and the halakhic way of life, and whose decision to convert has been thoroughly vetted through the requisite series of investigations and remonstrations. Given Judaism's complex connections between ethnicity and religion, this allows an individual to claim membership in an ethnic

---

1. Translated from German by Leah Chizek.

group by way of religious ceremony; at the same time, someone who is indifferent or even scornful toward the very idea of religion may still qualify as a Jew on religious grounds—indeed, this is even true in the exceptional case that such an individual's mother is equally indifferent, so long as she, too, can prove her own mother is Jewish. What is actually at stake, however, is a genealogical ancestry that cannot be annulled even if the mother has converted to another religion, such as Christianity or Buddhism. The Chief Rabbinate of Israel recognizes as Jews those individuals whose mothers converted to Christianity during the National Socialist era and chose not to revert after the war; their children were then recognized as Jews once they came of age. This rabbinical practice stands in peculiar contrast to the biblical sources to which Jews appeal when they wish to be reassured of their religion's ancient roots which are then gladly attributed to the patriarch Abraham, or "Abraham Avinu." Of course, Abraham—insofar as he is said to have existed at all—was no more a Jew than he was a Muslim, as the Koran claims.

At this point, then, two questions are in need of an answer: When did the Jewish religion originate, and how was the matrilineal principle established as its criterion for belonging? What can the history of religion tell us? Who were the ancient Jews?

Jehudim and Judaioi in the Ancient World

Historical documentation of the Jews begins with an act of calling them by name. This name, meaning *Jehudim* (or *Iudaioi* in Greek), is used in several later biblical texts as well as by a number of nonbiblical archaeological sources, chiefly coins. The name itself refers to a province of the Persian kingdom, Jehud, a small and otherwise unknown city in the district settled by the tribe of Dan. Among the biblical books in which this name can be found—as opposed, say, to references to Israel or the House of Jacob—are those of Esther, Ezra, Nehemiah, Jeremiah, and the second book of Kings. Each of these reveals an awareness of Judah's demise, Babylonian exile, the return from exile, and the events that later took place during the period of Persian exile. These books span the period from 537 BCE, when the Babylonian king Nebuchadnezzar conquered Jerusalem, destroyed Solomon's Temple, and led the country's upper classes into exile in Babylon (as was Assyrian custom), to 538 BCE, when the great Persian king Xerxes issued the edict permitting those who had been exiled to return to Jerusalem. One year later, the cornerstone was laid for the Second Temple, which was most likely finished and dedicated in 520 BCE. And toward the end of the fifth century BCE, just as the Greeks had successfully warded off an attack by the Persians, Judah's religious and political foundations were then laid by Ezra and Nehemiah, both of whom had been trained at the Persian court—Ezra as a priest, and Nehemiah as a court servant. At this point the small satrapy, which was largely centered in Jerusalem, continued to enjoy a certain degree of autonomy within the Persian kingdom although it was not politically independent.

Coins minted in the mid-fourth century testify to this general state of affairs, and the Jews are depicted by the book of Esther, on Babylonian clay tablets, and in papyri from a military colony in lower Egypt as a prosperous people, well-known beyond the small Persian satrapy of Jehud. In all likelihood, the books of Esther, Ezra, Jeremiah, and Nehemiah, as well as the second book of Kings, were based on older sources and composed some time during the third or fourth century BCE; the exception here is the prophetic book of Jeremiah, which was presumably composed two hundred and fifty years earlier, at the beginning of the sixth century BCE.

If one subscribes to this version of things, then the word "Jews" is mentioned for the first time by Jeremiah and was the result of an impassioned exchange he had had with Zedekiah, the last king of Judah at the time of Jerusalem's occupation. Zedekiah found himself in an argument with Jeremiah, who believed further resistance to the Babylonians' more powerful military would be futile, and refuted the prophet thus: "I am afraid of the Jews that are fallen to the Chaldeans, lest they deliver me into their hand, and they mock me" (Jer 38:19). Jeremiah, who later led the Jewish elite into exile, attempted to reassure the king, albeit without hiding from him the hardships of a future in exile. The Jews' debut as "Jews" on the historical stage consequently extended over a period of more than two hundred years—between the time of the First Temple's destruction in 587 BCE and Ezra's decree, which was likely issued in 400 BCE and ordered all male members of the Israelite tribe who had chosen to stay behind to divorce women belonging to other tribes for reasons of theology.

As for the creation of a semiautonomous political entity, coins from the late fourth century BCE substantiate biblical reports that suggest a Jewish "ethnogenesis" lasting around one hundred and fifty years. An ethnicity thus formed during this period as did a religion, both of which are attested to in the books of faith as well as through other information passed down by the ancient Israelites and kings of Judah. This development should also be regarded as something new to the extent that it would have been unthinkable without the experiences of an elite minority exiled in Babylon. The Jewish religion therefore originated neither in Israel nor in Judah but at the Babylonian court, and while the rebuilding of the temple may suggest the renewal of ties with a bygone of era of mythical kings, namely David and Solomon, Ezra's divorce edict describes something altogether different: a new foundation based on divine instruction and administered by a Gentile, the Persian king Xerxes. It was Xerxes who instructed Ezra, a scribe hailing from a distinguished family of clerics, to lead the descendants of exiled families wishing to return to Jerusalem and Judah: "And thou, Ezra, after the wisdom of thy God, that is in thine hand, set magistrates and judges, which may judge all the people that are beyond the river, all such as know the laws of thy god; and teach ye them, that know them not. And whosoever will not do the law of thy God, and the law of the king, let judgment be executed speedily upon him, whether it be unto death, or to banishment, or to confiscation of goods, or to imprisonment" (Ezra 7:25–26).

Xerxes had identified the god of Israel with the Babylonian sky god known to him, just as no small number of exiled Judaic peoples had experienced JHWH, the god known to them, in the forms and figures of the Babylonian-Persian gods. In any case, exegetical research on the Old Testament assumes that essential sections of the Torah, the five books of Moses, were produced during the period of Babylonian exile—not least of all because the book of Genesis conjures anthropomorphic visions of an all-powerful creator whose techniques resembled those of a potter and who, like an oriental despot, could call a whole world into existence at his own command, a world that also included the serpent designed to tempt Adam and Eve.

During the same period, the books of the prophets Malachi and Obadiah were composed in Babylon (or perhaps somewhat later in Jerusalem) as were the books of Wisdom, Job, and Proverbs, the love poetry that is the Song of Songs, and of course the book of Ruth—a veritable theological novella criticizing Ezra's divorce decree. The book of Ruth sings a praise of salvation for this pious woman from Moab, who pledges unconditional devotion to her Jewish mother-in-law. In doing so, it liberates the nascent Jewish religion from the dictates of tribal ancestry and proclaims its god the god of all humanity. Granted, the book of Ruth, insofar as it possesses any kernel of historical truth, mentions no conversion ceremony of any kind: Ruth becomes a member of her mother-in-law's tribe because she moves together with her to her rural community and finds a new spouse there. Beyond marriage, however, no further steps are necessary to become one with the people of Israel.

Together with the Jewish religion's monotheistic universalism, which originated in the fifth and sixth centuries BCE, it is above all else the experience of exile that is impressed upon it from very early on. Many psalms, in particular Psalm 137, evince strongly stylized narratives telling of both homesickness for Zion and the experience of banishment, which was simultaneously experienced as estrangement from God. The prophets Jeremiah and Ezekiel also articulate this experience in Babylon: as an authentic key figure in the Jewish diaspora, Jeremiah had moved from Jerusalem to Babylon. In Ezekiel's case, the emerging Jewish religion had him to thank for his visionary glimpses of God and the heavenly kingdom, as well as for the idea of resurrecting the dead. In any case, the book of Ruth is the first book of the Bible to call God the "Lord . . . to the living and to the dead" (Ruth 2:20).

Temples and Priests

Established as a religion at the same time that the Achaemenid Empire had assumed control, Judaism can be traced back to the old Israelite traditions of a group that had the court servants Ezra and Jeremiah at its center and the temple cult in Jerusalem as one of its primary sites of activity. What was new and unusual about this cult was its exclusivity. That ancient gods and goddesses were worshipped in sanctuaries was nothing out of the ordinary—witness, for example, the Temple of Artemis in Ephesus, Zeus in Dodona, and Apollo in Olympia, or that of the Egyptian sun god Ra in Memphis. What *was* new and unusual was that JHWH's worshippers in Jerusalem prayed and made sacrifices to him and him alone. In the process, they revisited a certain experiment that had failed several centuries earlier in the kingdom of the pharaohs: back then, the young pharaoh Amenophis IV, also known as Echnaton, had attempted to outlaw the worship of all but one god from the Egyptian pantheon—the sun god Aton. After many years of bloodshed and violent conflict with priests who worshipped other deities, Echnaton's attempt ultimately failed. And although truly convincing evidence for this cannot be put forward, this attempt readily qualifies—at the very latest in Freud's last book *Moses and Monotheism*—as the secret precursor to Jewish monotheism (to say nothing of the fact that biblical texts actually describe Moses as someone who came of age at the pharaoh's court). At the same time, biblical texts that document monotheism's origin in both states of old Israel and portray it as so many attempts to consolidate various cults are less than clear. Whether space was accorded for the existence of other gods—an honor meanwhile granted only to JHWH—or whether their existence was denied altogether is difficult to ascertain; and whether this was because JHWH's devotees merely refused to respect other gods or fundamentally contested their very existence, they were in fact the ones who, in the essentially polytheistic context of the Old World, appeared "godless" in one way or another. Meaningful and decisive for our own context at any rate is the fact that the Jerusalem-based temple cult was in need of a priestly caste. Though consisting of Cohenites and Levites, this priestly caste was first to assume worldly rule in the form of the Hasmonean kingdom for the time being and only later, following Roman conquest and the destruction of the Second Temple, in the Roman province of Judea.

Jews as Ethnos

There is much reason to believe that the period of Babylonian exile gave rise to monotheism's achievements—that is to say, to its chief assumptions that there is but one god and that he is worthy of worship. This systematic, theological, even philosophical monotheism is what first constitutes the newness and peculiarity of the Jewish religion. Emerging in the context of the Persian Empire and beyond Israel, Judaism maintained its cultic headquarters in Jehud, in Judea within the borders of a small satrapy or dependent vassal state, where this same god was worshipped. It is in this way that Judaism acquired its characteristic tension between the universal and particular, between diasporic existence on the one hand and the search for a geographic and religious homeland on the other. Eliminationist anti-Semitism, the politically organized hatred of Jews, also made its first appearances during the historical period of Judaism's consolidation. The book of Esther portrays the contemporary situation at the court of Xerxes and tells of Haman, the royal vizier who wished to see the Jews of Persia annihilated: "And Haman said unto king Ahasuerus, There is a certain people scattered abroad and dispersed among the people in all the provinces of thy kingdom; and their laws are diverse from all people; neither keep they the king's laws: therefore it is not for the king's profit to suffer them. If it please the king, let it be written that they may be destroyed: and I will pay ten thousand talents of silver to the hands of those that have the charge of the business, to bring it into the king's treasuries" (Esth 3:8–9).

The king drafted this decree, which expressly stipulated that all Jews including their wives and children were to be exterminated so that "the kingdom's affairs may always remain in good order unshaken" (Esth 3:13). To the credit of Esther, Xerxes' Jewish spouse, this first act of organized murder ever to be planned in world history was able to be successfully thwarted; Haman and his followers were hung and killed. Just how were the *Jehudim* understood, living as they did throughout Xerxes' entire kingdom, which stretched, after all, from Anatolia to the western border of present-day Afghanistan? The question remains. And how did they understand themselves? The book of Esther mentions a "people"—*Am* in the Hebrew text, and *ethnos* in the Greek. Does this refer to some kind of cult deviating from the Persian state religion, a distinct linguistic community, or perhaps even an actual settlement? While not a perfectly reliable source, the book of Esther assumes that the Jews lived dispersed from one another and thus did not represent a single settled community. Despite this, they also followed their own divergent laws, although this had nothing to do with cultic beliefs; rather, the bone of contention was simply the fact that these laws were "their own." Exactly which royals laws the *Jehudim* failed to observe is a matter that can no longer be resolved.

The founding era of Judaism ends with the conquest of Persia by Alexander the Great, the Macedonian king. The books of Chronicles, Ezra, Nehemiah, and the prophets Joel and Zachariah, as well as the wisdom books of Jonah and Tobias, all had their likely origins in Jerusalem prior to Alexander's conquest of the weak and overtaxed Persian kingdom.

An Early Polemic against Intermarriage?

The canonical Jewish Bible, the so-called Masoretic Text, introduces Malachi as the last of the prophets. Polemicizing one day against the temple priesthood, he summons God, who will punish the godless. Many interpreters read Malachi's fervid persecution of abomination through the lens of social history, understanding it as a resumption of Ezra's polemic against "mixed marriages," which only addressed the threat to the Jewish faith posed by marriage partners who prayed to other gods. Yet there were also those prophets who had interpreted the relationship between God and Israel using the metaphor of marriage, and a lot speaks in favor of understanding the statement below to mean that other gods and even goddesses—not just the imageless JHWH—were worshipped in the Temple of Jerusalem. This was witnessed by the prophet Ezekiel, who was also living in Babylon: "[F]or Judah hath profaned the holiness of the LORD which he loved, and hath married the daughter of a strange god" (Mal 2:11). Here, Malachi no doubt intended the proper biblical name Judah to refer to the Jews as a whole. Nonbiblical documents passed down from the Persian era also state that Jewish military colonists in lower Egypt gave JHWH a wife named Aschera to whom they also prayed. That this cultic practice would consequently undercut Ezra's strict commandment calling for endogamy is obvious.

Between the downfall of Judah, the edict of Ezra, and Alexander's conquest of Persia, a formative period in the history of the Jewish religion begins. Where the prophetic voice of Jeremiah welcomes exile along with the universalist expansion of old Israel's tribal religion, Malachi tells of the Jewish faith's need to forge stubbornly ahead, setting strict boundaries and focusing on its own internal affairs. Amid the interplay between these various ambitions, the tension between universalism and particularism—between diaspora and Zion—was to witness developments pivotal to the future of Jewish self-understanding. Indeed, the subsequent history of the Jewish people demonstrates that a group's fate is shaped by much more than their ideas alone; rather, it is frequently subject to external, often undesirable influences and powers. Since at least the third century, the Jews had been well-known to their contemporaries, who were now under Hellenistic influence. As such, they went from being a largely subjective, imagined community to one that now possessed an objective historical significance.

Belonging

Although Ezra's divorce decree only states that Jewish men must leave their Gentile marriage partners, both Ezra and Malachi in fact appear to argue that spouses—or more precisely, *wives*—could only be members of the *Jehudim* providing they worshipped no other god apart from the God of Israel. The question, then, is what happens in yet another situation: namely, the marriage of a Jewish *woman* to a Gentile *man*. That there is a gaping hole here cannot be overlooked: indeed, this is the strongest evidence yet that the matrilineal principle was not yet valid in Ezra's day—in other words, during the founding period of the Jewish religion. If belonging to the Jewish *ethnos* was determined by the father's ancestry, as in all other Mediterranean cultures, then it is necessary to ask why Gentile women had to be sent away. A systematic answer to this question is only given six centuries later in the protocols of the Mishnah. But even so: Can it be concluded from Ezra that Jewish women did not need to part ways with their Gentile husbands, or were such ties perhaps nonexistent? And if they did exist, were they regarded as something trivial and insignificant, or did the young Jewish religion now see something special in marriage—certainly no sacrament in the Catholic sense, but a high-ranking source of legitimation just the same—that determined the role of offspring as bona fide members of the community? One thing, at least, can be indirectly concluded from Ezra's edict: in order to become a member of the religiously observant *ethnos* of the *Jehudim*, a son or daughter had to be the offspring of a sanctified closed marriage, which is to say a marriage between two Jews. The *Jehudim* were hardly alone in introducing such a provision. Some one hundred kilometers to the west, in Athens, the statesman Pericles introduced a similar statute around the same time stating that only children born to two Athenian citizens, husband and wife, could acquire Athenian citizenship.

So far then, it can only be ascertained that the criterion for a legitimate marriage between Jews is not just a matter of being born to a Jewish mother.

Legitimacy—Kiddushin

The requirement, known as *Kiddushin*, that a Jewish marriage be properly sanctified did not yet include the matrilineal principle. In fact, religious and historical sources allow no doubt that the matrilineal principle was established during the Rabbinic era, hence only after the destruction of the Second Temple and probably prior to the defeat of the Bar Khokba Revolt. In a pathbreaking monograph on this subject entitled *The Beginnings of Jewishness. Boundaries, Varieties, Uncertainties*, Shaye J. D. Cohen demonstrates that aside from their religious customs the Jews could not be distinguished from anyone else in any way prior to 90 CE. For that matter, there was also no public auditing procedure that could determine whether someone had officially converted to Judaism (so long as one disregards the male obligation to be circumcised).

The traditional passages delineating the matrilineal principle are found in the Mishnah, Kiddushin 3:12, which deals with the status of children conceived out of wedlock, and in Yevamot 4:13, which also discusses the status of a *mamzer*. Cohen meticulously analyzes seven possible reasons for the adoption of the matrilineal principle: the Tanakh (scripture), Ezra, uncertain paternity, the intimacy of the mother-child bond, the residual of a primitive matriarchal society, and the prohibition of forbidden mixtures. He ultimately concludes that the most likely reason was merely silent acquiescence to Roman law, which assigned mothers complete custody of their children under all circumstances. Yet in the end, and in light of the fact that only the patrilineal principle was valid among Jews until the time of the Mishnah, Cohen is also forced to concede: "Why, then, did the rabbis break with previous practice? I do not know."[2]

Admittedly, the answer may well be just where Cohen seeks it: in the form of Pericles' laws concerning Athenian citizenship and the Roman political sphere. Yet despite his intense scrutiny of key passages from the Mishnah, Cohen may have overlooked an essential piece of information. As it says in Kiddushin 3:12:

> Wherever there is potential for a valid marriage and the sexual union is not sinful, the offspring follows the male. And what [fem.] is this? This is the daughter of a priest, Levite, or Israelite who was married to a priest, Levite, or Israelite . . . And any woman who does not have the potential for a valid marriage with this man but has the potential for a valid marriage with other men, the offspring is a *mamzer*. And what [masc.] is this? This is he who has intercourse with any of the relations prohibited by the Torah. And any woman who does not have

---

2. Cohen, *Beginnings of Jewishness*, 305.

the potential for a valid marriage either with this man or with other men, the offspring is like her.³

Yevamot 7:5 contains a similar statute in which it is determined that "(If) the daughter of an Israelite (was married) to a priest, or (if) the daughter of a priest (was married) to an Israelite, and she bore him a daughter; and (if) that daughter went and was married to a slave or to a gentile and bore him a son—he is a *mamzer*."⁴ Still another passage from the Mishnah, Bikkurim 1:4–5, ensures even more confusion regarding the matter by stipulating, for example, which individuals bring fruit to the altar but do not recite prayers during the harvest festival. A convert is required to bring fruit but may not recite prayers, since God's promise in Deuteronomy 26:3 does not apply to converts—that is, unless one's mother is from Israel. But what is this supposed to mean? In what circumstances can one speak of a convert whose mother is Jewish?

In equal measure, this is also means that "[a] woman who is the daughter of converts may not marry into the priesthood, unless her mother is of Israel" (Mishnah: *m. Bik.* 1:4–5).⁵ What is meant by the fact that the daughter of converts has a mother from Israel? Is one to assume that people from Israel belong to a faith other than that of the God of Israel? Without being able to resolve these questions here, the special significance accorded to the relationship between Israel and its priesthood should be reconsidered—for I suspect that this tense relationship provides the solution to the riddle behind the matrilineal principle.

High Priests, the Pharisees, and a Queen

In doubtful cases of *Kiddushin*, Talmudic sources make frequent and conspicuous mention of the daughter of a certain high priest. As can be deduced, her marriage wielded considerable political influence during the era of the Cohenite priesthood, when the temple still stood as in the time of Hellenism and Hasmonean rule and even into the time of the Julian Empire. It is also known that, during the Hasmonean dynasty, there was a bitter competition between temple priests and the increasingly influential Pharisees, and that the ruling Hasmonean dynasty even

---

3. Quoted in ibid., 273–74.
4. Quoted in ibid., 276.
5. Quoted in ibid., 309.

supported the Pharisees at the expense of the priesthood at times. So it was in the case of the Hasmonean queen Salome Alexandra, who is known in Hebrew as Shlomtzion and was the last Hasmonean ruler before Judea lost its political independence.

Writes Flavius Josephus in *The Antiquities of the Jews*, "Alexandra . . . acted as her husband had suggested to her, and spake to the Pharisees, and put all things into their power, both as to the dead body, and as to the affairs of the kingdom, and thereby pacified their anger against Alexander, and made them bear goodwill and friendship to him; who then came among the multitude, and made speeches to them, and laid before them the actions of Alexander, and told them that they had lost a righteous king."[6]

A little further down, Josephus affords the queen a good deal of praise: "A woman she was who showed no signs of the weakness of her sex, for she was sagacious to the greatest degree in her ambition of governing; and demonstrated by her doings at once, that her mind was fit for action, and that sometimes men themselves show the little understanding they have by the frequent mistakes they make in point of government."[7]

By appointing her son—who also backed the Pharisees—as high priest (*Kohen Gadol*), the queen allowed the Pharisees to assume actual control of the country. As Josephus notes, "So she had indeed the name of the regent, but the Pharisees had the authority; for it was they who restored such as had been banished, and set such as were prisoners at liberty, and, to say all at once, they differed in nothing from lords."[8]

A leading role for any Jewish house of royalty—Idumaean Herodians, according to the Hasmoneans—ended once and for all with the destruction of the temple. Judaism was then reestablished by the Pharisees' rabbis and scholars of scripture as an aristocracy of scholars with its headquarters in Javne and, later, in Uscha and Galilee. They were therefore in a position to appropriate the Hasmonean legacy at a time when it was no longer clear, as Josephus claims, just who the descendants of the Zadokite dynasty were.[9] As is well-known, the rabbonim

---

6. Flavius Josephus, *Antiquities of the Jews* 13.16.1 (434). Parenthetical numbers refer to page numbers of the English translation.

7. Ibid., 13.16.6 (436).

8. Ibid., 13.16.2 (434).

9. Bickerman, *Jews in the Greek Age*, 144.

in the Pirkei Avot substituted a different line of tradition and heritage for the cohanim's Aaronic line of descent: from Moses, through Joshua, and down to the men of the Great Assembly (Mishnah: *m. Avot.* 1:1).

A Hypothesis

One could suggest—and I want to conclude with this supposition—that the rabbonim who came to power through Queen Alexandra and a war that was lost to the Romans did not have the female of the species to thank for this. In their reorganization of Judaism, I suspect that the rabbonim systematically denied political demands by the high priest as well as the priesthood's claims to legitimacy in order to install themselves—the scholars—in their place. In Rabbinic Judaism, nothing of the cohanim's erstwhile power remained but the privilege of being the first to have been called to the Torah. This shift also meant that the Jewish caste society was transformed into a meritocratic one (i.e., in the service of an educated republic based on learning). In my estimation, the matrilineal principle played a decisive role in this process: since it was no longer important which caste a Jewish man or woman belonged to, and since everything depended solely on Jewish ancestry *sans phrase*, the birth privileges associated with caste status obviously lost their force. Admittedly, Rabbinic Judaism paid a high price for doing away with the clerical caste system: in the same moment priestly power and charisma were abrogated, the public influence that women had so clearly possessed during the Hellenic period and to which the Hasmoneans had also attested was abrogated as well. Women were now forced into a peculiar status oscillating somewhere between that of a human being and a house pet.[10] Perhaps it is no coincidence, then, that the fourth pericope of Avot, which culminates by praising the scholars for whom the house is now to be readied, is followed in the fifth by the words of Jersualem's Jose ben Jochanan, who speaks out against the dangerousness of women: "Make your house open wide, and make the poor as children of your house. And do not increase conversation with the woman—He causes badness to himself, and neglects the words of Torah, and in his end he inherits Gehenna" (Mishnah: *m. Avot.* 1:5).

As is known—and to which no small number of Talmudic midrashim including Beruriah, Imma Shalom, and Yalta attest—the wives

10. Wegner, *Chattel or Person*.

of the rabbonim by no means let this setback occur without resistance; it is to the credit of the Talmud, its authors, and its editors that the memory of their opposition is kept alive. Nonetheless, the late classical monotheisms—Rabbinic Judaism, Christianity, and Islam—constituted themselves in and through the exclusion of women. And paradoxically, it is the matrilineal principle in Judaism—comparable in this sense to the Catholic Marian cult of virginity—that has played such a decisive role in this.

Bibliography

Bickerman, Elias J. *The Jews in the Greek Age*. Cambridge, MA: Harvard University Press, 1988.
Cohen, Shaye J. D. *The Beginnings of Jewishness: Boundaries, Varieties, Uncertainties*. Berkeley: University of California Press, 1999.
Flavius Josephus. *The Antiquities of the Jews*. Translated by William Whiston. Lawrence, KS: Digireads.com, 2010.
Mishnah [Hebrew]. 6 vols. Edited by Hanoch Albeck. Jerusalem: Bialik Institute, 1952–1958.
Wegner, Judith Romney. *Chattel or Person? The Status of Women in the Mishnah*. Oxford: Oxford University Press, 1988.

Race, Gender, and Religious Fundamentalism

Debates between Christians and Jews at the End of the Weimar Republic

The Case of Hans Blüher and Hans-Joachim Schoeps[1]

CLAUDIA BRUNS

In history, debates about Christianity and Judaism did not take place on the religious level alone. In early twentieth-century Germany in particular, interreligious controversies were tightly intertwined with gender and racist discourses. In this article, I want to elaborate on the question whether racist elements in Christian-Jewish dialogue can be read as signs of fundamentalist tendencies, that is, to what extent a connection exists between fundamentalism, racism, and gender. We might suspect that by no means *every form* of fundamentalism contains or must contain racist elements, but that all racism appearing in the guise of religious discourse has the effect of increasing its fundamentalist nature. Perhaps that is why it is so difficult nowadays to speak of fundamentalist movements without falling into fundamentalist patterns of argumentation themselves. Racist presuppositions slip quickly

---

1. Translated from German by Pamela Selwyn.

into discussions of the religious Other. Racist and religious discourses not infrequently enter into an "unholy alliance." The sociologist of religion Martin Riesebrodt recently and convincingly referred to Samuel Huntington's argumentation about the "clash of civilizations" as in itself fundamentalist. According to Huntington, religions exist in diametrical opposition to one another in homogenized spaces along an East-West schema; this plays down the tensions *within* a given religion and turns those between different religions into insurmountable barriers, thereby introducing cultural racism into religious discourse.

It is no accident that Huntington's bestseller brings up associations of Spengler's early twentieth-century *Untergang des Abendlandes* (*Decline of the West*, 1918/22), since he regards himself as a modern-day disciple of Spengler.[2] Similarly, the public controversies over the role of Islam in Germany that have attracted so much media attention recall debates during the Weimar Republic in which the relationship between Jews and Christians was discussed as a "national question." Then as now, the treatment of religious affiliation was simultaneously a debate on the racialized and gendered collective identity of the German nation.

In the following, I would like to examine the religious disputation between a Jew and a Christian, both of whom experienced a strong personal turn toward religion during the era of the Weimar Republic and had roots in the German youth movement.[3] One of them speaks of a veritable "conversion" to Christianity, the other of rediscovering his Jewish roots. However, one of them, Hans Blüher (1888–1955), evolved into an anti-Semitic Protestant, while Hans-Joachim Schoeps (1909–1980), twenty years his junior and a Prussian conservative, was soon referred to in reviews as a "revelationist Jewish theologian," although German-Jewish religious philosopher and historian would be a more fitting description.[4] Based on the debate between the two men, which was published in 1933 under the title *Streit um Israel* (Dispute over Israel) (Blüher/Schoeps), I will show in this article how deeply the categories of race, gender, and national community had penetrated religious

---

2. Hempel, "Schoeps."

3. Ibid.; Schoeps, *Ja—nein—und trotzdem*; Bruns, "Eros, Macht und Männlichkeit."

4. Kroll, "Wider den Zeitgeist"; Hillerbrand, "Schoeps"; Faber, "Deutschbewusstes Judentum." For Blüher's biography, see Bruns, "Politics of Eros"; Hergemöller, "Blühers Männerwelten."

discourse at the end of the Weimar Republic and how they enforced its fundamentalist tendencies.[5]

It is remarkable that the entire discussion between Schoeps and Blüher revolves around religious derivations of community from "blood" and the male "seed." That one *is* a Jew by virtue of birth, blood, and seed, but *becomes* a Christian by virtue of baptism is at the center of concern. Membership in a collective seems at once so shaken and yet so highly desirable that it becomes an obsession explicable only on the highest metaphysical and existential plane. At this moment in history, religious and national political discourses were becoming ever more tightly intertwined.

At the same time, the positions in the disputation (particularly Blüher's) exhibit fundamentalist traits. This is particularly apparent if we follow Riesebrodt's view that fundamentalisms are characterized by a radical critique of certain manifestations of modernity (social critique) and juxtaposed with the model of an ideal social order, as well as rooted in an interpretation of the present in the light of the history of salvation.[6] Blüher, at least, was also concerned with a particular approach to the "truth" of the Holy Scripture. This truth was ascertainable not by historical-critical methods but solely through a special cognitive process accessible only to a small, select group. In addition, Blüher and Schoeps regarded themselves as religious laymen who nevertheless felt called upon to speak in the name of and to radically renew their religions, whose official institutions and representatives had failed. The two also speak from an elitist position typical of fundamentalist approaches, convinced of belonging, respectively, to the "legalist *remnant*" or the "primary race" that could assert a sole claim to the truth.

We would nevertheless be justified in asking whether their dispute was not better categorized as an aspect of "religious-nationalist movements," which are distinguished in the literature from genuine fundamentalisms. Juergensmeyer characterizes religious-nationalist movements as politically oriented and fixated in particular on ethnic or national differences, which applies in the case discussed here. The reli-

---

5. See also Lease, "Wer war hier Christ"; Lease, *Odd fellows*.

6. Riesebrodt, "Fundamentalismus," 19; see also LeVine, "What Is Fundamentalism"; Heilman, "Jews and Fundamentalism"; Ingber, "Fundamentalismus im Judentum"; Armstrong, *Im Kampf für Gott*; Antoun, *Understanding Fundamentalism*; Kienzler, *Der religiöse Fundamentalismus*.

gious regulation of ways of life is generally less central. While religious fundamentalism allows for conversion, ethnic-nationalist movements do not.[7] Nevertheless, the lines between fundamentalism and religious nationalism are fluid, and hybrid forms are frequent, so that the case presented in this essay may reveal such a hybrid form, since religious argumentation is actually in the foreground here.

Scholars have also debated whether fundamentalism, especially in its religious-nationalist variant, is not primarily a *political* reaction to social and economic changes that has only coincidentally assumed a religious form. Riesebrodt rightly considers this to be a "fundamental misjudgment,"[8] since religion is more than mere outer appearance. Religion decisively shapes the fundamentalist milieu by playing a key role in determining its identity formation, its expectations of solidarity, and its political interests. The kind of discourse in which political questions are discussed also makes a significant difference: whether the questions of membership in a religiously, nationally or gender-coded collective are treated and transported in a partisan political, scientific, or religious discourse is *not* unimportant, because each of these discourses has a logic of its own and provides and structures the framework for potential negotiation processes.

The New Religious Movements and the Case of Blüher and Schoeps

I would like to start by returning to our case study and its two protagonists for a closer look. Riesebrodt has suggested that fundamentalism arises from the "dynamic of new group and class formation in the context of social restructuring processes. Changes that people experience as dramatic cast doubt on traditions and no longer allow traditionalists to take them for granted."[9] This applies in particular to the period of the Weimar Republic. As enthusiastically as they had entered World War I, Germans found themselves severely disillusioned by the final defeat of 1918. The experience of hardship and death, destruction and hunger, and the ultimate tally of some seventeen million dead, 9.7 million of them

---

7. Riesebrodt, "Fundamentalismus," 21.
8. Ibid.
9. Ibid., 19.

soldiers, including nearly two million (young) men from Germany, gave an undreamt-of boost to religious and metaphysical questions.

In 1921, Richard Heinrich Grützmacher (1876–1956), professor of Protestant theology in Erlangen, noted, "In our present day, religion has regained relevance for the formation of a worldview."[10] Religiosity outside the churches became more differentiated and individualized. At the same time, a wide variety of religious associations, groups, and leagues emerged.[11] In the *völkisch* or racist-nationalist milieu alone some seventy different religious organizations existed between 1890 and 1945.[12] Some of these groupings were strongly Christian-oriented (for instance the so-called German Christians), while others understood themselves as "neo-pagan" and rejected all things Christian. Many, such as the Monistenbund or "Union of Monists," sought a synthesis between modern scholarship and religion and worked towards a syncretism of science and faith.[13]

Grützmacher counted Hans Blüher among the "critics and re-creators of religion in the twentieth century" alongside the religious philosophers Heinrich Scholz (1884–1956), Max Scheler (1874–1928), and the professor of Protestant church history Albert Hauck (1845–1918), as well as the philosopher of life and culture Count Hermann von Keyserling (1880–1946), philosopher Leopold Ziegler (1881–1958), author Houston Stewart Chamberlain (1855–1927), and the anthroposophist Rudolf Steiner (1861–1925). Blüher's positions on religious philosophy represented a "particular type of religious critique and re-creation of religion at the beginning of the twentieth century" and were thus worthy of closer attention.[14] While sharply criticizing his ahistorical biblical exegesis, Grützmacher nevertheless believed Blüher's positions to be typical of the "modern era" and expected that he "would surely

10. Grützmacher, *Kritiker und Neuschöpfer*, 3; Bertz, "Jüdische Renaissance"; Kläcker, "Erneuerungsbewegungen."

11. Linse, "Säkularisierung," 120. Many of these movements were anti-modernist and ambivalent in their effects. Schieder also observes that the nineteenth century is "characterized less by a dramatic decline in religion" than by an "increase in religiosity outside the churches" (Schieder, "Sozialgeschichte," 18).

12. Cancik and Puschner, *Antisemitismus*; Schnurbein and Ulbricht, *Völkische Religion*; Nanko, *Glaubensbewegung*; Schnurbein, *Religion*.

13. Linse, "Säkularisierung"; Hering, "Säkularisierung, Entkirchlichung"; Figl, "Säkularisierung und Fundamentalismus."

14. Grützmacher, *Kritiker und Neuschöpfer*, 44. For a more detailed analysis of Blüher's religious racism, see Bruns, "Die 'metaphysische Pathologie' des Juden."

prove popular among the broad mass of the reading public, especially those with no knowledge of Greek." Presumably, wrote Grützmacher, most would acknowledge "this 'laying of foundations' as a result of scholarship."[15]

In fact, a series of enthusiastic reviews shows that Blüher's religious writings, including the disputation with Schoeps, met with a lively and surprisingly positive response. Writing from the perspective of 1922, Keyserling saw a connection between his publications and the new religious awakening and messianic expectations that followed the war.[16] After all, at this time, Blüher also moved in the circles of the highest church dignitaries surrounding the exiled Kaiser Wilhelm who were still dreaming of his return to the throne and the resacralization of Prussia.

Alongside the search for religious meaning, tough political conflicts were also being fought out between right and left. While the Revolution enjoyed initial successes and the workers' and soldiers' councils gained political power, on the other side of the divide new, extraparliamentary forms of political organization oriented toward the soldierly ideal also emerged. These included the newly formed youth leagues on both the left and the right. From the remnants of the prewar *Wandervogel* youth movement arose the more tightly and hierarchically organized *Bündische Jugendbewegung* of the Weimar Republic, which now also separated boys and girls and racialized religious groups from one another.[17] The exclusion of Jewish youths, who then organized groups of their own, had already occurred before the First World War.[18] As part of the *Freideutscher Werkbund*, Schoeps was one of fewer than two hundred fifty unbaptized Jewish members of the youth movement.[19] This development notwithstanding, Jewish and Christian young people experienced many of the upheavals in similar ways. Both groups sought the roots of their own religion and spawned movements of religious renewal and self-styled awakening that were also supported by young people and spread in the life-reform milieu. Both groups experienced conflicts between renewal and tradition as well as fundamentalist at-

---

15. Grützmacher, *Kritiker und Neuschöpfer*, 44.
16. Keyserling, *Das Erbe*.
17. Bruns, *Politik des Eros*; Bruns, "Politics of Eros."
18. Winnecken, *Ein Fall von Antisemitismus*; Bruns, *Politik des Eros*, 373–86.
19. Rheins, "Deutscher Vortrupp," 209.

tempts at a "conservative revolution."[20] Both engaged in a search for new means of claiming origins and roots that incorporated a modernized reinvention of traditions.

Hans Blüher was one of these young conservative revolutionaries. He had belonged to the *Wandervogel* movement and enjoyed great success and a wide public response as the author of writings on the foundations of the movement in homoeroticism and male bonding. At the beginning of the Weimar Republic, Blüher subscribed to the doctrine of Jesus Christ's *arete* and elite kingdom, which was reserved for the few and the best.[21]

Woven into this new reading of the New Testament was a turn from gender to racial discourse. While before the war distancing himself from women's emancipation had been a central objective for the anti-feminist Blüher, the "women's question" now appeared to have been largely "resolved." The war had clearly restored the soldierly virtues of masculinity and thus of gender difference, so that women's emancipation was at first no longer perceived as a central threat.

Blüher thus stated in his monograph *Die Aristie des Jesus von Nazareth* (The Arete of Jesus of Nazareth, 1921) that "Nature has given man the guarantee that he will not someday feel overrun by his female sexual characteristics; the primary race, however, has no guarantee of being spared secondary racial events. That is why the situation of mankind as a whole is a desperate one."[22] The dominant anti-feminist gender discourse had been transferred unnoticed into a racial discourse with anti-Semitic implications, which at the same time promoted a hierarchical class structure—one headed by the "intellectual aristocracy" of the educated middle class. According to Blüher, the bipolar split in humanity now ran along the lines of primary and secondary "races." To Blüher's dismay, "racial difference" was harder to pin down to biological than to cultural and religious traits.[23] No good or bad behavior would be of any

---

20. Breuer, *Ordnungen*; Mohler, *Die konservative Revolution*.

21. Bruns, "Die 'metaphysische Pathologie' des Juden."

22. Blüher, *Die Aristie*, 42; Kläber, "Blühers Christologie"; Matthias, "Blüher und das Christentum."

23. Blüher, *Die Aristie*, 52. The notion of "race" was indeed not a clearly biological one, but from the beginning of racism was imbued with cultural categories. See Weingart et al., *Rasse, Blut und Gene*, 91–103, 230–32. "As difficult as it is today to disentangle the two original races of mankind in a precise *biological* sense—too much

use to human beings, but only "a new act of creation by Nature." There was no route to the kingdom of heaven other than "natural belonging." According to Blüher's interpretation of the Bible, "all of mankind is called but . . . they are fooled, for only few are chosen."[24] The redemptive turning point is like an "organ that functions only in the primary race."[25] Many would have to disappear to bring forth a new race, that of the "Son of Man."[26] In Blüher's assessment, humanity was engaged in "a losing battle." The creation of the human species was a big "mistake" of nature "until the coming of the Son of Man."[27] Only the "primary race" still had the right to live. The great majority of the "secondary race" was inferior and dangerous, for the "primary race" often fell "victim to the bared teeth of the secondary."[28] He sought to derive this basic idea from the Gospel of John and the Apocrypha.

For Blüher, Jesus became the central figure in a properly understood Christianity. Johannes Weiss's (1863–1914) "consistent eschatology" and Albert Schweitzer's (1875–1965) "research on Jesus" had confirmed him in this.[29] The focus was no longer on Jesus the historical person—liberal theology had abdicated its authority—but on his myth, the "eschatological line" in the life of Jesus, which would restore his grandeur.[30]

Associated with this was the shift from a psychoanalytic and (homo)sexological discourse on male bonding to one rooted in re-

mixing has already occurred—their disparate nature becomes absolutely clear if their essence is projected onto the spiritual (*geistige*) dimension" (Blüher, *Die Aristie*, 40; emphasis added). Here Blüher could refer to the well-known positions of the French anti-Semite Count Joseph Arthur de Gobineau, who attributed what he saw as the severe decline in the nobility of mankind to racial mixing. See Zerger, *Was ist Rassismus*, 36–39.

24. Blüher, *Die Aristie*, 141.

25. Ibid., 57.

26. Ibid., 80.

27. Ibid., 19. "All the other species of animal are successful in building their nests and dens. They do well in all their undertakings . . . only human beings have to fight with constant experiences of failure . . . is it possible that nature may have made a mistake in creating human beings . . . at least until the coming of the Son of Man?" (ibid., 12).

28. Ibid., 59. "The human species is the most brutal and the worst of all creatures. It is split into two races that misunderstand each other and diverge wildly, and the best specimens of the whole type succumb to melancholy" (ibid., 183).

29. Ibid., 117.

30. Ibid., 119.

ligious studies. And yet one can trace analogies and interferences in the patterns of argumentation and exclusion, which are similar in the two discourses. While anti-feminism revolved around the exclusion of women from the arena of political representation, Blüher's religiously-based anti-Semitism sought to exclude Jews from positions in the state and military and thus from control over the national community, which was defined as genuinely "German Germanic."

Hans-Joachim Schoeps (1909–1980) became acquainted with Blüher's works on male bonding and later his religious writings in the context of the youth movement, which he enthusiastically joined in 1923 at the age of fourteen. Schoeps came from a family of German Jews loyal to the Kaiser who felt more drawn to Prussian tradition than the Jewish religion.[31] His father, who worked as a general practitioner in Berlin, had gained honors and medals as a military doctor during the First World War. Schoeps himself describes how he gradually "grew into" Judaism (especially after meeting Eberhard Beyer—a student of Karl Holl, professor of church history and Lutheranism—in 1926) despite the religious indifference of his parents, which he attributed to his "basically conservative instincts."[32] He felt repelled by nineteenth-century liberalism and believed that "Jewish beliefs needed to be completely reconceptualized."[33] For a time, while part of the Freideutsche Jugend (Free German Youth) movement, he was associated with a group of new religious Protestants. During his time as a student at the University of Heidelberg in 1928, Schoeps was accepted as a member of the more hierarchically-organized *bündisch* youth movement, Deutsche Akademische Freischar, became the *Bundesführer* of the Freideutsche Kameradschaft (F. K.) a year later, and was attracted to the burgeoning movement of the Conservative Revolution as well as the Prussian monarchy.[34] The emphasis of the F. K. was on "spiritual tasks" and the search for a new *Volkstum* within an authoritarian state, drawing from divergent conservative spokesmen such as Wilhelm Dilthey, Martin Heidegger, Rudolf Bultmann, Carl Schmitt, Othmar Spann, and

---

31. Schoeps, *Rückblicke*, 72.
32. Ibid., 71; Rheins, "Deutscher Vortrupp," 209.
33. Schoeps, *Rückblicke*, 73.
34. Faber, *Deutschbewusstes Judentum*, 103–5; Lease, "Wer war hier Christ" 223.

Wilhelm Stapel, among others.[35] On 26 February 1933, less than four weeks after Hitler's appointment as chancellor of the *Reich*, Schoeps founded the Deutscher Vortrupp, Gefolgschaft deutscher Juden (D. V.), hoping to reaffirm Jewish participation in the movement of "national regeneration" by creating a separate Jewish youth movement founded upon strict nationalist principles.[36]

Schoeps's commitment to a conservative revolution was accompanied by his interpretation of Judaism, which gave his subsequent political attitudes a particular thrust.[37] Through his contact with Beyer, Schoeps learned more about Protestant approaches to religious questions, so that he became interested in his own (Jewish) heritage and aimed to integrate the two components into his thinking. He began to study the Jewish philosopher Salomon Ludwig Steinheim (1789–1866), whose anti-rationalist approach set him apart from both liberal and Orthodox Jewish thinkers of his era—an isolated position with which Schoeps identified. He decided to study religion at the University of Leipzig with Joachim Wach, completed his doctoral dissertation in 1931 on the topic of the history of modern Jewish religious philosophy (*Geschichte der jüdischen Religionsphilosophie in der Neuzeit*), and published his first major theological monograph, *Jüdischer Glaube in dieser Zeit*. Here he tried to "point the way towards a thorough reorientation of Jewish religious thought" using methods and addressing problems raised by Søren Kierkegaard and Karl Barth and was attacked by both Jewish liberals and Zionists in Germany.[38] Trying to develop a system of religious belief from an anti-Zionist perspective that would allow Jewish youth to remain loyal to both their German "fatherland" and their Jewish heritage, he aimed to demonstrate the compatibility between Judaism and German Protestantism.[39]

Around this time, Schoeps penned a first scathing critique of Blüher's religious anti-Semitic writings[40] in the newspaper of the Central-Verein, a German-Jewish organization dedicated to combat-

35. Schoeps, *Ja—nein—und trotzdem*, 82.
36. Rheins, "Deutscher Vortrupp," 207–8.
37. Ibid., 210.
38. Ibid., 211.
39. Ibid., 212.
40. Schoeps was referring in particular to Blüher's recent (1931) publication: Blüher, *Die Erhebung Israels*.

ing anti-Semitism.⁴¹ Blüher thereupon challenged Schoeps, who was twenty years his junior, to a disputation in which their positions would alternate in longer essays. Written in 1932, these essays were published in the book *Streit um Israel* (Dispute over Israel) and appeared under the imprint of Blüher's regular publishing house, the conservative Hanseatische Verlagsanstalt. A few months after its appearance in 1933, it was withdrawn from the market by the publishing house itself. After the Nazi Party (NSDAP) came to power in March, the publication of a religious dispute between a Christian and a Jew, and particularly a Jewish author, was obviously no longer viewed as opportune. Nevertheless, it elicited a substantial response together with Blüher's recently published *Die Erhebung Israels gegen die christlichen Güter* (Israel's Revolt against the Goods of Christianity, 1931).

"Dispute over Israel"

1. The Fundamentalist Conservative Revolution as a Modern Movement with an Anti-Modernist Thrust

Schoeps and Blüher certainly had some things in common, which is perhaps the reason why they entered into a debate in the first place. Both came from the youth movement and wrote enthusiastically about homoerotic male bonding; both belonged to the "conservative revolutionary" camp in politics and were dedicated to Prussia and the monarchy "by the grace of God." A further commonality was their rejection of the Enlightenment, liberalism, and above all Bolshevism, but also relativism, egalitarianism, and pluralism. Based on their basic religious stance, both of them were dedicated to resacralizing a world pushed to the brink by the Enlightenment and democracy. According to Blüher, even modern natural science and sexology had been ruined: "the best scientific descriptions of external processes" remained "utterly obscure" and could "only be illuminated by the concealed and nameless reconnection (*religio*), which the researcher's inner being has to the things he is studying."⁴² Darwin's theories were ultimately also only a "purely

---

41. Schoeps, "Soll Homosexualität strafbar bleiben."
42. Blüher, *Die Aristie*, 55–56.

metaphysical myth" and "no more 'scientific' than the sentence 'And God made the beasts of the earth according to their kinds.'"[43]

Such religiously justified resistance to certain transformations of the modern age is quite typical of fundamentalist currents.[44] Usually, they have recourse to premodern traditions that are purportedly immune to enlightened emancipation processes. Following Riesebrodt, we could speak of a reinterpretation of tradition, which is often not merely reformed but also radicalized and even revolutionized.[45] At the same time, an "exact" return to allegedly eternally valid, sacred principles, commandments, or laws is supposed to help overcome the crisis.[46]

It also becomes clear, however, that the objective is not a return to the Middle Ages but rather a mixture of the selective acceptance and rejection of modern institutions and ideologies. The biblical dictum that only "few are chosen" is translated into a modern "theory of two races," which had not previously been a genuine element of the biblical Christian tradition. It is quite typical of fundamentalists to borrow from other ideologies, in this case nationalism or fascism, and to seek not merely to overcome the modern natural sciences but also to reconcile science and religion.[47] To that extent, we can describe fundamentalism as a deeply modern movement with an anti-modernist thrust. Its strong resemblance to the extraparliamentary movement of the Conservative Revolution is no accident.

2. The Function of Blood and Gender in the Model of an Ideal Order

Blüher and Schoeps's shared objective was to save the world by creating a religiously-based elite. Schoeps speaks of a small "legalist remnant," distinct both from the Zionists and the mass of apostate liberal Jews—and certainly from Jews like Freud, Marx, and Trotsky, whom he personally considered "demonic." Blüher, in contrast, put his faith in the few elect men of the "primary race," who alone were destined to succeed Jesus and establish his "kingdom." While for Schoeps an act, the observance of laws,

---

43. Ibid., 76.
44. Prutsch, *Fundamentalismus*, 59.
45. Riesebrodt, "Fundamentalismus," 19.
46. Ibid., 18.
47. Ibid., 20.

marked the difference between the groups of Jews, whether an individual belonged to the inferior mass or the elect few was for Blüher determined by fate and scarcely subject to influence. The Christian religion should ultimately be understood not legalistically but mystically. According to Blüher, there was no freedom to choose the good.

Here, too, Blüher brings racial predisposition into play. Thus he believed that the North Germans had especially good racial prerequisites for accepting and internalizing Christ's message. The Jews, in contrast, were *per se* incapable of accepting Christ's doctrine of salvation. The divine plan for salvation, which was also tantamount to a great apocalypse, had chosen a different fate for Jews. They were condemned to play the role of the Anti-Christ and to embody the eternal adversaries of Christendom. Only the Jewish religion could have spawned the idea that revelation is consistent with human reason, because Judaism posited a "relationship of compensation" between man and God. Freud, Marx, and Trotsky were the tip of the iceberg and ultimately "demonic powers." In light of the corruption and forsakenness of the world, Blüher implies that one day, in a distant, paradisiacal epoch, the separation of the races could be overcome, since the split of humanity into two races was ultimately the world's great drama and disaster. After an apocalyptic end, at some point only the "best" would exist, and all others would have disappeared.

Such a coherent interpretation of the world with a dualist-Manichaean worldview is characteristic of fundamentalist movements.[48] Bassam Tibi speaks of an "eschatological drama" in which the fundamentalists see themselves as warriors of light itself.[49] In the existential struggle between divine and satanic powers, compromise and pluralism can only mean ruin. It is quite typical that general decline is blamed on concrete groups. The traitors are usually the agents of change and presumed beneficiaries of modernization—in Blüher's case, the Jews.[50] Blüher stresses here that his anti-Semitism springs not from age-old wrath and "mere affect" but rather from religious understanding and insight into the history of salvation.

---

48. Prutsch, *Fundamentalismus*, 59.
49. Tibi, *Fundamentalismus im Islam*, 15.
50. Riesebrodt, "Fundamentalismus," 23.

For Blüher, blood plays a very particular role in this apocalyptic interpretation of the history of salvation. For him, blood and seed are Jewish "organs of faith" "for the unmediated reception of revelation." Since God made a covenant with the Jews, he sanctified their blood, and this sanctification goes far beyond an ethnological foundation of the Jewish community, which is never a "mere religion"; indeed, it extends to the divine itself and is thus of a wholly different quality than anything that Christians could ever attain. A person could choose to join the Christian community through baptism, but Jews are such by virtue of birth and God's choosing. This gives Jews a sort of racial surety or *Rassenbürgschaft*, unattainable by Christians.[51] According to Blüher, transubstantiation during the Eucharist was a transitory affair in comparison. Jews were also seen as bound to each other by the sacred blood, though, and could never leave this covenant. That was what made them so special and so demonic. Even in the diaspora, Jews were still *one* people. For that reason, they could (in Blüher's view) never become part of the German people. In short, Jews appeared to possess everything desirable: a divinely guaranteed, indissoluble collective that would exist until the end of time even without a state. To be sure, Schoeps contradicts Blüher at this point. He submits that the sanctification of the blood merely guarantees a "*possibility* of redemption," which has to be continually reinforced by piety and obedience to the laws; and he believes that the Germans are also no closer to God, since the Redeemer did not maintain "branch offices" for individual peoples. After all, according to Schoeps, "Jesus died on the Cross and was not a Germanic duke leading his armed servants to Valhalla."[52]

For Schoeps, too, however, the covenant with God was indissoluble and Israel a "divine institution of revelation composed of flesh and blood." Every Israelite is described as a "son of God" and bears the predisposition for redemption within himself "through his corporeality"; he possesses in Schoeps's view an "organic disposition to receive revelation."[53] Nevertheless, Jews were not responsible for one another and also differed from each other; therefore Schoeps distanced himself

---

51. Blüher and Schoeps, *Streit um Israel*, 18.
52. Ibid., 119.
53. Ibid., 55.

from actions of apostate Jews such as Freud and Marx, who in his view were truly "demonic."

This did not convince Blüher, however. He was obsessed with the idea of a magical blood cohesion that still distinguished Jews "physically" from other peoples and fatefully tied them together even after three thousand years. And even Schoeps remarks in a footnote that there were "undoubtedly" "physical and constitutional differences" between Jews and other groups. A reviewer notes that while Blüher followed a pagan "sacred myth," Schoeps could not decisively best his opponent because he himself adhered to a "blood monism" including a "biological founding of the sacred," so that it is not surprising that the debate broke off without a winner.[54]

Along with the reference to the racialized idea of a special religious blood cohesion the gender dimension also played an important role in their vision of an ideal social order. In most fundamentalist movements, the apocalyptic Manichaean worldview, as described here, leads to an idealization of patriarchal authority and morality.[55] The family is regarded as a holy institution and clear relationship of authority in which the wife should be subordinate to her husband and responsible for home, hearth, and children. This gender order is assigned significance for the history of salvation. Only a return to patriarchal principles could overcome the crisis of the present and its moral decadence.[56]

The debate discussed here, however, invokes the family as a holy institution far less than it does the concept of "male bonding" (which was developed in the youth movement and came to be known by the German term *Männerbund*). After the First World War it was transferred to the religious sphere, whether in the communion of Christian disciples, as Blüher put it, or in Schoeps's writings in the Old Testament covenant with God, which is passed down solely through the generational flow of male seed.[57] In both instances, male bonding mirrors the divine order of the world. Citing the Apocrypha, Blüher also interprets Jesus Christ (literally) as a "fertile provider of seed" and "brilliant Creator" who came to "destroy the works of femininity." The capacity to

54. Koch, "Streit um Israel," 65.
55. Howland, *Religious Fundamentalisms*; Bendroth, *Fundamentalism & Gender*.
56. Riesebrodt, "Fundamentalismus," 25.
57. Faber, "Theokratie," 69.

"propagate his works" was reserved for the German character, which thus demonstrated its masculine nature.[58] At the same time, the figure of the son plays a particular role. For Blüher, the hope of a new society—a new, both physically- and metaphysically-grounded human "species"—is concentrated in the eternal son: As the son of God, Jesus Christ rose to become not just the "turning point" in the "living substance" but also sensed the coming of the kingdom as an "*organic feeling in his own body*."[59] The new Christian artist-genius would thus appropriate Nature in such a way that he himself could bring forth Nature. The capacity for creaturely procreation would have been transferred to him, the *male genius*.

Schoeps makes no mention of the matriarchal line, which actually plays a major role in the Jewish tradition. To be sure, he criticizes the vitalist thrust of the male-bonding elements of Blüher's theory, but ultimately both men sought the redemption of the world in the male-bonding order, which they believed was the realization of an apparently godly, meaningful order.

3. Interpretation of Secular History via the History of Salvation

Biblical figures often play a central role in world history as viewed from a fundamentalist perspective. For Blüher, the event of Jesus Christ and his adversaries explains the wicked and strife-torn condition of the modern world. He places the secular history of events in the context of the history of salvation and virtually equates the former with the latter. Schoeps criticizes Blüher's confusion of the history of salvation with actual history. It would be arrogant of him to believe that he has direct access to the history of salvation. In his opinion, God is still the judge, over the apostates as well. Nevertheless, Schoeps's epistemic interest lies in exploring how the history of creation and human history interpenetrate and determine one another. And both men cite the past as a time of true redemption, while loading the future with millenarian and apocalyptic expectations.[60] A "modern view of history as a continual growth of freedom, prosperity, and control over nature" is juxtaposed with a "scenario of increasing . . . decay rooted in the history of salva-

58. Blüher, *Die Aristie*, 30.
59. Ibid., 28.
60. Prutsch, *Fundamentalismus*, 59.

tion"; history appears as degeneration, as a falling away from divine law and sacred tradition.⁶¹ This scenario frequently leads to a specifically fundamentalist interpretation of historical events with a considerable potential for radicalization.⁶²

4. Reviews and Reactions to the Dispute between Schoeps and Blüher

The many positive reviews of the disputation between Blüher and Schoeps in the 1930s are interesting not least because a number of Christian magazines and church newspapers felt compelled to offer their opinions alongside right-wing extremist publications such as the *Stahlhelm*. Regardless of their political parties or religious or secular affiliations, reviewers came to sometimes surprisingly similar conclusions. Astonishingly enough, almost all reviews stressed that Blüher's positions were convincingly arguing for a radical anti-Semitism in metaphysical terms and approved the expressed anti-Semitism as such, though for different reasons and to varying degree. Blüher's position was "no common street anti-Semitism," noted the Prussian Lutheran monthly *Monatsblatt der Vereinigung der Evangelisch-Lutherischen innerhalb der preußischen Landeskirche* (formerly the *Evangelische Kirchenzeitung*), since he did not place race "above all else" or promote "enticing people away from Christianity."⁶³ Positive emphasis was given to the fact that Blüher, in contrast to "pure" racists, argued in religious terms and nevertheless exhaustively demonstrated the "secret influence of Jewry." The *Stahlhelm* reviewer on the other hand called Blüher's work a "wake-up call to both Catholics and Protestants" to "regard and combat Jewry as the shared, great anti-Christian foe." Here, Blüher's anti-Semitism was seen as positive because it was "expressed in an unprecedented sharpness" and due to its potential to weaken the Christian churches as Blüher managed to convincingly combine both, the racial and the theological discourse: "Since Blüher analyses the role of Jewry in history from a racial, but also from a theological-political standpoint, his writings are not only unassailable and truly dangerous for the Jewish

---

61. Riesebrodt, "Fundamentalismus," 23.
62. Ibid., 27.
63. Anonymous, "Hans Blüher."

people, but also bring down the Christian churches."⁶⁴ Others affirmed the theological perspective in order to come to terms with problems of race. In *Stimmen der Zeit* (published by Herder Verlag), Anton Koch argued that one could not "come to grips with the Jewish question with positivism and liberal 'tolerance.'" It was impossible "without physics and metaphysics," that is, "without theology."⁶⁵ To that extent, reviewers welcomed the disputation.⁶⁶

Some Christian writers criticized Blüher from a theological standpoint, however, and accused him of "neo-Hellenic paganism." Writing in the *Theologisches Literaturblatt* (Theological Literary Magazine), Hartling insisted that God's mercy was dependent on blood only from a Jewish (and not from a genuinely Christian) perspective.⁶⁷ Others—more traditionally—believed that the only "solution" to the dispute was Jewish conversion to Christianity, while Jews such as the well-known rabbi Joseph Carlebach criticized Blüher's anti-Semitic notion of truth.⁶⁸

Few non-Jews came to the defense of Jews. The conservative author Oskar A. H. Schmitz, who was close to the circle around the poet Stefan George and described himself as an "ideal mixture" of a Jewish mother and an "Aryan" father, tried to formulate a compromise between the different positions. He proposed a distinction between "desirable and undesirable Jews" as an alternative to the anti-Semitism that Blüher himself referred to as "radical."⁶⁹ After all, in his view, Jews could "still" improve and "turn themselves" around—an approach that was also not free of ambivalence and anti-Semitic implications.

64. Anonym, "Die Erhebung Israels."
65. Koch, "Streit um Israel," 65.
66. See, for example, the following reviews: W. R., "Streit um Israel"; R., "Streit um Israel"; Meinhold, "Religion—Theologie—Kirche"; Anonymous, "Streit um Israel"; Glaser, "Hans Blüher"; Müller, "Antimessianismus"; Anonymous, "Vom Büchertisch"; Niekisch, "Die Erhebung Israels."
67. Hartling, Review of *Streit um Israel*, 151.
68. Carlebach, "Hans Blüher"; Schriftleitung, "Anmerkungen."
69. Schmitz, "Wünschenswerte Juden"; idem, "Judenfrage."

Conclusions

We can conclude that the Christian-Jewish disputation between Schoeps and Blüher of 1933 is characterized by the following fundamentalist elements: a radical critique of modernity and its manifestations such as liberalism, egalitarianism, and rationality; the utopia of a racially pure, religious, and self-assured society in conjunction with a Manichaean, apocalyptic worldview; and the claim to be in possession of the truth of holy scripture, accessible only to the few who belonged to the primary race. Jesus becomes a figure of the "primary race," his *arete* is proof of the consistency of spiritual and natural, biological traits. "Blood" is a central theme in the dispute: it organizes the national and religious certainty of redemption and is not coincidentally located at the intersection of natural science and religion, modernity and tradition.

The extent to which fundamentalist movements are characterized by a specific relationship to politics is controversial. In this case, however, it is obvious that the religious discourse treats the foundations of the collective order—one in which the Germans believed themselves to be the elect and sought to occupy the imaginary position of the Jews. Because it was assumed that Christians and Jews enjoyed a special affinity, it was also considered that they shared a similar, or at least an interconnected destiny. Taken to the extreme, this meant that the Germans could only become "German" to the extent that the Jews became "Jewish" (according to the view of the German anti-Semite Paul de Lagarde, whose positions had some influence in the middle classes and the youth movement).[70] The fiction of a symbiosis became a reverse mimicry, since the Jewish religion appeared to have everything the Christian faith lacked: the certainty of being chosen, particularity, and the possibility of remaining "pure" and "unmixed," that is, of not disappearing (even without a state); to have a fixed identity and demonic powers; and to represent an indissoluble unity. While the Jewish "Other" was initially branded as weak and "feminine" when he (still) embodied the spirit of defeat immediately following World War I, later—after his promotion to a masculine and demonic force—, the aim was to supplant and succeed him.

The distance posited between God and humanity in Judaism is undermined and negated by the concept of an immediate "blood covenant" with God. And this appears to be typical not least of a Christian

---

70. Bruns, *Politik des Eros*, 385–86.

position that proceeds from an abolition of this distance when man becomes divine in the guise of the son of God, who here is quietly turned into the incarnation of German man.

The supposed transformation of pagan Eros into Christian love that Blüher sees in Christianity represents not an ethical law or morality, but rather a vitalist force that manifests the divine in the physically beautiful body and thereby creates a new, modernist boundary between the elect and the disinherited, the spiritual and the mass, which runs along the lines of religious physiognomy. Participation in *arete* is not coincidentally conceived as a communion of disciples and an associated resacralized conception of the state, which—beyond the boundaries of the religious—also represents the commonality between the two disputants. Schoeps, too, sees a particular predisposition toward redemption in blood and seed. He, too, believes in the divine theocratic state, which however functions less through vitality than through laws, which in turn derive directly from God.

Although Schoeps certainly recognized the vitalization in Blüher's manner of thinking and distanced himself from it, their shared experience of the youth movement and a certain adoration for the author of the homoerotic male-bonding concept let him enter the discussion. His aim to demonstrate a certain closeness between Judaism and German Protestantism in order to path the way for the Jewish youth to remain loyal to both—Prussia and their Jewish heritage—nevertheless remained the decisive motivation for him to engage in the religious dispute. Although the dispute was not quite leading to a reconciled end, Schoeps still tried to close the disputation of 1933 with an ironical remark by saying that God in his infinite goodness must have a sense of humor in order to bear the disputation between the two of them.

The life paths of the two men subsequently diverged radically. Schoeps, accompanied by a troop of young Jewish men, tried unsuccessfully to gain an audience with Hitler in order to convince him of the Prussian sentiments of Jewish youth. He was forced to flee to Sweden in 1938. His parents were deported and died at Auschwitz and Theresienstadt. Blüher, in contrast, was left unmolested under National Socialism. After the war he even managed to gain recognition as a "victim of fascism" based on his good relationship with Jews such as Schoeps, which gave him access to the much sought-after "Ration Card One." Schoeps, still a strong nationalist, already returned to Germany in 1946 and became professor of religious and intellectual history at the University of Erlangen in 1950.[71] Not long thereafter, he tried to connect with conservative circles but was soon excluded, not least because of his public support for the abolition of discrimination against homosexuals.[72] Disappointed, Schoeps saw to it that Blüher's works on (homosexual) male bonding were reprinted in postwar Germany. Blüher himself, who died in 1955, was discussed in the press as a homeopath, philosopher, and Kant scholar. His ideas on male bonding, but also his anti-Semitism, went largely unmentioned in postwar Germany.

In retrospect, the debate between Schoeps and Blüher at the beginning of the 1930s recalls not only the debate on Jewish emancipation around 1800 but also the immigration debate that has been unleashed anew in recent years in Germany. In particular, notions of a "Jewish gene" and a fixed "Muslim character" parallel earlier discussions of "blood." The search for the racial "substance" of religion has clearly lost little of its allure. Even today, religious and racial ordering systems are still closely intertwined. An invisible, assimilated "Other," however, appears to have taken on a newly dangerous quality of late, since he could be living amongst us as a "sleeper." From this perspective, the "nationalist rampage," as Schmitz clear-sightedly called it in 1926, is apparently a response that remains close at hand today.

Thilo Sarrazin's much-discussed book *Deutschland schafft sich ab* (*Germany Does Away with Itself, 2010*) also expresses fears that the very existence of the nation is threatened because there are too many non-Christians—in this case, Muslims—living in the country, a topic that catapulted Sarrazin onto the list of the bestselling non-fiction titles since 1945. Once again, the German nation is being conceptualized as an ethno-racial unit created above all through religious difference. Once again, a political problem is being wrapped in the garb of national-religious apocalypse. "We" are faced with nothing less than doom and annihilation. The remedy of a return to national values and a wave of births among ethnic-German women academics (who in the process also incidentally find their way back to subordinate positions), is part and parcel of this idea. In the name of religious conflicts, older forms of (cultural and eugenic) racism, which perhaps never wholly disap-

71. Schoeps, "Hitler ist nicht Deuschland."
72. Schoeps, "Soll Homosexualität strafbar bleiben"; Keilson-Lauritz, "Hans-Joachim Schoeps."

peared, have been reactivated. Even today, the "nomos of election" can easily become the "physis of biology," as Schoeps put it.[73]

Bibliography

Anonymous. "Die Erhebung Israels gegen die christlichen Güter." *Der Stahlhelm. Helden und Zeiten* 15/4 (Apr 17, 1932) 17.

Anonymous. "Vom Büchertisch, Hans Blüher: 1. Die Erhebung Israels gegen die christlichen Güter, 2. Der Standort des Christentums in der lebendigen Welt." *Niederdeutsche Kirchenzeitung. Evangelisch-lutherisches Halbmonatsblatt für Kirche und Volkstum in Niederdeutschland* 2/6 (Mar 15, 1932).

Anonymous. "Streit um Israel. Ein jüdisch-christliches Gespräch. Von Hans Blüher und Hans Joachim Schoeps." *Der deutsche Vorwärts* 2 (Apr 1933).

Anonymous [Sup. D. Dr. Matthes?]. "Hans Blüher: Die Erhebung Israels gegen die christlichen Güter und der Standort des Christentums in der lebendigen Welt." *Monatsblatt der Vereinigung der Evangelisch-Lutherischen innerhalb der preußischen Landeskirche* (bekenntnistreue Gruppe). Früher *Evangelische Kirchenzeitung*. Literarische Beilage zu 2/3 (Mar 1932).

Antoun, Richard T. *Understanding Fundamentalism: Christian, Islamic, and Jewish Movements*. Walnut Creek, CA: AltaMira, 2004.

Armstrong, Karen. *Im Kampf für Gott: Fundamentalismus in Christentum, Judentum und Islam*. München: Siedler, 2004.

Bendroth, Margaret Lamberts. *Fundamentalism & Gender, 1875 to the Present*. New Haven: Yale University Press, 1993.

Bertz, Inka. "Jüdische Renaissance." In *Handbuch der deutschen Reformbewegungen*, edited by Diethart Kerbs and Jürgen Reulecke, 551–64. Wuppertal: Hammer, 1998.

Blüher, Hans. *Die Aristie des Jesus von Nazareth: Philosophische Grundlegung der Lehre und der Erscheinungen Christi*. Prien: Kampmann & Schnabel, 1921.

———. *Die Erhebung Israels gegen die christlichen Güter*. M. e. Vorwort v. Hans Blüher [Weihn. 1931] u. e. bebilderten Anhang zu Martin Buber, Friedrich Gundolf u. zu „der Presse." Hamburg: Hanseatische Verlagsanstalt (Ringbücherei), 1931.

Blüher, Hans, and Hans-Joachim Schoeps. *Streit um Israel: Ein jüdisch-christliches Gespräch*. Hamburg: Hanseatische Verlagsanstalt, 1933.

Breuer, Stefan. *Ordnungen der Ungleichheit: Die deutsche Rechte im Widerstreit ihrer Ideen 1871–1945*. Darmstadt: Wissenschaftliche Buchgesellschaft, 2001.

Bruns, Claudia. "Eros, Macht und Männlichkeit: Männerbündische Konstruktionen in der deutschen Jugendbewegung zwischen Emanzipation und Reaktion." In *Jugendbewegte Geschlechterverhältnisse*, edited by Meike Sophia Baader and Susanne Rappe-Weber, 25–54. Schwalbach: Wochenschau-Verlag, 2012.

———. "The Politics of Eros. The German "Männerbund" between Anti-Feminism and Anti-Semitism in the Early Twentieth Century." In *Masculinity, Senses, Spirit*, edited by Katherine M. Faull, 153–90. Aperçus. Lewisburg, PA: Bucknell University Press, 2011.

---

73. Blüher and Schoeps, *Streit um Israel*, 27.

———. *Politik des Eros: Der Männerbund in Wissenschaft, Politik und Jugendkultur 1880–1934*. Vienna: Böhlau, 2008.

———. "Die 'metaphysische Pathologie' des Juden: Erkenntnistheoretische Dimensionen eines religiösen Rassismus um 1920." In *Lebendige Sozialgeschichte: Gedenkschrift für Peter Borowsky*, edited by Rainer Hering and Rainer Nicolaysen, 278–95. Wiesbaden: Westdeutscher Verlag, 2003.

Cancik, Hubert, and Uwe Puschner, editors. *Antisemitismus, Paganismus, Völkische Religion*. München: Saur, 2004.

Carlebach, Joseph. "Hans Blüher oder der neue antisemitische Wahrheitsbegriff." *Der Israelit: Centralorgan für das orthodoxe Judentum* 73/27 (1932) 1–3.

Faber, Richard. *Deutschbewusstes Judentum und jüdischbewusstes Deutschtum: Der historische und politische Theologe Hans-Joachim Schoeps*. Würzburg: Königshausen & Neumann, 2008.

———. "'Theokratie von unten versus Theokratie von oben': Die Antipoden Hans-Joachim Schoeps und Jacob Taubes." In *Wider den Zeitgeist: Studien zum Leben und Werk von Hans-Joachim Schoeps (1909–1980)*, edited by Gideon Botsch et al., 63–92. Hildesheim: Olms, 2009.

Figl, Johann. "Säkularisierung und Fundamentalismus." In *Religiöser Fundamentalismus: Vom Kolonialismus zur Globalisierung*, 2nd ed., edited by Clemens Six et al., 33–51. Innsbruck: Studienverlag, 2005.

Glaser, Ludwig. "Hans Blüher: Die Erhebung Israels gegen die christlichen Güter. Der Standort des Christentums in der lebendigen Welt. Streit um Israel." *Allgemeine Weltrundschau*, April 30, 1933, 743.

Grützmacher, Richard Heinrich. *Kritiker und Neuschöpfer der Religion im zwanzigsten Jahrhundert: Keyserling, L. Ziegler, Blüher, Chamberlain, Steiner, Scholz, Scheler, Hauck*. Leipzig: Deichert, 1921.

Hartling, D. von. Review of *Streit um Israel. Ein jüdisch-christliches Gespräch*, by Hans Blüher und Hans Joachim Schoeps. *Theologisches Literatur-Blatt* 10 (1934) 151.

Heilman, Samuel C. "Jews and Fundamentalism: Transnationalism versus Fundamentalism." *Journal of Ecumenical Studies* 42/1 (2007) 29–41.

Hempel, Wolfgang. "Hans-Joachim Schoeps und die deutsche Jugendbewegung—Texte." In *Wider den Zeitgeist: Studien zum Leben und Werk von Hans-Joachim Schoeps (1909–1980)*, edited by Gideon Botsch et al., 213–26. Hildesheim: Olms, 2009.

Hergemöller, Bernd-Ulrich. "Hans Blühers Männerwelten. Fragmente, Widersprüche, Perspektiven." *Invertito* 2 (2000) 58–84.

Hering, Rainer. "Säkularisierung, Entkirchlichung, Dechristianisierung und Formen der Rechristianisierung bzw: Resakralisierung in Deutschland." In *Völkische Religion und Krisen der Moderne: Entwürfe "arteigener" Glaubenssysteme seit der Jahrhundertwende*, edited by Stefanie von Schnurbein and Justus H. Ulbricht, 117–41. Würzburg: Königshausen & Neumann, 2001.

Hillerbrand, Hans J. "Hans-Joachim Schoeps als Religionswissenschaftler." In *Wider den Zeitgeist: Studien zum Leben und Werk von Hans-Joachim Schoeps (1909–1980)*, edited by Gideon Botsch et al., 45–62. Hildesheim: Olms, 2009.

Howland, Courtney W., editor. *Religious Fundamentalisms and the Human Rights of Women*. New York: Palgrave, 2001.

Huntington, Samuel P. *The Clash of Civilizations and the Remaking of World Order.* New York: Simon & Schuster, 2003.

Ingber, Michael. "Fundamentalismus im Judentum und in der Jüdisch-Israelischen Gesellschaft im Staat Israel." In *Religiöser Fundamentalismus: Vom Kolonialismus zur Globalisierung,* 2nd ed., edited by Clemens Six et al., 91–115. Innsbruck: Studienverlag, 2005.

Juergensmeyer, Mark. *The New Cold War?: Religious Nationalism Confronts the Secular State.* Berkeley: University of California Press, 1993.

Kaiser, Jochen-Christoph. "Erneuerungsbewegungen im Protestantismus." In *Handbuch der deutschen Reformbewegungen,* edited by Diethart Kerbs and Jürgen Reulecke, 581–94. Wuppertal: Hammer, 1998.

Keilson-Lauritz, Marita. "Hans-Joachim Schoeps, Hans Blüher und der Männerbund. Überlegungen zu Hans-Joachim Schoeps und dem Thema Homosexualität." In *Wider den Zeitgeist: Studien zum Leben und Werk von Hans-Joachim Schoeps (1909–1980),* edited by Gideon Botsch et al., 177–98. Hildesheim: Olms, 2009.

Keyserling, Hermann. "Zu Hans Blühers Aristie des Jesus von Nazareth" (1922). In *Das Erbe der Schule der Weisheit: Unveröffentlichte Essays und Buchbesprechungen,* introduced and selected by Arnold Keyserling, 1:129–31. Vienna: Palme, 1981.

Kienzler, Klaus. *Der religiöse Fundamentalismus: Christentum, Judentum, Islam.* 2nd ed. München: Beck, 1999.

Kläber, Kurt. "Blühers Christologie." *Die Tat* 13/10 (1922) 796–99.

Kläcker, Michael. "Erneuerungsbewegungen im römischen Katholizismus." In *Handbuch der deutschen Reformbewegungen,* edited by Diethart Kerbs and Jürgen Reulecke, 7–56. Wuppertal: Hammer, 1998.

Koch, Anton. "Streit um Israel." *Stimmen der Zeit* 7 (1932/1933) 64–66.

Kroll, Frank-Lothar. "Wider den Zeitgeist. Zum hundertsten Geburtstag des Historikers Hans-Joachim Schoeps." *Mitteldeutsches Jahrbuch für Kultur und Geschichte,* Sonderheft, 16 (2009) 127–40.

Lease, Gary. "Wer war hier Christ, wer Jude? Das Gespräch zwischen Hans-Joachim Schoeps und Hans Blüher." In *Das jüdisch-christliche Religionsgespräch,* edited by Heinz Kremers and Julius H. Schoeps, 114–30. Sachsenheim: Burg, 1988.

———. "Who Was the Christian, Who the Jew? The Dialogue between Hans-Joachim Schoeps and Hans Blüher." In *"Odd fellows" in the Politics of Religion: Modernism, National Socialism, and German Judaism,* 211–31. Berlin: de Gruyter, 1995.

LeVine, Mark. "What Is Fundamentalism, and How Do We Get Rid of It?" *Journal of Ecumenical Studies* 42/1 (2007) 15–28.

Linse, Ulrich. "Säkularisierung oder neue Religiosität? Zur religiösen Situation in Deutschland um 1900." *Recherches Germaniques* 17 (1997) 117–41.

Matthias, Leo. "Hans Blüher und das Christentum." *Der neue Merkur: Monatshefte* 5/11 (1922) 775–78.

Meinhold, Joh. "Religion—Theologie—Kirche: Hans Blüher; Hans Joachim Schoeps. Streit um Israel." *Deutsche Literaturzeitung* 5/17 (1934) 769–72.

Mohler, Armin. *Die konservative Revolution in Deutschland 1918–1932: Ein Handbuch.* Hauptband und Ergänzungsband (mit Korrigenda) in einem Band

(Diss. Basel, 1949). 4th ed. Darmstadt: Wissenschaftliche Buchgesellschaft, 1994.
Müller, Ferdinand. "Antimessianismus." *Kölnische Volkszeitung*, Jan 28, 1933.
Müller-Jung, Joachim. "Sarrazins Biologismus. Phantasma 'Juden-Gen.'" *Frankfurter Allgemeine Zeitung*, Aug 30, 2010, n.p. Online: http://www.faz.net/aktuell/feuilleton/debatten/integration/sarrazins-biologismus-phantasma-juden-gen-11028466.html.
Nanko, Ulrich. *Die deutsche Glaubensbewegung: Eine historische und soziologische Untersuchung*. Marburg: Diagonal, 1993.
Niekisch, Ernst. "Die Erhebung Israels gegen die christlichen Güter." *Widerstand: Zeitschrift für nationalrevolutionäre Politik* 7 (1932) 26–29.
Prutsch, Markus Josef. *Fundamentalismus: Das "Projekt der Moderne" und die Politisierung des Religiösen*. 2nd ed. Vienna: Passagen, 2008.
Puschner, Uwe. *Die völkische Bewegung im wilhelminischen Kaiserreich: Sprache—Rasse—Religion*. Darmstadt: Wissenschaftliche Buchgesellschaft, 2001.
R. "Streit um Israel. Ein jüdisch-christliches Gespräch von Hans Blüher und Hans Joachim Schoeps, Hamburg 1933." *Die Christliche Welt*, Mar 18, 1933, n.p.
Rheins, Carl J. "Deutscher Vortrupp, Gefolgschaft deutscher Juden 1933–1935." *Publications of the Leo Baeck Institute: Year Book* 26 (1981) 207–29.
Riesebrodt, Martin. "Was ist 'religiöser Fundamentalismus'?" In *Religiöser Fundamentalismus: Vom Kolonialismus zur Globalisierung*, 2nd ed., edited by Clemens Six et al., 13–32. Innsbruck: Studienverlag, 2005.
Sarrazin, Thilo. *Deutschland schafft sich ab: Wie wir unser Land aufs Spiel setzen*. München: Deutsche Verlags-Anstalt, 2010.
Sarrazin: Eine deutsche Debatte. Edited by Deutschlandstiftung Integration. 2nd ed. München: Piper, 2010.
Schieder, Wolfgang. "Sozialgeschichte der Religion im 19. Jahrhundert: Bemerkungen zur Forschungslage." In *Religion und Gesellschaft im 19. Jahrhundert*, edited by Wolfgang Schieder, 11–28. Stuttgart: Klett-Cotta, 1993.
Schmitz, Oscar A. H. "Die falsch gestellte Judenfrage" (1923). In *Das geistige Deutschland angesichts der jüdischen Frage: Positionen 1922–1938*, edited by Oliver Humberg and Stephan Hötzel, 49–57. Velbert: Humberg & Fresen, 1994.
———. "Wünschenswerte und nicht wünschenswerte Juden." *Der Jude*, Sonderheft, 1 (1925) 17–33.
Schnurbein, Stefanie von. *Religion als Kulturkritik: Neugermanisches Heidentum im 20. Jahrhundert*. Heidelberg: Winter, 1992.
Schnurbein, Stefanie von, and Justus H. Ulbricht, editors. *Völkische Religion und Krisen der Moderne: Entwürfe "arteigener" Glaubenssysteme seit der Jahrhundertwende*. Würzburg: Königshausen & Neumann, 2001.
Schoeps, Hans Joachim. "Antwort an Hans Blüher [Die Erhebung Israels gegen die christlichen Güter]." *Central Verein-Zeitung* 11/6 (1932) 47.
———. *Ja—nein—und trotzdem: Erinnerungen, Begegnungen, Erfahrungen*. Mainz: Hase & Koehler, 1974.
———. *Rückblicke. Die letzten dreißig Jahre (1925–1955) und danach*. 2nd ed. Berlin: Haude & Spener, 1963.
———. "Soll Homosexualität strafbar bleiben?" *Der Monat* 15/171 (1962) 19–27.

Schoeps, Julius H. "'Hitler ist nicht Deutschland': Der Nationalsozialismus, das Exil in Schweden und die Rückkehr von Hans-Joachim Schoeps in die ehemalige Heimat." In *Wider den Zeitgeist: Studien zum Leben und Werk von Hans-Joachim Schoeps (1909–1980)*, edited by Gideon Botsch et al., 227–48. Hildesheim: Olms, 2009.

Schriftleitung des Central-Vereins. "Anmerkungen zur Debatte zwischen Blüher und Schoeps um Hans Blühers 'Die Erhebung Israels gegen die christlichen Güter.'" *Central Verein-Zeitung* 11/6 (1932) 46.

Schwarz, Patrik, editor. *Die Sarrazin-Debatte: Eine Provokation—und die Antworten.* Hamburg: Die Zeit, 2010.

Spengler, Oswald. *Der Untergang des Abendlandes: Umrisse einer Morphologie der Weltgeschichte.* 2 vols. Vienna: Braunmüller, 1918; München: Beck, 1922.

Tibi, Bassam. *Fundamentalismus im Islam. Eine Gefahr für den Weltfrieden?* Darmstadt: Primus, 2002.

Weingart, Peter, et al. *Rasse, Blut und Gene: Geschichte der Eugenik und Rassenhygiene in Deutschland.* 2nd ed. Frankfurt: Suhrkamp, 1996.

Winnecken, Andreas. *Ein Fall von Antisemitismus. Zur Geschichte und Pathogenese der deutschen Jugendbewegung vor dem Ersten Weltkrieg.* Köln: Wissenschaft & Politik, 1991.

W. R. "Streit um Israel." *Deutsches Adelsblatt* (1933).

Zerger, Johannes. *Was ist Rassismus? Eine Einführung.* Göttingen: Lamuv, 1997.

Antifundamentalism as Fundamentalism

Reading Thilo Sarrazin through Joseph McCarthy
Some Thoughts on Supremacy, Secularism,
Gender, and Culturalization[1]

GABRIELE DIETZE

Thomas Meyer, one of the most influential German theorists of fundamentalism, perceives of the latter as a "revolt against modernity," engendered by the dialectics of this very same modernity, which "produces its own antithesis as fundamentalism in times of great societal crisis."[2]

Other theorists of fundamentalism claim just the opposite and assert together with Shmuel Eisenstadt that "fundamentalism is a thoroughly modern phenomenon,"[3] but they still come to the same diagnosis of crisis: "Fundamentalist movements tend to arise in periods of rapid social and cultural change, especially in situations in which there

1. Translated from German by Leah Chizek.
2. Meyer, *Fundamentalismus*, 7.
3. Eisenstadt, "Fundamentalism," 299. For an overview of contemporary theories on fundamentalism, see Riesebrodt, *Fundamentalismus als Protestbewegung*. He distinguishes between theorists of ongoing secularization, who see fundamentalism either as an assault against modernity (Meyer, *Fundamentalismus*), an attempt to adapt to modernity (Gellner, *Muslim Society*), or an effect of deficient religious markets (Stark and Bainbridge, *Theory of Religion*).

develop ... growing differentiation, growing diversity of ways and styles of life."[4] Societies in crisis tend to give rise to *political fundamentalism*, which, following Meyer, is a mode or a metapolitics: "which comes from a position of absolute truth, be it from above or from within, and which demands the right to oust the rules of democracy, political relativism, the inviolability of human rights, tolerance, pluralism, and room for error."[5] These particular kinds of political fundamentalism will be the subject of my article. I will focus here on two societies, each in a different historical period:

1. The post-1945 United States during its rise as a global power and as the Soviet Union emerged as its major antagonist.
2. Late twentieth- and early twenty-first-century Germany as it transformed from a society defined by an autochthonous population into a multicultural country shaped by immigration.

These liminal periods can be distinguished by strong polemics against allegedly dangerous forms of "fundamentalism" introduced by unwelcome antagonists: orthodox communism as *ideology* in the first case, and Islam as *culture* in the second. Both of these arguments understand themselves to be strictly antifundamentalist critique, yet—and this is my central argument—the "antifundamentalist" position in each case is marked by the very defining characteristics of fundamentalism.

It is a well-known strategy to reproach strong and passionate modes of criticism by adopting the very same dogmatism these reproaches are intended to address. But the cases at hand exhibit "strategic fundamentalisms," which, while initially peculiar, eventually become normalized and are transformed into ontologisms. Both movements but especially the latter—the critique of Islamist fundamentalism—mobilize individuals and political groups with liberal or even leftist identities in addition to the expected conservative constituencies. Their common political repertoire is a series of performative gestures that supposedly reveal criminal doings, unmask villains, and identify structural injustice and systemic oppression. The means to the desired political end is the rhetoric of investigation, clarification, and illumination—in other words, the rhetoric of enlightenment.

4. Eisenstadt, "Fundamentalism," 272.
5. Meyer, *Fundamentalismus*, 157.

In *Dialectic of Enlightenment*, Theodor W. Adorno and Max Horkheimer uncompromisingly stated that "Enlightenment is totalitarian."[6] I do and will not follow Adorno/Horkheimer in any detail, whose ultimate concern here is the critique of instrumental reason and the exclusionary power of disintegrating rationality. But by modifying their statement somewhat to say that "Enlightenment *can* be totalitarian," I will nonetheless adapt their dictum as a motto—as the guiding light of my investigation, so to speak.

Anticommunism

Critiques of fundamentalism particularly tend to become totalitarian—let's call it fundamentalist—in cases when the fundamentalism under attack is cast as the defining difference, the "constitutive outside"[7] *to* or the other side *of* a central binary opposition structuring a society's identity. Most of the second half of the twentieth century was dominated by the East-West conflict, which was translated into antagonistic dichotomies such as capitalism versus communism, one-party dictatorship versus representative democracy, and individualism versus collectivism. On the basis of certain agreed-upon features, Soviet as well as Maoist style communism has been characterized as "secular ideological fundamentalism"[8] or "secular religion."[9]

Orthodox communism's production of truth led to the prosecution of dissenters as "traitors," forcing them through blackmail and torture into "confessing" their alleged treason at Stalinist show trials. Given these historical facts, it is all the more striking that one of the most powerful Western anticommunist (and therefore supposedly antifundamentalist) enterprises, US senator Joseph McCarthy's famous House Committee on Un-American Activities (1945–1961), was staged as a mind-controlling public inquisition quite similar in style to the Soviet

---

6. Adorno and Horkheimer, *Dialektik*, 10.

7. The Derridean notion of "constitutive outside" has been used in work expanding on Gramsci's political theory; Laclau and Mouffe, *Hegemony*, 127–34. Judith Butler has also employed it to inquire into the "constitutive outside" required in the construction heteronormativity; Butler, *Bodies*, 157.

8. Meyer, *Fundamentalismus*, 162: "säkulär-weltanschauliche[r] Fundamentalismus."

9. Gellner, "Fundamentalism," 278.

show trials. McCarthy framed his anticommunist propaganda by using a rigid either-or rhetoric that thereby stressed a second binary—atheism and Christianity—not yet mentioned: "Today we are engaged in a final, all-out battle between communistic atheism and Christianity. The modern champions of communism have selected this as the time, and ladies and gentlemen, the chips are down—they are truly down."[10] One can speak of McCarthyist anticommunist fundamentalism as a kind of derivative fundamentalism, or fundamentalism of the second order. McCarthy's criticism of orthodox communism was not inappropriate in some of the arguments he provided, but he ultimately crossed the line by suspecting every middle-of-the-road liberal of high treason. The victims of this culture of suspicion were school teachers, Hollywood script writers, trade unionists, civil servants in the army and in the federal administration, and last but not least a poisoned public sphere. Journalist Edward R. Morrow, who, in 1954, finally worked up the courage to counter McCarthyism's witch hunt, said on the television news show *See It Now*: "His primary achievement has been in confusing the public mind, as between the internal and the external threats of Communism. We must not confuse dissent with disloyalty . . . We will not be driven by fear into an age of unreason . . . And whose fault is that? Not really his. He didn't create this situation of fear; he merely exploited it—and rather successfully."[11] It is interesting that the only theorist I came across who theorizes antifundamentalism as fundamentalism in any detail, Mark Jürgensmayer, likewise refers to fear in developing his concept: "In many parts of the world not fundamentalism but the fear of it has become a problem; in some cases this fear has led to a violation of human rights."[12]

Occidentalism as the Meta-Racism of Elites

Fear of Islamic fundamentalism is one of the major elements feeding present anti-Muslim resentment in Europe in general and Germany in

10. Speech in Wheeling, West Virginia, Feb 9, 1950, quoted in http://en.wikiquote.org/wiki/Joseph_McCarthy, accessed Nov. 23, 2011.

11. "See It Now: A Report on Senator Joseph R. McCarthy," Mar. 9, 1954, CBS-TV, see transcript: http://www.lib.berkeley.edu/MRC/murrowmccarthy.html, accessed Sept 9, 2011.

12. Jürgensmeyer, "Antifundamentalism," 353.

particular. But the fear of a potentially terrorist political religion after 9/11 and the wars in Iraq and Afghanistan are not the only issues in the neo-Orientalist conglomerate, which came into being as the East/West divide crumbled after the collapse of the Socialist bloc. An Orient/Occident binary replaced anticommunism as the unifying ideology and put anti-Muslim resentment at the center of European self-affirmation. Derived from Edward Said's Orientalism as the invention of an Oriental Other, I would like to call this process of constructing European supremacy over and against an imagined Orient *Occidentalism*.[13]

Occidentalist German rejection of Muslim migration and long-standing denial of citizenship for migrants was met with a culturalist[14] vision of all Muslims as traditionalist, zealously religious, patriarchal, women-oppressing, and hate-preaching, despite social data regularly confirming that only 5 percent of the five million strong Muslim population (citizens or not) lean toward an orthodox strand of the Islam faith.[15] The Green Party and other actors and agencies of civil society promoted multiculturalism, in line with the definition in the 2010 annual report of the Council of Experts of German Foundations on Integration and Migration: namely, to "[learn] to tolerate heterogeneity and difference as a normal state of affairs."[16] But these liberalizing discourses were always counteracted by xenophobic ones.

Beyond the state agencies and lawmakers who maintain a pattern of structural discrimination through legislation in the form of immigration laws, Muslim questionnaires, rules for the reunion of families, mandatory integration courses, and so on, a very diverse constellation of public intellectuals started to publish political manifestos against Islam in general and against Muslim migration to Germany in particular around 2005: German Turkish female intellectuals criticizing the position of women in Islam such as Necla Kelek and Seyran Ates were

13. Said, *Orientalism*. For a more extensive discussion of the term "Occidentalism," see Dietze, "Occidentalism." My usage is different to Buruma and Margalit, who employ the term for Eastern resentment toward the West (Buruma and Margalit, *Occidentalism*) but in tune with Latin American postcolonial critics such as Coronil or Mignolo, who speak of "Beyond Occidentalism" or "(Post)Occidentalism."

14. For the inherent racism of culturalist perspectives, see Mamdani, *Beyond Rights Talk*.

15. Figures quoted in Herrmann and Wierth, "Gene."

16. Sachverständigenrat deutscher Stiftungen, *Einwanderungsgesellschaft*, 16.

supported by mainstream feminists such as Alice Schwarzer, foreign correspondents such us Gerd Konzelmann and Peter Scholl-Latour, and structurally liberal German Jewish intellectuals such as Henryk M. Broder and Ralph Giordano, as well as more right-wing conspiracy theorists such as Ulf Ulfkotte.[17] This discursive production of Occidentalism was and is very visible on talkshows and keeps a high profile in print media debates in daily and weekly newspapers, serious and yellow press alike.[18] Sabine Schiffer has distilled some of the selective figures of thought that occur in this kind of criticism of Islam: tuning out, emphasizing, repeating, and *pars pro toto* symbolism.[19]

Even if these manifestos have had perhaps two or three reprints, nothing even comes the close to the success of Thilo Sarrazin's book *Deutschland schafft sich ab. Wie wir unser Land auf das Spiel setzen* (Germany Does Away with Itself. How We Are Placing our Nation in Jeopardy). Published in August 2010, it had sold 1.3 million hard copies by January 2012 (paperback forthcoming) and is the best-selling political book ever in the history of the Federal Republic of Germany.[20]

Why is it that anti-Islamic resentment is suddenly so much in the foreground of political debate since Sarrazin's publication? While I certainly cannot provide fully sufficient or exhaustive answers in this very complex matter, I will offer two elements of explanation. The first argument has to do with Sarrazin's status as a onetime leading member of several powerful administrations: after studying economics, he served in state government and the federal ministry of economics, as state senator for finances in the city government of Berlin, and finally as the vice president of the German Federal Reserve Bank. He does not fit the profile of a disgruntled intellectual, feminist, or aging investigative journalist in search of taboo-breaking publicity. Instead, he is a power holder and has used his clout before in public and legislative affairs.

Listening to *him* say that immigration was wrong and that multiculturalism has shipwrecked autochtonous (Kanak Attac uses the

---

17. Just to give some titles: Ates, *Der Multikulti-Irrtum*; Broder, *Hurra, wir kapitulieren!*; Kelek, *Die fremde Braut*; Lachmann, *Tödliche Toleranz*; Schwarzer, *Gotteskrieger und die falsche Toleranz*; Ulfkotte, *SOS Abendland*.

18. See an analysis of the Islam-critical formation as a group in Schneiders, "Schattenseite."

19. Schiffer, *Darstellung des Islam*.

20. For the figures, see Schirrmacher, "Frau Merkel."

term "bio-German") Germans, leaving them on the brink of becoming outnumbered and forcibly Islamicized in the near future, has provided large segments of the general public with an enormous psychological outlet. Polls have long indicated resentment toward migrants in over 50 percent of the population.[21] But published opinion (not including tabloids), as well as state agencies—formerly led by Social Democrat/Green Party as well as Social Democrat/Christian Democrat coalition governments (the former is referred to colloquially in Germany as the "red/green," the latter as the "red/black" coalition)—have more or less successfully managed to contain resentment and reroute things in the direction of an acceptable and accepted diversity (the percentage of persons expressing resentment over immigration sank below 50 percent in 2009). Open xenophobia was discarded by most authorities, and some "winds of change" even whispered that Germany is not only an immigration state, but that immigration itself is desirable and necessary, and that diversity might even enrich the country.

The new coalition of Christian Democrats (CDU/CSU) and Free Democrats (FDP) that assumed control of the federal government in 2009 reverted to a strategy of scapegoating minorities, targeting recipients of social security first and then migrants, who allegedly resisted *integration* in addition to being recipients of social security. Sarrazin's book was packaged as a dissident, taboo-breaking enterprise but was welcomed by the public as a "message from above," as a license to tell the "truth" that allowed for the expression of legitimate feelings. In my view, racism very often works like an ever-present bacterial culture: secured in a laboratory, it might not cause evil, but brought out in the open and fertilized by caretakers in high places, it inflames and infects. *Stern* journalist Hans Ulrich Jörgens writes, "The case of Sarrazin is the largest collateral media damage I can think of [in the history of the BRD]."[22]

Coming back to the general argument, I see a synergetic effect, which has resulted from current xenophobic federal politics as well as Sarrazin's book. The supposedly reasonable discourse to "integrate or leave," officially sponsored by the state and Sarrazin's allegedly dissident

21. Answering the question "Do you think there are too many foreigners in Germany?" the following percentage of people answered "yes": in 2003, 59.1 percent; 2004, 59.8 percent; 2005, 61.2 percent; 2006, 59.3 percent; 2007, 54.7 percent; 2008, 52.0 percent; and 2009, 45.8 percent; Leibold, "Fremdenfeindlichkeit," 154.

22. Jörges, "Ungeheuer."

discourses, serve to strengthen and intensify each other. The populace is not the actor in this game but the cheering crowd; a government in danger of losing elections takes refuge in appealing to the imagined cultural identity of an autochthonous population. One could also say that they construct an occidentalist identity superior to the Muslim world both within and beyond the country in order to quell economic and cultural panic. To drive the argument one step further: I would say that Occidentalism is not only the Achilles' heel for those who have lost out in the process of modernization, as social scientists would have us believe,[23] but also—and maybe even more so—a so-called meta-racism of elites,[24] for it is the elites who ignite the process and profit from resentment by riding the waves of populist sentiment.

Sarrazin's Sayings and his Fundamentalist Edge

Before I finally come back to the question of the fundamentalism of antifundamentalism, I will briefly review the most important ideas from Sarrazin's widely (and wildly) discussed book. His general thesis is as follows, and I quote him in his own words: "The great majority of Arabs and Turks are neither willing to integrate nor capable of doing so. I don't have to acknowledge anyone who lives off the state, rejects this same state, fails to care sensibly for his children's education, and constantly turns out new little headscarf maidens."[25] Translated into demographic terms, this diagnosis is then construed so as to make the following claim (once again in his own words): "It has been scientifically proven that fifty to eighty percent of intelligence is hereditary. What I'm saying is therefore the result of plain and straightforward logical analysis: if those with less than average intelligence have a higher fertility rate, then the average intelligence of the entire population sinks."[26] It's not only the average intelligence of Germany that is threatened but its cultural identity as well, as this last direct quotation indicates: "I don't want the

---

23. Such an argument would affirm the notion of "losers of modernization" (*Modernisierungsverlierer*), see Jäger, *Die rechtsextreme Versuchung*. For a somewhat more skeptical analysis, see Spier, *Modernisierungsverlierer*.

24. For further elaboration of the term, see Dietze, "Occidentalism," 98–99.

25. See the interview with Thilo Sarrazin "Klasse statt Masse," *Lettre International*.

26. See the interview with Thilo Sarrazin, "Sind Muslime dümmer," *DIE ZEIT*.

land of my grandchildren and great-grandchildren to become predominantly Muslim, Turkish and Arabic to be widely spoken, women to wear headscarves, and the patterns of daily life to be determined by the call of the muezzins."[27] I will not analyze or criticize this social Darwinist demography and its eugenic taint (one could just as well say scientific racism) in any detail, because I think it speaks for itself. It is a very well-known nativist pattern, driven by the fear that an autochthonous population will one day become outnumbered by immigrants. This narrative, long present in nineteenth-century Malthusian thought and Social Darwinism during the nineteenth and twentieth centuries, fell out of favor in the wake of Nazi eugenics and the Holocaust but was recycled by American social scientists Richard J. Herrnstein and Charles Murray in *The Bell Curve* in 1994; more recently, it has reemerged in the form of right-wing populist manifestos throughout Europe as well, where it is also espoused by Jean-Marie Le Pen in France, Geert Wilders in the Netherlands, and Christoph Blocher in Switzerland.

What interests me more is Sarrazin's connection to fundamentalism. One can call the aforementioned pseudoscientific narrative racism, but there is nothing specifically fundamentalist about it. Rather, fundamentalism is instantiated where Sarrazin refers to the foundations of his thought. Having been attacked as fundamentalist, he openly adopts the term:

> "*Certain points are nonnegotiable* [Sarrazin's emphasis]. What's more, any set of values has something fundamentalist about it in the end; this is just as true for the basic ideas of the Enlightenment and the resulting separation between church and state . . . Any manner of fundamentalism is trapped if it is supposed to justify itself since it has no more ground to fall back on, and this applies to 'final doctrines' [*letzte Glaubenssätze*] (see further down) as much as it does to any belief in human rights, civic freedoms, and enlightenment. Accusing Islam's critics of fundamentalism consequently amounts to nothing. After all, it's true."[28]

Here we come to a crucial point in the "enlightened" critique of fundamentalism. Sarrazin seriously misconceives Enlightenment as a belief system with a set of irreproachable axioms. This misunderstand-

27. Sarrazin, *Deutschland*, 308.
28. Ibid. 274.

ing revises Enlightenment so that it is no longer defined by the emancipatory practice of leading oneself from Kantian "self-imposed immaturity" (*selbstverschuldete Unmündigkeit*) to freedom but rather by an ontology with normative strands. Secularity is one of the decisive features of the European version of this kind of Enlightenment dogmatism. In contrast to the United States, which sees itself as a society descended from religious dissenters and where religious freedom and observance are thus considered central values, European Enlightenment understood itself as a struggle against religious (read: Catholic) dogmatism, inquisition, and the divine right of kings.[29]

Secularism

Insisting on the secular nature of occidental societies is a tendency that has recently come under criticism by postcolonial theorists and anthropologists of religion. One of the most important such critics is the anthropologist and postcolonial theorist Talal Asad, who was born in Saudi Arabia to a Polish Pakastani diplomat father, himself a Jewish-born convert to Islam, and a Saudi Muslim mother. Motivated by the severity and (unacknowledged) assumption of its own universality with which the Occident acted in a number of very different conflicts with political Islam, Asad's critique spans from the Rushdie controversy to the subject of suicide bombing. In the former case, he claims to expose the voice of colonial disciplining in the British reflex, and his consideration of the latter challenges Western reactions with the question as to why aggression in the name of God is more alarming to the Western public than killing in the name of secular nations or democracy.

If we consider the extensive reception of Asad's work to be the major contemporary opponent to the Western cultural war against Islam, we cannot avoid encountering a variety of aggressive or at least irritated reactions to the question above, which has itself undergone several reformulations. Judith Butler's remarks in the volume *Is Critique Secular?* (2009) keenly address this issue: "If Asad's questions upsets us . . . we become aware of the contingent conditions under which we feel shock, outrage and moral revulsion. And since we can only make sense of why we feel so much more horror in the face of one mode of death-dealing

29. For further explanation on the difference between "enlightened" religiosity in the US and European antireligious secularism, see Casanova, "Secularization."

than in the face of another through recourse to implicitly racist and civilizational schemes organizing and sustaining affect differentially, we end up feeling shock by our lack of shock . . . We realize, that we have already judged or evaluated the worth of certain lives over others."[30] In his work *Genealogies of Religion* (1993), Asad thwarts the Western notion of secularity as an emancipation movement won in a battle against despotic religion. He shows that the term religion as we understand it today first developed with the construction of the "Great Other of liberal tolerance."[31] He argues, moreover, that the secular public sphere originating from this battle is not a space of Habermasian communication aspiring to be free of domination (*herrschaftsfreie Kommunikation*) but rather one which places secular worldviews above religious ones and thus produces religious, Islamic non-humans.[32]

Similar to Asad but in another vain, the philosopher and theologian Heiner Bielefeldt questions the alleged secularism of Western society in general; he speaks instead of "baptized secularity."[33] By appropriating the biblical saying "[r]ender to Caesar the things that are Caesar's, and to God the things that are God's" (Mark 12:17) as the original model for the "separation of powers" and the "separation of church and state," some theorists understand Enlightenment as a genuinely Christian enterprise.[34] Thilo Sarrazin concurs with Rüdiger Safranski, who perceives present-day Christianity as a "civil religion" with a secular faith in "inalienable human rights" as well as in "the separation of church and state."[35]

Following this line of thinking, people of a non-Christian orientation do not have any legitimate space available to them in the framework of a constitutional order now defined as Christian.[36] Muslim migrants

30. Butler, "Sensibility," 108.

31. See Asad, *Genealogies*.

32. For further elaboration on Asad's thought provoking interventions, see Scott and Hirschkind, *Powers*. For Habermas's most recent stances on secularism, see Habermas, "Dialektik."

33. Bielefeldt, "Zwischen Kulturkampf und Integralismus," 480.

34. Pannenberg, "Civil Religion," quoted in Bielefeldt, "Menschenrechte," 480.

35. Sarrazin, *Deutschland*, 275, quoting Safranski, "Heiße und kalte Religionen."

36. Nowadays Christian heritage is more broadly defined as "Judeo-Christian" heritage. Given recent German history, it cannot be seen without a certain irony that Chancellor Merkel called upon "Judeo-Christian tradition" (*jüdisch-christliche Tradition*) in 2010; see "Merkel verweist auf christlich-jüdische Tradition."

in particular, whose religion is seen as structurally incapable of Enlightenment, fall victim to exclusion. Against this understanding of enlightenment, Bielefeld maintains that the separation of church and state in the wake of religious wars was *not* designed to appoint and support the state as an agent enforcing Christian "baptized" secularism but as a mediator granting religious pluralism.[37] Sarrazin's triumphalist affirmation of the fundamentalist nature of "final doctrines," human rights, and freedom misses the point of enlightenment—namely, to appease religious conflict—and is therefore fundamentalist but not on the same grounds he himself thinks he is. His unenlightened fundamentalism is all the more dangerous because of its zealous politics of social exclusion.

Sexual Politics of Anti-Islamist Fundamentalism

Classical modern fundamentalisms, as Riesebrodt has developed so convincingly in his book *Fundamentalismus als patriarchalische Protestbewegung*[38] (Fundamentalism as Patriarchal Protest Movement), is based on a masculinity in crisis, which resists modernism's particularism by affirming power over the family and especially over women. The antifundamentalisms discussed here dwell on sexual politics, which is always race politics as well. On the surface, anticommunism seems to circumvent the gender question but openly used its powers of intimidation to keep black resistance against US racial apartheid in check.[39]

The gender question in McCarthyism was dealt with on a more subtle level: in the age of enforced domesticity that lasted from the late forties to the early sixties, it would have been difficult in any case to slander communist regimes whose rhetoric supported the emancipation of women, at least in the workforce and in certain public service sectors dealing with children. Although there were some arguments about gender in anticommunist subdiscourses that criticized alleged gender equality in the Eastern bloc for masculinizing women who worked as miners and construction workers, gender generally did not matter much.

37. Bielefeldt, "Zwischen Kulturkampf und Integralismus," 486–87.
38. Riesebrodt, "Fundamentalismus, Säkularisierung."
39. Berg, "Black Civil Rights," 81–82. For example, in an opportunistic move in 1947, the civil rights organization NAACP ended its support of the UN initiative *An Appeal to the World* after the Soviet Union offered to support the African American struggle.

This changed dramatically with occidentalist antifundamentalism of the Sarrazin brand. The gender question took center stage, focusing on the image of the oppressed Muslim woman: forced to wear headscarves and enter marriages, and threatened with honor killings by "oriental patriarchs." This development marked a distinct discursive phenomenon, which can be referred to as the "culturalization" of ethnic and religious difference[40] and, in particular, the "culturalization of gender relations."[41] The term culturalization refers to claims that late modern racisms are characterized by their decoupling from biological or "chromatic" markers. It is in this sense that neo-racism[42] is said to argue in terms of "culture." However, the term culture in this case is not intended as a flexible concept in continuous flux and deemed capable of modernizing and adapting to new surroundings; rather, it connotes a static notion that is territorially bound to its origins and typically regarded as archaic and traditional. Wendy Brown summarizes the cultural *dispositif* of neo-racism with the following: "'we' have culture while culture has 'them,' or we *have* a culture while they *are* culture. Or we are democracy while they are culture [Brown's emphasis]."[43]

Within such logics, gender regimes and especially women are made to embody an alleged cultural stasis. It follows that Western condemnation of female genital mutilation (FGM), for example, without contextual knowledge of particular places, times, and power structures, comes to indicate a supposed African backwardness.[44] Similarly, the Muslim practice of veiling—conflated with the much less invasive habit of wearing a headscarf—is made to represent Islamist oppression of women in a so-called oriental patriarchy. The image of the veiled woman is furthermore and simultaneously held to signify alleged Islamist fanaticism, hate preaching, and terrorism. Perhaps unsurprisingly, this discourse is not designed to further the "liberation" or secularization of Muslim women but rather to install that which is accordingly denoted "Muslim culture" as the "constitutive outside"[45] of Occidentalism.

40. Chanock, "Culture."
41. Rommelspacher, "Dominante Diskurse."
42. Balibar, "Neo-Rassismus."
43. Brown, *Regulating Aversion*, 17.
44. Narayan, "Essence of Culture."
45. See n6 above.

While equating Muslim women with a supposedly static and archaic culture on the one hand, this discourse makes the claim that the emancipation of Western women has already been achieved on the other. Any allegation of sexism can thus be denied and transferred to the "oriental patriarch." Accordingly, Margret Jäger calls this neo-orientalist pattern the "ethnicization of sexism."[46] Consisting of Western male dominance, sexism, and the culturalization (read: racialization) of a homogenized image of Muslim persons, this matrix produces something I have elsewhere called the "occidentalist gender pact."[47] By stigmatizing "oriental" women as oppressed, occidental women are performatively staged as already emancipated. Or, to put it differently: the occidental gender pact is a peace treaty between the protagonists of an unfinished revolution (Western women) and the occidental sex-gender system at the expense of Muslim women.

Epitomized by the headscarf, this generalized figure operates as a condensation in the psychoanalytical sense, or as a "collective symbol"[48] of cultural supremacy that pushes white women up the ladder of civilization. One could also claim that the image of the woman wearing a headscarf is an apotropaic sign of the deficits of women's emancipation in the Western world—deficits that are felt but not acknowledged. The culturalization of gender relations results not only in fundamentalist claims of an allegedly homogenous Muslim womanhood; in a similarly fundamentalist maneuver, "enlightened" occidental femininity is made static, unproblematic, and undifferentiated as well. Both conceptions are presented as defining features of a hierarchy of civilizations in which religious traditionalism is inferior to secular and democratic "emancipation," which rests at the top. The two opposing concepts that constitute this line of thought are neither thought of as individual nor historical, but presented as static signifiers for either "archaic" or "enlightened" societies.

Conclusion

The two versions of antifundamentalist fundamentalism mentioned above share quite an array of similar features. Both discourses operate in four dimensions: Firstly, they are paranoid constructions of hege-

46. Jäger, *Fatale Effekte*.
47. Dietze, "Occidentalism," 99–100.
48. Link, "Kollektivsymbolik."

monic majorities in crisis, executed by acting (McCarthy) or former state agents (Sarrazin). Secondly, they target a group of people *within* society and organize a pattern of discrimination (liberals in the postwar US and Muslim migrants with and without German citizenship). Thirdly, both fundamentalisms work as smokescreens hiding serious social injustice in their very own country. It is mostly overlooked that, at its peak, McCarthyism overshadowed racial apartheid.[49] (This is one of the reasons why prominent black leaders at the time such as W. E. B. Du Bois, Paul Robeson, Richard Wright, Ralph Ellison, Harry Belafonte and last but not least Angela Davis were attracted to Soviet-style party communism as one of the very few possible allies in their fight for racial justice). Frequently overlooked with regard to anti-Muslim fundamentalism is the fact that the culturalization *of* and focus *on* Muslim gender regimes renders deficits in Western struggles for gender justice and emancipation invisible.

Finally, by performing ritualistic self-assurance and self-affirmation, both versions of antifundamentalist fundamentalism generate supremacy. Where McCarthyism is concerned, it was the alleged ideological supremacy of Western freedom and democracy (in fact, white supremacy at home). Where European Occidentalism is concerned, the rhetoric of antifundamentalist fundamentalism seeks to prove the superiority of Western enlightenment, secularism, and "emancipation." The latter is all the more important in that it works not only to impede multiculturalism at home but also prevent postcolonial challenges from being considered and ultimately realized—challenges intended to "provincialize Europe," "decenter Eurocentrism," and move "beyond Occidentalism."[50]

Antifundamentalist fundamentalisms (or fundamentalism of the second order) differ from classical fundamentalisms of the Christian Protestant, Jewish Orthodox or Islamist creeds in that they are secular and see themselves as enlightened and enlightening—recall Adorno's statement that "Enlightenment is totalitarian." Together with classical fundamentalism, they share a circular logic of argumentation, unchal-

---

49. Some publications have lately begun to close the gap. For the conflation of the Red Scare and racism in the South, see Woods, *Black Struggle*; for the "opportunism" of the NAACP to join the camp of liberal anticommunism to keep the civil rights organization safe from red-baiting, see Berg, "Black Civil Rights."

50. Coronil, "Beyond Occidentalism"; Chakrabarty, *Provincializing Europe*; Conrad, *Jenseits des Eurozentrismus*.

lenged foundations, unacknowledged metaphysical grounding, and a structural lack of reflexivity. And because they perceive their countries to be in danger, to be in a state of emergency or exception, they undermine the very principles they pretend to defend: tolerance (I prefer to say acceptance and recognition of difference and diversity), freedom of speech, movement and expression, and human rights.

Bibliography

Adorno, Theodor W., and Max Horkheimer. *Die Dialektik der Aufklärung. Philosophische Fragmente.* 7th ed. Frankfurt: Fischer, 1980.

Asad, Talal. *Genealogies of Religion: Discipline and Reasons of Power in Christianity and Islam.* Baltimore: Johns Hopkins University Press, 1993.

Asad, Talal, et al. *Is Critique Secular? Blasphemy, Injury, and Free Speech.* Berkeley: University of California Press, 2009.

Ates, Seyran. *Der Multikulti-Irrtum: Wie wir in Deutschland besser zusammenleben können.* Berlin: Ullstein, 2007.

Balibar, Etienne. "Gibt es einen 'Neo-Rassismus'?" In *Rasse, Klasse, Nation: Ambivalente Identitäten*, edited by Etienne Balibar and Immanuel Wallerstein, 23–38. Hamburg: Argument, 1990.

Berg, Manfred. "Black Civil Rights and Liberal Anticommunism: The NAACP and the Early Cold War." *Journal of American History* 94/1 (2007) 75–96.

Bielefeldt, Heiner. "'Westliche' versus 'islamische' Menschenrechte? Zur Kritik an kulturalistischen Vereinnahmungen der Menschenrechtsidee." In *Facetten islamischer Welt: Geschlechterordnungen, Frauen- und Menschenrechte in der Diskussion*, edited by Mechthild Rumpf et al., 123–42. Bielefeld, Germany: transcript, 2003.

———. "Zwischen laizistischem Kulturkampf und religiösem Integralismus: Der säkulare Rechtsstaat in der modernen Gesellschaft." In *Politisierte Religion: Ursachen und Erscheinungsformen des modernen Fundamentalismus*, edited by Heiner Bielefeld and Wilhelm Heitmeyer, 474–92. Frankfurt: Suhrkamp, 1998.

Broder, Henryk M. *Hurra, wir kapitulieren! Von der Lust am Einknicken.* Berlin: Pantheon, 2006.

Brown, Wendy. *Regulating Aversion: Tolerance in the Age of Identity and Empire.* Princeton: Princeton University Press, 2006.

Buruma, Ian, and Avishai Margalit. *Occidentalism: The West in the Eyes of its Enemies.* New York: Penguin, 2004.

Butler, Judith. *Bodies That Matter: On the Discursive Limits of "Sex."* New York: Routledge, 1993.

———. "The Sensibility of Critique: Response to Asad and Mahmood." In Talal Asad et al., *Is Critique Secular? Blasphemy, Injury, and Free Speech*, 101–36. Berkeley: University of California Press, 2009.

Casanova, José. "Secularization Revisited: A Reply to Talal Asad." In *Powers of the Secular Modern: Talal Asad and His Interlocutors*, edited by David Scott and Charles Hirschkind, 12–30. Stanford: Stanford University Press, 2006.

Chakrabarty, Dipesh. *Provincializing Europe: Postcolonial Thought and Historical Difference*. Princeton: Princeton University Press, 2000.
Chanock, Martin. "'Culture' and Human Rights: Orientalising, Occidentalising, and Authenticity." In *Beyond Rights Talk and Culture Talk: Comparative Essays on the Politics of Rights and Culture*, edited by Mahmood Mamdani, 15–36. New York: St. Martin's, 2000.
Conrad, Sebastian, and Shalini Randeria, editors. *Jenseits des Eurozentrismus. Postkoloniale Perspektiven in den Geschichts- und Kulturwissenschaften*. Frankfurt: Campus, 2002.
Coronil, Fernando. "Beyond Occidentalism: Toward Nonimperial Geohistorical Categories." *Cultural Anthropology* 11/1 (1996) 51–87.
Dietze, Gabriele. "'Occidentalism,' European Identity, and Sexual Politics." In *Study of Europe*, edited by Hauke Brunkhorst and Gerd Groezinger, 89–116. Baden-Baden: Nomos, 2010.
Eisenstadt, Shmuel N. "Fundamentalism, Phenomenology, and Comparative Dimensions." In *Fundamentalisms Comprehended*, edited by Martin E. Marty and Scott R. Appleby, 259–76. Chicago: University of Chicago Press, 1995.
Gellner, Ernest. "Fundamentalism as a Comprehensive System: Soviet Marxism and Islamic Fundamentalism Compared." In *Fundamentalisms Comprehended*, edited by Martin E. Marty and Scott R. Appleby, 277–87. Chicago: University of Chicago Press, 1995.
———. *Muslim Society*. Cambridge: Cambridge University Press, 1981.
Habermas, Jürgen. "Dialektik der Säkularisierung." *Blätter für deutsche und internationale Politik* 4 (2008) 33–46.
Hall, Stuart. "Rassismus als ideologischer Diskurs." In *Theorien über Rassismus*, edited by Nora Räthzel, 7–16. Hamburg: Argument, 2000.
Herrmann, Ulrike, and Alke Wierth. "Die Gene sind schuld." *taz*, Aug 31, 2010. Online: http://www.taz.de/1/archiv/digitaz/artikel/?ressort=tz&dig=2010/08/30/a0130&cHash=597af159e9.
Herrnstein, Richard J., and Charles Murray. *The Bell Curve: Intelligence and Class Structure in American Life*. New York: Free, 1994.
Jäger, Johannes. *Die rechtsextreme Versuchung*. Münster: LIT, 2002.
Jäger, Margret. *Fatale Effekte: Die Kritik am Patriarchat im Einwanderungsdiskurs*. Duisburg: DISS, 1996.
Jörges, Hans U. "Ein Ungeheuer wird freigesetzt." In *Sarrazin: Eine Deutsche Debatte*, edited by Deutschlandstiftung Integration, 154–56. München: Piper, 2010.
Jürgensmeyer, Mark. "Antifundamentalism." In *Fundamentalisms Comprehended*, edited by Martin E. Marty and Scott R. Appleby, 353–66. Chicago: University of Chicago Press, 1995.
Kelek, Necla. *Die fremde Braut: Ein Bericht aus dem Inneren des türkischen Lebens in Deutschland*. Köln: Kiepenheuer & Witsch, 2005.
"Klasse statt Masse. Von der Hauptstadt der Transferleistungen zur Metropole der Eliten." *Lettre International* 86 (2009) 197–201. Online: http://www.pi-news.net/wp/uploads/2009/10/sarrazin_interview1.pdf.
Lachmann, Günther. *Tödliche Toleranz: Die Muslime und unsere offene Gesellschaft*. München: Piper, 2005.

Laclau, Ernesto, and Chantal Mouffe, editors. *Hegemony and Socialist Strategy: Towards a Radical Democratic Politics*. New York: Verso, 1985.
Leibold, Jürgen. "Fremdenfeindlichkeit und Islamophobie: Fakten zum gegenwärtigen Verhältnis genereller und spezifischer Vorurteile." In *Islamfeindlichkeit: Wenn die Grenzen der Kritik verschwimmen*, 2nd ed, edited by Thorsten Gerald Schneiders, 149–59. Wiesbaden: VS, 2010.
Link, Jürgen. "Kollektivsymbolik und Mediendiskurse." *KultuRRevolution* 1 (1982) 6–21.
Mamdani, Mahmood, editor. *Beyond Rights Talk and Culture Talk: Comparative Essays on the Politics of Rights and Culture*. New York: St. Martin's, 2000.
"Merkel verweist auf christlich-jüdische Tradition." *RP Online*, Oct 6, 2010, n.p. Online: http://www.rp-online.de/politik/merkel-verweist-auf-christlich-juedische-tradition-1.2292287.
Meyer, Thomas. *Fundamentalismus: Aufstand gegen die Moderne*. Hamburg: Rowohlt, 1989.
Mignolo, Walter. "(Post)Occidentalism, (Post)Coloniality, and (Post)Subaltern Rationality." In *The Pre-Occupation of Postcolonial Studies*, edited by Fawzia Afzal-Khan and Kalpana Seshadri-Crooks, 86–118. Durham, NC: Duke University Press, 2000.
Narayan, Uma. "Essence of Culture and a Sense of History: A Feminist Critique of Cultural Essentialism." In *Decentering the Center: Philosophy for a Multicultural, Postcolonial, and Feminist World*, edited by Uma Narayan and Sandra Harding, 80–101. Bloomington, IN: Indiana University Press, 2000.
Pannenberg, Wolfhart. "Civil Religion? Religionsfreiheit und pluralistischer Staat: Das theologische Fundament der Gesellschaft." In *Die religiöse Dimension der Gesellschaft: Religion und ihre Theorien*, edited by Peter Koslowski, 63–75. Tübingen: Mohr, 1985.
Riesebrodt, Martin. *Fundamentalismus als patriarchalische Protestbewegung: Amerikanische Protestanten (1910–28) und iranische Schiiten (1961–79) im Vergleich*. Tübingen: Mohr, 1990.
———. "Fundamentalismus, Säkularisierung und die Risiken der Moderne." In *Politisierte Religion: Ursachen und Erscheinungsformen des modernen Fundamentalismus*, edited by Heiner Bielefeldt and Wilhelm Heitmeyer, 67–90. Frankfurt: Suhrkamp, 1998.
Rommelspacher, Birgit. "Dominante Diskurse: Zur Popularität von 'Kultur' in der aktuellen Islam-Debatte." In *Orient- und IslamBilder: Interdisziplinäre Beiträge zu Orientalismus und antimuslimischem Rassismus*, edited by Iman Attia, 245–67. Münster: Unrast, 2007.
Sachverständigenrat deutscher Stiftungen für Integration und Migration. *Einwanderungsgesellschaft 2010: Jahresgutachten 2010 mit Integrationsbarometer*. Online:http://www.svr-migration.de/wp-content/uploads/2010/05/einwanderungsgesellschaft_2010.pdf.
Safranski, Rüdiger. "Heiße und kalte Religionen." *DER SPIEGEL* 3 (2010) 119–21. Online: http://www.spiegel.de/spiegel/print/d-68703778.html.
Said, Edward. *Orientalism: Western Concepts of the Orient*. New York: Pantheon, 1978.

Sarrazin, Thilo. *Deutschland schafft sich ab: Wie wir unser Land aufs Spiel setzen*. 7th ed. München: Deutsche Verlags-Anstalt, 2010.

Schiffer, Sabine. *Die Darstellung des Islam in den Medien: Sprache, Bilder, Suggestionen. Eine Auswahl von Techniken und Beispielen*. Würzburg: Ergon, 2005.

Schirrmacher, Frank. "Frau Merkel sagt, es ist alles gesagt." *Frankfurter Allgemeine Zeitung*, Sept 19, 2010, n.p. Online: http://www.faz.net/s/Rub546D91F15D9A404286667CCD54ACA9BA/Doc~E4DC2AE94A2ED43A8A1FD9A6FD6533C12~ATpl~Ecommon~Scontent.html.

Schneiders, Thorsten Gerald. "Die Schattenseite der Islamkritik: Darstellung und Analyse der Argumentationsstrategien von Henryk M. Broder, Ralph Giordano, Necla Kelek, Alice Schwarzer und anderen." In *Islamfeindlichkeit: Wenn die Grenzen der Kritik verschwimmen*, edited by Thorsten Gerald Schneiders, 403–32. Wiesbaden: VS, 2010.

Schwarzer, Alice, editor. *Gotteskrieger und die falsche Toleranz*. Köln: Kiepenheuer & Witsch, 2002.

Scott, David, and Charles Hirschkind, editors. *Powers of the Secular Modern: Talal Asad and His Interlocutors*. Stanford: Stanford University Press, 2006.

"Sind Muslime dümmer?" *DIE ZEIT*, Aug 26, 2010, n.p. Online: http://www.zeit.de/2010/35/Sarrazin/.

Spier, Tim. *Modernisierungsverlierer? Die Wählerschaft rechtspopulistischer Parteien in Westeuropa*. Wiesbaden: VS, 2010.

Stark, Rodney, and William Sims Bainbridge. *A Theory of Religion*. New York: Lang, 1987.

Ulfkotte, Udo. *SOS Abendland: Die schleichende Islamisierung Europas*. Rottenburg: Kopp, 2008.

Woods, Jeff. *Black Struggle, Red Scare: Segregation and Anti-Communism in the South, 1948–1968*. Baton Rouge: Louisiana State University Press, 2004.

Citation and Censorship

The Politics of Talking About the Sexual Politics of Israel[1]

JASBIR PUAR

This paper was presented at the "Fundamentalism and Gender" conference at Humboldt University on December 4, 2010. The talk was presented despite last-minute accusatory and offensive communications with the conference organizing committee, which expressed concern about the title of the talk (originally "Beware Israeli Pinkwashing"), and complained that the focus on the Israeli-Palestinian conflict had nothing to do with the conference theme, nor the author's prior work. They stated that they did not understand how her 2007 book *Terrorist Assemblages: Homonationalism in Queer Times* related to Israel or why the author was discussing Israel at all given that, as they understood it, her work focused on feminist and queer critiques of US national/diasporic formation post-9/11. They were exclusively interested in the critique of the Western construction of the Muslim other. They also suggested that the talk was anti-Semitic, based on reading an op-ed the author published in *The Guardian* in July 2010 titled "Israel's gay propa-

---

[1]. This article is a reprint of Jasbir Puar, "Citation and Censorship: The Politics of Talking About the Sexual Politics of Israel." *Feminist Legal Studies* 19/2 (2011) 133–42. With kind permission from Springer Science and Business Media. © Springer Science+Business Media B.V. 2011.

ganda war." These concerns were communicated just two weeks prior to the conference, even though the paper title and information had been submitted in June of 2010.

One day prior to the start of the conference, the Director of the PhD Research Training Group "Gender as a Category of Knowledge" and also a conference organizing committee member, Professor Christina von Braun, gave an interview to Alan Posener, a well-known journalist in Berlin. While Posener is a self-described champion of Muslim rights in Europe, his contributions in the interview with von Braun reflect one example of the complex ways that anti-Muslim assumptions can be refunctioned and masked within neoliberal discourse. In this interview von Braun made derogatory comments about the author's work and person, stating that the author had "lost her marbles"[2] if she deemed Israel a totalitarian state, and claimed that the author's analysis suffered because it was based on activist work. Von Braun also reiterated the conference committee's statement that the author's prior work on sexuality and nationalism was quite interesting, but the critique of pinkwashing was unrelated. The author withdrew from the conference. After the organizing committee claimed that Alan Posener misstated von Braun's words, and after the author requested a public apology, a written retraction from von Braun, and a new moderator, she agreed to give her lecture. Professor Ulrike Auga made the public apology on behalf of the organizing committee right before the author's talk. In January 2011 the author received an "apology" from von Braun, which confirmed that she did indeed make the above comments in the interview. Puar is still waiting for the public written retraction of the article.

In the essay that follows, the author cites both Auga and von Braun's work to show the continuities between their positions and hers, and also cites from von Braun's interview with Alan Posener. She also demonstrates the (rather obvious) linkages between her work in *Terrorist Assemblages* (where she notes that some of the earliest forms of Islamophobia in queer organizing is mobilized through the Israeli-Palestinian conflict) and the current debates about pinkwashing and homonationalism in Israel.

What I want to do in this essay is attempt to convey to you the richness and complexity of a dialogue about the relationship of gay and lesbian sexual rights to the Israel-Palestine conflict. I'm going to do this

2. Posener, "Geschlecht als Wissenskategorie."

in three parts: the first part surveys the literature on sexual rights within the Israeli-Palestinian conflict; the second part examines implications of this regional framing of sexual rights for diasporic locations, specifically the US and Canada, by surveying the "Brand Israel" campaign; and, the third section discusses some of the locational politics of this debate in the context of Germany.

A Long History of Homonationalism in Israel?

A growing body of academic scholarship argues that the status of gay and lesbian rights and the politics of Israel and Palestine are inextricably linked, or to quote Gil Z. Hochberg, that the relations between "the politics of homophobia" and "the politics of occupation" are intractable.[3] As Ulrike Auga and Christina von Braun have noted in the introduction of their edited collection, *Gender in Conflicts: Palestine—Israel—Germany*, "[i]n a situation of conflict, societies tend to 'defame' the 'conduct' of women belonging to the other society; they accuse the 'other' women of either sexual libertinism or of sexual narrow-mindedness, both seen as opposed to one's own 'normality.'"[4] While unfortunately this collection from 2006 does not have any of the numerous examples already brewing of this dynamic as it relates to homosexuality in the region, the cover of the book does have an interesting photo of the Gay Pride March in Jerusalem on Christopher Street Day, 2004, depicting a graffiti wall with the words "No Pride in Palestine" as the most prominent scrawl legible in English. A concern for how, not only women, but now especially homosexuals, have become the symbols of civilisational aptitude. In other words, the biopolitical relationship between gay, lesbian, queer sexualities and nationalism has indeed been relevant for some time. As anthropologist Rebecca L. Stein notes, the rise of the gay equality agenda in Israel is concomitant with the increasing repression of the Israeli state towards Palestinians. She writes: "During the 1990's, Israel's gay communities were being recognized in unprecedented ways in Israeli legal spheres, while changing Israeli policies vis-à-vis the occupied territories were creating new forms of un-recognition for its Palestinian population: gay communities were enjoying new forms of social mobil-

---

3. Hochberg, "Israelis," 510.
4. Auga and von Braun, *Gender in Conflicts*, 2.

ity within the nation-state while the literal mobility of Palestinians from the occupied territories was being increasingly curtailed."⁵

These gains in the 1990s—what is called "Israel's gay decade"—included: protection against workplace discrimination, increasing institutionalisation of same-sex partner benefits, and greater inclusion in the Israeli Defence Forces. On the other hand, the 1993 Oslo Accords started strictly delimiting the presence of Palestinian labour pools in Israel and produced increasingly segregated living and working zones, multiplied existing surveillance systems and security checkpoints, and generally reduced the visibility and mobility of Palestinians and contact that they had with Israeli Jews. Renowned Israeli architect Eyal Weizman (2002) has done brilliant work on how the Oslo Accords created what he calls "the politics of verticality"—the dividing up of space from a two dimensional here-versus-there to a three dimensional system of air space, ground space, underground space, sacred space, checkpoint space, that basically tripled the amount of space that could be surveilled, controlled, and fought over.⁶

Stein asks, "How might one read these two political histories in concert?"⁷. This formulation—of the relationship of the rise of gay and lesbian legal rights as well as popular visibility that happens in tandem with increasingly xenophobic policies in regards to minority communities within the nation-state and the Others that threaten the borders of the nation-state from outside—is exactly what I have theorised, within the context of the United States, as well as some European states, as "homonationalism".⁸ In some ways Jewish studies scholars have been looking at the production of homonationalism as it operates in Israel for quite some time now. Alisa Solomon was amongst the first to argue that the notion of the progressive status of gays and lesbians in Israel has fomented rivalries and divisions between orthodox and secular Israeli Jews. In a 2003 volume titled *Queer Theory and the Jewish Question*, edited by leading Jewish Studies scholars Daniel Boyarin, Daniel Itzkovitz, and Ann Pellegrini, Solomon states: "In today's Israeli culture war, queerness—or at least the tolerance of queerness—has acquired a new

---

5. Stein, "Exploxive," 521.
6. Weizman, "The Politics."
7. Stein, "Exploxive," 521.
8. Puar, *Terrorist Assemblages*.

rhetorical value for mainstream Zionism: standing against the imposition of fundamentalist religious law, it has come to stand for democratic liberalism."[9] In this formulation, Solomon is clear that queerness has become another ground upon which the cohesion of an Israeli Zionist state is possible. A wonderful book by Adi Kuntsman looks at how, within Israeli queer communities, there is a hierarchy between more mainstream Israeli queer Jews, and Russian Israeli queers, and that the fissures between different factions do not result in equal access to the benefits of gay equality.[10]

Despite these internal contradictions however, as Amal Amireh notes, "the positive rhetorical function of queerness . . . goes beyond those internal cultural wars (between secular Jews and religious Jews) into the wider culture war between Israelis and Palestinians, where it functions to consolidate a fractured Zionist consensus".[11] As von Braun points out in her recent interview with Alan Posener, this use of gay rights to reiterate the terms of the Israeli-Palestinian conflict—those terms being that Israel is civilised, liberal, and progressive in relation to the backwardness of Palestinian society—is certainly not a new observation (I never claimed that it was "new.").[12] What is "new," however is how these debates are being connected to transnational feminist studies and queer theory. In this regard, I want to laud the recent publication of a special issue of the *GLQ: A Journal of Lesbian and Gay Studies*, titled "Queer Politics and the Question of Palestine/Israel," edited by Gil Z. Hochberg,[13] which contains fantastic essays that both historicise and contextualise the kinds of discursive and material practices that have proliferated and continue to produce Israel's claim to "gay friendliness" and "gay tolerance" as somehow independent of its repressive politics towards Palestinians. These essays look at the complex co-dependent intertwining of queerness and nationalism. So for example, Hochberg analyses the problematic Israeli patriotism produced through the mourning of the shooting of queer teenagers at the Israeli GLBT As-

---

9. Solomon, "Viva la Diva," 636.

10. Kuntsman, *Figurations*; although his analysis misreads the relationship between homonationalism and gay rights. See also Gross, "Israeli GLBT Politics."

11. Amireh, "Afterword," 637.

12. Posener, "Geschlecht als Wissenskategorie."

13. Hochberg, ed., "Queer Politics and the Questions of Palestine/Israel."

sociation in August of 2009;[14] Amalia Ziv highlights the work of Black Laundry, a queer group in Israel committed to anti-occupation activism[15] and "No Pride in Occupation" is a roundtable of activists, scholars, and activist-scholars in Israel, Palestine, and the diasporas who discuss the complexities of being queer in the region.[16]

The "Pinkwashing" Debate in the Diasporas

Now I want to elaborate upon a series of debates happening transnationally regarding what is widely termed in North American organizing contexts as "Israeli Pinkwashing". Jason Ritchie writes that "while the significance of tolerance of homosexuality as a marker of liberal democratic modernity has perhaps declined in recent Israeli political discourse—alongside the decline of Ashkenazi hegemony and the ascendancy of Mizrahi, religious, and ultranationalist politics—that narrative still retains considerable currency in the United States and Europe, where liberal Zionists, especially queer liberal Zionists, frequently deploy it to represent Israel as 'an oasis of liberal tolerance in a reactionary religious backwater.'"[17]

If it is the case, as Ritchie argues, that the production of the "Israeli gay tolerance/ Palestinian homophobia" binary is a recognised discursive tactic of the conflict today, the reasons for why this debate has now taken hold in diasporic contexts such as the US and Canada are multiple. In part, a critique of the US global war on terror cannot be so easily separated out from a critique of the Israel-Palestine conflict. Geographer Derek Gregory has written at length about the kinds of post 9-11 foreign policy decisions that further aligned the United States and Israel in an identification as both "victims" of Islamic fundamentalism and united in the war on terror. Gregory argues that the Israeli state used 9-11 as a moment to amplify its aggression against the Occupied Territories, and that the United States sanctioned this aggression even as they feared losing their Arab allies in their efforts to reign in Al-Qaeda.[18] Further, as Professor von Braun herself confirms in the interview

14. Hochberg, "Israelis."
15. Ziv, "Performative Politics."
16. Hochberg et al., "No Pride."
17. Ritchie, "How Do You Say," 559–60, citing Kirchick, "Queers for Palestine."
18. Gregory, "Defiled Cities."

with Alan Posener, Israel's have indeed been invested in the production of Muslim societies as backwards and repressed,[19] contributing in no small part to the discourses of the Muslim other as the terrorist other. Therefore, the critique of the US occupation of Iraq and Afghanistan, Islamophobia (both post 9–11, and in its recent rising forms), and Israeli policies towards Palestine are contiguous political positions.

To turn now to the specific diasporic articulations of Israel's "gay friendly" image: several years ago Israel invested in a large-scale, massively funded "Brand Israel" campaign, produced by the Israeli Foreign Ministry, to counter its growing reputation as a colonial power. Ranked 185 out of 200 nations in an East West Communications survey in terms of "positive perception," Israel beat Pakistan (186) but not Iran (184). Targeting global cities such as New York, Toronto, and London, the "Brand Israel" campaign has used events such as film festivals to promote its image as cultured and modern.

One of the most prominent features of the "Brand Israel" campaign is the marketing of a modern Israel as a gay-friendly Israel. Stand With US, a self-declared Zionist organisation, has been quoted in *The Jerusalem Post* as saying, "We decided to improve Israel's image through the gay community in Israel."[20] This "pinkwash-ing," as it is now commonly termed in activist circles, has currency beyond Israeli gay groups. Within global gay and lesbian organizing circuits, to be gay friendly is to be modern, cosmopolitan, developed, first-world, global north, and most significantly, democratic. Events such as WorldPride 2006 hosted in Jerusalem and "Out in Israel", recently held in San Francisco, highlight Israel as a country committed to democratic ideals of freedom for all, including gays and lesbians. It is important to note that homonationalism has scalar movement between local, national, and transnational sites; from the internal contradictions that homonation-alism produces within Israel, to the production of Israel as liberal and progressive in relation to the homophobia of Palestine, to the level of global transnational organizing where homonationalism translates—within a liberal telos of progress—onto this register as well.

Thus, Israeli pinkwashing is a potent method through which the terms of Israeli occupation of Palestine are reiterated—Israel is civilised,

19. Posener, "Geschlecht als Wissenskategorie."
20. Belzalel, "Prominent Gay Opinion-Shapers."

Palestinians are barbaric, homophobic, and uncivilised. This discourse has manifold effects: it denies Israeli homophobic oppression of its own gays and lesbians,[21] and it recruits, often unwittingly, gays and lesbians of other countries into collusion with Israeli violence towards Palestine. In reproducing Orientalist tropes of Palestinian sexual backwardness, it also denies the impact of colonial occupation on the degradation and containment of Palestinian cultural norms and values. Pinkwashing harnesses global gays as a new source of affiliation by recruiting liberal gays into a dirty bargaining of their own safety against the continued oppression of Palestinians, who are now perforce re-branded as "gay un-friendly." This strategy then also works to elide the presence of numerous Palestinian gay and lesbian organisations, for example Palestinian Queers for Boycott, Divestment and Sanctions (PQBDS).

Pinkwashing's effects are being widely contested, especially at gay and lesbian events and despite the censorship of gay and lesbian groups that actively oppose the Israeli occupation. The recent banning of the phrase "Israeli Apartheid" during Pride weekend by PRIDE Toronto, in response to pressure by the City of Toronto and Israeli lobby groups, effectively barred the group Queers Against Israeli Apartheid (QuAIA) from the pride parade. However, on June 23rd, 2010, the ban was rescinded in response to community activism and the twenty-three Pride Award recipients who returned their prizes in protest of the ban. Frameline's San Francisco LGBT Film Festival faced opposition from Queers Undermining Israeli Terrorism (QUIT), among other groups, for accepting Israeli government sponsorship. Last summer, after protests by Palestinian, Arab, Muslim, and other anti-Zionist factions, the US Social Forum in Detroit cancelled a workshop slated to be held by Stand With Us on "LGBTQI Liberation in the Middle East" that sought to promote images of Israel as a gay mecca at the expense of Palestinian liberation.

The transnational organizing that is taking place in relation to this issue is very broad and involves many activists and scholars in the United States, Canada, Palestine, Israel (no doubt in Berlin too), and spans from queer of colour communities, to Palestinian activists, both in and out of Palestine, to diasporic, as well as Israeli Jews, and Palestinians. And of course, Israeli activists such as Dalit Baum have been critical of the Brand Israel campaign as well, reiterating the notion that "the

---

21. Gross, "Israeli GLBT Politics"; Kuntsman, *Figurations*.

flourishing of gay rights in Israel is being used by the government to divert attention from its gross violation of human rights in the Occupied Territories"[22]. So you can see that the constituencies that are involved in these discussions cannot be reduced to a single position: they cannot be summarily dismissed through the reductive accusations of being racist, homophobic, or anti-Semitic; they cannot be rendered within a Manichean division between right and wrong. Further, all of these organisations peaceably participate in this transnational organizing with a respect accorded to the variety of locational, national and ideological differences among them.

A final twist to the diasporic production of pinkwashing—it is hardly produced by the Brand Israel campaign alone. It is increasingly the case that a stance against Israeli state-violence towards Palestinians is advocated and sanctioned, but then accompanied by an additional condemnation of Muslim sexual cultures. This has become a standard rhetorical framing produced by liberal supporters of the Palestinian cause. (Note, as another example, the messaging of OutRage!, Britain's premier queer human rights organisation, at a Free Palestine rally in London, May 21, 2005: "Israel: Stop persecuting Palestine!" "Palestine: Stop persecuting Queers!") This framing has the effect, however unintended, of analogising Israeli state oppression of Palestinians to Palestinian oppression of their gays and lesbians, as if the two were equivalent or contiguous. As numerous postcolonial scholars have convincingly demonstrated, the production of "homophobia" in a location dealing with epistemological and material violence of colonial occupation through the use of sexuality to affirm racial and cultural superiority cannot be considered "cultural" alone. Rather, it is at least in part a by-product of cultural domination.

It is important to consider the way that the debate about Israel and Palestine continues to anchor what I have called a homonationalist politics of sexual rights in North America and why this is significant. What is at stake is not a normative decision about whether Israel is gay-friendly or whether Palestine and other regions of the Middle East are homophobic. There is no question that Israel's legal record on gay rights suggests a certain notion of liberal "progress"; Palestinian queers that live in the Occupied Territories also articulate how difficult it is to

---

22. Ziv, "Performative Politics," 537.

be "openly" gay. But, as this scholarly literature and this political organizing demonstrates, this is only the beginning of the story. As I have argued elsewhere, the "Woman Question" is now being supplemented with the "Homosexual Question."[23] That is, in the colonial period, the question of "how do you treat your women?" as a determining factor of a nation's capacity for sovereignty has now been appended with the barometer of "how well do you treat your homosexuals?"

Academic Censorship, Anti-Semitism, and Transnational Feminist Alliances

I want to bring to a close my comments with some remarks about the purported "controversy" about this talk, a controversy that might in other locations be simply called "an academic debate" or even a political disagreement, but not the basis for attempts to censor, micromanage, or otherwise vilify someone's work. It is a controversy that could have easily been avoided, as far as I am concerned, had open communication happened in a timely and direct fashion, instead of through third parties and interviews with anti-Muslim reporters. In general, I have had the good fortune of hearing from many people in Europe, all over North America, and Israel and Palestine, who have enthusiastically welcomed this discussion on sexual rights as they function in the Israeli-Palestinian conflict. For those who have attempted in various ways to censor or silence this talk, on the basis that "in the German context" it is anti-Semitic to be critical of oppressive Israeli state practices towards the Palestinians, it has become clear to me that the desires to silence such a debate are, in fact, the very evidence of the need for this conversation to happen. I think it is worth thinking about the accusation of anti-Semitism for a moment: from whom it comes, who benefits, and what kind of work it does. I follow, along with Judith Butler and numerous other Jewish intellectuals both inside and outside of Israel, that it is crucial to retain a distinction between anti-Semitism, which is a form of racism directed at Jewish peoples that is deeply embedded in biologically deterministic notions of race, and a critique of Israeli state practices (which is not the same thing as a stance against the existence of the Israeli state). In fact, the conflation of anti-Semitism with a posi-

23. Puar, "Israel's Gay Propaganda War."

tion against the Israeli oppression of Palestinians is precisely what the definition of Zionism is. Furthermore, it is most important to retain this distinction because otherwise the accusation of anti-Semitism becomes empty, loses its political force, and becomes a blanket alibi for a repression of a complicated conversation around the Israeli-Palestinian conflict. We need the term anti-Semitism to mean something other than "critical of Israel" because anti-Semitism still exists. Without this important and hardly semantic distinction, the charge of anti-Semitism becomes a strong projection of the history of the Holocaust onto the bodies of "outsiders" like myself, those not directly interpellated by that history, as a classic form of psychoanalytic disavowal; I accuse you of doing what I am afraid I might be doing myself, what I very much so fear doing, what I don't want to do myself (interestingly enough, this projection of the accusation of anti-Semitism onto "others" mirrors the production of migrants in Germany as the prime carriers and transmitters of anti-Semitism). As members of a German society with a history of racial genocide and suppression of dissenting voices and bodies via extermination, perhaps it is worth thinking twice about the kinds of transnational academic feminist alliances that are rendered impossible when the accusation of anti-Semitism is used indiscriminately, and when used to censor, in the midst of predominantly white academics, a self-identified queer woman of colour, an international speaker for whom a different locational politics is absolutely necessary (and for whom accounting for the "German context" is not exactly her job—otherwise, why bother to invite an international speaker who works in the field of American Studies in the first instance?).

What I have offered today is not anti-Semitic. I would argue that it is not even a critique of Israeli state practices per se. Rather, it is an analysis of how sexual politics and national politics are irreducibly intertwined with each other, and how this works in the particular case of the Israeli-Palestinian conflict. As I have made clear in my work in *Terrorist Assemblages*, this is reflective of a neo-liberal phenomenon happening in many, many national locations; I am thus not "picking" on Israel, as has been voiced by those who differ with me politically. I have not, contrary to the claims of the organizing committee of this conference and in the interview with Professor von Braun, called Israel a totalitarian state. I will quote the relevant passage from the Guardian piece: "While Israel may blatantly disregard global outrage about its wartime activities, it nonetheless has deep stakes in projecting its image as a liberal society of tolerance, in particular homosexual tolerance. These two tendencies should not be seen as contradictory, rather constitutive of the very mechanisms by which a liberal democracy sanctions its own totalitarian regimes."[24]

The fact that this passage keeps being misread as calling the Israeli state totalitarian is a classic symptom of this kind of projection. The difference between a totalitarian state and what Giorgio Agamben calls the "state of exception" is precisely about the way in which liberal democracy and totalitarianism meet at a threshold to excuse liberal democracy from its own rule of law. Agamben has called the post 9–11 period in the United States, where the "writ of habeas corpus" (that is, the right to a fair trial) was suspended for "enemy combatants" despite being on US soil, legitimated in the name of a liberal democracy, the most extreme state of exception in US history.[25] This is absolutely a different political formation than that of a totalitarian state.

From what I have observed in my limited experience in Germany, the crucial question facing progressives is, can a critique of anti-Muslim racism and a critique of anti-Semitism co-exist? Is it possible to articulate a critical, progressive stance against anti-Muslim racism without this positioning automatically reduced to being "against Jews" or "anti-Semitic"? If a particular "anti-Deutsche position" is critical of the German state for its history of racial genocide during the Holocaust and understands German racism as exceptional, it makes little sense for this very same position to endorse the state practices of yet another, not only racist, but also, apartheid state.

For those of you who are committed to a critique of anti-Muslim racism and Islamophobia, both here and globally, and yet do not see Israeli state oppression of the Palestinians as part of the production of that racism, that position—this fissuring—is simply untenable for any critical left politics in the United States that stands against US and other forms of imperialism. This is perhaps a locational distinction between the United States and Germany that cannot simply be dismissed as "wrong." I take the locational distinction seriously and without dismissal; I only ask that you do the same.

24. Puar, "To be Gay."
25. Agamben, *State of Exception*.

Bibliography

Agamben, Giorgio. *State of Exception*. Chicago: University of Chicago Press, 2005.

Amireh, Amal. "Afterword." *GLQ* 16/4 (2010) 635–48.

Auga, Ulrike, and Christina von Braun, editors. *Gender in Conflicts: Palestine—Israel—Germany*. Berlin: Lit, 2006.

Belzalel, Mel. "A Group of Prominent Gay Opinion-Shapers from around the World to Attend TA Parade on Friday." *The Jerusalem Post*, June 10, 2009, n.p. Online: http://www.jpost.com/Israel//Article.aspx?id=144736.

Gregory, Derek. "Defiled Cities." *Singapore Journal of Tropical Geography* 24/3 (2003) 307–26.

Gross, Aeyal. "Israeli GLBT Politics between Queerness and Homonationalism." July 01, 2010. *Bully Bloggers*. No pages. Online: http://bullybloggers.wordpress.com/2010/07/03/israeli-glbt-politics-between-queerness-and-homonationalism/.

Hochberg, Gil Z. "Israelis, Palestinians, Queers: Points of Departure." In "Queer Politics and the Questions of Palestine/Israel," edited by Gil Z. Hochberg, special issue, *GLQ* 16/4 (2010) 493–516.

Hochberg, Gil Z., editor. "Queer Politics and the Questions of Palestine/Israel." Special issue, *GLQ* 16/4 (2010).

Hochberg, Gil Z., Haneed Maikey, and Samira Saraya Rima. "No Pride in Occupation: A Roundtable Discussion, 2010." In "Queer Politics and the Questions of Palestine/Israel," edited by Gil Z. Hochberg, special issue, *GLQ* 16/4 (2010) 599–610.

Kirchick, James. "Queers for Palestine?" *Advocate*, Jan. 28, 2009, n.p. Online: http://www.advocate.com/politics/2009/01/28/queers-palestine.

Kuntsman, Adi. *Figurations of Violence and Belonging*. Oxford: Lang, 2009.

Posener, Alan. "Geschlecht als Wissenskategorie." Starke-Meinungen.de, Dec. 1, 2010. Online: http://starke-meinungen.de/blog/2010/12/01/geschlecht-als-wissenskategorie/.

Puar, Jasbir. "Israel's Gay Propaganda War." *The Guardian*, July 01, 2010.

———. *Terrorist Assemblages: Homonationalism in Queer Times*. Durham, NC: Duke University Press, 2007.

———. "To be Gay and Racist Is No Anomaly." *The Guardian*, June 02, 2010.

Ritchie, Jason. "How Do You Say 'Come Out of the Closet' in Arabic? Queer Activism and the Politics of Visibility in Israel Palestine." In "Queer Politics and the Questions of Palestine/Israel," edited by Gil Z. Hochberg, special issue, *GLQ* 16/4 (2010) 557–76.

Solomon, Alisa. "Viva la Diva Citizenship: Post-Zionism and Gay Rights." In *Queer Theory and the Jewish Question*, edited by Daniel Boyarin et al., 149–65. New York: Columbia University Press, 2004.

Stein, Rebecca L. "Explosive: Scenes from Israel's Gay Occupation." In "Queer Politics and the Questions of Palestine/Israel," edited by Gil Z. Hochberg, special issue, *GLQ* 16/4 (2010) 517–36.

Weizman, Eyal. 2002. "The Politics of Verticality." *Open Democracy*, Apr 24, 2002. Online: http://www.opendemocracy.net/ecology-politicsverticality/article_801.jsp.

Ziv, Amalia. "Performative Politics in Israeli Queer Anti-Occupation Activism." In "Queer Politics and the Questions of Palestine/Israel," edited by Gil Z. Hochberg, special issue, *GLQ* 16/4 (2010) 537–56.

Body, Life, and Biopolitics

Queer Theologies and Sacred Bodies

Lisa Isherwood

In this chapter, I wish to consider two bodies that feminist theology has regarded as being intimately linked in a downward spiraling under the weight of patriarchally constructed theology: these are the bodies of the sexually marginalized, and the body of the earth itself. Using the method of "queering," it is possible to see these bodies, view them differently, and from here offer a challenge to mainstream thinking. Indeed, I would suggest it becomes possible to offer a more biophilic approach to life and the theology that springs from it. A Christian fundamentalist approach to both these issues may vary slightly but is in essence very similar; that is to say, the sexually marginalized are rebelling against the heterosexual pattern that God set in place in Genesis for the perpetuation of the species and the positions of male and female, the male ruling over the female as head of his house and family. The earth, while being the creation of God, has lost its exalted place in prelapsarian theology in which we see that many temptations lie in the created order. Fundamentalist theologies diverge when it comes to considering what this may imply, but for most there is the basic belief that when Christ comes back to earth, which by then may have been ravaged by the wars and plagues welcome under this scheme, it will be renewed and made perfect for inhabitation by the saved. This leads many fundamentalist theologies to suggest that the earth should be stripped of all resources as quickly as possible, since this will bring prosperity for some now and a quicker end to the earth, as well as the return of Christ; others stand on the side of a stewardship model, which suggests that the earth is under the control of man, and so some degree of care should be afforded to it; ultimately, however, it is imperfect and will be renewed.

The political implications of these approaches to both the sexually marginalized and the earth are, I think, clear to see. What may be less clear is the effect that such restricted and negative thinking has exercised in the area of theology for centuries. It is the aim of this paper to demonstrate that the bodies of the marginalized and the body of the earth are sacred and, when viewed as such, enable a more creative and flourishing form of theology to emerge and in turn enable a more positive form of political thinking. Central, of course, to the theologies mentioned above is the notion of a monotheistic deity who holds all perfection within himself, sets in place rules and regulations for humans, and has dictated the very existence of the earth itself. It is this mono-thinking that has exerted itself beyond the bounds of theology and taken its toll on economics and politics from the macro- to the microlevel. It is this insistence on the "One" that has created many "Others" along the way and in so doing sets in place many exclusions and divisions. An examination of monotheism itself is not the purpose of this essay, but it does need to be borne in mind as the essay progresses that it is the lurking "Oneness" that has stripped out the appreciation of the sacred in its diverse forms and manifestations. It is in an attempt to find once again the sacred in marginal human bodies and the earth itself that I turn to queer theory and its application within theology.

Queer Theory and Theological Revolutions

The word *queer* comes from Indo-European roots meaning "across, to transverse, to move to." Queering is a method by which we expose and engage with the untidy edges, with the bits that do not fit a neat system. By trespassing and transgressing, by mining submerged knowledges, queering attempts to change the way we see and act. It is a refusal to be normalized into oblivion by the deadening systems of a binary opposite world; it is a contradiction and a fluid revolution. Queer, then, should no longer be understood as a noun marking an identity we have been taught to despise but rather as a verb destabilizing any claim to identity. It has come to symbolize the moving around or crossing of boundaries in order to gain another view of tradition. The straight mind is one that is divided within itself because it has to cut out so much that is real in order to maintain the illusion of unity, a unity ironically based in dualism—in the hetero of the straight mind. The queer mind lives with opposites and indeed embraces contradictions as a way of moving toward a deeper understanding of what may be real. It is, then, an extremely useful hermeneutical device with which to subvert the rigid doctrinal discourses of Christianity and release people from their worst excesses.

An example of how this works can be found in Marcella Althaus-Reid's notion of the Bi-Christ, which in theory overcomes mono-relations in sexuality and beyond.[1] A Bi-Christ, a figure who is not bi in the sense of sexual preference but rather in terms of thought and life, is a challenge to the way in which Western theology and society is constructed. Althaus-Reid sees this Christ as fluid and full of contradictions—a gospel-based picture, in fact. She argues that the gospels present us with the Prince of Peace and the one who whips the traders from the temple, the one who talked to the women at the well and could not change the impurity laws regarding menstruation. When we take these stories as starting points for Christology, we go in contradictory directions; but far from wishing to harmonize these points of tension, Althaus-Reid wants us to embrace them as the fluid movements of Christology.[2] Taking the evidence before us and asking challenging questions allows false harmonies to be stripped away and a new and exciting picture to emerge.

Althaus-Reid gives illuminating examples of how the monorelational pattern works. Firstly, the hetero-Christ even defines sexual relations that are not heterosexual: the gay man is seen as effeminate, and the lesbian as either butch or femme. These are heteronormative categories, which prohibit naming the diverse range of sexual identities[3] that actually operate within people's lives. Heteronormativity stabilizes categories and colonizes experience in order to keep some control, if only by ostracizing. The second example shows how mono-relations lead to economic oppression. Using the colonization of Africa as an example, Althaus-Reid points out that the relationship under one (mono) heavenly Father could never be equal—*that* father was not flexible enough.

---

1. Althaus-Reid, *Indecent Theology*.
2. Ibid., 112–20.
3. Ibid., 116.

The exclusion of "otherness" meant that the needs and desires of the other do not enter the equation, and exploitation steps in. Althaus-Reid argues that the Bi-Christ dismantles the mono-relations of naming, organizing, exploiting, and owning that underpin economic, racial, and sexual exclusions, as well as the worlds this leads to. The Bi-Christ allows other ways to think and be, other ways to build the world, and other ways to understand the sacred. This destabilizing of the mono-God, which Althaus-Reid enables with her reading of the Bi-Christ, has enormous political implications, as she suggests: for there is no longer One reality that is seen as legitimate and best. Instead, the mono begins to dissolve as other voices and bodies step into the picture—sites of revelation where the sacred shines through.

A further lived reality that challenges the mono-reality in a more subtle way is the lived experience of transpeople: those who are either transgendered, transsexual, or transvestite. Since they are not tied to what Daniel Maguire calls "pelvic orthodoxy,"[4] they therefore move beyond many accepted gender orthodoxies. This could be questioned in the case of transsexuals, who may feel compelled to change sex in order to fit a gender identity. Virginia Mollenkott suggests that the challenge offered to gender orthodoxy by transpeople is needed not only to remind religious congregations of human diversity but also of the fact that all of us, in all our diversity, are made in the image of one dazzlingly diverse Spirit. Here is a radical challenge to religious fundamentalism through just the mention that such sexual outsiders may offer anything to churches or hold within them anything of the nature of God. This form of human diversity is outside the remit of fundamentalist religion, which believes that God created genders as well as sexes that are fixed and distinct and thus able to feed into the unequal power relations also felt to be attached to sex and gender through a narrow reading of the Genesis and other stories. In the story of Genesis, complementarity is believed to be in the mind of God; the female, a secondary and supplementing feature of humanness, comes from the rib of the male, made for his comfort and under his control. This control is even signaled by the missionary position of sex, which is seen as the only acceptable position since it clearly demonstrates the relation of the sexes to each other, with the male active and on top, the female passive and beneath. Any

---

4. Maguire, "Religion," 188.

blurring of the gender divide is thus a great sin against both the nature of God and the way the world is meant to operate under that God. Many fundamentalists take this to mean that women may not have contraceptive access, sex education, the right to divorce, jobs, or, if they do work, equal pay. We thus see that any challenge to the rigid sex and gender divides at the heart of much Christian fundamentalist theology and ethics goes beyond simply including marginalized bodies; it also means rethinking society, politics, and even economics.

While offering communion to a six-foot-seven male body builder in full drag, then, what challenge is presented by a married, heterosexual male priest who plucks his own eyebrows, wears make-up, and dons ladies' underwear—Basque and all—in order to show off the newly acquired breasts beneath his vestments? This is a situation known to me and one I think is theologically challenging. Do we have the edges of our concept of gender and love moved? What kind of challenge is this priest to us, with his penis and his newly acquired breasts? As the dazzling glory of God, what does this do to our narrow theological methods? We see love that is not tied to the "correct" body parts, an understanding of gender not limited by physical attributes, and an example of the many forms of heterosexuality not allowed by the rigid performance requirements of fundamentalist Christian gender relations. I find it a challenging example because it is, after all, a heterosexual example and thus one that fundamentalists might have to look at before dismissing it as perverted.

Elisabeth Stuart[5] contends that the Eucharist erases sex altogether, indeed that the Eucharist is itself transsexual since it takes sex into the realm of the symbolic and offers many displacements. Through its celebration, we are able to move more easily toward a new identity, one that is unstable and non-sexed. Stuart argues that transpeople must be welcomed and honored in church circles but must also take up the Eucharistic challenge of erasure. In other words, they must not take comfort in a new identity but realize that it, too, is unstable and has no ultimate meaning; they must live through it by resisting rather than reaffirming gender scripts. B. K. Hipsher[6] argues that precisely because a transgender image of God is so unsettling to people, we are compelled to argue for it since it gives fullness to the idea of ongoing incarnation. She says,

---

5. Stuart, "The Priest," 131.
6. Hipsher, "God."

"We need a *trans*-God ... one that *trans*gresses all our ideas about who and what God is and can be, one that *trans*ports us to new possibilities for how God can incarnate in the multiplicity of human embodiments, one that *trans*figures our mental images from limitations, one that *trans*forms our ideas about our fellow humans and ourselves, one that *trans*cends all we know or think we know about God and about humanity as the *imago Dei*."[7]

Virginia Mollenkott[8] reminds us that the visible expression of diversity's full range is not encouraged in churches, arguing that while the "straight civil partnered gay/lesbian couple" may be accepted in some church circles, the leather Daddy with his bitch boy is less welcome. There is rarely a question of how the theology these diverse bodies inhabit may expand the theological landscape we ourselves have been encouraged to inhabit. Are they unwelcome even in liberal circles because what we see in front of us is actually a painful reminder of how Christian theology has viewed the human relation to God, with humans required to submit to many sufferings and degradations in praise of his name? Or is it because the power we invest in dominant masculinity is challenged by the bitch boy, content to be where he is? Ken Stone says this model is familiar to us in the writings of the prophets in the figure of the occasional feisty boy, such as Jeremiah.[9] It is clear that what these marginal bodies do is challenge the politics underlying the theology in a way that coupled, "straight" lesbian and gay people perhaps do not; the latter are more easily assimilated by the dominant societal norm and thus do not rock the boat. Of course, neither group would find a welcome in fundamentalist circles, but it is worth considering that even those groups who see themselves as theologically liberal are constrained by deeper political ties held in place by gender expectations and performance.

Ellison argues that "compulsory coupling" fits the dominant capitalist ethos but does not lend itself to our full becoming as humans and should therefore be held up for theological critique. It makes us dependent on one other for the fulfillment of our needs, limits our range and the importance we place on friendship, and weakens our ties with

---

7. Ibid., 99.
8. Mollenkott, "We Come Bearing Gifts."
9. Stone, *Practicing*, 77.

the wider community.[10] Ellison comments, "Heterosexual marriage is therefore far from being a free and voluntary personal choice; it is a political requirement for normative status in this culture."[11] Because it acts as the glue for hierarchical systems, he wonders why gay and lesbian people would wish to emulate it. Ellison furthermore declares that within such an arrangement, power is eroticized in patriarchal sexual relations, and that what we learn through these acts of intimacy is carried into the world in such a way that we do not object to the exertion of power in all aspects of life—we have been physically acclimatized to it; we may even desire it. Ellison believes that the way ahead may be by prioritizing the Song of Songs in which eroticism—not marriage—becomes "worship in the context of grace"[12]; erotic ecstasy, he says, is both our gift and our prophetic task.[13] The notion that ecstasy—that pleasure—can be the base for a theology in search of justice may upset the anti-body, spiritually-based notions we have hitherto worked with. But can we simply disregard the thousands of people who testify to justice, love, warmth, and care, so often experienced as life transforming in the arms of strangers, where they feel free to explore and fulfill their desires? It would be foolish to declare that all such people were making a political statement, but if Ellison is correct in his assertion, then it may be less than wise for sexually marginalized people to dash headlong into demanding normative status within church and society.

Queer Theory and Cosmic Revolutions

Although it may seem a little strange to place the earth/cosmos alongside the sexually marginalized when considering the impact of fundamentalist theology, it is actually a very logical thing to do. As mentioned earlier, much fundamentalist theology, despite understanding all creation to have come forth from the command of God, nevertheless considers it all in need of an overhaul due to the Fall, and so all is open to corruption; natural disasters are often viewed as the punishment of God, and many see world's destruction as a necessity in order to herald the second coming of Christ. This kind of model also tends to harbor

10. Ellison, *Erotic Justice*, 84.
11. Ibid., 27.
12. Ibid., 71.
13. Ibid., 122.

terror toward any aspect of the earth that may appear chaotic. Various attempts to find divine order have been made, and unsurprisingly, the findings have been in line with the theological beliefs of those who undertook the task. One better-known example of not facing the evidence is the suggestion that fossils are made by the devil in order to mislead the believer. I wish to argue that, while it is not named as such by many of those working in the field, the new cosmology, as well as its impact on theology, may also be called queer; that is to say, the body of the cosmos is another queer body for the reason that profound engagement with it pushes us to the edges of our theological constructs and even across them. The abstractly constructed world that much theology creates cannot remain untouched once we delve into the cosmic story itself, yet this is profoundly shocking for those who wish to maintain a fundamentalist approach to religion and theology. We will see as the essay progresses just what the challenge the cosmic story poses to fundamental theology and how this may impact the politics that fundamentalism is so wedded to. Further, the earth itself—and by extension the cosmos—has often been viewed as female by the scientists investigating it. At times, their investigative language even reads like a sadomasochistic sexual assault: Francis Bacon felt free to dismember the earth in order that *she* would give up her secrets and thereby allow human kind total dominance over what had once held it captive. Carolyn Merchant summarizes Bacon's position as follows: "The new man of science must not think that the 'inquisition of nature is in any part interdicted or forbidden.' Nature must be 'bound into service' and made a 'slave,' put 'in constraint' and 'molded' by the mechanical arts."[14] This is also how Merchant describes the way the extraction of resources was viewed: "The new mining activities have altered the earth from a bountiful mother to a passive receptor of human rape . . . Digging into the matrices and pockets of earth for metals was like mining the female flesh for pleasure."[15] For some early scientists, this desire for control did have a religious dimension in that they wished to take back the control they believed had been lost through the actions of Eve; but in so doing, they ensured the earth had no face, no soul, and, as they also believed, no power. As we shall see, this religio-scientific approach is not only far from satisfactory; it is also

14. Merchant, *Death of Nature*, 169.
15. Ibid., 39.

illusory and, I would argue, against the divine process. However, this is just another aspect of the dualistic thinking inherent in fundamentalist theology that furthers the notion we are above nature and, once we control it, that we will have fulfilled another God-given human task.

The first challenge offered when engaging with our enfleshed cosmic story is to move ourselves away from a search for perfect origins and back to beginnings. There is no place from which we were cast out but rather a place that grew us, nurtured us, and generously gave and gives us life. Yet fundamentalist Christians still tend to build theology around the notion that our home is elsewhere, a place we once dwelt and have had rebought for us by the redemptive death of Jesus. This is a place that has also set in stone the sex, gender, and power relations between two distinct sexes and the rest of the created order, with man being in charge of everything from the female to all that lives. Engaging with the cosmic story challenges this notion of perfect origins and, as Edward Said[16] reminds us, that beginnings are always relative, contested, and historical, whereas origins are absolute and power laden. Beginnings, then, give the Christian theologian the chance to decolonize this space of origins in creation and the inevitable creator sitting apart and, as Catherine Keller puts it, to challenge "the great supernatural surge of father power, a world appearing zap out of the void and mankind ruling the world in our manly creator's image."[17] We are thrown back to cosmic beginnings, to the void and chaos, and we are asked to make our theology from there—to understand who we are and who we might be from *tohu wabohu*, the depth veiled in darkness. Once we give agency to void and chaos, there can be no creation from nothing. Creation ceases to be a unilateral act, and the divine speech in the pages of Genesis is no longer understood as a command uttered by the Lord ruling over creation; instead, as Keller tells us, "let there be" is a whisper of desire, and what comes forth emanates from all that already is rather than appearing from above and beyond. In this shift, we also see the possibility for incarnation to be understood as the rule for rather than the exception to creation, for the whisper desires enfleshment.[18] Significantly, Keller moves us from creation out of nothing to a place where the divine is

---

16. Said, *Orientalism*, 93.
17. Keller, *Face of the Deep*, 6.
18. Ibid., 56.

more humble and entices ever-unfolding acts of becoming, grounded in the chaos at the heart of the cosmos. In so doing, she destabilizes fundamentalist notions of the great father God who dictates every outcome and has a blueprint for every living creature, opening the way for an exciting, divine-filled journey of becoming—a divine process, perhaps, that embraces the becoming of all in its particular place. This has significant impact in terms of sex and gender theologies as well as for those wishing to conceive of a redemptive narrative as set apart from the essence of the cosmos. By introducing chaos back into the Genesis story as a good force and one foundational in our lives, Keller sends shock waves through a fundamentalist theology that has no place for chaos in its well-ordered world, with its Father God who sets all in place. She is, of course, being truer to the script of Genesis itself, albeit distant from the way in which, since the time of Augustine, these texts have been used to place fear in the hearts of men—literally men who learn to fear the power of women, who bring the destruction of paradise and the Fall of man, as well as the wrath of God, which cannot be calmed by anything less than the death of his own Son. The fundamentalist readings also fill the created order itself with things of terror for the Christian, who is not to seek knowledge within it but to be above and untouched by it for the sake of his soul. The reading of divine origins places the fundamentalist in a narrowly prescribed world with rigid boundaries while Keller's reading—though she does not call it queer—throws open the doors, inviting endless and creative engagement with all that there is; it sees neither edges nor divisions, understanding everything to be the energy of which all is made including the divine itself.

Eco-philosopher Val Plumwood[19] is less concerned with sex and gender and the impact of engaging with chaos on a hitherto ordered theology and more concerned with the way fundamentalist theologies have allowed abusive and destructive treatment of the earth. She insists that while we understand ourselves as something other than the rest of the created order, we will inevitably see this as being "better" or "higher," and that this false consciousness leads to alienation and destruction. She is quick to point out to us the logical absurdity of such a position; monological relationships will eventually weaken the provider, the earth on which we rely. In Plumwood's view, we need to move to a dialogue

---

19. Plumwood, *Environmental Culture*.

between mutually recognizing and supporting agents, to realize we live in a communion of subjects rather than a collection of objects. It is perhaps this suggestion that fundamentalist theology would find the most absurd, since it does not recognize agency of any kind in the created order; yet on further reflection, this is strange, since agency was considered part of the downfall in the Genesis account. Plumwood argues that removing agency from the cosmos, a technique we have so often used in our colonial history in relation to the discovery of "new lands," makes it and all that lives in it an empty space, one that can be used for profit by maximizing its development potential. She reminds us of the effect of this way of thinking, in which nature is no longer viewed as a creator of our environment and the land as well as those who depend most directly on it are relegated to the realm of the "Other." Although Plumwood does not say it, the relationship between fundamentalist theology and the development of savage capitalism[20] is a well-argued one; if God the great creator has given the earth to man, then man is charged with making it work for him. The ways in which this has turned into an imperial theology, with its exploitation of lands and people regarded as less than human, is also well argued in this hierarchical scheme.[21] By arguing for the recognition of interdependent and mutually supportive subjects, Plumwood opens up a critique of the way in which theology has been implicated in exploiting the earth and its peoples for the accrual of capital. Her intervention is also timely, given that we see the growth of what is known as prosperity theology. This form of theology once again makes the distinction between Christians and others and sets out an agenda according to which the blessed may profit at the expense of those who are understood as not blessed. Once again, we see that this form of Christianity enables its followers to act as though they do not belong to this world and are certainly not part of a communion of subjects; according to this scheme, the blessings gained through exploitation will never have consequences in this world since the believer will be taken to yet another world in which prosperity can continue for eternity, with no thought of diminishing earth resources or the near slavery of millions of producers.

---

20. Weber, *The Protestant Ethic*.
21. See, for example, McClintock, *Imperial Leather*.

Plumwood argues that far from a prosperity theory, we should return to what she calls the "heart of stone" in order to overcome the "sado-dispassionate rationalism of scientific reduction."[22] This involves a reenchantment of the realm designated as material: the rematerialization of spirit as matter that speaks. She warns that this project should not slide into the world of the romantic and that in order to guard against this it needs to be ever mindful of the spirit/matter dualism, resisting it at every turn. Western culture has placed speaking matter in the rarefied world of fairy tale and legend from where it cannot really impact ethical or philosophical thinking, and yet it is this world we need to foreground if we are to return intentionality and agency to matter. By journeying to the heart of stone, we have to walk a different path, one that moves stone (the material world of nature) from the background of consciousness to the foreground, from silence to speech, and from the ordinary to the extraordinary, to the wonderful and even to the sacred. This move is necessary in order to challenge the false consciousness of the Western world, so rooted in our Christian heritage, which tells us we no longer live in nature but in culture. The political and economic implications of this, I think, are quite clear. What impact would such thinking have on logging companies, chemical companies, and the bodies of those who labor to make $2.50 T-shirts? And what would it do to a fundamentalist theology that has no place for a spirit-filled material world and finds it difficult to understand the material as sacred? As a liberation and queer theologian, I find the difficulties fundamentalist theology has with such notions somewhat at odds with the tradition we have inherited. Our Christian stories have within them all sorts of material transformations, from flesh and blood to bread and wine, and from human to cosmic spirit; this is a truly complex and enchanted vista. Of course, the dualist theological stance held by much fundamentalist theology has narrowed these stories' vision through a tight-knit working of metaphysics that removes their power to transform. We have stopped telling these stories as though they spoke of our birthright of *dunamis* and given them away by interpreting them as tales of heroic Gods and their power to save us through *their* magical powers and actions. Keller and Plumwood throw open the way for us to see that the animate and inanimate are both agents in the cosmos and engaged in mutually em-

---

22. Plumwood, *Feminism*, 67.

powering (redemptive) acts of transformation. This has a significant impact on theology and the way it is challenged to view all manner of the material order, from the cosmos to the individual person: all are seen as sacred, made of the energy of which the divine is made. Keller refers us to 1 Cor 12:4–6 and its reference to the body of Christ in which we are moved from one dead body of Jesus to an ongoing interactive body. The writer uses *energia*, and we are told that God is the same One who is All in All (*ho energon ta panta en passim*); this, Keller says, is the God of entanglement, not of dualist distance.[23] By implication, this is the divine that, in making all such distinctions due to race, religion, gender, or sexuality, appears blasphemous and still furthers disrespect for the earth, and all coexisting animate and inanimate subjects may be added to the same blasphemy.

Those who wish to believe that the way the world should be was laid down in the beginning by the distant voice of the commander God have more in store for them from the pen of Keller. She states that we know the cosmos did not emerge from Platonic forms but rather from tehomic chaos; there was no blueprint. Rather, there is and continues to be a glorious outpouring of surprise and novelty. This, she says, makes the notions of a static God and static ethics little more than nonsense, and so she proposes a tehomic ethic—one that enables us to bear with chaos, neither liking nor fostering it, but recognizing that *there* is the unformed future, and hence quite a challenge to Omega Points and fully formed paradises.[24] This unformed future consists of repetitions, but from very early in cosmic development, every repetition also became a transgression; our bodies and that of the cosmos are in constant flux as they regenerate and change, and so they are in essence transgressive. Keller is arguing, then, that in reality nothing is stable; all is an entanglement of constant becoming, and this is the sacredness of things. In the language of queer theology, then, the ever-changing world and the shape-shifting of its gendered and sexed subjects is as much the activity of the divine as any other unfolding, creative, and chaotic process in the cosmos. To fix these things is against the nature of the cosmos and, as I have argued elsewhere, against the understanding of the Gospel,[25] and so

23. Keller, "The Energy," 26.
24. Ibid., 25.
25. Isherwood, "Fucking Straight."

church and society must be challenged whenever a rigid system is used to underpin political agendas.

Of course, we can see how the theology emanating from the new cosmology offers a challenge to the economic system under which we labor as well as arguably to the international relations we fail to foster. John F. Haught explains that there are three persistent elements in cosmic evolution: gratuity, extravagance, and surprise.[26] This, he believes, suggests that we should move toward a more humble and receptive mode of accepting all as a gift and changing our lifestyle accordingly. Perhaps it could be argued that a gift economy may have operated in early Christianity, but those days are long gone, with Christian theology underpinning the development of Western capitalism, as we have seen. There is no doubt that the world would benefit from an economic system based on universal extravagant giving, a gift economy modeled on the cosmos itself as a challenge to the power-driven models we have that bring misery and death to millions. Here then, perhaps, is the challenge for Christian theologians: to counter prosperity theology with a theology of extravagant giving in which we include the earth itself as a subject that demands respect and compassion!

Bibliography

Althaus-Reid, Marcella. *Indecent Theology: Theological Perversions in Sex, Gender and Politics*. London: Routledge, 2001.

Ellison, Marvin Mahan. *Erotic Justice: A Liberating Ethic of Sexuality*. Louisville: Westminster John Knox, 1996.

Hipsher, B. K. "God is a Many Gendered Thing: An Apophatic Journey to Pastoral Diversity." In *Trans/Formations*, edited by Marcella Althaus-Reid and Lisa Isherwood, 92–104. London: SCM, 2009.

Isherwood, Lisa. "Fucking Straight and the Gospel of Radical Equality." In *The Sexual Theologian: Essays on Sex, God and Politics*, edited by Marcella Althaus-Reid and Lisa Isherwood, 47–57. London: T. & T. Clark, 2004.

Keller, Catherine. "The Energy We Are: A Meditation in Seven Pulsations." In *Cosmology, Ecology and the Energy of God*, edited by Donna Bowman and Clayton Crockett, 11–25. New York: Fordham, 2012.

———. *Face of the Deep: A Theology of Becoming*. London: Routledge, 2003.

Maguire, Daniel C. "Religion and Reproductive Policy." In *God Forbid: Religion and American Public Life*, edited by Kathleen M. Sands, 185–202. New York: Oxford University Press, 2000.

---

26. O'Murchu, *Evolutionary Faith*, 31.

McClintock, Anne. *Imperial Leather: Race, Gender and Sexuality in the Colonial Context*. London: Routledge, 1995.
Merchant, Carolyn. *The Death of Nature. Women, Ecology and the Scientific Revolution*. San Francisco: Harper & Row, 1980.
Mollenkott, Virginia Ramey. "We Come Bearing Gifts: Seven Lessons Religious Congregations Can Learn from Transpeople." In *Trans/Formations*, edited by Marcella Althaus-Reid and Lisa Isherwood, 46–58. London: SCM, 2009.
O'Murchu, Diarmuid. *Evolutionary Faith: Rediscovering God in Our Great Story*. Maryknoll, NY: Orbis, 2004.
Plumwood, Val. *Environmental Culture: The Ecological Crisis of Reason*. London: Routledge, 2002.
———. *Feminism and the Mastery of Nature*. London: Routledge, 1993.
Said, Edward. *Orientalism*. New York: Vintage, 1979.
Stone, Ken. *Practicing Safer Texts: Food, Sex and Bible in Queer Perspective*. London: T. & T. Clark, 2005.
Stuart, Elisabeth. "The Priest at the Altar: The Eucharistic Erasure of Sex." In *Trans/Formations*, edited by Marcella Althaus-Reid and Lisa Isherwood, 127–38. London: SCM, 2009.
Weber, Max. *The Protestant Ethic and the Spirit of Capitalism*. London: Harper Collins Academic, 1930.

Seminal Reasoning

Ultra-Orthodoxy and the Biopolitics of Medically Assisted Reproduction in Israel

Carmel Shalev

Introduction

Israel is known for its widespread utilization of assisted reproductive technologies (ART) and its innovations in related clinical practices. It boasts by far the highest rates in the world of medical intervention for the treatment of infertility.[1] This embracement of medically assisted reproduction (MAR) derives from compound political, historical, social, and religious factors. The perception of an existential threat to the survival of the Jewish people, against the backdrop of the Holocaust and in view of the geopolitics of conflict in the Middle East, is at the root of a pronatalist demographic policy. Family is a central social institution in Jewish culture, and the suffering associated with childlessness—recalling the biblical matriarchs—is a reverberating theme in contemporary Israeli culture.[2]

---

1. Collins, "International Survey"; De Mouzon et al., "World Collaborative Report."

2. Kahn, *Reproducing Jews*; Birenbaum-Carmeli, "Cheaper than a Newcomer"; Birenbaum-Carmeli and Carmeli, *Kin*.

With regard to medical treatment for infertility, there is a historical affinity between the Jewish people and the practice of medicine.[3] Scientific knowledge and technological progress were pillars of the earliest vision of Zionism,[4] and Israel's scientists have pioneered new frontiers in ART research and development. Its public is trustful of science and progress[5] and open to accepting and consuming technological novelties. In addition, Israelis place a high value on health, and medicine seems to epitomize the boon of applied science. Public funding is available for almost unlimited cycles of ART interventions, and the jurisprudence of the Supreme Court has recognized a positive "right to parenthood" that derives from an innate existential desire for genetic continuity.[6]

Religious factors also play a central role in Israel's cultural preoccupation with reproduction and its embracement of ART,[7] as well as in other matters of life and death, such as end-of-life medical care[8] or the definition of death for the purpose of organ transplantation.[9] The innovations of Western medical practice in the second half of the twentieth century—from the creation of embryos in vitro at the beginning of life to the prolongation of dying from old-age at its end—raise a plethora of ethical and moral questions that challenge long-standing religious and moral sensibilities about the meaning of life and death. In response, rabbinical scholars have drawn upon traditional sources and teachings to try and provide answers within the framework of Jewish medical ethics. While Israel's court system is based on a jurisprudence of liberal democracy, it is defined constitutionally as a "Jewish democracy," and rabbinic authorities exert a strong influence on policy, regulation, and legislation in matters of bioethics.

The secular propensity for hi-tech medicine is supported by the traditional Jewish value of *tikkun*—healing the world. It is the role of human beings to mend, repair, and improve the world and correct defects in nature. There is also a therapeutic imperative to prevent suffering and to heal (*rafo yerape*) that has its source in a biblical text (Exod

3. Hirsch, "Jews and Medicine."
4. Herzl, *Altneuland*.
5. Hashiloni-Dolev, "Between Mothers."
6. Shalev, "Reflections," 333–36; Shalev and Gooldin, "Uses and Misuses."
7. Sperling, "Commanding the Directive."
8. Barilan, "Revisiting the Problem"; Shalev, "Reclaiming the Voice."
9. "Brain-Respiratory Death Bill."

21:19). In the case of reproductive medicine, these values are reinforced by a fundamental tenet of the Jewish worldview—the commandment to "be fruitful and multiply." This explains the generally positive attitude toward the use of ART, not merely as a remedy for childlessness but as a means for repeated childbearing and the creation of multi-sibling families. At the same time, there are halakhic constraints on the manner in which ART may be used.

First, rabbinic beliefs about kinship and lineage (*yichuss*) shape the construction of legal paternity and maternity vis-à-vis the offspring of ART.[10] These beliefs often lead to outcomes that seem paradoxical from a secular humanist point of view—suffice it to mention here the principle of matrilineal descent in a patriarchal social system that otherwise confers status through patrilineage (for which Micha Brumlik offers an interesting and original explanation in this volume), or the preference for using sperm from non-Jewish rather than Jewish donors in artificial insemination (AI).[11]

Second, halakhic prohibitions on adultery and incest (which embody a gendered double standard) and the feared consequence of stigmatizing the offspring of forbidden relations (*mamzerut*) have a major impact on Israeli law and policy regarding permitted reproductive relations in the use of ART.[12] It is well known that these concerns about forbidden relations, lineage, and kinship are explicit themes in the public debate around the regulation of ART in Israel, because the offspring of illicit relations or intermarriage suffer serious halakhic impediments to marriage and all matters of marriage for Jews are subject to rabbinical control under Israeli law.

However, the focus of the present article is on a third paradigm of rabbinic thought, which is not actually expressed in the public discourse about ART: the biblical prohibition against "wasting seed" or "spilling seed in vain." While concern about the embryo's moral status is a major theme in Christian religious attitudes toward the uses of technologies associated with medically assisted reproduction, halakhic attitudes appear to stem from the primary value attributed to sperm and semen. As we shall see, this sensitivity comes to light in the adaptation of ART

10. Kahn, *Reproducing Jews*.
11. Mei-Ami, "Sperm Donation."
12. Shalev, *Halakha*.

clinical practice to the requirements of ultra-Orthodox Jewish couples; it also plays a role in the debate about cloning and embryonic stem cell research. (In the halakhic worldview, a fertilized egg outside a woman's womb is not called an embryo and is not regarded as human. At the same time, cloned human embryos are preferred over fertilized eggs as a source of stem cells for research because cloning does not require the extraction of sperm.[13]) The preoccupation with seed is a subtle theme which explains a variety of rules laid down by halakhic authorities as conditions for the use of ART. As a result of the significance attached to sperm, there is moreover a propensity to favor highly sophisticated reproductive technologies that entail subjecting women's bodies to invasive medical interventions over less intrusive alternatives.

It should be noted that Jewish law is pluralistic and there are different schools of Jewish thought. We therefore need to ask: When we speak of the influence of religion on the biopolitics of MAR in Israel, which school of thought are we referring to, and what are its main features? This article suggests that Israel's law and policy governing MAR is shaped by an ultra-Orthodox Jewish rendition of halakha that manifests characteristics of religious fundamentalism.

Ultra-Orthodox Judaism

Pluralism is an innate feature of Jewish thought and law, and disagreement between scholars and decision makers (*poskim*) is quintessential to the literary canon known as halakha. Traditionally, Jewish discourse is a complex intellectual exercise that draws upon a broad array of authoritative texts layered in a hierarchical canon of literary sources. The highest authority is ascribed to the biblical texts of the Torah (Five Books of Moses), which are believed to derive their validity directly from the word of God through divine revelation at Mount Sinai. The next layer is the Talmud, comprised of the Mishna and the Gemara. The Mishna committed into writing the oral traditions of Jewish law based on the biblical texts (ca. 220 CE), and the Gemara recorded rabbinic discussions about Mishnaic texts that took place over the next three hundred years. Both these texts are characterized by arguments among sages over the application and interpretation of rules of law. There are additional layers of commentaries on these texts and medieval codifica-

13. Steinberg, "Stem Cell Experiments."

tions, as well as centuries of rabbinic responses to particular questions and decisions in individual cases until the present day. Rabbinic discourse is therefore casuistic and pluralistic and contains a wide array of divergent practical opinions that result from reading, interpreting, and applying the same texts and precedents.[14]

Moreover, in contemporary times there are different schools of Jewish thought and practice—ultra-Orthodox, Orthodox, Conservative, Reconstructionist, and Reform or Liberal. These schools vary in their attitudes to Western education, women, and secular Jews and non-Jews, as well as in their interpretation of the halakhic canon and the degree to which they view it as binding. Even among those who strictly follow halakha, the opinions of rabbinic decision makers vary between strictness and lenience on diverse matters, so it is impossible to state a uniform position on any subject. From a political perspective, the major influence in Israel over issues of state and religion—including in the area of reproduction—is exercised by the ultra-Orthodox minority, which is the most zealous school of thought. Rabbinical leaders of the ultra-Orthodox community also disagree on multiple matters, but, as we shall see, the rule of thumb that has been adopted in the making of secular policy and law about ART is to err in favor of strictness rather than lenience in order to be on the safe side.

Ultra-Orthodox Judaism, also known as *haredi*,[15] is fundamentalist in several respects. The basis of its worldview is the notion of an abyss separating Jews from Gentiles. The unique essence of the chosen Jewish people is of "a nation which dwelleth alone" (Num 23:9) and faces a non-Jewish world that seeks its destruction.[16] This leads to a separatism that also insulates ultra-Orthodox society against the influence of modern culture, including the lifestyle and worldview of secular Jews, by opposing secular education and abstaining from media and the internet. Instead, ultra-Orthodox Judaism seeks to maintain a form of religious community that supposedly existed in pre-Holocaust Europe, based on the belief that the traditional lifestyle guarantees the survival of the Jewish nation. Hence, it is anti-Zionist: it views the notion of

---

14. Jakobovits, "Jewish Views," 120; Zohar, *Alternatives*, 9.

15. The term *haredi* has its root in the Hebrew word *hared*, which means fearful (or anxious) in its common contemporary usage. As a synonym for ultra-Orthodox Judaism, it signifies God-fearing, exceptionally devout, and strictly observant of the halakha.

16. Friedman, "Haredi Society."

a Jewish state which fails to conform to halakha as a profanation and rejects the authority of the democratic values, processes, and institutions that make up Israel's constitutional governance—secular liberalism, universal human rights, the rule of law, and the separation of state powers. Rather, members of the ultra-Orthodox Jewish community live according to the dictates of their rabbi, derived from his interpretation of the halakhic literary canon.[17] The authority of the rabbi extends to matters of personal choice, from voting in parliamentary elections to undergoing infertility treatment.

In addition, ultra-Orthodox society is patriarchal and strictly segregated along lines of gender. Friedman has characterized it as a "society of scholars" (*hevrat lomdim*) in which men are dedicated to devotional study, while women function not only as wives and mothers but also as breadwinners, working to support large families and supplement the social welfare stipends from the state upon which they are dependent.[18] While women are allowed to cast a vote, they are denied the right to be elected to public office. Similarly, the halakhic rules of reproduction are essentially gendered. For example, the paramount norm to "be fruitful and multiply," which is the very first commandment in the Bible, appears in the text as a directive to man and woman alike (Gen 1:27–28). However, it evolved into a gendered obligation that applies to men only, despite a dissenting opinion, fueled by the covert assumption that a woman's natural function is to bear and raise children.[19]

Despite the fact that ultra-Orthodox Jews refute the legitimacy of Israel's democracy, they interact with it not just as passive recipients of economic support but also as active stakeholders in government and legislation. In all matters of life and death, marriage and divorce, and Jewish identity (the question "Who is a Jew?"), they exert far-reaching influence over all members of Israeli society. To pass legislation on any of these subjects, it is necessary to have the backing of haredi political parties, while haredi politicians make decisions only after consulting with and receiving instructions from their respective rabbinical authorities. Different parties bow to different luminaries who often disagree

---

17. Shahak and Mezvinsky, *Jewish Fundamentalism*.
18. Friedman, "Haredi Society."
19. Ir-Shay, "Family Planning," 97–98, 120.

with each other.[20] In the realm of bioethics, including reproduction, the rabbinic influence is mediated not only by the ultra-Orthodox political parties but also by experts on halakha and medicine, who act as unofficial spokesmen for ultra-Orthodox authorities on parliamentary committees, ad hoc policymaking bodies, and other fora of public debate.

Forbidden Relations and the Taint of Mamzerut

Considering that a major concern of ultra-Orthodox Judaism is to preserve the unique nature of the Jewish people, ART's acceptability is contingent upon adopting measures to guarantee the integrity of the biosocial body. Traditional rules of reproductive relations, kinship, and lineage must be observed if the offspring are to qualify for membership in the collective corpus. Even among the ultra-Orthodox rabbinic authorities, however, there are differences of opinion about the legitimacy of ART procedures and the eligibility of offspring.

Halakhic laws of kinship and lineage (*yichuss*) have two prime objectives. The first objective is to establish rules of endogamy and forbid intermarriage between Jews and non-Jews.[21] The second objective is to establish internal restrictions on marital or sexual-reproductive relations. In relation to ART, adultery and sibling incest are the relevant categories of forbidden relations. With regard to adultery, the question is whether the prohibition applies to reproductive relations in which there is no sexual intercourse; as for sibling incest, there is the fear of unwitting marriage between half-siblings, a potential consequence of anonymous gamete donations.

The source of the prohibitions on adultery and incest is biblical (Lev 18:6–20), and transgressing these prohibitions incurs severe penalties: offenders are subject to capital punishment (Lev 20:10–20), and the offspring of such unions suffer the stigma of *mamzerut*. The biblical text says that a *mamzer* "shall not come into the assembly of the Lord" even down to the tenth generation (Deut 23:3), meaning forever. The commentaries explain that they are not eligible to marry a Jewish person; they may marry only other *mamzerim* or converts to Judaism. Because the impediment to marriage within the Jewish congregation is inherited, it amounts in effect to excommunication. These rules continue to be pertinent in the

20. Shahak and Mezvinsky, *Jewish Fundamentalism*.
21. Zohar, "From Lineage."

present day, since matters of personal status in Israel including marriage fall under the jurisdiction of religious courts. In other words, the marital eligibility of Israeli children born to Jewish parents as a result of ART is determined by these halakhic rules, so that the taint of *mamzerut* is a matter of concern even for secular Israeli Jews.

Halakhic rules also inform the legal regulation of ART practices in Israel in a direct manner. The most conspicuous example is found in relation to third-party reproduction, which has been the subject of legislation in two statutes: the Surrogate Mother Agreements Law of 1995 and the Egg Cells Donation Law of 2010. Both statutes provide that, as the rule, only unmarried women may act as surrogate mothers or egg cell donors. The stratification of women into married and unmarried—with the latter providing reproductive services to the former—is reminiscent of the madonna-whore dichotomy that characterizes patriarchal social orders.[22] Even though secular Israeli society is sexually liberal and there is a general tolerance of single-mother families, marriage usually provides advantages of economic security and emotional support for women, so that designating unmarried women as reproductive laborers creates conditions ripe for potential exploitation. Moreover, the stratification of married and unmarried women stems from a gendered double standard that underlies the prohibition of adultery, which applies to married women but not married men. According to Jewish law, a child born to a married woman from a man who is not her marital partner is a *mamzer*; but this stigma does not apply to the extramarital child of a married man so long as the mother is not married to another.[23]

What is more, the adoption of the distinction between unmarried and married women by the secular legislature reflects a choice to regulate ART according to the views of the strictest *poskim*. There are differences of opinion among the rabbis as to whether the use of ART with third party donors creates the problem of *mamzerut*, since sexual intercourse is not involved. One prominent authority, R. Moshe Feinstein, ruled unequivocally that *mamzerut* results only from forbidden sexual relations and not from reproductive adulteration (i.e., the mere "mixing of alien genetic material" [gametes]).[24] Another authority, R. Eliezer

22. Shalev, *Birth Power*, 26–32.
23. Shalev, *Halakha*.
24. Halperin, "Definition of Parenthood," 187.

Waldenberg, takes the similar position that there can be no adultery without illicit sexual relations.[25] These opinions even reflect the majority view. Nonetheless, the secular legislature chose to follow the more cautious and restrictive approach, which appears to arise from concerns about "communal purity."[26] Dr. Mordechai Halperin, a rabbi, gynecologist, and leading expert on halakhic medical ethics, explained this choice as follows: "Since the taint of *mamzerut* is irremediable and very serious, even in the case of doubt, it is necessary to ascertain a broad halakhic consensus before permitting a married surrogate mother. A lack of consensus could lead to the birth of an offspring with a social and religious defect, which might not always be rectifiable."[27]

Ten years later, in the parliamentary debate over the enactment of a statute on egg cell donations, the same expert, now in his capacity as the official in charge of bioethics at the Israeli Ministry of Health, used similar terms to explain the rule that only unmarried women may volunteer to donate egg cells:

> There are decisions of almost all the great *poskim* of the latter generation . . . who ruled unequivocally that *mamzerut* is the consequence of adultery and incest, and not of alien genetic adulteration . . . However, in the matter of *mamzerut*, because of the grave character of the problem, we are usually sensitive. In order to prevent the possibility that another rabbi 20 years from now will give a different directive and will cast an unjustified taint on the offspring, we must make every effort today to prevent such a situation. Therefore, the law takes this into account, for instance in the matter of a married egg donor. The law says that the ideal situation is for the donor to be single, so as to prevent the possibility of someone saying something else 20 years from now.[28]

It is important to note that this extremist position is contrary to the traditional approach of rabbis throughout the generations. The moral discomfort about punishing children for their parents' sins led to the requirement of the strictest evidentiary standards, which made it almost impossible to prove *mamzerut*. Accordingly, in 2000, the rabbini-

---

25. Zohar, *Alternatives*, 74.
26. Kaplan Spitz, "Mamzerut," 567.
27. Levi, "Surrogacy," 5.
28. Knesset Committee, Protocol 393.

cal assembly of the Conservative-Masorti Movement decided to make *mamzerut* functionally inoperative by refusing to entertain evidence of it.[29] The concession of Israel's legislature to minority ultra-Orthodox views, so as to preclude any remote question of doubt (*khashash safek*) as to the children's capacity for marriage, not only violates their human rights but also goes against the consistent trend of previous generations in which rabbis sought to minimize the disability of *mamzerut*.

Ultra-Orthodox views about proper reproductive relations influence the regulation of ART in Israel in further ways, including the establishment of statutory registries of offspring from surrogacy agreements and egg cell donations to which rabbinic marriage registrars have access.[30] Control over the constitution of the biosocial Jewish body is also exerted by recommending that children born with the assistance of non-Jewish women through transnational third-party reproduction be converted to Judaism due to halakhic disagreement about the construction of Jewish motherhood.[31] Whereas the debates that are typical of Jewish thought traditionally allowed for pluralism and flexibility in individual cases, the theoretical halakhic disputes now inform policy but also create uncertainty, which in turn becomes a tool for exercising power and control over reproducing adults, who then prefer to stay on the safe side for the sake of their children.

29. Kaplan Spitz, "Mamzerut."

30. Note that these registries are neither intended nor designed to guarantee the right of MAR children to know their biological origins; rather, their main purpose is to establish rabbinical control over the private lives of individuals. Discussion of the pros and cons of identifiable gamete donor registries lie beyond the scope of this article. Suffice it to say that the potential violation of the rights to privacy and to marriage because of the stigma of *mamzerut* might outweigh the benefits of a registry in Israel. From a human rights perspective, the dangers of half-sibling marriage can be prevented by less invasive means of voluntary genetic testing (Shalev, *Halakha*, 68–69).

31. The Surrogate Mother Agreements Law and the Egg Cells Donation Law both assume that Jewish lineage is conferred by the birth mother. However, of recent, the question which mother—the genetic mother or the birth mother—confers Jewish lineage has become a matter of dispute, perhaps because of the increasing numbers of postmenopausal women who have given birth to children with the assistance of egg cell donors from outside Israel (Shalev and Werner-Felmayer, "Patterns of Globalized Reproduction"). To be on the safe side, conversion of the baby is recommended in the case of a child born to a Jewish woman from a non-Jewish egg cell donor (Sherlo, "Egg Cell Donation").

The Koshering of ART Clinical Practice

The halakhic worldview has also influenced the clinical practice of MAR in cases where the recipients of care are themselves observant Jews. For example, ultra-Orthodox anxieties about the consequences for kinship of unintended mismatching of sperm, eggs, and embryos have led to the introduction of halakhic supervisors (*mashgikhot*), who monitor all laboratory procedures in fertility clinics that involve the handling of reproductive genetic material and overlook kosher[32] conditions for the use of ART.[33]

What is more, the involvement of rabbinic experts in the clinical practice of infertility medicine for observant Jewish couples often means that women undergo medical interventions because of halakhic requirements, without any medical indication per se and with relatively little discussion of the effects of the procedures on their health and well-being.[34] That is to say, halakhic interference in the medical clinic constructs the ways in which female bodies are used and misused so as to mediate reproductive technologies.

For example, halakhic concerns related to the laws of female "impurity" (*niddah*) create a kind of "halakhic infertility," which is treated hormonally even though a woman with this "condition" is perfectly healthy and physiologically fertile. The source of this problem is the length of abstinence prescribed by halakha following menstruation. During the period of impurity, no physical contact is allowed between the spouses. Sexual activity is allowed to resume only after seven days of cleanness and after the woman has immersed herself in a ritual bath (*mikveh*). For women with relatively short menstrual cycles, ovulation might occur during the days of ritual impurity, so that they cannot conceive because of the halakhic restrictions on sexual intercourse. The result of "halakhic infertility" is that women are treated with hormones so as to standardize their menstrual cycles.[35]

---

32. *Kosher* is a term primarily used to designate the foods that may be eaten under rabbinic dietary law, but it is also used to designate the properness or legitimacy of an activity.

33. Kahn, *Reproducing Jews*, 114–16.

34. Ivry, "Kosher Medicine."

35. Haimov-Kochman et al., "Infertility Counseling."

A key factor in "the koshering of medical care" for infertile couples is the injunction against "the destruction of seed" (*hashkhatat zera*),³⁶ which lies at the root of the prohibitions of masturbation, homosexuality, and contraception. The term "seed" (*zera*) is also used in the biblical source for the prohibition against adultery (Lev 18:20), although this is not reflected in English translations of the verse.³⁷ As we shall see, "seed" is a central concept in halakhic discourse and a key to understanding the ultra-Orthodox mindset with regard to medically assisted reproduction. For example, R. Eliezer Waldenberg, who opined that there can be no adultery without sexual relations, nonetheless denounced artificial insemination with donor sperm (AID) in the following terms: "placing into the womb of a married woman the seed of another man—is a great abomination."³⁸

In the clinical context of infertility treatment, semen is normally obtained through masturbation, whether for analysis to assess the causes of infertility or for its treatment by means of artificial insemination (AI) or IVF; however, the halakhic injunction against destroying seed or spilling it in vain means that extravaginal ejaculation is prohibited even when done for the ultimate purpose of reproduction. There are certain technical solutions to this predicament. For example, semen can be collected from the woman's cervix after the couple performs sexual intercourse. If this fails to produce satisfactory results, semen can be collected after coitus interruptus with a specially designed condom.³⁹ Ivry offers an account of one doctor who treated a couple whose rabbi refused to sanction the kosher condom and told the woman to stand up after sex and "to drip into a cup."⁴⁰

In other words, women undergo unnecessary bodily intrusions and privacy invasions due to halakhic interference in evidence-based standards of medical care for the treatment of infertility. While this oc-

36. Ivry, "Kosher Medicine."
37. The prohibition of adultery comes after a long list of prohibitions against "uncovering nakedness" in incestuous relations (Lev 18:6–19). In relation to adultery, the Hebrew text uses an unusual combination of words which mean literally "you shall not give your 'laying down to seed' (*schovte'cha le'zara*) with your fellow's wife." The King James Version of the Holy Bible translates this verse, "thou shalt not lie carnally with thy neighbour's wife."
38. Zohar, *Alternatives*, 74.
39. Haimov-Kochman et al., "Infertility Counseling."
40. Ivry, "Kosher Medicine," 671.

curs at the level of clinical care only in the case of observant patients who adhere to rabbinic authority, the ultra-Orthodox influence at the level of policy and law affects all individuals who wish to use ART in Israel. We shall see that halakhic sensitivity about seed explains a propensity to accept and even prefer the use of sophisticated hi-tech reproductive medicine that subject women's bodies to invasive medical interventions over less intrusive lo-tech measures. A particular example of this propensity can be found in the directives issued by the Israeli Ministry of Health regarding sex selection for non-medical purposes by means of preimplantation genetic diagnosis (PIGD), which was allowed for the first time in "the cohen case."

The Cohen Case

In 2002, an ultra-Orthodox couple in their twenties who were unable to have children because the husband had no sperm in his semen—that is, he suffered from azoospermia—asked the ministry of health's legal advisor to approve the use of PIGD after in vitro fertilization of the wife's egg cells with donor sperm, so as to select female embryos for implantation. Under Israeli law, abortion on grounds of sex selection is illegal, but the legal advisor nonetheless approved the couple's request. Her decision created a precedent for permissible uses of PIGD, since the couple presented without any medical indication for undergoing the procedure. Rather, the reason behind this unusual request related to the husband being a *cohen*.[41] The legal advisor explained that, without sex selection, this couple could not have had children at all, and "sometimes we have to adapt to the spirit and tradition of the people."[42] In the haredi community, infertility is seen as a disability and a source of great shame. The stigma could affect the prospects of family members for arranged marriage, and in any event intimate family affairs are kept secret. But in this case it would be extremely difficult to keep the use of donor sperm a secret, because of the fact that the husband was a cohen.

A cohen is a male who is a patrilineal descendent of the select tribe of priests originating in Aaron, the brother of Moses, who exercised political power and performed special sacrificial rituals in the days of the Temple in Jerusalem. To this day, cohens retain special status in or-

41. Siegel Itzkovich, "Israel allows Sex Selection."
42. Traubman and Shadmi, "Precedent in Israel."

thodox religious practice and fill a unique role in synagogue prayer services after they turn thirteen, the age of bar mitzvah. For example, it is customary to call up a cohen for the first portion of the weekly reading of the Torah, and there is a point in the orthodox prayer service where the cohens rise and face the congregation to deliver a priestly blessing—but only boys act as cohens. In the present case, however, this would mean that the secret of the donated sperm would have to come out. Since the child was not the father's biological offspring, he would not be allowed to take part in the services as a cohen, and the secret would become public. On the other hand, girls do not participate actively in synagogue prayer services, so if the child was female the couple could keep it a secret that she was not the biological offspring of her father. For this reason, the couple wished to select the sex of the embryo so as to guarantee that a girl would be born. The community would not know that she was not the couple's natural child, nor would there be any need to tell the girl herself.

Western bioethics takes a cautious approach toward the use of PIGD because it provides a technical platform for the engineering and enhancement of embryos. Therefore, the rule is that PIGD should be employed only to prevent the birth of a child suffering from a serious disease. If the disease is sex-linked, there is a therapeutic indication for the use of PIGD for sex selection, but otherwise such use is not allowed. Article 14 of the European Convention on Human Rights and Biomedicine (1997) thus states that "[t]he use of techniques of medically assisted procreation shall not be allowed for the purpose of choosing a future child's sex, except where serious hereditary sex-related disease is to be avoided."[43] Another reason for reservations about the use of PIGD is that women should not undergo the intrusive procedures and risks entailed in IVF without medical justification.

One comment on the cohen case suggests that the shame of male infertility in a haredi community is a form of suffering much like that which prompts others to undergo cosmetic surgery;[44] but in the case of cosmetic surgery, the procedure affects the body of the suffering person, whereas in the present case it is another person—the wife—who undergoes the medical intervention. Furthermore, the root cause of suffering is not a

---

43. "Convention for the Protection of Human Rights," Council of Europe, Article 14.

44. Weitzman and Harari, "Revisiting Sex Selections."

medical one but a patriarchal society in which male self-esteem is caught up with virility and women's bodies are enlisted to keep up pretenses. The solution also presents a patriarchal prejudice, since the preference for a girl derives paradoxically from the inferior status that underlies her exclusion from equal participation in public religious life. In other words, rather than addressing social issues by appropriate means, medicine is recruited to reinforce the fundamentalist stereotypes and prejudices that lie at the core of the predicament in the first place.

From a medical point of view, concern for women's bodily integrity, health, and well-being ought to indicate the exhaustion of all less invasive measures before resorting to IVF. One might therefore ask: Why was the couple not offered the alternative of AI with sperm from a donor who is also a cohen? The status of a cohen passes from father to son, so if the sperm donor were a cohen and a boy child were born, the child would also be a cohen. This would not only eliminate the need for sex selection but also make it unnecessary for the woman to undergo invasive IVF procedures, since AI with donated sperm would suffice to achieve a pregnancy.

It is quite likely that the possibility of solving this couple's predicament by using AI with sperm from a cohen donor never even occurred. This is because the rabbis generally disapprove of using sperm from a Jewish donor, even in the case of unmarried women where there is no concern about *mamzerut*, due to concern about the blurring of paternity with anonymous donations[45] and the subsequent fear of future half-sibling marriages.[46] The ultra-Orthodox preference for non-Jewish sperm donors is a consequence of a fiction in Jewish law that says there is no relation to the child if the biological father is non-Jewish;[47] by virtue of the same fiction, if the children are not legally affiliated with the father and have different mothers (recipients of sperm from the same non-Jewish donor), they are not regarded as legal siblings.[48]

---

45. Zohar, *Alternatives*, 72.

46. Halperin, "Definition of Parenthood," 187. The concern about the blurring of paternity and the fear of half-sibling marriages could be averted by registries of sperm donations, like those established under the legislation on surrogacy and egg cell donations. It is somewhat of a mystery why sperm donor registries do not exist in Israel. This requires further research, which lies beyond the scope of the present article.

47. Levi, "Surrogacy."

48. The health risks of half-sibling procreation nonetheless persist, but if the

This case raises several points. First, it provides one more illustration of the ways in which the clinical practice of infertility medicine in Israel is adapted to meet ultra-Orthodox demands. Second, it served as a precedent for an administrative directive issued by the ministry of health in 2005, which permits the use of PIGD for sex selection for non-medical purposes in other exceptional cases as a matter of general policy.[49] Third, it demonstrates a preference for the use of sophisticated ART that entail significant intrusions into women's bodies over less invasive therapeutic interventions. Indeed, Kahn suggests that the use of IVF as opposed to AI is preferred for married women because of sensitivities about sperm stemming from the biblical prohibition of adultery: "[a] clear halakhic distinction can be made between the act of sperm being introduced into a woman's reproductive tract, which can be understood to be unequivocally prohibited, and the act of an embryo being introduced into her, for which there is no clear prohibition. In other words, the prohibition against adultery is only against putting 'seed' in thy neighbor's wife; it is not against putting an embryo in her. Thus IVF and embryo transfer are preferred by some rabbis as a form of fertility treatment that do not violate the literal Halakhic precepts against adultery."[50]

As we shall see below, similar reasoning related to the significance of seed may explain yet another instance of the halakhic propensity for hi-tech reproductive interventions—that is, a rabbinic preference for reproductive cloning over IVF, and for stem cell research with cloned human embryos rather than with fertilized egg cells.

The Significance of Seed

As mentioned above, rabbinic involvement in the clinical care for infertile ultra-Orthodox couples reveals a concern about masturbation. In the halakhic imagination, masturbation signifies a waste of the reproductive potential of sperm. This view underlies the condemnation of homosexuality as well as restrictions on the use of contraceptive measures.[51] In halakhic discourse, the improper emission of sperm or

sperm donor is non-Jewish, the statistical probability of this occurring is far less.
    49. Shalev and Hashiloni-Dolev, "Bioethics Gouvernance," 159.
    50. Kahn, *Reproducing Jews*, 103–4.
    51. Ir-Shay, "Family Planning."

semen (*zera*) is referred to as the "waste of seed" (*hashkhatat zera*) and is regarded as a capital offense. The prohibition against "spilling seed in vain" (*hotza'at zera le-battala*) is so severe that according to Maimonides, the great medieval codifier of Jewish law, masturbation is tantamount to killing a human being (Mishneh Torah, Hilkhot Issurei Biah 21:18).

The source of the prohibition against discharging semen without reproductive purpose is in the biblical story of Onan (Gen 38:1–10) from which the term "onanism" (masturbation or coitus interruptus) is derived. In this story, "seed" (*zera*) means issue, progeny, or offspring. The sin of onanism occurs because Onan refuses to fulfill the duty of levirate (*yibbum*) in order to guarantee the genetic continuity of his elder brother, who died without having begotten any children. It is not insignificant that the story concerns the sons of Judah, who was the patriarchal head of the most important of the twelve tribes descending from the children of Israel (Jacob). Onan was Judah's second son and was expected to marry Tamar, his elder brother's widow, so as to "raise up issue [*zera*]" for the childless deceased. According to the text, Onan refused to fulfill his fraternal duty because he "knew that the issue would not be his." The commentators explain that the firstborn child of a levirate marriage carries the name of the deceased, as if it were his offspring. So whenever Onan slept with "his brother's wife," he "wasted [his seed] on the ground [*shikhet artza*]" (Gen 38:9), presumably by withdrawal and extravaginal ejaculation. The story of Tamar does not end here—indeed, she is the heroine of a tale of deception and intrigue in which she tricks Judah so as to become the founding mother of the line of King David.[52] Here, however, God punishes Onan by taking his life.

In the halakhic view, therefore, wasting seed is a serious offense that incurs capital punishment and amounts to shedding blood (Talmud, Nidah 13a). Similarly, there is the view that a man's failure to fulfill the commandment to be fruitful and multiply is equivalent to murder.[53] This is in stark contrast to the halakhic view of the human embryo. That is to say, while halakha accords the utmost importance to seed, it is relatively lenient about the value of prenatal life. In the halakhic view, the human embryo gains moral value as a matter of gradual development from "mere water" (*maya b'alma*) during the first forty days of pregnan-

---

52. Ramon, "Lion Heart."
53. Ir-Shay, "Family Planning," 98.

cy (Talmud, Yevamot 69b) to full human status after birth.[54] Therefore, the value of the life of an unborn child and that of the pregnant woman are distinctly unequal. If a woman is having difficulty in childbirth and her life is at stake, there is a clear duty to save her life before that of the fetus, so long as the child has not emerged for the most part from the birth canal (Mishna, Ohalot 7:6).[55]

What is more, according to Steinberg, a prominent expert on halakhic medical ethics, only within the womb does the embryo develop into an entity of value, so that a fertilized egg in a petri dish (a blastocyst) is not considered to be an embryo. Therefore, it is erroneous to speak of "embryonic" stem cells, because the cluster of cells in the blastocyst before implantation is not called an embryo. This is learned from analogy to a hypothetical discussion about the killing of a golem, which concludes that this would not amount to murder because a golem is not brought into the world through gestation in a woman's womb. Yet even if a fertilized egg does not have any title to life, there are other pertinent halakhic considerations, including the prohibition against wasting seed. For example, a blastocyst may be used as a source of stem cells only if the egg cell was fertilized initially for infertility treatment but is no longer needed for that purpose. This comports with a generally accepted international norm that human embryos should not be created for the sole purpose of research. However, the halakhic rationale is not related to any sensitivity about the moral status of the embryo but rather to the concern that if an egg was fertilized solely in order to produce stem cells for research, then this would entail the improper emission of sperm.[56]

---

54. Jakobovits, "Jewish Views." The primary source for the value of prenatal life is a chapter in the Bible that addresses various incidents of personal injury, or what we might call the law of torts. The particular verses (Exod 21:22–23) concern the case of a pregnant woman who gets hurt in the course of a brawl between some men, so that she suffers a miscarriage and loses the fetus. The rule is that if the woman survives the incident, the attacker must compensate her husband for the loss of the fetus by paying for the damage as if it were property; if the woman suffers fatal injury and dies, then the man responsible for her death is guilty of a capital crime. The conclusion that the sanction for killing an unborn child is payment of damages rather than a death sentence indicates that the unborn child is not considered to be a full human life (*nefesh*).

55. "If a woman is in hard labor, one cuts up the child within her womb and extracts it member by member, because her life comes before the life of the child. But if the greater part has already come out, one may not touch it, for one may not set aside one life for another life" (Mishna, Ohalot 7:6).

56. Steinberg, "Stem Cell Experiments," 274–76.

By the same halakhic logic, research with stem cells obtained from cloned human embryos appears to be preferable to research with stem cells from surplus IVF embryos, since cloning embryos by means of nuclear cell transfer requires no sperm at all. Furthermore, reproductive cloning—which raises so many objections in the Western ethical discourse[57]—might even be preferred over methods of infertility treatment that involve the collection of sperm. From a halakhic point of view, there is nothing inherently prohibited in asexual reproduction, and cloning does not represent a negative meddling with nature (referred to as witchcraft). The product of cloning would moreover enjoy the full status of a human being rather than be regarded as a golem, because it would be born of a woman. Nevertheless, there are some unresolved questions about the determination of fatherhood: specifically whether the definition of fatherhood is the consequence of contributing sperm, or whether paternity can arise from contributing genetic material that is contained in the nucleus of a mature cell. As opposed to AI of a married woman with donor sperm, however, the issue of *mamzerut* may be rendered moot in the case of cloning, even where the egg cell is provided by a married woman and the cell nucleus is obtained from a Jewish man who is not her husband, because "the situation does not involve sperm from an outside donor but rather complex genetic material."[58] In other words, not only does the halakhic view fail to find fault with human cloning on any matter of principle; it actually considers it to be advantageous in certain respects since it circumvents the halakhic problems associated with the improper emission of seed. It may follow that sophisticated cloning technology could be preferred over the relatively non-invasive intervention of AI with donor sperm for the treatment of male infertility.

Conclusion

The influence of halakha on the law and policy of ART in Israel is well-known. In this article, I have argued that while Jewish law is characteristically pluralistic, the regulation of third-party ART practices in Israel (egg cell donations and surrogate mother agreements) is in fact guided by strict ultra-Orthodox interpretations of halakha. In the ultra-Orthodox view of the world, a major concern is to preserve the unique

57. Shalev, "Reflections."
58. Steinberg, "Human Cloning."

essence of the Jewish people and the integrity of its bio-social body. While it embraces the use of ART as a means to fulfill the fundamental commandment to be fruitful and multiply, it also lays down multiple conditions as to how these means may or may not be employed in conformity with biblical paradigms of forbidden sexual relationships.

In effect, these conditions lay down rules of *kashrut*—that is, propriety and legitimacy—for the use of ART on two levels: law and policy in general, and clinical practice for ultra-Orthodox couples. With regard to law and policy, halakhic considerations determine the legitimacy of reproductive relationships in terms of the eligibility of adults to collaborate to bring a child into the world, depending on their ethnicity and on the marital status of the women. Likewise, halakhic considerations determine the fitness of the offspring to marry as full members of the collective. At the clinical level, halakhic demands have led to the introduction of rabbinical supervision of quality control services established in hospital laboratories especially for ultra-Orthodox couples in order to prevent mishaps or mix-ups in the handling of gametes and fertilized eggs. Similarly, infertility clinics have adopted extraordinary treatment protocols that involve unnecessary invasions of women's bodies so as to accommodate the ultra-Orthodox concern that seed not be "spilled," including the design of a special medical device that legitimizes otherwise forbidden collection of sperm.[59]

Discussions of the halakhic influence over definitions of legal kinship have a tendency to focus on the prohibition of adultery, the transgression of which is punished by visiting upon the offspring the taint of *mamzerut*. The gendered norm that forbids adultery indeed explains why unmarried women are designated to provide reproductive services for others under Israeli law. Furthermore, concerns about *mamzerut* as a result of half-sibling marriages between the offspring of anonymous third-party reproductive collaborations underlie the establishment of statutory registries to keep track of the children—not because there is recognition of the children's right to know their biological origins but in order to allow inspection by rabbinical marriage registrars so as to prevent forbidden marriages.

---

59. The idea of designing and using a special perforated condom instead of masturbation or coitus interruptus is similar to the idea of designing and using a special timer for discontinuing life support machines at the end of life rather than pulling the plug (Shalev, "Reclaiming the Voice").

At the same time, this article suggests that the preoccupation of the ultra-Orthodox halakhic imagination with male seed is also a key to understanding attitudes toward ART in Israel. Interestingly enough, a further reading of the biblical source of the prohibition of adultery (Lev 18:20) reveals that it too uses the word "seed" (*zera*), in contrast with the preceding verses which prohibit various incestuous relations by reference to "uncovering nakedness" (*erva*). Concern about the proper and improper emission of seed comes to light from observing the ways in which the medical practice of infertility treatment has been adapted for the use of ultra-Orthodox couples. Even though the purpose of ejaculation in the infertility clinic is for reproduction, ultra-Orthodox rabbis insist that if sperm is not emitted inside the woman's vagina, it amounts to wasting seed or spilling seed in vain. As a result, ultra-Orthodox women undergo intrusive bodily procedures for the purpose of determining whether the cause of the couple's infertility is found in the male partner. The same concern about extravaginal ejaculation explains why the highly sophisticated technological notion of reproductive cloning, at least in theory, appears to be preferred over the relatively simple lo-tech option of AI with donor sperm. A preference for subjecting women's bodies to hi-tech interventions so as to solve quandaries originating from sensitivity about male fertility is also demonstrated by the cohen case. In addition, this case illustrates how the accommodation of ultra-Orthodox demands for extraordinary uses of ART creates a precedent that then serves as ground for making general policy for all persons, regardless of their religious affiliation or faith.

While rights of access to ART in Israel are governed by a liberal and permissive jurisprudence, the regulatory mechanisms adopted by legislators and policy makers are guided by fundamentalist and gendered rules that embody ultra-Orthodox interpretations of halakhic tenets of sexuality and reproduction. The ultra-Orthodox influence on law and policy is not explicit but implicit within the mechanisms of state power that enforce rules controlling the reproductive agency of women and the human rights of their children. This article suggests that ultra-Orthodox views not only determine the legitimacy of third-party reproductive practices under Israeli law but also play an important role in favoring and encouraging the use of sophisticated reproductive technologies that require subjecting women's bodies to intrusive medical interventions.

The article posits that rabbinic approval and embrace of invasive infertility treatments such as IVF and reproductive cloning are associated not only with the fundamental commandment to be fruitful and multiply but also with the high value the halakhic worldview places on seed. This stands in contrast to the Western preoccupation with the moral status of new forms of human embryonic life, that is, with the frozen fertilized eggs that exist outside the womb, suspended in time and space in hospital laboratories around the globe, and with the human rights of the women who undergo these various medical interventions as patients, egg cell donors, or surrogate mothers. This leads to an absurdity from a feminist point of view: for while sperm appears to be an abundant natural resource that is readily available and easily accessible—certainly when compared to egg cells—it gains the status of a most precious essence that must not be wasted in the ultra-Orthodox imagination. The result is a postmodern fundamentalism that instrumentalizes women's bodies in order to mediate highly sophisticated medical interventions for the purpose of preserving male seed.

Bibliography

Barilan, Michael Y. "Revisiting the Problem of Jewish Bioethics: The Case of Terminal Care." *Kennedy Institute of Ethics Journal* 13/2 (2003) 141–68.

Birenbaum-Carmeli, Daphna. "'Cheaper than a Newcomer': On the Social Production of IVF Policy in Israel." *Sociology of Health & Illness* 26/7 (2004) 897–924.

Birenbaum-Carmeli, Daphna, and Yoram S. Carmeli, editors. *Kin, Gene, Community: Reproductive Technology among Jewish Israelis*. Oxford: Berghahn, 2010.

"Brain-Respiratory Death Bill [Hebrew]." *Hatza'ot Chok Knesset* Jan 22, 2008, 120.

Collins, John A. "An International Survey of the Health Economics of IVF and ICSI." *Human Reproduction Update* 8/3 (2002) 265–77.

"Convention for the Protection of Human Rights and Dignity of the Human Being with regard to the Application of Biology and Medicine: Convention on Human Rights and Biomedicine." Council of Europe, Oviedo, Apr 04, 1997. Online: http://conventions.coe.int/Treaty/en/Treaties/Html/164.htm.

De Mouzon, Jacques, et al. "World Collaborative Report on Assisted Reproductive Technology, 2002." *Human Reproduction* 24 (2009) 2310–20.

Friedman, Menachem. *The Haredi (Ultra-Orthodox) Society: Sources, Trends and Processes*. Research Series 41. Jerusalem: Jerusalem Institute for Israel Studies, 1991. Online: http://www.jiis.org/.upload/haredcom.pdf.

Haimov-Kochman, Ronit, et al. "Infertility Counseling for Orthodox Jewish Couples." *Fertility & Sterility* 93/6 (2010) 1816–19.

Halperin, Mordechai. "The Definition of Parenthood and the Right to Find Biological Roots." In *Moral Dilemmas in Medicine*, edited by Raphael Cohen-Almagor, 161–88. Jerusalem: Van Leer Institute, 2002 [Hebrew].

Hashiloni-Dolev, Yael. "Between Mothers, Fetuses and Society: Reproductive Genetics in the Israeli-Jewish Context." *Nashim: A Journal of Jewish Women's Studies & Gender Issues* 12 (2006) 129–50.

Herzl, Theodor. *Altneuland—Old-New Land* (1902). Translated by Paula Arnold. Haifa: Haifa Publishing, 1960.

Hirsch, Dafna. "Jews and Medicine." In *New Jewish Time: Jewish Culture in a Secular Age. An Encyclopedic View*, edited by Yirmiyahu Yovel and David Shaham, 1:318–22. Jerusalem: Keter, 2007 [Hebrew].

Ir-Shay, Ronit. "Family Planning: A Halakhic-Gender Perspective." *Nashim* 12 (2006) 95–128.

Ivry, Tsipy. "Kosher Medicine and Medicalized Halacha." *American Ethnologist* 37/4 (2010) 662–80.

Jakobovits, Immanuel. "Jewish Views on Abortion." In *Jewish Bioethics*, edited by Fred Rosner and J. David Bleich, 118–33. New York: Hebrew Publishing, 1979.

Kahn, Susan M. *Reproducing Jews: A Cultural Account of Assisted Conception in Israel*. Durham, NC: Duke University Press, 2000.

Kaplan Spitz, Elie. "Mamzerut." In *Responsa 1991–2000*, edited by Kassel Abelson and David J. Fine, 558–86. New York: Rabbinical Assembly, 2000. Online: http://www.rabbinicalassembly.org/sites/default/files/public/halakhah/teshuvot/19912000/spitz_mamzerut.pdf?phpMyAdmin=GoIs7ZE%2CH7O%2Ct%2CZ1sDHpI8UAVD6.

Knesset Labor, Welfare, and Health Committee. "Protocol 393," Mar. 04, 2008.

Levi, Shelly. "Surrogacy in Israel: A Review of Halakhic Aspects." Knesset Department for Information and Research, Aug. 2006. Online: http://www.knesset.gov.il/mmm/data/pdf/m01565.pdf [Hebrew].

Mei-Ami, Naomi. "Sperm Donation in Israel." Knesset Research and Information Center, Mar. 2005. Online: http://www.knesset.gov.il/mmm/data/pdf/m01527.pdf [Hebrew].

Ramon, Einat. "The Lion Heart of Tamar." In *Kor'ot MiBreshit: Creative Women Write About the Book of Genesis*, edited by Ruth Ravitzky, 293–300. Tel Aviv: Yedi'ot Aharonot, 2003 [Hebrew].

Shahak, Israel and Norton Mezvinsky. *Jewish Fundamentalism in Israel*. London: Pluto Press, 1999. Online: http://members.tripod.com/alabasters_archive/jewish_fundamentalism.html#1n.

Shalev, Carmel. *Birth Power: The Case for Surrogacy*. New Haven: Yale University Press, 1989.

———. "*Halakha* and Patriarchal Motherhood: An Anatomy of the New Israeli Surrogacy Law." *Israel Law Review* 32/1 (1998) 51–80.

———. "Reclaiming the Patient's Voice and Spirit in Dying: A Perspective from Israel." *Bioethics* 24/3 (2010) 134–44.

———. "Reflections on Human Dignity and the Israeli Cloning Debate." In *The Contingent Nature of Life: Bioethics and Limits of Human Existence*, edited by Marcus Düwell et al., 323–44. Dordrecht: Springer, 2008.

Shalev, Carmel, and Sigal Gooldin. "The Uses and Misuses of In-Vitro Fertilization in Israel: Some Sociological and Ethical Considerations." *Nashim* 12 (2006) 151–76.
Shalev, Carmel, and Yael Hashiloni-Dolev. "Bioethics Governance in Israel: An Expert Regime." *Indian Journal of Medical Ethics* 8/3 (2011) 157–60.
Shalev, Carmel, and Gabriele Werner-Felmayer. "Patterns of Globalized Reproduction: Egg Cells Regulation in Israel and Austria." *Israel Journal of Health Policy Research* 1 (2012), n.p. Online: http://www.ijhpr.org/content/1/1/15.
Sherlo, Yuval. "Egg Cell Donation: Halakha in Practice." *Moreshet*. Online: http://www.moreshet.co.il/web/shut/shut2.asp?id=116954 [Hebrew].
Siegel Itzkovich, Judy. "Israel Allows Sex Selection of Embryos for Non-Medical Reasons." *BMJ* 330 (2005) 1228.
Sperling, Daniel. "Commanding the 'Be Fruitful and Multiply' Directive: Reproductive Ethics, Law and Policy in Israel." *Cambridge Quarterly of Healthcare Ethics* 19/3 (2010) 363–71.
Steinberg, Avraham. "Human Cloning." In *Encyclopedia of Jewish Medical Ethics* 1:509–20. Jerusalem: Feldheim, 2003.
———. "Stem Cell Experiments: Medical, Ethical and Halakhic Aspects." In *Research Ethics*, edited by Ruth Landau and Gabi Shefler, 267–78. Jerusalem: Magnes, 2007 [Hebrew].
Traubman, Tamara, and Haim Shadmi. "A Precedent in Israel: Choosing in Advance the Sex of the Baby." *Ha'Aretz*, Oct 18, 2002. Online: http://news.walla.co.il/?w=//295978. [Hebrew].
Weitzman, Gideon, and David Harari. "Revisiting Sex Selection in Jewish Law." IDEAS: Institute for Jewish Ideas and Ideals, Mar. 22, 2010. Online: http://www.jewishideas.org/articles/revisiting-sex-selection-jewish-law.
Zohar, Noam J. *Alternatives in Jewish Bioethics*. Albany: State University of New York Press, 1997.
———. "From Lineage to Sexual Mores: Examining 'Jewish Eugenics.'" *Science in Context* 11/3–4 (1998) 575–85.

Daughters are Diamonds

When Honor Precludes Reflexivity

Shafinaaz Hassim

This article explores the ways in which "reflexivity of the self" is inhibited in cultures where "honor" is valued, using a small sample of South African Muslim women, whose families originated from India. The concept of "honor" refers to a particular way in which patriarchal structures are conceptualized in some settings. "Family honor," for example, is one constituent of this. The upholding of family honor is seen as a means to maintain the political order, which rests on the broader system of patriarchy. One is made to question the kind of practices considered legitimate in dealing with violations of cultural and familial codes of honor.

Current case studies show that, in extreme situations, the actual physical removal of those who go against the grain of desired behaviors through "honor killings" is socially legitimated by deeply held cultural beliefs, as is the case in contemporary Pakistan. In an honor killing, the honor entailed in the status quo requires protection from any form of subversion. Its defendants seek to eradicate any (perceived) threats to its existence. Hence, when we say that women are killed for the sake of *honor*, we also need to understand what underpins the idea that there is a *duty* to uphold patriarchal structures. In addition, the killings act as a mechanism of terror, which is meant to inspire fear in potential transgressors. It is the very nature of this fear to deny the individual capacity for self-reflexivity.

Honor and Social Behavior

While extreme examples such as those in Pakistan draw attention to the kind of cultural memory and prevalent thought processes in situations concerning "honor," the South African cases that I refer to are far less tangible and extreme. Nevertheless, these ideas of duty and fear may be prevalent even in less "extreme" situations, where murder does not occur but ideas of honor are still fiercely protected. They seem to occur at a psychological level, in the form of stigma and social sanction; the individual may be singled out for daring to deviate from the status quo together with their immediate family upon whom they may rely and from whence comes a qualitative form of support. If, at any point, the immediate family condones the act(s), then this is bound to affect the internal equilibrium of the family unit. The setting of limits and the exertion of pressures may come into play; the sanctioning of particular behaviors can act as an extremely harsh and effective form of social control.[1]

The following considerations are based on my study titled *Daughters are Diamonds*.[2] This research suggests that social behavior among the Indian Muslims in South Africa locates itself in the preservation of patriarchal custom and tradition, which is so deeply embedded in everyday life that its undertaking is almost always mistaken for religious obligation. South African Indian Muslim society draws on a social amalgam of ancestral Indian cultural belief and morally-defined religious norms. The basis of the Islamic polity and way of life is antithetical to the classical conception of the separation of church and state in Western political ideology. Christendom renders "unto Caesar the things which are Caesar's and to God the things which are God's."[3] Islam as a religion presents itself as a complete way of life. This compels Muslims to practice all features of life seen to correspond within it. Cultural belief, traditionalist values, and religion are transposed and inform thoughts and actions. Hence, entrenched cultural acts glean social endorsement

---

1. Hassim, *Daughters*.
2. Ibid.
3. Lewis, *Political Language*, 2.

from being viewed as a duty or an obligation to divine command. Islam denounces the exploitation and control of people of either sex.

The framework for this study asserts that the individual capacity for self-reflexivity is a basic and natural right, as well as the precondition for modern social life. The internalization of values of honor leads many women to expect that deviance from acceptable norms will bring social sanction and stigma. This form of "conditioning" has debilitating outcomes for closing the gap between opportunities and actual achievements. The aim of this research, then, is to explore the perpetuation of gender stereotypes and notions of honor in South African Indian Muslim society, as well as the degree to which they impact the mindsets of people from traditionalist cultures. The statement that "women are diamonds" is often used by Indian Muslim traditionalists to justify the seclusion of women. In this view, that which is valuable should be hidden in safekeeping. The metaphor of the diamond is used to illustrate the objectification of daughters in honor-bound societies and the limits put on the administration of their lives in keeping with the code of honor. This study is a commentary on the notion that, in keeping with this honor code, there is a fine line between maintaining the dignity of a people and infringing on the rights of the individual. It also asks whether women are able to carve out a space for themselves within which a fully reflexive life may be lived in spite of the restrictions placed on them.[4] "The Indian sees himself not merely as the father of a family, but as the founder and head of succeeding generations bearing his name in honour and wealth. He will establish a family trust, make his pilgrimage to Mecca if he is a Moslem, and put his name in large letters on the properties he has built. He becomes a pillar of society during his lifetime and a benefactor of his family at his death."[5]

Family honor is the leading thread through the journey this essay undertakes. The concept of family honor draws from the social identity and status awarded to families and clans, probably over generations. In order to maintain this often prestigious place in society, a number of behaviors and expectations are taught to individual members, male and female. In many instances, the maintenance of this social status is important in setting structures for future generations. On the other hand,

---

4. Hassim, *Daughters*.
5. Calpin, *Indians*, 105, quoted in Ebr.-Vally, *Kala Pani*, 89.

the rigidity implied by such structures can prove to be limiting to the individual. My research focuses on how South African Indian Muslim women perceive and experience the opportunities, challenges, and obstacles facing them. It also looks at the extent, if at all, to which traditionalist culture creates or influences a gap between opportunity and achievement for South African Indian Muslim women.

It is the aim of this research to explore the ways in which the reflexivity of the self is inhibited in cultures where "honor" is valued. What it tests are the limits to freedom of choice allowed to the individual. While moral limits are expected to be set, the question here is whether there are limits that extend far beyond moral boundaries and what implications this social structure has for the individual in developing and achieving goals. As two sides of the coin of social order, male domination and female subordination both impact individuals regardless of gender. The construction and articulation of honor (*izzat*), affects men just as it affects the life decisions and choices available to women. The sociological honor code is constructed in a way that ensures women symbolize this code, and the male members of their family are afforded the responsibility of administering the lives of the objects of honor in order to maintain the family's status within the social unit, or *kutum-qabila*.

The study is set against the backdrop of honor killings in Pakistan. This is not to imply a direct comparison between the extreme case study of honor killings and the experiences of South African Indian Muslim women; rather, it is to illuminate the patriarchal mindset that infringes on the rights and liberties of women in a number of ways, based on the assumption that Muslims of Indian origin, whether in South Africa or Pakistan, share a common cultural heritage. In the extreme case of Pakistan, women who deviate are murdered or physically disfigured; in the South African case, they face social sanction and stigma. This decreases their chances of achieving goals. In the more extreme case, we are more easily able to discern the motivations and rationalizations for—and even resistance to—the attack on individual liberties. In addition, we can illuminate the multicultural social fabric of contemporary South Africa and the residual effects various cultures have on both the network of people and their constructions of individual and national biography.

Academics in the fields of legal jurisprudence and human rights continue to debate the apparent contradictions between notions of gender equality and respect for culture and tradition, especially since the formulation of the new constitution in South Africa. Here, the loss of self-reflexivity is about the loss of newfound freedoms—it rests on oppressive structures within the scope of democratic promise.

This study, then, essentially explores the perpetuation of gender and family stereotypes in South African Indian Muslim society and assesses the degree to which this affects people from traditionalist backgrounds. It thus asks whether and how women are able to carve out a space for themselves within which a fully reflexive life may be lived.

The Loss of Reflexivity

"The payment of honour in daily life is accorded through the offering of precedence (so often expressed through an analogy with the head), and through the demonstrations of respect which are commonly associated with the head whether it is bowed, touched, uncovered or covered . . . Decapitation recognized that there was something worth chopping off. Even where polite society has outlawed physical violence it retains the ritual slap on the face as a challenge to settle an affair of honour, and it was commonly admitted that offences to honour could only be redeemed through blood."[6]

What is meant by the "loss of reflexivity"? For the purpose of this research, we can identify three main mechanisms through which it operates: terror, stigma, and the internalization of values.

1) Terror

Walter suggests that terror "may mean, on the one hand, the psychic state—extreme fear—and, on the other hand, the thing that terrifies—the violent event that produces the psychic state."[7] With this in mind, he acknowledges the importance of unpacking the "process of terror, the act and the fear together in reaction to each other."[8] The systematic proliferation of terror creates instability, anxiety, and fear in its victim target population, and the only condition under which such a situation can be avoided is with the removal of injustice from the political sphere and insidious acts of horror from the psyche of the people. The

---

6. Pitt-Rivers, "Honour," 25.
7. Walter, *Terror*, 5–6.
8. Ibid.

underlying message of the campaign of terror is that rebellion invites its perpetration upon the individual, that abiding by the unspoken laws allows a space within which the individual may carve out some semblance of a "life." The institutionalization of fear allows for the continuation, then, of a system of psychological manipulation and subsequently disallows the self-reflexive capacity of citizenship. So-called honor killings become the deterrent for behavior that is unacceptable to the current status quo, and such acts are furthermore justified in the service they provide by protecting the honor of draconian patriarchal systems entrenched within the family and society. The use of terror is relevant to this study in that it denies self-reflexive capacity. This violation of the individual's human and moral rights becomes second nature in the efforts to maintain the dominant culture. While a contradiction exists between the notion of universal human rights and the arguments of cultural relativists, there is no uncertainty that acts of instilling terror run deeply against the grain of human liberties in an absolute sense.

2) *Stigma*

Notions of stigmatization, or deviance-labeling,[9] have similar implications for denying autonomy to the victims. For Schur, "being female" already carries a degree of stigma because of the ways women are devalued in the sociopolitical arena: "Such categorical devaluation is reflected in and reinforced by numerous applications to women of substantively specific deviance labels ... we might even say that women have served as 'all-purpose' deviants within our society ... These presumed offenses emerge when women are perceived as having violated specific gender system norms—by behaving or even presenting themselves in ways deemed inappropriate for females."[10] Schur suggests that women's social subordination makes them more vulnerable to stigmatization, and "spoiled identity"[11] in turn reinforces that they be socially subordinated and subsequently makes the achievement of goals far more difficult.

---

9. Schur, *Labeling Women Deviant*.
10. Ibid., 7.
11. Goffman, *Stigma*.

3) Internalization of Values

At the heart of these practices, which endorse particular kinds of stigma, are entrenched notions of power and authority within the family. Power is the "possibility of imposing one's will upon the behaviour of other persons" without actually having to exercise this power.[12] The internalization of deeply held cultural beliefs often allows for the domination of some over others. This relationship of authority over subordinates obviously reduces individual liberty and equality. However, having acknowledged and accepted the authority of their husbands, wives in many traditional societies went further; they themselves legitimated the social system of patriarchy.

Subsequently, they endorsed their own limited authority in almost every sphere of life. For Weber, the patriarch thus rules through "traditional authority," constituted by "widely held norms and values that both men and women accept."[13] It should be acknowledged, though, that the occurrence of such relations has not remained in the pre-industrial past. Many people continue to hold onto a culturally-based belief in male domination "as part of the natural order of family life."[14] Indeed, research shows that these relations of inequality, seen from the viewpoint of many traditionalist settings, "are relations not of domination and subordination but of protection and dependency."[15]

Modesty and Shame in Relation to Honor

"Individuals must achieve social status by living up to the cultural ideals entailed by the code of honor, in which the supreme value is autonomy. The weak and dependent, who cannot realize many of the ideals of the honor code, can still achieve respect and honor through an alternative code, the modesty code."[16] This is what constitutes a society governed by high ideals of morality and personhood. It suggests that the individual immersed in it is virtuous and autonomous. If honor derives from the values of autonomy, "then there are many, most notably women,

12. Bendix, *Max Weber*, quoted in Cherlin, *Public and Private Families*, 289.
13. Cherlin, *Public and Private Families*, 289.
14. Ibid., 290.
15. Abu-Lughod, *Veiled Sentiments*, 85.
16. Ibid., 78–79.

who because of their physical, social and economic dependency are handicapped in their efforts to realise these ideals."[17] Abu-Lughod says further that even though there are relative displays of "some of the virtues of autonomy under certain conditions, their path to honor in this system is different."[18] She finds that there exists a significant relationship between honor and modesty. Women in particular are expected to exhibit a great degree of modesty in their conduct toward those who are able to have a greater sense of the perfect ideal (i.e., their social superiors, who are mostly men and then some older women). "To have moral worth, [women] must show modesty."[19] Abu-Lughod identifies that the 'soundness' in the interpretation of sexual modesty within this social unit, is illustrated in its capacity to rationalize honor killings and women's veiling. The conceptualization and experience of the modesty code as "shame" pertains to a society that assigns great value to honor, mainly in the form of social esteem and respectability. More than the available understandings of guilt and shame from the individual point of view, be they from biological factors or socialization agents or perhaps from both, the notion of self-evaluative and self-conscious emotion has implications for the development of the individual as a unit of that moral society. In analyzing the effects of culture, ideology, and power, I refer to the impact on autonomy and self-reflexivity that can be noted due to the socialization tendencies of other "self-conscious emotions" such as shame, guilt, and embarrassment. When shame is given a community consciousness or public emphasis, it translates the bounds of violating self-conceptions of standards and limits, taking on a wholly different status. The kind of "shame" that is culturally expected of the individual self, immersed within a social unit that derives its discourse from that particular culture, is a preemptive one. It is not a reactive state borne of an experience but a preemptive understanding of adverse implications to the honor or *izzat* of the self, the family, and the community/clan (*kutum-qabila*). Guilt and shame motivate moral behavior by enacting and engaging in avoidance behavior "the tendency to act morally in order to avoid the feelings of guilt that one knows would result if one had failed

---

17. Ibid., 33.
18. Ibid.
19. Ibid.

to act as such."[20] This confirms a "complex interplay between the experience of guilt and the motivation of moral and pro-social behaviour."[21]

Subsequently, this translates into the honoring of perceived moral commitments and invariably validates the upholding of unequal ideals of the status quo. Abu-Lughod's research is helpful for understanding the imperative of modesty as a socially constructed reply to the question of the interplay between the realms of men and women, a relationship construed as unequal to some and as that of protector-dependent to others: "Autonomy or freedom is the standard by which status is measured and social hierarchy determined."[22] The social construct of levels of dependency and the arbitrary control of resources and properties allow a distinction to be made between the hierarchies of varying positions of autonomy. This differentiation is then used to validate the social statutes.[23]

Liberty, Consent, and the Disorder of Women

According to Pateman, standard interpretations of classical texts prevent political theory from acknowledging the exclusion of women from the public realm. Political orders are constructed in the image of everything that is antithetical to the female form. If we argue that the exclusion of women from the public sphere is not complete, then we at least have to agree that what little incorporation there might be is essentially different from the inclusion of men. Pateman observes particularly that "[t]he contract theorists constructed sexual difference as a *political* difference, the difference between men's natural freedom and women's natural subjection."[24] Rousseau's emphatic declaration that political order relies on the exclusion of women from the body politic makes his version of self-governance an exclusively male domain. He takes as his justification the premise that women are "a permanently subversive force within the political order."[25] He argues that "[t]he influence of women, even good women, always corrupts men, because women are 'naturally' incapable

---

20. Lindsay-Hartz et al., "Differentiating Guilt and Shame," 290.
21. Ibid.
22. Abu-Lughod, *Veiled Sentiments*, 79.
23. Ibid., 85.
24. Pateman, *Disorder*, 5.
25. Ibid., 17.

of attaining the status of free and equal individuals, or citizens, and incapable of developing the capacities required to give consent."[26]

This poses an immediate question for the notion of participatory democracy, since consent becomes the sole prerogative of one sex.[27] Pateman also notes that "motherhood is seen as the antithesis of the duties of men and citizens."[28] The gendering of both public and private domains, of the economy or state on the one hand and domestic life on the other, is reminiscent of this, as well as widely critiqued by feminists. Pateman moreover suggests that the idea of a "common bond uniting 'individuals' participating in the economy and the practice of contract" is in fact a myth.[29] The bond that does exist is a social contract allowing them to be "united by the interests that they share *as men* in their jurisdiction over women, interests that are protected by the laws and policies of the state"[30] or by the culture or society that endorses them.

Hourani contends that the legal and ethical frameworks in the Arab countries, which largely upheld the primacy of the male, were being challenged by the late twentieth century.[31] Islamic laws of personal status were interpreted anew. Tunisia abolished polygamy, and elsewhere in the Arab world it became a rarer custom. In countries like Tunisia and Iraq, it had become easier for women to request a divorce, while in other Arab countries men retained both the "right" to dissolve a marriage without legal procedure or reason and the right to custody of the children. In some cases, laws of inheritance were reinterpreted and the minimum age of marriage was raised.

One particularly strong observation Hourani makes is that "[e]ven when laws changed, social customs did not necessarily change with them. New laws could not always be enforced, particularly when they came up against deeply rooted social customs which asserted and preserved the domination of the male. That girls should marry early, that their marriages should be arranged by the family, and that wives could easily be repudiated were firm rooted ideas, preserved by wom-

26. Ibid., 76.
27. Ibid., 13.
28. Ibid., 11.
29. Ibid., 7.
30. Ibid.
31. Hourani, *History*.

en themselves; the mother and the mother-in-law were often pillars of the system."[32] Through narrative, Goodwin explores how socially-endorsed power relations affect women in terms of the expectations and regulations that have been culturally entrenched over decades.[33] The violations referred to in this overview such as rape, disfiguration, and murder are explicit in their physical form and have the ability to leave enduring psychological scars. On the other hand, this essay looks at the stigma and ostracization of people (women) who do not conform to particular socially-defined expectations, as well as at the kind of limitations this has for their development as individuals. This also relates to the concept that family honor is a direct product of social conformity, and I therefore proceed to question the (loss of) rationale in upholding that status of "honor" at any expense.

Honor killings suggest that the female is a symbol of her family honor and that any marring of this symbolism requires that she (the symbol) should be "removed." The idea, then, that women are linked with honor is thus not a matter of esteem; rather, it is a gross project of objectification, institutionalizing control over and exploitation of women's human and moral rights. The social and cultural endorsement of such acts by the very people who form the moral fabric of that society serves only to veil the immorality of such acts, be they in the form of physical violence or entrenched attitudes. More significantly, they heighten the dangerous implications of relations of power and control that seek legitimacy in the name of democracy or, worse yet, in the form of divine sanction. This calls into question the nature of repressive regimes and the systems of subjugation they perpetuate, and this in turn impacts on the reflexive potential of citizenship. History shows us ample instances of acquiescence—for example, by the populace in Nazi Germany or in Russia under Stalin. The totalitarian and terror-filled ideologies that feed into such systems need to be analyzed in terms of the kind of oppressive relations that ripple down the scale of the social hierarchy and into the family, carrying through the generations. In this way, we can uncover the kinds of social control and the inequalities that arise. Themes of reference center on the notion of patriarchy as a basis for society. Patriarchy is focused not on the behavior of women but on the expected and acceptable models of behavior. These

---

32. Ibid., 441.
33. Goodwin, *Price*.

expectations, then, set limits and exert pressures on maintaining the sociopolitical order.

"The [Muslim] Moroccan Fatima Mernissi, in *Beyond the Veil*, argues that sexual inequality [in Morocco] was based upon, or at least justified by, a view of women as having a dangerous power which must be contained; this, she suggested, was a view which was incompatible with the needs of an independent nation in the modern world."[34] The impact on contemporary mindsets is thus of particular importance when we consider the paradox of a society that continues to endorse a premodern form of social control while at the same time trying to parallel the rest of the world in its technological advancements (e.g., Jordan, where democratic principles seem to be accessible only to the elite; at the grassroots level, cultural imposition and honor killings continue unabated). The case of Pakistan is somewhat different in the extent to which culture and religion play a role in endorsing particular social intercourse. This case study provides a platform from which to debate notions of individual liberty and the right to dignity.

Analyzing the Findings

It is interesting to note the way in which women are socialized to subordinate positions as well as their internalized notions of honor (*izzat*) and what is relevant for the family and generations to come (*khandaan*), as well as for the household community sphere (*kutum-qabila*) in terms of their different roles and the expectations of them. Furthermore, I explore the concept of patience (*sabr*) as a socialization agent and also as a form of social control, as opposed to its intended goal of spiritual uplifting and developing an individual who enjoins the tenets of patience with good moral living.[35]

The study is structured around the biographical narratives of six women from the Indian Muslim community in Johannesburg. Each of these women, regardless of her age or level of education, proved to be a philosopher in her own right. Mira (27) is a progressive, career-oriented woman who faces the task of reconciling her parents' wish that she marry someone of their choice with her own more liberal conception of life; one which, until now, they have fully supported. Fiona (35),

34. Hourani, *History*, 442.
35. Hassim, *Daughters*.

Fiza (42), Sima (44), and Salma (46) are all married with children. Zara (59) has never been married but has instead spent her life rearing both her siblings and their children.[36] "[T]he interpersonal context revealed in women's personal narratives suggests how women's lives are shaped through and evolve within relationships with others. Feminists have long noted the special reliance of women upon the resources of networks of family and kin, and the important role women play in nurturing and maintaining such networks. Indeed, this reliance may well be a function of women's relative powerlessness."[37]

Andrea Rugh reminds us that "exaggeration is not foreign to these narratives," and that the stories are "presented as the women see themselves, woven through with their corrections, additions and omissions of time past, and cast in the mould of their developed themes."[38] What we seek, then, is not "the truth," since "this is but one of the many truths that reside in the drama of human events. Each woman is aware of how critical it is to present oneself to the world effectively. Not only she herself gains from this kind of glorified presentation, but so do all the others—parents, husbands, children, relatives—that make up the extended self and suffer the consequences or reap the rewards of one another's accomplishments."[39] In a social setting comprised of customs that make a woman the custodian of a communal honor, the pressure to glorify this presentation is no doubt deeply ingrained. "As she grows up, a girl is assigned child-care (and household) responsibilities and is made aware that her sex is a potential source of shame and dishonor. She is constantly told that she is inferior to her brothers and that 'you are a woman and you are going to someone else's house where you had better know how to behave.'"[40]

Zara (59) defines the concept of household honor, or what she refers to as *ghar jo izzat*, as follows: "It means respect. [He] didn't want anyone to say anything against the family and especially against him, so he was strict ... He used to say [about regulating the behavior of the daughter-in-law in the family]: '*ijjat pachhi; pehla ijjat. maru chuna keh*

36. Ibid.
37. Personal Narratives Group, *Interpreting Women's Lives*, 20.
38. Atiya, *Khul-Khaal*, ix.
39. Ibid.
40. Kabir, "On the Women's Liberation Movement," quoted in Callaway and Creevey, *Heritage*, 34.

nu ai pachhi chuna keh di ai. I don't want that.' [First (my/our) honour, then (their) honour. (Because) people will say that first she's (my/our) daughter-in-law, then they will say that she's (their) daughter]" (Zara, 59, unmarried).

In addition to her upbringing, age at marriage, and family's class status, each woman's present role within her family affects the nature and range of decision making allowed to her. For example, Salma (46), married at nineteen, gives insight into her situation: "I got engaged in November and married in January. It was the end of my young days. I only agreed [because] my grandfather gave my mother hell about keeping a daughter in the house and maybe entertaining my ideas of studying" (Salma, 46). About her mother she reveals: "As far as she was concerned, housework was more important for females... to her studying wasn't important; to her, 'izzat' was more important, you know. She made it very difficult for me to study for my matric finals" (Salma, 46).

Women in more affluent households may not be required to work in order to supplement the family income. Financial dependence removes an essential source of power and opportunity in making decisions.

Conversely, Sima (44) is required to involve herself in the family business alongside her husband due to financial necessity, and over time she obtains a growing amount of freedom in the decisions regarding the lives of her children. Financial success elevates her status in the extended family and especially in the eyes of her mother-in-law. This is a contrast to the earlier stages of her married life, when she was not allowed to take part in discussions between her husband and his mother regarding communal decisions that invariably affected her. She remembers that, for the sake of respect toward her mother-in-law, she was unable to accompany her husband to his weekly cricket matches on many occasions. Instead, she was expected to remain behind in the kitchen.[41]

In the case of each of the married women I interviewed, there exists a definite sense of the crucial relationship with the figure of the mother-in-law and the impact that this person has on their respective relationships with their husbands (and often, even with their own children). For example, both Fiza (42) and Sima (44) mention that when they were first married, their husbands were expected to hand over their entire paychecks to their mothers, and personal spending required

---

41. Hassim, *Daughters*.

them to request their mothers' permission. Fiza (42) suffered depression throughout the first two years of her marriage because she struggled to establish a bond with her husband. She felt that she was not able to relate to her mother-in-law either, even though she spent most of her waking hours with her. She furthermore attributes the learning difficulties experienced by her child to her depression. Together, mothers and mother-in-laws form a social system in their own right in maintaining the transfer of expectations and social controls.

The study also looked at the kinds of religious and cultural texts that may inform social expectation. The primary religious text referred to is the Qur'an, while the cultural texts referred to a range of material published on the Indian and Pakistani subcontinent. This latter form of literature is readily made available to South Africans in *madrassas* as well as in community bookshops. Religious and cultural texts often serve as agents of socialization and establishing a guide for expected and accepted behaviors. While religious texts tend to justify the upholding of morality, cultural texts tend to be responsible for the contradictions and misgivings operating in everyday modern social life as we know it. This is because the interpretation of authentic religious texts from a cultural standpoint tends to lend them a patriarchal bias that is contradictory and hence problematic. The line of difference between the two is blurred, and people often tend to confuse the obligation of religion with the sentiment of tradition. The practices that limit the autonomy in an individual's life are explained as adhering to religious obligation. The line between the religion of Islam as a way of life and traditionalist thinking that derives from the Indian culture becomes blurred, and a woman internalizes this transposed network of ambiguity as a natural condition. She naturalizes her own dependency and subordination as part of her greater link with Faith. In so doing, she becomes the perfect candidate for perpetuating the system later on in life as a mother or mother-in-law.[42]

Scholars Revisit the Historical Text of the Qur'an

> "From the cradle . . . and for the duration of a lifetime . . . the practising Muslim lives by the Qur'an. The verses in the Qur'an

---

42. Ibid.

which were revealed to the Prophet Muhammad in the seventh century and the traditions connected with his life provide the Believer with a system of laws, obligations and moral values, and constitute a code of conduct and distinctive way of life . . . Despite the recognition given by the Prophet to the rights of women, the patriarchal nature of pre-Islamic society . . . continued to predominate and many of the enlightened ideals enshrined in the Qur'an were largely overridden by the customary laws which operated."[43]

The life experience of women in Islam is shaped by the patriarchal interpretation of the Qur'an. Divine sanction is justification for the prescribed norms and rules for acceptable behaviors and guidelines for avoiding taboos. A number of scholars revisit the classical interpretation and provide the logic that previous interpretations were embedded in a context where the basis of patriarchies was never considered in terms of the unequal status it afforded women. Because of this, previous readings are steeped in patriarchal rhetoric that poses problems for the implementation of social laws regarding women and adversely affects their experience of life:

> "[I]n spite of the diversity of Muslim cultures and societies, women in many societies have to endure similar forms of sexual inequality and discrimination. These range from cultural mores and psychological attitudes that condone bigotry or violence towards women, to laws that refuse to recognize them as legal and moral agents on a par with men, to the restriction or denial of political-economic rights and resources to them relative to men. What is more, discrimination, and even oppression, [is] often justified by recourse to sacred knowledge or, more accurately, knowledge claiming to derive from religion, including from Islam's Scripture, the Qur'an."[44]

Asma Barlas identifies a central concern facing women in Muslim societies, which is "the prevalence of discriminatory and misogynistic practices and ideologies (howsoever defined) which prevent them from realising their full human potential and, in some cases, from being able to meet even their most basic needs for survival."[45] She finds "the ten-

---

43. Hall and Ismail, *Sisters*, 39.
44. Barlas, "Muslim Women," 117–18.
45. Ibid., 118–19.

dency to read misogyny and discrimination *into* Islam, particularly into the Quran" rather problematic and hence worthy of analysis.⁴⁶ Barlas' work culminates in a recent academic work titled *"Believing Women" in Islam: Gender and Patriarchy in the Qur'an* and aims to allow readers a view of the Qur'an which is not tainted by Western media stereotypes or by Muslim cultural practice. She asserts that "Muslims came to read inequality and patriarchy into the Qur'an to justify existing religious and social structures and demonstrates that the patriarchal meanings ascribed to the Qur'an are a function of who has read it, how, and in what contexts."⁴⁷

"As numerous scholars have pointed out, patriarchal and sexual patterns in Muslim states are a function also of the nature of the state and political economy, cultural practices that may have nothing to do with Islam, the history of a particular society, women's social class, the choices available to them, etc."⁴⁸ The teachings of the Qur'an, she contends, are egalitarian and antipatriarchal in nature.⁴⁹

Wadud proposes that in terms of Qur'anic injuncture, "there is no essential difference in the value attributed to women and men . . . Man and woman are two categories of the human species given the same or equal consideration and endowed with the same or equal potential . . . The Qur'an encourages all believers, male and female, to follow their belief with actions, and for this it promises them a great reward."⁵⁰ "Muslim progressives have long argued that it is not the religion, but patriarchal explication and implementation of the Qur'an that have kept women oppressed . . . The Qur'an does not prescribe one timeless and unchanging social structure for men and women."⁵¹ Wadud's argument affirms that "the Qur'an holds greater possibilities for guiding human society to a more fulfilling and productive mutual collaboration between men and women than as yet attained by Muslims or non-Muslims."⁵²

Barlas raises a number of questions as she interrogates the notion of patriarchal readings of the Qur'an and suggests that, indeed, the cul-

46. Ibid., 119.
47. Barlas, *Believing Women*, blurb.
48. Barlas, "Muslim Women," 118.
49. Barlas, *Believing Women*.
50. Wadud, *Qur'an*, 15.
51. Ibid., blurb.
52. Ibid.

tural derivatives of interpretation leave us with problematic implications for the way of life shaped for men and women respectively.[53] In one interview, the respondent questions her "equation of patriarchy with *zulm* [violation], rightly pointing out that since most people view patriarchy as universal and 'natural,' they are unlikely to share [Barlas'] definition of it as a form of *zulm* [violation] against women. Isn't it hubris, she asks further, to suggest that there has been something quite misguided about Muslim readings of Islam for a millennium and a half?"[54] Her research goes on to grapple with real-life concerns: "[H]ow can Muslims revise gender roles? Won't people resist egalitarian readings of the Quran? Can there be a meaningful dialogue between Muslim feminists and the standard bearers of patriarchy? These questions reveal real anxiety that the issue of Muslim women's rights not just remain at the level of theoretical discussions."[55]

Conclusion

The six women who form the core of this project were interviewed about more than their life circumstances. They revealed a great deal about the experiences and concepts which frame their thinking and decisions. These fall on a continuum. At one end of the continuum are those who felt extreme pressures upon them to conform and did conform; at the other end were those who felt these pressures in a milder form and were able to negotiate a better range of choices for themselves.

That male honor and female modesty are linked in intrinsic ways as this study discovers, is and continues to be a problematic finding, suggesting that the locus of power remains skewed in favor of men; also largely detrimental to the status of women. The discovery raises important questions about the patriarchal bias of social codes and behaviour, as well as the general perpetuation of gender crimes, domestic violence and so-called 'corrective rape' of perceived deviants of narrowly regulated masculinity and femininity. For as long as woman is seen as the object relating to male honor, a possession in crude sense, she will be open to vilification and abuse, and her autonomy grossly limited.

---

53. Barlas, "Muslim Women."
54. Ibid., 136.
55. Ibid., 137.

There is no simple correlation; there are no predictable patterns in the post-modern drama of human events. A network of social factors accosts each woman (and man) along the path of life. This network consists of multiple controls and multiple opportunities that the individual has to find his or her way through. These are among the numerous social features that invariably affect the continuum of differing degrees of reflexivity and autonomy allowed to the individual.[56]

There is a continual effort to infuse post-apartheid South African society with new literature on the diversity of life in and specifically on emerging cultural conceptualizations of life in the new era. While this remains limited, and may have proven a limit to the frame of reference for this study, it also points to the need for further research of this nature with regard to the various traditionalist settings in South Africa.

Bibliography

Abu-Lughod, Lila. *Veiled Sentiments: Honor and Poetry in a Bedouin Society*. Berkeley: University of California Press, 1988.

Atiya, Nayra. *Khul-Khaal: Five Egyptian Women Tell Their Stories*. Cairo: American University of Cairo, 1993.

Barlas, Asma. *"Believing Women" in Islam: Unreading Patriarchal Interpretations of the Qur'an*. Austin: University of Texas Press, 2002.

———. "Muslim Women and Sexual Oppression: Reading Liberation from the Qu'ran." *Macalester International* 10 (2001) 117–46.

Bendix, Reinhard. *Max Weber: An Intellectual Portrait*. New York: Doubleday, 1960.

Callaway, Barbara, and Lucy Creevey. *The Heritage of Islam: Women, Religion and Politics in West Africa*. Boulder, CO: Rienner, 1994.

Calpin, George H. *Indians in South Africa*. Pietermaritzburg: Shuter & Shooter, 1949.

Cherlin, Andrew J. *Public and Private Families*. New York: McGraw-Hill, 1996.

Ebr.-Valley, Rehana, editor. *Kala Pani: Caste and Colour in South Africa*. Cape Town: Kwela, 2001.

Goffman, Erving. *Stigma: Notes on the Management of Spoiled Identity*. New York: Touchstone, 1963.

Goodwin, Jan. *Price of Honour*. London: Warner, 1995.

Hall, Marjorie J., and Bakhita Amin Ismail. *Sisters under the Sun: The Story of Sudanese Women*. London: Longman, 1981.

Hassim, Shafinaaz, *Daughters are Diamonds: Honour, Shame & Seclusion—A South African Perspective*. Wandsbeck, Germany: Reach, 2007.

Hourani, Albert. *A History of the Arab Peoples*. London: Faber & Faber, 1992.

Jeffery, Patricia. *Frogs in a Well: Indian Women in Purdah*. London: Zed, 1979.

---

56. Hassim, *Daughters*.

Kabir, Zainab. "On the Women's Liberation Movement: Myth and Realities." Paper presented at the Conference of Muslim Sisters' Organisation, Kano, Nigeria, 1985.
Lewis, Bernard. *The Political Language of Islam*. Chicago: University of Chicago Press, 1988.
Lindsay-Hartz, Janice, et al. "Differentiating Guilt and Shame and Their Effects on Motivation." In *Self-Conscious Emotions: The Psychology of Shame, Guilt, Embarrassment, and Pride*, edited by June Price Tangney and Kurt W. Fischer, 274–300. New York: Guilford, 1995.
Mernissi, Fatima. *Beyond the Veil: Male-Female Dynamics in a Modern Muslim Society*. Cambridge: Schenkman, 1975.
Minturn, Leigh. *Sita's Daughters: Coming Out of Purdah*. New York: Oxford University Press, 1993.
Pateman, Carole. *The Disorder of Women*. Oxford: Polity, 1989.
Personal Narratives Group, editor. *Interpreting Women's Lives: Feminist Theory and Personal Narratives*. Bloomington, IN: Indiana University Press, 1989.
Pitt-Rivers, Julian. "Honour and Social Status." In *Honour and Shame: The Values of Mediterranean Society*, edited by Jean G. Péristiany. Chicago: University of Chicago Press, 1966.
Schur, Edwin M. *Labeling Women Deviant: Gender, Stigma and Social Control*. New York: McGraw-Hill, 1984.
Tangney, June Price, and Kurt W. Fischer, editors. *Self-Conscious Emotions: The Psychology of Shame, Guilt, Embarrassment, and Pride*. New York: Guilford, 1995.
Vreede-de Steurs, Cora. *Parda: A Study of Muslim Women's Lives in Northern India*. Assen: Royal Van Gorcum, 1968.
Wadud, Amina. *Qur'an and Woman. Rereading the Sacred Text from a Woman's Perspective*. Oxford: Oxford University Press, 1999.
Walter, Eugene Victor. *Terror and Resistance: A Study of Political Violence*. New York: Oxford University Press, 1972.

"No Other Means"?

Fundamentalisms, Religion, Survival, and Biopolitical Counterdiscourses[1]

ULRIKE AUGA

Introduction

Normative concepts of gender and sexuality have emerged in various respects as key features of religious fundamentalisms. Enforced inscription into gendered hierarchies is used as an opportunity to construct diverse "others" as well as confident "self-identities" while at the same time dismissing how discursive power determines one's own position.

1. Hegemonic "Western" Christian discourse and public discourse of a supposedly secular nature both legitimate their sense of moral superiority on the basis that they grant greater "freedom" and agency to women; at the same time, however, they fail to acknowledge their own violent inscription of norms, which regulate gender while also exerting forceful interventions into life more generally. The hegemonic discourse of "Western" democracies presumes a separation between religion and state while forgetting that sovereign power deals in matters deeply informed by politically-charged theological categories.

---

1. Translated from German by Leah Chizek.

2. Counterdiscourses in the context of "Western" knowledge criticize the exclusionary effects produced by the interlinkages of nation, state, and capitalism through the use of essentialized categories of knowledge including gender, race, and class. Even where these categories have been subject to systematic deconstruction, their relationship to the category of religion remains troubling. Leftist and feminist discourses observe that individual and collective life are sustained by norms of gender, sexuality, and desire; in doing so they can also show how patriarchal or hierarchical orders—symbolic, ethical, and legal—inform the greater part of a theological discourse that is historically conservative. The consequence is that leftist, feminist, and queer theory not only attribute the hierarchical encoding of gender norms to religious practice per se, but also contest the very possibility of subject formation and agency in the religious sphere.

3. Postcolonial theory has long pointed out that religion's role in colonization, decolonization, and neocolonization has been underestimated; additionally, it has also underscored the violent aspects of enforcing European secularism. Yet at the same time, many postcolonial approaches criticize epistemic violence without overcoming their own violent inscriptions of agency.

In order to undo this violence, it seems essential to identify various manifestations of power while taking care not to inadvertently vilify religion. I will begin by reviewing the various inscriptions of and intersections between sovereign and epistemic power. At issue are theologies that attempt to forcefully regulate life as well as those varieties of secularism that do not consider the role the religious sphere plays in subject formation and agency. What I call a "critical biotheology" can assist in exposing the relationship between power and knowledge production. In addition, however, this means taking "religious knowledge and religious praxis" seriously by recognizing the religious sphere as an equally valid counterspace that can also allow for subject formation, agency, and the critical production of knowledge.

The Return of Religions and Fundamentalist Violence

Since the last third of the twentieth century, the world has been confronted by the actions of fundamentalist movements that call into question the dominance of "Western" secular values, be it in Jerusalem, New York, London, or Oslo.[2] Today radical fundamentalism can be observed across every great tradition of faith.[3] The impressive worldwide renaissance of religion and its prominence in the public sphere is surprising to many, and the more militant forms this has taken unsettling.[4] The monolithic universalism of the Scientific Revolution is being challenged by a turn toward the Western phenomenon of "reenchantment" and the continuous devotional practice of the marginalized.[5] Yet the Western myth of modernization has taught us to take for granted the ongoing advance of secularization and privatization.[6] Many have assumed that national ideologies or civil religions would replace religious traditions.[7] And still others have expected religious values to influence modern societies in new and unexpected ways.[8] Hardly anyone, however, imagined that religion would become a power so capable of successfully creating new religious subjects and winning public influence.[9] In any case, as Martin Riesebrodt puts it, it has been confusing that this has not been the result of "socio-politically or culturally 'progressive' forms" of religion, "like Latin American liberation theology, with its synthesis of Christianity and Marxism, but rather conservative or fundamentalist forms with a strong emphasis on patriarchal authority and social morals. This depicted a backward-looking world, one in which the underclasses didn't become revolutionary but pious, and

---

2. Juergensmeyer, *Terror*; Baudler, *Gewalt*.
3. Armstrong, *Battle for God*.
4. Claussen, *Zurück zur Religion*; Weimer, *Credo*.
5. Berman, *Reenchantment*; Partridge, *Re-Enchantment of the West*.
6. See Bryan Wilson's classic formulation of the secularization process: "that process by which religious institutions, actions and consciousness loose their social significance" (Wilson, *Religion in Social Perspective*, 149). See also Inglehart, *Modernization*, 8; Luckmann, *Religion*.
7. Bellah, *Beyond Belief*.
8. de Vries and Sullivan, *Political Theologies*.
9. Herbert, *Religion and Civil Society*.

women weren't emancipated from patriarchalism but submitted to it, often voluntarily."[10]

If one tries to find the reasons for this, the usual answer is to stress the relationship between modernity, secularization, and the revitalization of religion. In the West, twentieth-century fundamentalism first emerged as the backlash against a scientific and secular culture and was to spread throughout the world. Yet fundamentalist movements themselves have also been influenced by modernity and scientific rationalism. Modernization has led to a society polarized by a wide and seemingly irreconcilable gap in worldviews—that is to say, the gap between secular and religious societies, both of which have had their own individual experiences with violence in the past and still feel threatened today. To some, modern "Western" culture has been experienced as an invasion of their own cultural contexts by a foreign imperialist power; others recall the Holocaust. And still others live under the influence of the "martyrdom flights" on 9/11.

Fundamentalism exerts a powerful influence on contemporary society and will continue to play an important role in the future, both at home and abroad. The most forceful aspects of its development must be met with an appropriate response. Violent suppressing it would be the worst such response.

The Dilemma of Politico-Theological Discourse in Light of Religion's Return

One frequently encounters the argument that religion in itself is dangerous.[11] Contemporary public discourses commonly make a connection between Christianity and violence, as well as between violence and religion more generally. Often, this comes down to equating violence with religion, Christianity, and the Bible.[12] At stake are not simply criticisms specific to Christianity but to religion's hegemonic, monotheistic,

---

10. Riesebrodt, *Rückkehr*, 9–10.

11. In the face of devastating religious wars, philosophers in the seventeenth and eighteenth centuries had to accept that monotheistic faith necessarily harbored violence toward those of different faiths. René Girard influentially questions the religious use of violence referring to the cycle of holiness and the use of violence in ritual scapegoating. Girard, *Violence*.

12. Palmer, *Is Religion Killing*; Collins, *Bible*.

and patriarchal tendencies, which can be seen in the parallel structure of debates about the relationship between violence, Christianity, and the Bible, as well as those about Islam and the Quran. In his attempt to clarify the relationship between monotheism and violence, for example, Jan Assmann works out the violent aspects of Jewish, Christian, and Islamic monotheism; yet he cuts his discussion short by focusing exclusively on the issue of apostasy, much as Hans G. Kippenberg has done.[13] In a similar fashion, Jack Palmer's claim that Biblical and Quranic texts are intrinsically violent conflates violence with religion while ignoring tradition and hermeneutics.[14] Many more examples could also be used to demonstrate how overly detached critical approaches to religion take a restrictive, even blinkered view of contemporary religious practice. In a welcome and stark contrast to this, Karen Armstrong protests, "At the end of the twentieth century, the liberal myth that humanity is progressing to an ever more enlightened and tolerant state looks as fantastic as any of the other millennial myths we have considered in this book. Without the constraints of a 'higher,' mythical truth, reason can on occasion become demonic and commit crimes that are as great as, if not greater than, any of the atrocities perpetuated by fundamentalists."[15]

By the same token, public or political theology rarely manages to find sufficient explanations for contemporary violent phenomena. This comes down to the interplay between various forms and contexts of violence and the centrality of religious topoi, not only in fundamentalist but also democratic contexts where state and religion are supposedly separated. As Sigrid Weigel emphasizes:

> Above all, the failure of political theology in light of contemporary phenomena concerns those actors newly emerging on the stages of war and conflict, where international law, civil strife, and the war between religions mingle and merge. It concerns terrorism in the guise of religion, in particular the figure of the martyr or suicide assassin, the topos of the 'just' or even 'holy war' deployed by both sides. And it concerns the enmeshment of religious and criminal discourse informing each side's images of the enemy as much as it does the legitimizing of actions

---

13. Assmann, *Moses*; Assmann, *Monotheismus*. On the state of research into monotheism in religious studies see Lang, "Monotheismus." See also Kippenberg, *Gewalt*, 17–18, as well as the innovative volume by Schneider, *Beyond Monotheism*.

14. Palmer, *Is Religion Killing*, xiv.

15. Armstrong, *Battle for God*, 367.

by falling back on universal concepts like freedom, fairness, human worth, or human rights.[16]

This leads to questions about the relationship between (bio)power, violence, and sovereignty in real existing democracies. As pivotal as it is, the notion of sovereignty is also ambivalent. In contemporary usage, it initially appears to be a "political" concept referring to a state's capacity for self-determination; this idea was already familiar in the Middle Ages, when it seemed quite natural and was sanctioned by prepolitical notions of divine truth. Sovereignty was furthermore linked to a set of theological concepts without which any explanation, understanding, or idea of power seemed inconceivable. In this way, political philosophy constructs the notion of the king's two bodies: mortal and human, this same king also rules as an immortal, divinely-appointed authority, the head of God's eternal kingdom.[17] Following the king's death in the French Revolution, the idea of sovereignty remained very much alive, although its form had to change.

Carl Schmitt famously emphasized that "any significant concepts of modern state theory are secularized theological concepts. Not only because of their development which saw their transposition from theology into political theory and by which, for example, the all-mighty God became an omnipotent lawmaker but also in their systematic configuration which need be recognized by any sociological study of these concepts."[18] This is not the place to revisit the famous debate between Carl Schmitt and Walter Benjamin on the meaning of sovereignty. Yet so much can be said for our purposes: whereas Benjamin regards the exclusionary practices produced by the state of exception as the latter's most important function, the ability to enact the state of exception in the first place is sovereignty's most important feature according to Schmitt. Benjamin does not simply reproduce Schmitt's notion of sovereignty; instead, he knowingly appropriates it so as to critically examine and revise it.[19] For Schmitt, making a decision about the state of exception is tantamount to actually creating it and thus creating a situation that renders a sovereign power's absolute ability to act both visible and effec-

16. Weigel, *Walter Benjamin*, 77.
17. Kantorowicz, *The King's Two Bodies*.
18. Schmitt, *Political Theology*.
19. Benjamin, "Kritik der Gewalt"; Benjamin, *Origin of German Tragic Drama*.

tive. To put it more precisely, Schmitt becomes a representative for secularization and not its critic, according to Sigrid Weigel. This happens despite the fact that he silently goes about investing political concepts with theological significance. Weigel argues against the Schmittian figure of *transposing* theological concepts, which she characterizes as the "secularized theological," since in her understanding of the relevant passages in Schmitt "no further allowances are then made for religious themes *following* a complete transposition of theological concepts into other registers."[20] This is then said to be especially problematic, since what is obscured "from the field of vision in this type of political theology [is] religion, paradoxically enough." This has two consequences: First, the question as to "whether and which traces of religious violence have an impact on 'secularized theological concepts' of politics" is left unconsidered; and secondly, any possibility to "envision different types of relationships between politics and theology" beyond the notion of transposition Weigel equates with a loss of meaning is dismissed.[21]

Benjamin, by contrast, finds strict separation of the theological and political spheres essential, even though he is also interested in the possibilities theology has to offer as opposed to politics. It is therefore necessary to detect the traces of religious power influencing the "secularized theological concepts" of politics. This also allows Benjamin to reclaim the *theological imagination as a site of non-violent and peaceable agency.*

Sovereignty and Biological Citizenship

There is much more at stake than just the symbolic construction and naturalization of gender and religion through political regulation. Speaking more broadly, the issue is how sovereign power intervenes into the lives of all individuals in order "to decide [on] life and death."[22] Today, life in and beyond the configurations of the state is bound to a sovereign biopower that offers people possibilities for empowerment even as it threatens them with destruction. People are thereby bound

20. Weigel, *Walter Benjamin*, 69.
21. Ibid., 70.
22. Foucault, *Society*, 258; idem, *Security*; idem, *Birth*. Georgio Agamben transforms Foucault's biopolitics in a thanatopolitics in his Homo Sacer project. Agamben, *Homo Sacer*. See also the necessary feminist critique—which suggests "standing by Foucault": Deuber-Mankowsky, "Homo Sacer."

to an ambivalent form of power that produces both sovereign subjects and social outcasts. The processes by which those marginalized become empowered are complex, however, and do not just disappear once equal legal footing is achieved. Instead, marginalized (groups) continue to be associated with marginalized knowledge and forced into interdependent, essentialized categories such as "gender," "sexuality," "race," "religion," "class," "nation," and so forth. As power, sovereignty becomes both violent and effective time and again whenever the right structures are in place and allow it to have an impact.[23]

The establishment of and debate over the notion of "biological citizenship" underscores how national as well as transnational regulations increasingly reinforce access to or even exclusion from life-sustaining commodities.[24] For that matter, it is becoming increasingly clear that the ability to secure certain rights and even basic liberties is always reliant upon citizenship. The *legal constructs* of a given polity, however, are connected primarily to hegemonic, religious, and hierarchical constructs organized on the basis of gender.

The modern Western nation-state is based on ties between birth, territory, and order, and has its origins in the spatialization of a legal order that registers life as birth.[25] Michel Foucault describes how Western modernity ultimately conceives of the territorial state as a "population state." Accordingly, the modern state-as-biopower subjects natural, reproductive life to its own interventions: "Biopolitics therefore can only be conceived of as 'bioregulation by the state.'"[26]

Toward the end of the seventies, Foucault developed the concept of governmentality in order to describe the regulation of individuals by *late capitalist* societies. The modern state is described as a complex

---

23. Put simply, biopolitics is concerned with the state's (vested) political interests in the life and bodies of its inhabitants, who form the "population" over which it presides and are subject to state's attempts to leverage this population's potential through laws, facilitation, screenings, and so forth in order to maintain its health, its capacity for efficient reproduction, etc. Foucault suggests that these politics are always intertwined with powers of moral and discipline, originally stemming from ecclesial sexual morals concerned with individual subjects' conducts, at times autonomous from the state, that in turn then also exert influence, partially and not necessarily, over laws and prohibitions and thus gain entrance into the politics of the state.

24. Petryna, *Life Exposed*.

25. Foucault, *Security*.

26. Ibid., 494.

combination of technologies that facilitate both individualization and totalization.[27] Through the secularization of Christian technologies of confession—what Foucault calls "pastoral power"—particular modes of subjectivation fundamental to capitalist socialization were brought into being.[28] Foucault explains, "[b]y 'governmentality' I understand the ensemble formed by institutions, procedures, analyses and reflections, calculations, and tactics that allow the exercise of this very specific, albeit very complex, power that has the population as its target, political economy as its major form of knowledge, and apparatuses of security as its essential technical instrument."[29] These "apparatuses of security" constitute a technology designed to safeguard the collective from internal dangers;[30] in other words, the "enemies" of a nation who purportedly pose the greater threat to security are no longer "foreign elements" on the outside, but "abnormals" within.

In *Terrorist Assemblages. Homonationalism in Queer Times*, Jasbir K. Puar describes how the configuration of the American nation-state is symbolically reorganized together with its sense of national belonging in times of neoliberal expansion using strategies like "counterterrorism" and what she calls "securitization."[31] Puar also describes how interrelated notions of religion and sexuality play a role in this process, which is emerging as a global paradigm. If the symbolic order is historically based on heteronormativity, this is now accompanied by homonormative ideologies as well. This illustrates how neoliberal politics succeeds in integrating select queer subjects into the nation-state, particularly through legal strategies of recognition. Such subjects become acceptable by refashioning them as agents of life and productivity rather than continuing to stigmatize them as "agents of death." The inclusion of *some* queer subjects nevertheless comes at the expense of creating another population of orientalized terrorist bodies. Encouraged by the sense that a state of exception exists, this notion of homonormativity persistently relies upon closely connected ideals of race, class, gender,

27. Ibid.
28. Ibid.
29. Ibid., 144.
30. Ibid.
31. Puar, *Terrorist Assemblages*.

and nation.³² Allegations of homophobia among racialized and religicized "others" assist in the production of a geopolitical sphere where neoliberal agendas can be pursued³³ under the pretense of tolerance and human rights.³⁴

Sovereign Power, Epistemic Violence, and the Possibilities of Subaltern Articulation

How is resistance dealt with in the face of this complex nexus of sovereign power and epistemic violence? In the context of post- and neocolonial criticism, the question of resistance first concerned itself with the voice and representation of the subaltern. Spivak famously looks at the phenomenon of widows' self-immolation in order to criticize how colonial perspectives contribute to the discursive production of an asymmetrical, gendered subject. In *Can the Subaltern Speak?*, she concludes that the subaltern female subject has no voice.³⁵

Since then, several authors have questioned the strength of the Foucauldian Western subject's position while attempting to underscore how marginalized subjects remain figures of productivity and agency. Hardt and Negri, for example, portray the "multitude" leading an existence that is exploited and precarious, albeit still productive. One contentious topic is the way suicide terrorism serves as a means of expression and communication for the subaltern. Says Spivak, "Suicidal resistance is a message inscribed on the body when no other means will get through. It is both execution and mourning, for both self and other. For you die with me for the same cause, no matter which side you are on. Because no matter what side you are, there are no designated killees in suicide bombing. No matter what side you are on, because I cannot

---

32. Puar doesn't deploy "race" according to a "colorline." She writes: "I deploy 'racialization' as a figure for specific social formations and processes that are not necessarily or only tied to what has been historically theorized as 'race'" (ibid., xii).

33. Ibid., 28. Suggestions that German immigration tests check the attitudes of "foreigners" toward homosexuality proceed in a similar fashion.

34. On the difficulty and misuse of the concept of tolerance, see Brown, *Regulating Aversion*.

35. Spivak, *Can the Subaltern Speak*. See also Said, *Orientalism*.

talk to you, you won't respond to me, with the implication that there is no dishonour in such shared and innocent death."[36]

The stance taken by some, such as Achilles Mbembe in "Necropolitics" or Adriana Cavarero in *Horrorism*, has been one of radically assuming the position of wounded and destroyed bodies. While I acknowledge these positions for naming contemporary violence, they lack any further perspective.[37] In *On the Postcolony*, Mbembe brilliantly describes the dynamics of power and subjectivity in Africa, yet on the whole his work remains essentially pessimistic and lacks any vision of possible solutions.[38]

Jasbir Puar claims that by utilizing what she calls a "queer praxis of assemblage," she seeks to reread the terrorist body, which she says is typically misunderstood "as culturally, ethnically, and religiously nationalist, fundamentalist, patriarchal, and homophobic" and in this way, she attempts to undermine the rhetoric of the war on terror according to which one is either "with us or against us."[39]

With this theoretical framework in mind, I would now like to address the following points:

1. The kind of resistance formulated here only allows for limited subject formation and limited agency. Following Julia Kristeva, Manuel Castells differentiates between resistance that persists in its resistance from that which envisions new and open-ended forms of community and social engagement.[40] Resistance which persists as such remains mired in violence. Yet it seems as if Spivak, Mbembe, and Puar all utilize this reductive notion of resistance, which is why they necessarily perceive of agency as something violent.

2. Spivak, Mbembe, and Puar also appear to take their departure point for imagining subject formation and agency from a universalized notion of resistance. Their subjects are queer and fragmented; while on the defensive, they nevertheless remain firmly within the parameters of Western discourse. Only because they imagine agency in reference to the normative and exclusionary

36. Spivak, "Class and Culture," quoted in Puar, *Terrorist* Assemblages, 218.
37. Cavarero, *Horrorism*.
38. Mbembe, "Necropolitics." See also Mbembe, *Postcolony*.
39. Puar, *Terrorist Assemblages*, 221.
40. Castells, *Information Age*, 360.

framework of Western discourses do their marginalized subjects have—to speak with Spivak—"no other means."[41]

3. Puar argues that "opening up to the fantastical wonders of futurity is the most powerful of political and critical strategies."[42] Assemblages allow for the inclusion of all kinds of unknown resistance now as well as in the future, although today it seems as if Puar's queer futurity has erupted in the form of terrorist assemblages. It is not clear how subject formation can be thought through together with the formation of the queer collective. But as José Muñoz reminds us in *Cruising Utopia*, queer futurity and even queerness are not there yet. He furthermore points to the fact that we should understand "queerness as collectivity."[43]

4. My last point concerns the notion of religion. While the authors criticize the Western construction of orientalized Muslim terrorist bodies, they themselves do not take seriously the creation of new knowledge through religious imaginations, conceptions, and practices for the sake of a more solidaric social imagination.

Secularism(s) as Fundamentalism(s)

Returning now to Walter Benjamin, his stance can be characterized as one that is "neither theological nor secular." His way of thinking is said to originate "in appreciation for Biblical language, for the notion of divine order and the idea of redemption, albeit without having any particular confessional ties."[44] The fact that concepts of divine order, which have a significance of their own, cannot be transposed onto concepts of worldly order is a fulcral point in Benjaminian thought.[45] And while Benjamin's writings do not reveal a cohesive theory of secularization, his use of concepts like "justice" (*Gerechtigkeit*) or "redemption" (*Erlösung*) criticize political philosophy's appropriation of religious

---

41. Spivak's idea of "unlearning" of one's own epistemological violence is a useful idea, whereas her stance toward the category of "religion" remains open to critique.
42. Puar, *Terrorist Assemblages*, 222.
43. Muñoz, *Cruising Utopia*, 11.
44. Weigel, *Walter Benjamin*, 12.
45. Benjamin is more interested in questions that theology has allowed to escape its interpretative scrutiny; ibid., 12–13. See also Weber, "Ausnahme."

concepts. Benjamin's dialectic of secularization points early to the significant ways secularized theological categories produce exclusions in a national context; at the same time, it also reveals how theological concepts themselves become truncated.

A revision of secularization discourses can also be observed at the turn of the twenty-first century. The classic sociological *theory of secularization* begins by observing religion's loss of (institutional as well as individual) significance in Western societies and brings this to bear on the phenomena of modernization. Current research continues to discuss a complex network of causes for this—from the tendencies toward rationalization that developed even within Judaism and Christianity (Max Weber) to various processes of differentiation, individualization, and socialization, and not least of all the impacts of science and technology.[46] These developments all transform religion's social status and ensure that something like a common "sacred canopy" no longer exists. Yet the present-day discipline of religious sociology still finds itself debating the influences pluralization and individualization have had on secularization.[47] As for modernization, its influence on institutionalized religion's loss of relevance is considered indisputable (so say the representatives of *individualization theory*, at least), although this loss is not regarded as affecting unique and individual religious attitudes.[48] Religion does not disappear; it simply changes its face and can now be found in the form of less institutionalized religious groups and movements (the new age movement, esotericism, meditation, etc.), as well as in the form of culture, art, or sport, all of which are chosen and combined in a syncretistic manner by individuals according to their personal affinities. Given the new appeal of fundamentalism and religious event culture (e.g., World Youth Day 2005, church conventions, the papal cult of celebrity, and the renewed interest in religion worldwide), it has also been discussed for several years

46. Bruce, *God is Dead*, 4–6.

47. Proponents of *market theory* object with regard to the current U.S. situation in analogy to economic theory, that a greater plurality of religions in a "religious market" brings about stimulating competition and a higher demand for the religious. Stark and Bainbridge, *Future of Religion*; Stark and Bainbridge, *Theory of Religion*; Stark and Finke, *Acts of Faith*; Iannaccone, "Rational Choice."

48. Luhmann, *Funkion der Religion*; Luckmann, "Privatisierung"; Davie, *Sociology of Religion*. For a critical discussion, see Pollack, "Individualisierung." For a classic discussion of the concept of individualization, see Beck, *Risikogesellschaft*.

now whether an actual "return of religion" has taken place or whether religion simply has greater visibility today owing to the mechanisms of a media society.[49] José Casanova has disputed in particular the element of privatization in *secularization theory*: he distinguishes between a public religion that advances liberal values and civil society (e.g., Catholicism in Poland, Brazil, or the United States) and official religions that are backward-looking and take the past as their model (for example, in Egypt or Iran).[50] Here, the emphasis is on the one hand the meaning religion possesses in and for the public sphere; on the other is the need to distinguish how religion becomes so effective in the first place. Throughout these debates, the very concept of religion has become the subject of considerable controversy.[51]

For my own discussion, I would like to focus on the newer critique of secularism. Debates in anthropology and other disciplines illustrate how a normative connection is made between secularity and an Enlightenment narrative of progressive modernity that is said to promise reason, freedom, peace, and progress—a narrative one can then define as *secularism*. Janet Jakobsen and Ann Pellegrini characterize secularism as "a political project that deploys the concept of the secular, and it may do so regardless of the empirical state of secularization."[52] Understood this way, secularity is then viewed as the answer to violence motivated by religion or otherwise mobilized in response to political Islam. This secularist narrative traces the theme of progress back to the religious wars of the sixteenth and seventeenth centuries, which could supposedly only be settled by appealing to reason and the Enlightenment, the forces that together with the nation-state first secured the individual's autonomy.[53] Yet the implicit set of values un-

---

49. Braun et al., *Säkularisierung*; Berger, *Desecularization*; for a critical voice, see Körtner, *Wiederkehr der Religion*, which lists additional relevant literature.

50. Casanova, *Public Religions*; Casanova, "Secularisation Revisited."

51. In addition to the aforementioned authors, see the overview and discussion in Wohlrab-Sahr, "Religionslosigkeit," as well as Pollack, "Was ist Religion." Compare on the other hand Bruce, *God is Dead*. With this, the theory of secularisation decidedly parts with philosophical critique of religions (Marx, among others), which in turn holds that with the extinction of capitalism religion, too, should perish.

52. Jakobsen and Pellegrini, "Introduction," 7.

53. Ibid., 4. This is where the implicit assumptions of Robert Bellah are demonstrated, according to whom secularization provides society with greater autonomy and the capacity to adapt. Bellah, *Beyond Belief*.

derlying this narrative also betrays its problematic side: deploying circular logic, secularism relies on a range of dichotomies that confirm each other and identify it with progressivism, universalism, rationality, and freedom, whereas religion is associated with regression, particularism, irrationality, and bondage.[54] A critique of this discourse need not be limited to demanding the separation of state and religion but must understand secularism as "a set of material and linguistic practices that work across multiple institutions"[55] (in the Foucauldian sense) and through which the very category of religion is also (re)produced in order to create a hierarchy of religions, as Tomuko Masuzawa argues.[56] "Other religions" are then subsumed into secular but still Christian-centered definitions of religion, or else isolated on the basis of exclusionary interests as David Chidester has shown.[57] A critique of the binary "religion versus secularity" can offer new perspectives—precisely in light of the most recent debates about Islam in Europe.[58] An additional facet of the current discussion is its interest in the relationship between secularity and nation-statehood. Charles Taylor links the theory of secularization to the modern nation-state: for Taylor, secularity comprises the *overlapping consensus* (Rawls) in a pluralistic modernity. Thus, for example, the right to life can be justified in different ways and must be socially negotiated ("background justifications") even though it is subject to the secular ethic that serves as the political principle for a modern and reasonable society.[59]

Talal Asad criticizes such hegemonic and potentially violent tendencies, which have erupted in post-9/11 America in the form of a new American nationalism and domestic intolerance: "[Secularism] is an enactment by which a political medium (representation of citizenship)

---

54. Jakobsen and Pellegrini, "Introduction," 6.

55. Ibid., 7.

56. Tomoko Masuzawa shows the difference between "Western" and "other" religions and demonstrates how the conceptualization of "world religions" reinscribes European Universalism. Masuzawa, *Invention*. See also Baird, "Late Secularism"; Baird, *Inventing Religion*.

57. Chidester, *Savage Systems*.

58. Jakobsen and Pellegrini, "Introduction," 10–11. See also Mahmood, *Politics of Piety*.

59. Taylor, "Modes of Secularism," 33–36, 69–71; Asad, *Formations*, 5. See also the discussion between Anderson, *Imagined Communities*, and Peterson and Walhof, "Introduction."

redefines and transcends particular and differentiating practices of the self that are articulated through class, gender and religion."[60] The pace of this debate quickened in 2003 with the publication of Asad's *Formations of the Secular. Christianity, Islam, Modernity*. For some time now, (critical) theory, (neo-)Marxist philosophy and even some—by them inspired—postcolonial approaches, have been criticized for treating religious concepts through the lens of Western theory production, thereby subjecting them to (Western) universalism.[61]

Subject Formations, Agencies, and Freedom in Religious Lives

Saba Mahmood's *Politics of Piety. The Islamic Revival and the Feminist Subject* (2005) offers an answer as to how the traditional division between the religious right and the secular left, or between religious and secular discourses, may be reconfigured, and how agency can be rethought free of violence. Using the example of a Muslim women's grassroots piety movement in Cairo, she attempts to illustrate how the ethical and political can be interwoven, as well as how spaces for subject formation (can) open up from directly within patriarchal places.[62] Mahmood is surprised by the sheer range of life forms and concepts of "human flourishing" she finds, in particular those arising from religious ideas and practices that have exceeded their own self-imposed limits on the imagination. This prompts Mahmood to reconsider her own feminist visions; she catches the language of theoretical analysis—leftist as well as feminist—in the act, so to speak, discerning how its ideas about religion rely on "notions of progressive and backward, superior and inferior, higher and lower." Such analyses are "littered with political plans for the reform and development of a situation like this one, which is understood as being worse than one's own living conditions."[63] And yet Mahmood wonders, "Do I even fully comprehend the forms of life

---

60. Asad, *Formations*, 5.

61. See the accusation of universalisms with regard to the concept of religion coming from postcolonial critique in Ashcroft et al., "Religion." It is interesting that only this second edition of *Post-Colonial Studies: The Key Concepts* includes "Religion" as a keyword, which underlines the growing importance of religion in current discourses.

62. Mahmood, *Politics of Piety*.

63. Ibid., 198–99.

that I want so passionately to remake?"[64] She then looks for opportunities to avoid "[rendering] unfamiliar lifeworlds into conceptual or communicable forms," since doing so means "to domesticate that which exceeds hegemonic protocols of intelligibility."[65] This has repercussions for one's own sense of self-perception, yet this is not a matter of self-assurance over and against the other but far more so a productive kind of destabilization: "[W]hat I mean to gesture at is a mode of encoutering the Other which does not assume that in the process of culturally translating other lifeworlds one's own certainty about how the world should proceed can remain stable. This attitude requires the virtue of humility: a sense that one does not always know *what* one opposes and that a political vision at times has to admit its own finitude in order to even comprehend what it has sought to oppose."[66] In these circumstances, feminist theory itself must be liberated from its own notions of "progressivism" and "liberalism." Solidarity, then, would mean to "ensue within the uncertain, at times opaque, conditions of intimate and uncomfortable encounters in all their eventuality."[67] The outcome of this is to rethink "analysis as a mode of conversation rather than mastery." This new mode of analysis "can yield a vision of coexistence that does not require making other lifeworlds extinct or provisional."[68]

How does Mahmood develop her approach? She starts by examining some of the tensions that can be found in the work of Judith Butler. Both Mahmood and Butler argue against agency's role in a predefined teleology of emancipatory politics: "The concept of agency should be delinked from the goals of progressive politics, a tethering that has often led to the incarceration of the notion of agency within the trope of resistance against oppressive and dominating operations of power."[69] Butler locates the possibility of agency within the structures of power, not outside of it. She emphasizes that the reiterative structure of norms serves not only to consolidate a particular discursive regime but also lays the groundwork for destabilizing it. This means there is no possibil-

64. Ibid., 198.
65. Ibid., 199.
66. Ibid.
67. Ibid.
68. Ibid.
69. Ibid., 34.

ity of "undoing" social norms independent of their "doing" in the first place. Butler speaks in line with Foucault: "[T]he paradox of subjectivation is precisely that the subject who would resist such norms is itself enabled, if not produced by such norm. Although this constitutive constraint does not foreclose the possibility of agency, it does locate agency as a reiterative or rearticulatory practice, immanent to power, and not a relation of external opposition to power."[70]

Mahmood reproaches Butler by pointing out that her investigations stick to "tracking the possibilities of resistance to the regulating power of normativity, and on the other hand to her model of performativity which is primarily conceptualized in terms of a dualistic structure of consolidation/resignification, doing/undoing of norms."[71] In light of her field work with the mosque movement, Mahmood stresses how "norms are not only consolidated and/or subverted . . . but performed, inhabited, and experienced in a variety of ways."[72] As such, any number of emergent subjectivities are left unconsidered by the (Butlerian) model outlined above.

Mahmood takes Foucault's analysis of an ethical model for conceptualizing agency beyond the limitations of a binary model that merely enacts and subverts norms. Drawing our attention to how external forms contribute to the development of human ethical capacities and specific modes of human agency, Foucault thinks of agency "(a) in terms of the capacities and skills required to undertake particular kinds of moral actions; and (b) as . . . bound up with the historically and culturally specific disciplines through which a subject is formed."[73] The paradox of subjectivation is that the capacity to act is created by concrete and particular relationships of subordination.

Foucault's approach necessitates raising questions about the relationship between moral codes and ethical conduct, questions that can only be answered by examining the *specific practices* through which historically specific moral norms are lived. Four elements are pivotal in Foucault's study of ethics and are useful for understanding key aspects

70. Butler, *Bodies that Matter*, 15.

71. Mahmood, *Politics of Piety*, 22. Butler develops her concept of agency primarily in contexts where norms are thrown into question or are subject to resignification. She has thus emphasized counterhegemonic modalities of agency.

72. Ibid.

73. Ibid., 29.

of the women's mosque movement and piety movements in general: (1) the "substance of ethics," (2) the mode of subjectivation, (3) the techniques of the self, and (4) telos, or the mode of being one aspires to.

Adapted to reflect the movement, this means: (1) substance: a divine plan; (2) mode of subjectivation: moral codes from the Quran; (3) techniques of the self: moral obligations invoked by (holy) texts and pedagogical literature and the adoption of practices for shaping moral conduct; and (4) telos: an individual's interpretation of moral codes, which allows her to discover how she may best realize the divine plan for her life as an individual.

Mahmood points out that "the meaning of agency must be explored within the grammar of concepts within which it resides."[74] We should therefore keep open the meaning of agency and allow it to emerge from "within semantic and institutional networks that define and make possible particular ways of relating to people, things, and oneself."[75]

Is Critique Secular?

In light this and other calls to take not only religion itself seriously but also the kinds of subject formation and agency that find space within it, the University of California in Berkeley has implemented a new program of study designed to bridge the conventional divides between modern European critical theory and non-Western and post-Enlightenment critical theoretical projects. The new program was inaugurated with a symposium entitled "Is Critique Secular?," which was followed by an eponymously titled volume in 2009 by Talal Asad, Wendy Brown, Judith Butler, and Saba Mahmood.[76] Here the authors consider the concept of "critique" in the philosophical sense as opposed to "criticism." Critique emerges in ancient Athens as *krisis*, a jurisprudential term: "*Krisis* integrates polis rupture, tribunal, knowledge, judgment, and repair at the same time that it links subject and object in practice."[77] The concept of "critique" has had different meanings throughout history. Nevertheless, it has always contained "a tacit presumption of reason's

---

74. Ibid., 34.
75. Asad, *Formations*, 78.
76. Asad et al., *Is Critique Secular?*
77. Koselleck, *Critique and Crisis*, 103.

capacity to unveil error"[78] and therefore produce new meaning. How did critique come to be defined as secular? It was "the Enlightenment presumption that the true, the objective, the real, the rational, and even the scientific emerge only with the shedding of religious authority or 'prejudice.'"[79] Kant claimed that everything must be subject to critique, even reason itself, hence the conviction that critique replaces "opinion or faith with truth, and subjectivism with science; that critique is, in short, secular."[80]

Marx used but also transformed Ludwig Feuerbach's critique of religion, regarding religious consciousness not merely as an error but a symptom of humanity's unfree existence. In brief, "Marx brings together in the notion of critique a comprehension of the Real identified as the material, a practice of objectivity identified with science, and the realization of true emancipation of religion, true secularism, in place of what he decries as 'merely theological criticism.'"[81] As Wendy Brown underscores, "It is this particular heritage from Marx, and the way it threads through German critical theory right up through Habermas, that has so overdetermined . . . the identification, of critique with secularism in the tradition of Western critical theory."[82]

These various observations further support Jakobsen and Pellegrini's point that "the choice between secularism and religion represents a false dichotomy. This is so because religious and secular formations are profoundly intertwined with each other. As a result, the easy presumption that secularism is necessarily more rational, more modern, freer, and less dangerous than religion is not sustainable."[83] Not only are there a variety of secularisms, then, but also different ways of formulating critique. Such approaches object to Western monopolization on the production of meaning, to say nothing of secularism, rationalism, freedom, or even democracy. They challenge the way "the rational, material, real, scientific, and human [try] both to explain and supplant [or even eradicate] the religious, the ideal, the unreal, the speculative, and

78. Brown, "Introduction," 9.
79. Ibid., 11.
80. Ibid.
81. Ibid., 12.
82. Ibid., 12–13.
83. Jakobsen and Pellegrini, *Secularisms*, 11.

the divine."[84] Clearly secularism is not a prerequisite for critique. On the other hand, if Western civilization's constructions of identity are rooted in the presumed convergence of Christianity, secularism, liberalism, and democracy, as Talal Asad and others have shown, then "Westerners" should think differently about their imagined global opposites.[85]

Critical Biotheology: An Outlook

In summary, several aspects of a critical biotheology would in my opinion greatly contribute to mediating between secularists, religious fundamentalists, and others of faith:

1. The connections between sovereign and epistemic power should be examined in their respective historical contexts.

2. Critical biotheology's task would be to ensure that concepts of sovereignty do not work with theological concepts that encourage violence and even preclude life and obstruct subject formation and agency. Theological concepts should not be appropriated by politics.

3. A crucial point seems to be the need to underscore how secularism is a form of epistemic violence that aggresses against the concept of religion and demand respect for religion and its adherents. At stake is not any kind of "solidarity critique" but the actual acceptance of subject formation and agency as it unfolds within the religious sphere. Moreover, it should be conceded on the premise of separating theory from politics that new concepts and meanings and lastly social imagination are also possible within a religious framework of knowledge.

4. Different conceptualizations of person, body, belief, freedom, and truth produce different opportunities. Instead of universalizing a "Western" emancipatory (counter)discourse, it should be acknowledged that resistances are contextual and that there are visions yet to be imagined, different perspectives, and alternative concepts of human flourishing.

---

84. Brown, "Introduction," 13.
85. Ibid.

5. In the context of counterdiscourses, whether secular or religious, it seems just as important not to operate with a reductionist notion of resistance. Resistance that persists as such and conceives of no project for social imagination and communal engagement threatens to become violent itself. Resistance and futurity belong together.

6. Finally, it is just as crucial to *openly* understand such projects and their future potentials.

Bibliography

Agamben, Georgio. *Homo Sacer: Sovereign Power and Bare Life*. Translated by Daniel Heller-Roazen. Stanford, CA: Stanford University Press, 1998.

Anderson, Benedict. *Imagined Communities: Reflections on the Origins and Spread of Nationalism*. London: Verso, 1983.

Armstrong, Karen. *The Battle for God*. New York: Knopf, 2000.

Asad, Talal. *Formations of the Secular: Christianity, Islam, Modernity*. Stanford: Stanford University Press, 2003.

Asad, Talal, et al. *Is Critique Secular?: Blasphemy, Injury, and Free Speech*. Berkeley: University of California Press, 2009.

Ashcroft, Bill, et al. "Religion and the Post-Colonial." In *Post-Colonial Studies: The Key Concepts*, 2nd ed., edited by Bill Ashcroft et al., 188–90. London, New York: Routledge, 2007.

Assmann, Jan. *Monotheismus und die Sprache der Gewalt*. Vienna: Picus, 2006.

———. *Moses der Ägypter: Entzifferung einer Gedächtnisspur*. München: Hanser, 1998.

Baird, Robert J. *Inventing Religion in the Western Imaginary*. Princeton: Princeton University Press (forthcoming).

———. "Late Secularism." In *Secularisms*, edited by Janet R. Jakobsen and Ann Pellegrini, 162–77. Durham, NC: Duke University Press, 2008.

Baudler, Georg. *Gewalt in den Weltreligionen*. Darmstadt: Wissenschaftliche Buchgesellschaft, 2005.

Beck, Ulrich. *Risikogesellschaft: Auf dem Weg in eine andere Moderne*, Frankfurt: Suhrkamp, 1986.

Bellah, Robert Neely. *Beyond Belief: Essays on Religion in a Post-Traditional World*. New York: Harper & Row, 1970.

Benjamin, Walter. *The Origin of German Tragic Drama*. Translated by John Osborne. New York: Verso, 1998.

———. "Zur Kritik der Gewalt" (1921). In *Gesammelte Schriften*, edited by Rolf Tiedemann and Hermann Schweppenhäuser, 2/1:179–203. Frankfurt: Suhrkamp, 1977.

Berger, Peter L. *The Desecularization of the World. Resurgent Religion and World Politics*. Washington, DC: Ethics and Public Policy Center, 1999.

Berman, Morris. *The Reenchantment of the World*. Ithaca, NY: Cornell University Press, 1981.
Braun, Christina von, et al., editors. *Säkularisierung: Bilanz und Perspektiven einer umstrittenen These*. Berlin: LIT, 2007.
Brown, Wendy. "Introduction." In Talal Asad et al., *Is Critique Secular? Blasphemy, Injury, and Free Speech*, 7–19. Berkeley: University of California Press, 2009.
———. *Regulating Aversion: Tolerance in the Age of Identity and Empire*. Princeton: Princeton University Press, 2006.
Bruce, Steve. *God is Dead: Secularization in the West*. Oxford: Blackwell, 2002.
Butler, Judith. *Bodies that Matter: On the Discursive Limits of "Sex."* New York: Routledge, 1993.
Casanova, José. *Public Religions in the Modern World*. Chicago: University of Chicago Press, 1994.
———. "Secularisation Revisited: A Reply to Talal Asad." In *Powers of the Secular Modern: Talal Asad and His Interlocutors*, edited by David Scott and Charles Hirschkind, 12–30. Stanford: Stanford University Press, 2006.
Castells, Manuel. *The Information Age: Economy, Society and Culture*. Vol. 2, *The Power of Identity*. Malden, MA: Blackwell, 1997.
Cavarero, Adriana. *Horrorism: Naming Contemporary Violence*. New York: Columbia University Press, 2009.
Chidester, David. *Savage Systems: Colonialism and Comparative Religion in Southern Africa*. Charlottesville, VA: University of Virginia Press, 1996.
Claussen, Johann Hinrich. *Zurück zur Religion: Warum wir vom Christentum nicht loskommen*. München: Pantheon, 2006.
Collins, John Joseph. *Does the Bible Justify Violence?* Minneapolis: Fortress, 2004.
Davie, Grace. *The Sociology of Religion*. London: Sage, 2007.
Deuber-Mankowsky, Astrid. "Homo Sacer, das bloße Leben und das Lager: Anmerkungen zu einem erneuten Versuch einer Kritik der Gewalt." *Die Philosophin* 25 (2002) 95–115.
de Vries, Hent, and Lawrence C. Sullivan, editors. *Political Theologies: Public Religions in a Post-Secular World*. New York: Fordham University Press, 2006.
Foucault, Michel. *The Birth of Biopolitics: Lectures at the Collège de France (1978–79)*. Translated by Graham Burchell. New York: Palgrave Macmillan, 2008.
———. *Security, Territory, Population: Lectures at the Collège de France (1977–78)*. Translated by Graham Burchell. New York: Palgrave Macmillan, 2007.
———. *Society Must Be Defended: Lectures at the Collège de France (1975–76)*. Edited by Arnold I. Davidson. Translated by David Macey. London: Penguin, 2003.
Girard, René. *La Violence et le Sacré*. Paris: Hachette, 2002.
Herbert, David. *Religion and Civil Society: Rethinking Public Religion in the Contemporary World*. London: Ashgate, 2003.
Iannaccone, Laurence R. "Rational Choice: Framework for the Scientific Study of Religion." In *Rational Choice Theory and Religion. Summary and Assessment*, edited by Alfred Young Lawrence, 25–44. New York: Routledge, 1997.
Inglehart, Ronald. *Modernization and Postmodernization: Cultural, Economic, and Political Change in 43 Societies*. Princeton: Princeton University Press, 1997.

Jakobsen, Janet R., and Ann Pellegrini. "Introduction: Times Like These." In *Secularisms*, edited by Janet R. Jakobsen and Ann Pellegrini, 1–38. Durham, NC: Duke University Press, 2008.
Jakobsen, Janet R., and Ann Pellegrini, editors. *Secularisms*. Durham, NC: Duke University Press, 2008.
Juergensmeyer, Mark. *Terror in the Mind of God: The Global Rise of Religious Violence*. 3rd ed. Berkeley: University of California Press, 2003.
Kantorowicz, Ernst Hartwig. *The King's Two Bodies: A Study in Mediaeval Political Theology*. 7th ed. Princeton: Princeton University Press, 1997.
Kippenberg, Hans G. *Gewalt als Gottesdienst: Religionskriege im Zeitalter der Globalisierung*. München: Beck, 2008.
Körtner, Ulrich H. J. *Wiederkehr der Religion? Das Christentum zwischen neuer Spiritualität und Gottvergessenheit*. Gütersloh: Gütersloher Verlagshaus, 2006.
Koselleck, Reinhart. *Critique and Crisis: Enlightenment and the Pathogenesis of Modern Society*. Cambridge, MA: MIT, 1988.
Lang, Bernhard. "Monotheismus." In *Handbuch religionswissenschaftlicher Grundbegriffe*, edited by Hubert Cancik, 4:148–65. Stuttgart: Kohlhammer, 1998.
Luckmann, Thomas. "Privatisierung und Individualisierung: Zur Sozialform der Religion in spätindustriellen Gesellschaften." In *Religiöse Individualisierung oder Säkularisierung: Biographie und Gruppe als Bezugspunkte moderner Religiosität*, edited by Karl Gabriel, 17–28. Gütersloh: Kaiser, 1996.
———. *Die unsichtbare Religion*. Frankfurt: Suhrkamp, 1991.
Luhmann, Niklas. *Funktion der Religion*. Frankfurt: Suhrkamp, 1982.
Mahmood, Saba. *Politics of Piety: The Islamic Revival and the Feminist Subject*. Princeton: Princeton University Press, 2005.
Masuzawa, Tomoko. *Invention of World Religions, or, How European Universalism was Preserved in the Language of Pluralism*. Chicago: University of Chicago Press, 2005.
Mbembe, Joseph-Achille. "Necropolitics." *Public Culture* 15/1 (2003) 11–40.
———. *On the Postcolony*. Berkeley: University of California Press, 2001.
Muñoz, José E. *Cruising Utopia: The Then and There of Queer Futurity*. New York: New York University Press, 2009.
Palmer, Jack. *Is Religion Killing Us? Violence in the Bible and Quran*. New York: Continuum, 2003.
Partridge, Christopher. *The Re-Enchantment of the West: Alternative Spiritualities, Sacralization, Popular Culture, and Occulture*. London: T. & T. Clark, 2006.
Peterson, Derek R., and Darren R. Walhof. "Introduction." In *The Invention of Religion: Rethinking Belief in Politics and History*, edited by Derek R. Peterson and Darren R. Walhof, 1–18. New Brunswick, NJ: Rutgers University Press, 2002.
Petryna, Adriana. *Life Exposed: Biological Citizens after Chernobyl*. Princeton: Princeton University Press, 2002.
Pollack, Detlef. "Individualisierung statt Säkularisierung? Zur Diskussion eines neueren Paradigmas in der Religionssoziologie." In *Religiöse Individualisierung oder Säkularisierung: Biographie und Gruppe als Bezugspunkte moderner Religiosität*, edited by Karl Gabriel, 57–85. Gütersloh: Kaiser, 1996.

———. "Was ist Religion?" *Zeitschrift für Religion* 3 (1995) 163–90.
Puar, Jasbir. *Terrorist Assemblages: Homonationalism in Queer Times*. Durham, NC: Duke University Press, 2007.
Riesebrodt, Martin. *Die Rückkehr der Religionen: Fundamentalismus und der "Kampf der Kulturen."* München: Beck, 2000.
Said, Edward W. *Orientalism*. New York: Vintage Books, 2003.
Schmitt, Carl. *Political Theology: Four Chapters on the Concept of Sovereignty*. Translated by George Schwab. Cambridge, MA: MIT, 1985.
Schneider, Laurel C. *Beyond Monotheism: A Theology of Multiplicity*. London: Routledge, 2008.
Spivak, Gayatri Chakravorty. *Can the Subaltern Speak?* Basingstoke, UK: Macmillan, 1988.
———. "Class and Culture in Diaspora." Keynote address at "Translating Class, Altering Hospitality" conference, Leeds University, UK, June 22, 2002.
Stark, Rodney, and Roger Finke. *Acts of Faith: Explaining the Human Side of Religion*. Berkeley: University of California Press, 2000.
Stark, Rodney, and William Sims Bainbridge. *The Future of Religion: Secularization, Revival, and Cult Formation*. Berkeley: University of California Press, 1986.
———. *A Theory of Religion*. New York: Lang, 1987.
Taylor, Charles. "Modes of Secularism." In *Secularism and Its Critics*, edited by Rajeev Bhargava, 31–53. Delhi: Oxford University Press, 1998.
Weber, Samuel. "Von der Ausnahme zur Entscheidung: Walter Benjamin und Carl Schmitt." In *Das Vergessen(e): Anamnesen des Undarstellbaren*, edited by Elisabeth Weber and Georg Christoph Tholen, 204–24. Vienna: Turia & Kant, 1997.
Weigel, Sigrid. *Walter Benjamin: Die Kreatur, das Heilige, die Bilder*. Frankfurt: Fischer, 2008.
Weimer, Wolfram. *Credo: Warum die Rückkehr der Religion gut ist*. München: Deutsche Verlags-Anstalt, 2006.
Wilson, Bryan R. *Religion in Social Perspective*. Oxford: Oxford University Press, 1982.
Wohlrab-Sahr, Monika. "Religionslosigkeit als Thema der Religionssoziologie." *Pastoraltheologie* 90 (2001) 152–67.

www.ingramcontent.com/pod-product-compliance
Lightning Source LLC
Chambersburg PA
CBHW050338230426
43663CB00010B/1905